Kent Library & Archives

D0521966

Action Stations Revisited

Action Stations Revisited

The complete history of Britain's
military airfields:
No. 3 South East England

David W Lee

Crécy Publishing Limited

First published in 2010 by Crécy Publishing Limited
All rights reserved

© David W Lee 2009
David W Lee is hereby identified as the author of this work in accordance with
Section 77 of the Copyright, Designs and Patents Act 1988

All rights reserved. No part of this book may be reproduced or transmitted in
any form or by any means electronic or mechanical, including photocopying,
recording or by any information storage without permission from the
Publisher in writing. All enquiries should be directed to the Publisher.

A CIP record for this book is available from the British Library

ISBN 9 780859 791106

Printed and bound in the UK by MPG Books Limited

Crécy Publishing Limited
1a Ringway Trading Estate, Shadowmoss Road, Manchester M22 5LH
www.crecy.co.uk

For Jeannie

CONTENTS

INTRODUCTION AND ACKNOWLEDGEMENTS

When I started to visit military airfields more than fifty years ago, the only way to find a particular site was to go to the settlement that gave the airfield its name and seek directions, since Ordnance Survey and road maps usually only showed an empty field. The wartime and Cold War security ethos was strong, and a 1950s visit to the Rolls-Royce Hucknall airfield resulted in an unplanned visit to the guardroom, a prolonged grilling, confiscation of a friend's film and a long walk back to where we had left our bicycles. When Volume 1 of *Actions Stations* appeared in 1979, for the very first time an aviation enthusiast could learn the history of an airfield and find it for himself. So when it was suggested that I might write one volume of the completely revised, updated and enlarged *Action Stations Revisited*, I was especially delighted that it covered the South East and Central area. Growing up shortly after the Second World War, it was the exploits of RAF fighter pilots, especially during the Battle of Britain, that first fired my interest in aviation. I produced a sample airfield with alacrity and soon signed a contract. That was nearly seven years ago and I am very grateful for the patience of the Crécy team, particularly Gill Richardson.

The information within these pages has been garnered from virtually every available source, but I must first acknowledge the debt I owe to the late Chris Ashworth. I am totally lost in admiration for just how he produced the original volume without the benefit of modern resources such as high-speed computers, broadband internet and Google Earth. For many decades I have been visiting, recording and collating information on airfields. Organisations like Air Britain and the Airfield Research Group have been an invaluable source of information, as have my friends and my extensive library, where I have made full use of the work of others as I trust they will of this volume.

Writing is essentially a solitary occupation and perhaps some authors have no need of outside assistance, but I could not have written this work without a great deal of help and support. Inevitably, I am not going to be able to record everyone's input, and if you do not get a mention, please forgive me. I am especially indebted to my long-time friend and Rolls-Royce colleague, Herbert Watson, who more than forty years ago first fired my interest in old derelict airfields. I am especially fortunate to live relatively close to Michael Bowyer, and without his sage advice and guidance this book would never have been completed. The superb airfield plans are the work of another good friend, Graham Simons, who ignored my comments that perfection was not necessary.

The photographs, the majority of which, I trust, will be new to most readers, come from a wide variety of sources. Many I took myself or have collected over the years, but the bulk of the early photographs come from the amazing Jack M. Bruce/G. Stuart Leslie collection, which is in the care of the Fleet Air Arm Museum. Without Stuart's knowledge of his archive and steady deluge of small photocopies, many of the Great War airfields would not be illustrated. I am also very grateful to my friends and museum colleagues in the FAAM for their cooperation at a time when they had much greater priorities. Two additional invaluable sources of Great War photographs have been William Casey and Pat Swan. Thank you both for allowing me access to your family photographs of W. A. Yeulett and H. J. Dyer. Another major source of photographs was Peter Green's wonderful collection. Friends who helped with the rest of the more than 250 photographs include Neville Cullingford, Roger Day, Pat Dufeu, Aldon Ferguson, Dick Hadlow, John Hamlin, Bob Jenner Hobbs (NA3T), Trevor Matthews, Trevor Mayes, John Moffat, Tony Moor and Ces Mowthorpe.

During my research I visited almost every airfield. Some were much easier to find than others, and in many cases without specialist local knowledge of the friends I hereby acknowledge, I could have never found them. These include Robin Brooks, Malcolm Finnis, Fred Giddings and Roger Hargreaves. I am particularly indebted to those who expedited my visit to the normally inaccessible sites, including Philip Greaves, Major Chris Gunning, Tony Knight, Stuart Marshall, David McAllister, Debs Pearson, David Thomas and colleagues, Captain Jason Watkinson and Richard Wright. Thank you all.

My proof-reading team include some of those whom I have already acknowledged above, but the load also fell onto Chris Lee-McCloud, Helen McFeely, Ross Sharp and John Strangward. Any faults you still find will be those I proofed!

Finally, I must mention my late wife, Jeannie, to whom this book is dedicated. She encouraged me to take on the task and losing her was a major factor in why it has taken so long to come to fruition.

David W Lee
Suffolk
July 2009

GLOSSARY

AA	Anti-Aircraft
AACU	Anti-Aircraft Co-operation Unit
AAIB	Air Accidents Investigation Branch
AAP	Aircraft Acceptance Park
AAS	Air Armament School
AASF	Advanced Air Striking Force
ABS	Air Base Squadron
(AC)	Army Co-operation
ADGB	Air Defence of Great Britain
AEF	Air Experience Flight
AES	Air Electrical School
AFC	Air Force Cross
AFDU	Air Fighting Development Unit
AI	Airborne Interception (radar)
ALG	Advanced Landing Ground
AMWD	Air Ministry Works Department
ANS	Air Navigation School
AOC(-i-C)	Air Officer Commanding (-in-Chief)
AONS	Air Observer and Navigation School
AOP	Air Observation Post
APC	Armament Practice Camp
ASR	Air Sea Rescue
ASL	Above Sea Level
AST	Air Service Training
ASV	Air-to-Surface Vessel (radar)
ASWDU	Air Sea warfare Development Unit
ATA	Air Transport Auxiliary
ATC	Air Traffic Control or Air Training Corps
ATDU	Air Torpedo Development Unit
ATS	Air Training Squadron
AVM	Air Vice Marshal
AWE	Atomic Weapons Establishment
AWRE	Atomic Weapons Research Establishment
BADU	Blind/Beam Approach Development Unit
BAF	British Air Ferries
BEA(C)	British European Airways (Corporation)
BEF	British Expeditionary Force
BG	Bomb/Bombardment Group (USAAF)

'Bomphoon'	Bomb-carrying Typhoon (slang)
BW(M) or (H)	Bomb/Bombardment Wing (Medium) or (Heavy) (USAAF)
CAA	Civil Aviation Authority
CAD	Computer Aided Design
Cab rank	Standing fighter patrol on immediate call for close tactical support
CAACU	Civilian Anti-Aircraft Co-operation Unit
CACU	Coast Artillery Co-operation Unit
CAF	Canadian Air Force
CAG	Civil Air Guard
C&M	Care and Maintenance
Channel Stop	Air operations to stop German shipping passing the Dover Straits
Chanak Crisis	Preventative action in Turkey 1922
C-in-C	Commander-in-Chief
Circus	Fighter escorted bombing raid to entice enemy response
CND	Campaign for Nuclear Disarmament
CO	Commanding Officer
COA	Cunliffe Owen Aircraft
Combination	Tug aircraft and towed glider
Co-op	Co-operation
CRO	Civilian Repair Organisation
Cross Bow	Bombing operations against V-1 flying bomb installations
DCM	Distinguished Conduct Medal
D/F	Direction Finding
DFC	Distinguished Flying Cross
DFM	Distinguished Flying Medal
DFW	Day Fighter Wing
'Doodlebug'	V-1 flying bomb (slang)
Drem Lighting	Airfield lighting system of outer markers and approach lights
DSC	Distinguished Service Cross
DSO	Distinguished Service Order
DZ	Dropping Zone
Eagle	RAF fighter squadron manned largely by American volunteers
E&RFTS	Elementary & Reserve Flying Training School
E&WS	Electrical and Wireless School
ECM	Electronic Counter Measures
EFTS	Elementary Flying Training School
ELG	Emergency Landing Ground
EM	Enlisted men (USAAF)
EO	Extra Over Blister hangar
Erpr	Erprobungsgruppe
ETPS	Empire Test Pilot's School
E/W	East/West
FAA	Fleet Air Arm
FBG	Fighter Bomber Group (USAAF)

FEW	Fighter Escort Wing (USAF)
FEAF	Far East Air Force
FG	Fighter Group (USAAF)
FIDO	Fog Investigation/ Intensive and Dispersal Operation
FIS	Flying Instructors' School
FIU	Fighter Interception Unit
Flak	Fliegerabwehrkannonen – German anti-aircraft gunfire
FPP	Ferry Pilots' Pool
FRU	Forward Repair Unit (RAF)
FRU	Fleet Requirements Unit (FAA)
FS	Fighter Squadron (USAAF)
FTS	Flying Training School
FW	Fighter Wing (USAAF)
GAMA	GLCM Alert and Maintenance Area
Gee	British radio navigation aid using ground transmitters and an airborne receiver
GLCM	Ground Launched Cruise Missile
GR	General Reconnaissance
GS	Gliding School and General Service (shed/hangar)
GSU	Group Support Unit
GTS	Glider Training School/Squadron
HD	Home Defence
HE	High Explosive (bomb)
HP	Handley Page
HQ	Headquarters
'Hurribombers'	Bomb carrying Hurricane fighters (slang)
IHTU	Inter-Service Hovercraft Trials Unit
JATO	Jet-Assisted Take Off (actually rocket-powered)
JG	Jagdgeschwader – German fighter group
Jim Crow	Reconnaissance patrols by armed fighters
JOAC	Junior Officers' Air Course
Kagohl	German bombing unit based in Belgium 1917-1918
LAA	Light Anti-Aircraft (gun)
LCC	Launch Control Centre
LG	Landing Ground
LZ	Landing Zone
MAP	Ministry of Aircraft Production
MCA	Ministry of Civil Aviation
MOD	Ministry of Defence
MoS	Ministry of Supply
MT	Motor Transport
MU	Maintenance Unit
NAAFI	Navy, Army and Air Force Institute
NAFDU	Naval Air Fighting Development Unit

NATO	North Atlantic Treaty Organisation
NCO	Non-Commissioned Officer
Noball	Operation against V-1 launch sites
N/S	North/South
OC	Officer Commanding
OCU	Operational Conversion Unit
OFU	Overseas Ferry Unit
Operation 'Anvil'	Amphibious invasion of southern France
Operation 'Jubilee	Combined operation at Dieppe in August 1942
Operation 'Market'	Airborne operation at Arnhem and Nijmegen in September 1944
Operation 'Overlord'	The invasion of Europe in June 1944
Operation 'Rutter'	Abandoned attack on heavy guns at Dieppe in July 1942
Operation 'Starkey'	Feint operation to persuade the enemy that an invasion of the Pas de Calais was in progress in September 1943
Operation 'Torch'	Invasion of French North Africa in October 1942
Operation 'Varsity'	Airborne operation to assist crossing of the Rhine in March 1945
OTU	Operational Training Unit
PAC	Parachute And Cable (installation), air defence equipment 1940
(P)AFU	(Pilots) Advanced Flying Unit
PIR	Parachute Infantry Regiment
POW	Prisoner of War
PR	Photographic Reconnaissance
PS&IOW	Portsmouth, Southsea & Isle of Wight (airline)
PSP	Pierced Steel Planking – metal sectional runway
Q-site	Decoy site with lighting to simulate an airfield at night.
RAAF	Royal Australian Air Force
RADAR	RAdio Detection And Ranging
RAE	Royal Aircraft Establishment
RAeC	Royal Aero Club
RAF	Royal Air Force
Ramrod	Day bomber raid escorted by fighters
Ranger	Deep-penetration sortie to engage targets of opportunity
R&SU	Repair and Salvage Unit
RAS	Reserve Aeroplane Squadron
RATO	Rocket Assisted Take-Off
RAuxAF	Royal Auxiliary Air Force
RCAF	Royal Canadian Air Force
RCM	Radio Counter Measures
RDF	Radio Direction Finding – cover name for what later was known as radar
RE	Royal Engineers
Recce	Reconnaissance
Reflex	USAF SAC bomber detachments on ground alert at overseas bases
RFC	Royal Flying Corps

RFS	Reserve Flying School
Rhubarb	Low-level fighter strike operation over occupied Europe
RLG	Relief Landing Ground
RNAS	Royal Naval Air Service
RNVR	Royal Naval Volunteer Reserve
ROC	Royal Observer Corps
Rodeo	Authorised name for a fighter 'sweep'
RS	Reserve Squadron
R/T	Radio Telephony
SAC	Strategic Air Command
SAR	Search And Rescue
SBAC	Society of British Aircraft Constructors – Aerospace Companies
SD	Special Duties
SEAFIS	South Eastern Area Flying Instructor's School
Serrate	Night fighter sortie to protect RAF bombers from German fighters
SFTS	Service Flying Training School
SHAEF	Supreme Headquarters, Allied Expeditionary Force
SHQ	Station Headquarters
SLG	Satellite Landing Ground
SoAG	School of Aerial Gunnery
SoFC	School of Flying Control
SoGR	School of General Reconnaissance
SoN&BD	School of Navigation and Bomb Dropping
SoNC	School of Naval Co-operation
SoTT	School of Technical Training
SOE	Special Operations Executive
Spartan	Exercise to evaluate procedures for fully mobile squadrons in 1943
StG	Stukageschwader – Ju 87 bomber unit
Strafe	Low-level gunnery attack on ground target
TAC	Tactical Air Command (USAAF)
Tac/R	Tactical Reconnaissance
TAF	Tactical Air Force as in 2TAF (RAF)
TAG	Telegraphist/Air Gunner (FAA)
TBR	Torpedo Bomber Reconnaissance
TCG	Troop Carrier Group (USAAF)
TCS	Troop Carrier Squadron (USAAF)
TCW	Troop Carrier Wing (USAAF)
TDS	Training Depot Station
TDU	Torpedo Development Unit
TEL	Transporter Erector Launcher
TFW	Tactical Fighter Wing (USAF)
'Tiffie'	Typhoon aircraft (slang)
TMW	Tactical Missile Wing
TS	Training Squadron

TT	Target Towing
TTU	Torpedo Training Unit
UAS	University Air Squadron
USAAC	United States Army Air Corps (from 2 July 1926)
USAAF	United States Army Air Force (from 20 June 1941)
USAF	United States Air Force (from 18 September 1947)
USAFE	USAF Europe
USAAS	United States Army Air Service (from 24 May 1918)
VHF	Very High Frequency
V-1	Vergeltungswaffe 1 – the Fieseler 103 flying bomb
VGS	Volunteer Gliding School
VR	Volunteer Reserve
WAAF	Women's Auxiliary Air Force
WAEC	War Agricultural Emergency Committee
WD	War Department
Window	Metal foil dropped to disrupt radar systems, later called chaff
WRAF	Women's Royal Air Force
WS	Wireless School
ZG	Zerstorer – German twin-engined fighter unit

EARLY WARNING

From Elizabethan times the British felt protected on their island, being surrounded by sea with the Royal Navy to ward off any foes. As any threat took days to materialise, Drake was secure in the knowledge that the chain of beacons spreading eastward from Cornwall, and their dedicated beacon lighters, would give him plenty of time to put to sea to counter the menace of the Spanish Armada. He had more than sufficient time to finish his game of bowls.

For centuries little changed until 25 July 1909 when, in just under 37 minutes, everything changed. At 04.41, a Frenchman called Louis Blériot took off in a monoplane of his own design from Les Baraques near Calais and, after a perilous 23 miles, landed in the Northfall Meadow behind Dover Castle. How ironic that after fighting the French for centuries, it was a Frenchman who revealed just how vulnerable we now were. As Sir Alan Cobham wrote, 'The day that Blériot flew the Channel marked the end of our insular safety and the beginning of the time when Britain must seek another form of defence besides ships.'

From having hours or even days of warning, the threat to British lives, liberty and property could now materialise in minutes. Sadly, Britain's military experts did not perceive the aeroplane as a possible threat. Only months before, the Imperial Defence committee had withdrawn funding from Cody's aeroplane in favour of airship development. The beginning of the First World War appeared to prove the committee correct, as it was one of Count von Zeppelin's rigid airships, LZ 38, that first bombed London on the night of 31 May 1915, killing seven and injuring another thirty-five East Enders. London was virtually defenceless, with just twelve anti-aircraft guns and a handful of totally inadequate aeroplanes. The 'early warning' system relied on telephone calls from military, police and similar bodies and was nigh-on useless. Usually, by the time a message got through even the slowest raider was on the way home.

By the following year, the observation system had been reorganised and streamlined. Early versions of sound locators were introduced to give advanced warning of the airship's approach. These were portable and comprised four 'ear trumpet' horns mounted on a framework. An example of the standard Mark 1 Sound Locator can be seen in the Canadian War Museum in Ottawa. By this means the Zeppelin threat was largely countered, only to be replaced by the Gotha and later by the Staaken Giant bombers. When twenty Gothas attacked London in broad daylight on 13 June 1917, killed 162 civilians and all returned home safely, the public outcry was deafening.

The Government turned to a Major General E. B. Ashmore to create a unified system to include observation, ground and air defences. A pilot who had commanded the RFC wing in France, attached to the 1st Army, Ashmore was well qualified for the task, and the defensive changes he created helped persuade the Gotha force to restrict their attacks to night. Despite these improvements, the reporting system, especially at night, remained of limited efficiency. A total reorganisation of the London-based observer network, the communications and control network, was instigated and extended outwards to give much greater advanced warning. Equipped with instruments to give the bearing of the intruder from the observer, the attacker's position was determined by triangulation at one of twenty-six sub-controls from two or more observing locations. The information was then passed through the London Air Defence Area (LADA) to the defending fighters and guns. The complete system, which would become the Observer Corps and a crucial link in the country's defence in 1940, was in place by the summer of 1918. The last German air raid on London had already taken place in May 1918, so the complete system was never fully tested during the Great War.

Sadly, although the need for an integrated air defence system was acknowledged in the War Office, the organisation that Ashmore had created was destroyed in the wholesale military reductions that followed the Armistice. From more than 200 fighter aircraft, just two squadrons survived, none of the 286 anti-aircraft guns and 387 searchlights was retained, and the observer/control network disappeared.

Following the Government's decision in 1923 to expand the RAF to fifty-two squadrons, a committee under Major General C. F. Romer was established to recommend a Command, Warning and Communication Structure. Major General Ashmore was a member of the Romer Committee and in 1924 instigated a trial observation system using voluntary special constables in an area between the Romney Marshes and Tonbridge. The chosen locations were Sutton Valence, Marden, Biddenden, Goudhurst, Cranbrook, Hawkhurst, Bethersden, Ham Street and Tenterden, with a control centre in Cranbrook. The first trial, on 12 August, involved a No 32 Squadron Sopwith Snipe flying from Kenley to Hawkinge. It, and subsequent day and night tests, proved that volunteers and a temporary network hired from the GPO at a cost of £82 could provide the basis of a air-defence control and reporting system.

A fuller test was made on 22 and 24 June 1925 involving more than forty observation posts in Kent and Sussex with control centres in Horsham and Maidstone. With the coverage extended to include Hampshire and Essex, the Observer Corps, with the Elizabethan beacon lighter as its symbol, was officially established in October 1925. The purpose of this chapter is not to tell the history of the Observer Corps (from 1941 the Royal Observer Corps), fascinating although it is, but to see how efforts to detect enemy aeroplanes beyond the range of human faculties have provided some amazing relics in this region.

From the first 'ear trumpet' portable sound detectors, experimental fixed acoustic 'mirrors' were built later in the Great War at Joss Gap, Kingsgate on the Thanet coast, and at Fan Hole, north of Dover. Both were concrete structures built into the cliff face and performed a useful role in giving advanced warning of the approach of the Gotha bombers on their way to London. Further experiments were curtailed by the Armistice, but began again in the 1920s. These involved both horizontal reflectors and the more familiar vertical sound mirror. The first of the new generation of mirror, 20 feet in diameter, was built on the Roughs at West Hythe. A report published in January 1924 of tests made in the previous September concluded that the mirror was 'at least ten times more effective than the unaided ear'. That was in ideal conditions, as strong winds, rough seas and coastal shipping could severely limit the effective range of the equipment.

Continued experimentation brought a series of differing designs and sizes. A 30-foot-diameter bowl mirror was constructed at West Hythe and a 20-foot slab mirror constructed at a new experimental station at Denge, south of Greatstone-on-Sea (TR075215). Another fixed slab mirror was erected at Abbot's Cliff, between Folkestone and Dover. Although a second bowl mirror of 30-foot diameter was completed at Denge in early 1930, plans for a much larger sound reflector had been under consideration since 1927. This monster mirror was a curved strip 200 feet long and was completed by mid-1930. By 1932, with all six mirrors having been tested, it was time to evaluate the system during the annual Exercises. It is obvious from the report of the 1932 Exercise that the Acoustic Detectors were fully integrated into a control and reporting system, although their efficiency varied significantly. The system was further refined in the 1933 and 1934 Exercises, but it would appear that only the Denge 30-foot and 200-foot, together with the Abbott's Cliff 20-foot mirrors, were used in the latter Exercise. Problems were beginning to become apparent at Denge, for the coastal road and associated housing was beginning to encroach between the site and the sea.

The final evaluation of the system, before large-scale construction of mirrors around the coast was implemented, was fixed for the July 1935 Air Defence of Great Britain Exercises. The test was primarily to speed up the passing of information to the control centres, then on out to the defenders.

My interest in these concrete relics was sparked at an Air Britain Aeromilitaria Special booklet written by David Collyer in the early 1980 called 'Kent's Listening Ears'. In that he describes the 1935 test at Denge, where the Air Member for Research and Development, AVM Hugh Dowding, was the principal visitor. While listening for the low buzz of distant aero engines, the operator in his cabin behind the wall heard a peculiar jingling together with a clopping noise. As other microphones detected this sound, a lone figure with horse and cart was suddenly spotted between the mirror and the sea. The startled milkman, delivering the daily pinta to newly built houses, was hurriedly chased away so that the exercise could begin!

This episode confirmed that, because of the expansion of housing along the coast, Denge was becoming unviable, but it also highlighted the limitations of acoustic detection. In good conditions, aircraft could be picked up at 10 miles range, but still with no method of establishing the height. It

The 20-foot slab mirror at Abbot's Cliff in September 1987. (DWL collection)

was far from perfect; but with the proven warning and control system it would have to do. Further experiments continued using a second 200-foot wall mirror on Malta, but a report of another, totally different, approach to the problem of early warning was being investigated.

Using the BBC's short-wave transmitters at Daventry, a small team of Government scientists led by Robert Watson-Watt had set up a pair of receivers on 26 February 1935 attached to an oscilloscope. This somewhat crude experiment proved that the radio waves were being reflected from a Handley Page Heyford bomber flying some 10 miles away, and the signal could be shown on the cathode ray tube. Conceived just in time, what was initially called RDF and later known as RADAR had been born. Developed into a crucial partnership with the Observer Corps, the system was an integral part of the victory achieved five years later during the Battle of Britain. But without the acoustic mirror experiments in long-range detection, the essential air defence and reporting system might never have been available to accept the information provided by radio waves.

My fascination with these concrete predecessors of radar led to an expedition to Kent in September 1987, accompanied by my son Chris and his ATC friend Andrew. Using 'Kent's Listening Ears' and OS maps as a guide, we first found the slab mirror at Abbot's Cliff near Capel (TR278387). Moving on to West Hythe, the 30-foot bowl mirror and its adjacent control building were located (TR132346) and photographed. We were then hoping to find the slab mirror at Hythe, but a farmer's stubble fire barred our way and we had to make a hasty retreat. We then travelled south towards the three mirrors at Denge, or Greatstone as their location is recorded in 'Kent's Listening Ears'. After parking just off the coast road we realised that there was extensive open water left by gravel extraction between us and the mirrors, and access was only possible by a long detour over the shingle. That was a long hard walk, but the effort was amply rewarded by the sight of three very different Sound Mirrors (TR077217). The first, a 30-foot bowl type, was in very good condition and even had the mast for the microphone still in place; the second, a 20-foot slab mirror, was perched precariously on the edge of the water. The most impressive was of course the 200-foot wall mirror, although the control cabin at the rear had collapsed, leaving an open hole in the centre of the wall through which the operator had spotted the errant milkman. The low evening light made photography difficult, but having recorded our visit we trudged back over the shingle to our car.

West Hythe's 30-foot-diameter bowl mirror still searches the skies. (DWL collection)

The historic importance of the Denge mirrors had been recognised in 1979, when they were made scheduled monuments, but no money was available to ensure their survival. Fortunately, in the early 2000s the Aggregates Levy Sustainability Fund was created to provide funds to mitigate the damage caused by aggregate extraction. With this and other financial resources, English Heritage was able to stabilise the foundations and isolate the mirrors on an island with a retractable bridge preventing further vandalism. Repairs to and conservation of the concrete continues. It is possible to see these historic structures through the Romney Marsh Countryside Project, which organises a number of conducted visits under the title of 'Echoes from the Sky Walks'. The tramp across the shingle still requires good footwear, but it will be worth it.

All three mirrors at Denge are silhouetted by the low September sun. (DWL collection)

With its foundations undermined by
gravel extraction, the 20-foot slab
mirror was at risk in September 1987.
(DWL collection)

By 1987, the operator's
cabin behind the 200-
foot wall had collapsed.
(DWL collection)

Below: The operator's
window looks down
onto an empty
microphone channel.
(DWL collection)

Kent Library & Archives

Relics of the wartime radar stations can be found around this area, the most famous being the three surviving Chain Home masts at Swingate near Dover, but a much more modern 'radar' installation can be found between Fareham and Southampton at Swanwick. Called the London Area Control Centre, Swanwick is part of National Air Traffic Services (NATS) and is one of the largest and most advanced air traffic control centres in the world. Designed as a replacement for the West Drayton facility, it went operational on 27 January 2002, nearly ten years and 5.25 million man hours since the initial contract was awarded to IBM in October 1992. After a further five years the relocation of the West Drayton staff and services was completed in 2007.

The three surviving Chain Home radar masts and the RFC memorial at Swingate Down, Dover. (DWL collection)

Swanwick's statistics are impressive; a staff of almost 650 includes nearly 550 civil and military controllers and assistants who control 200,000 square miles of airspace above England and Wales. On a summer's day, up to 6,000 flights are controlled in what is the busiest airspace in the world. The Operations Room covers 2,000 square metres and is three times the size of that at West Drayton. This most impressive facility ensures that the congested airspace over the South East remains safe.

From the concrete sound mirrors, through RDF and Chain Home to the latest aircraft tracking technology, the South of England has it all.

The spacious operations room of the National Air Traffic Service at Swanwick in Hampshire. (NATS)

Military Airfields of South-East England

South East England has some of the UK's earliest aerodromes, but space for many of the Great War sites that had no subsequent use could not be found. The 'Main features' information is applicable to December 1944 unless otherwise stated. Usually the main runway is listed first and accommodation figures are an indication of what was available, usually on site. OS map references relate to the 1:50,000 series.

001 Aldermaston, Berkshire
002 Andover, Hampshire
003 Appledram, Sussex
004 Ashford (Great Chart), Kent
005 Bekesbourne, Kent
006 Bembridge, Isle of Wight
007 Blackbushe, Hampshire
008 Bognor, East Sussex
009 Brenzett, Kent
010 Capel, Kent
011 Chailey, East Sussex
012 Chattis Hill, Hampshire
013 Chilbolton, Hampshire
014 Coolham, West Sussex
015 Cowdray Park, West Sussex
016 Deanland, East Sussex
017 Dover/Guston Rd and Dover/St Margarets, Kent
018 Dover/Marine Parade, Kent
019 Dunsfold, Surrey
020 Dymchurch, Kent
021 Eastbourne, East Sussex
022 Eastleigh, Hampshire
023 Farnborough, Hampshire
024 Ford, West Sussex
025 Foreland, Isle of Wight
026 Friston, East Sussex
027 Frost Hill Farm, Hampshire
028 Funtington, West Sussex
029 Godmersham Park, Kent
030 Gosport, Hampshire
031 Grain, Kent

032 Great Shefford, Berkshire
033 Greenham Common, Berkshire
034 Hamble, Hampshire
035 Hammerwood, East Sussex
036 Hawkinge, Kent
037 Headcorn, Kent
038 High Halden, Kent
039 Hythe, Kent
040 Kingsnorth (Airship), Kent
041 Kingsnorth (ALG), Kent
042 Larks Barrow, Hampshire
043 Lasham, Hampshire
044 Lashenden, Kent
045 Lee-on-Solent, Hampshire
046 Lenham, Kent
047 Leysdown, Kent
048 Lydd, Kent
049 Lympne, Kent
050 Manston, Kent
051 Marlborough, Wiltshire
052 Marwell Hall, Hampshire
053 Membury, Berkshire
054 Merston, West Sussex
055 Newchurch, Kent
056 Newhaven, East Sussex
057 New Romney/Honeychild, Kent
058 New Romney/Littlestone, Kent
059 Odiham, Hampshire
060 Overton Heath, Wiltshire
061 Polegate, East Sussex
062 Portsmouth, Hampshire

063 Pulborough, West Sussex
064 Ramsbury, Wiltshire
065 Ramsgate, Kent
066 Reading/Coley Park, Berkshire
067 Rustington, West Sussex
068 Selsey, West Sussex
069 Sheerness, Kent
070 Shoreham, West Sussex
071 Slindon, West Sussex
072 Soberton, Hampshire
073 Somerton, Isle of Wight
074 Southbourne, West Sussex
075 Staplehurst, Kent
076 Swingfield, Kent
077 Tangmere, West Sussex
078 Telscombe Cliffs, East Sussex
079 Theale, Berkshire
080 Thorney Island, Hampshire
081 Throwley, Kent
082 Tipnor, Hampshire
083 Walmer, Kent
084 Wanborough, Wiltshire
085 Welford, Berkshire
086 Westgate, Ken
087 Westenhangar, Kent
088 Westhampnett, West Sussex
089 Wittersham, Kent
090 Woodchurch, Kent
091 Worthy Down, Hampshire
092 Wroughton, Wiltshire
093 Wye, Kent

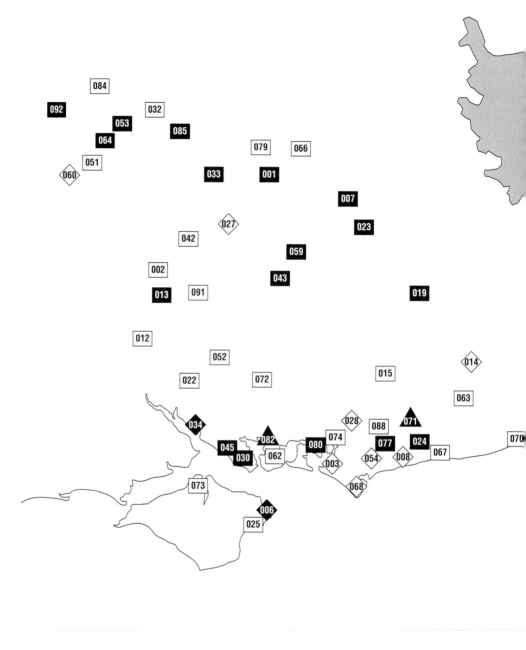

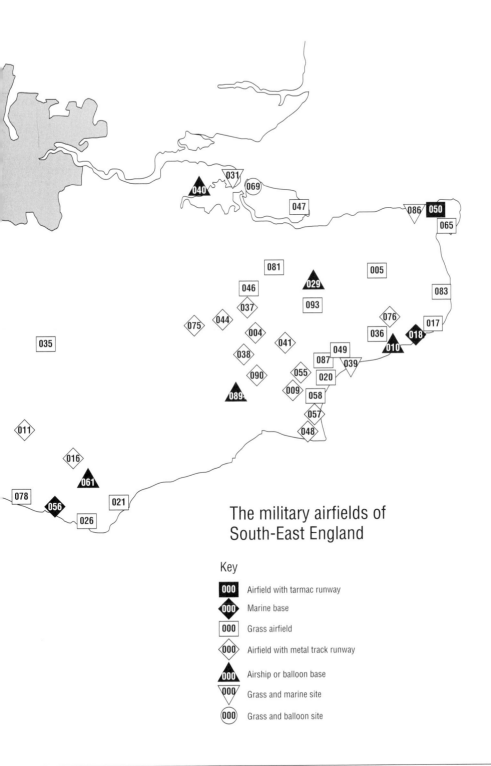

The military airfields of
South-East England

Key

000	Airfield with tarmac runway
000	Marine base
000	Grass airfield
000	Airfield with metal track runway
000	Airship or balloon base
000	Grass and marine site
(000)	Grass and balloon site

THE AIRFIELDS

ALDERMASTON, Berkshire

51°21N/01°08W 340ft asl; SU600635. 1.5 miles south east of Aldermaston village off A340

Aldermaston! A name that will mean nothing to virtually all the young voters of today, but which to older generations was synonymous with the then all-pervading threat of nuclear annihilation. From the early 1950s the Western Powers and the Soviet Union faced each other in the nuclear weapon stalemate of the Cold War with its strategy of Mutually Assured Destruction and an appropriate acronym of MAD! Aldermaston was Britain's Atomic Weapons Research Establishment and, from the late 1950s, it became the venue of the annual 'Ban the Bomb' marches organised by CND, the Campaign for Nuclear Disarmament. At that time the fear of nuclear weapons was such that more than 10,000 people would join the march from Aldermaston to London, led by Monsignor Bruce Kent and the controversial Canon Collins, with up to ten times that number finally gathering in Trafalgar Square. Unlike most 'Action Stations', Aldermaston's 'war' continues and security remains intense, but the ending of the Cold War does mean that some of the site's highly secret but vital work can now be revealed.

The story begins in September 1939 when Aldermaston Court was bought by Associated Electrical Industries to provide a safer alternative to its London head office. Before it could move in, the manor house was requisitioned for use by the Women's Land Army, and in 1941 the house became a Training Camp for the ATS. On 2 April 1941 HM Queen Elizabeth visited the unit to inspect the women under training and it is rumoured that her daughter, then Princess Elizabeth, received her driver mechanic's instruction at Aldermaston. The airfield's history also begins in 1941 when the land to the south of the Court was requisitioned, although this would entail the re-routing of part of the A340 Basingstoke road. Allocated to No 92 Group as a bomber OTU, the Class A specification airfield was built during the spring and summer of 1942 with an extensive bomb dump constructed to the west of the airfield. Designated as a parent station, four T2 hangars were erected in the technical area, which almost encircled the Falcon Inn.

The airfield opened on 1 July 1942. However, the planned Wellingtons never arrived, since Americans in the shape of the 60th TCG, Eighth Air Force, began to take up residence from early August. The four squadrons, the 10th, 11th, 12th and 28th TCS, were equipped with the C-47 and C-53 versions of the Douglas DC-3 commercial transport. They were joined by a battalion of paratroopers who were housed in a 'tent city' surrounding the village of Tadley. The villagers were issued with passes that they had to show at the picket posts on the entrance roads. The local physician, Dr Holmwood, had a lucky escape during an emergency call-out one night. With his mind on other things, he failed to stop at a check point and his Vauxhall received four bullets in its boot before he realised his error.

The Tadley villagers were not the only civilians within the airfield boundary. The AMWD Clerk of Works, Mr G. Wilson, lived with his family in what had been a gamekeeper's cottage of the Aldermaston estate, but now totally surrounded by the airfield's technical site. It appears on the 1945 Record Site Plan, just off the original road leading into the airfield from the Falcon Inn, as an unnumbered solid black outline together with a smaller building, which was probably the 'privy'. Mr Wilson's young daughter, Pat, now Mrs Pat Dufeu, has vivid memories of the airfield. She recalls that the cottage lacked any modern facilities, including electricity, despite being right in the middle of a modern airfield. The first aircraft they saw was a Whitley, which had managed to land at night on an incomplete runway. Before she went to school in Newbury, her father took her to see the aircraft and one of the crew showed her inside. Her only memory is that it was very dark. For much of the war, No 4 hangar was empty and she and her brother used to play there in wet weather. In drier conditions the many blast shelters were another playground. She remembers that the Americans were very good to them, giving them sweets and ice cream; her father also had a PX ration, which helped with his cigarettes. As Clerk of Works, Mr Wilson had to know all the facts and figures about 'his' airfield, but not everyone accepted his word. When he failed to convince someone of the length of the perimeter road, he had his whole family out one night walking around the perimeter with a 100-foot tape. With just a pair of wartime slit torches, they were lucky not to get shot!

For three months, the 60th practiced paratroop drops at Aldermaston, now designated USAAF Station 467. It wasn't all hard work for, on 26 October 1942, the Group was visited by the movie actor Edward G. Robinson, famous for his gangster roles. Just a week later, on 3 November, the station was sealed, with no one allowed in or out. The precautions were in preparation for what became Operation 'Torch', the landings in French North Africa. The 60th TCG provided thirty-nine aircraft, leaving Aldermaston on 6 November via St Eval and Predannack in Cornwall to pick up their paratroopers before continuing on to North Africa.

Their replacement, the 315th TCG, also an Eighth Air Force unit, began to arrive from 12 December. Its two squadrons, the 34th TCS with the C-53 troop transport and the 43rd TCS with the double-door C-47, were initially employed in a general transport role. The Americans were joined on 14 February 1943 by a temporary detachment of No 3 GTS while its base at Stoke Orchard was waterlogged. Equipped with Master tugs and Hotspur gliders, they gave the 315th some experience in glider towing before departing after just six weeks. Shortly after, the appearance of numerous packing crates heralded the arrival of the unit's own Waco CG-4A assault gliders, and training moved into high gear. With so much activity in the Mediterranean, it was inevitable that the 315th would be involved. On 25 May the majority of the unit's aircraft and personnel were temporarily deployed to North Africa to participate in the invasion of Sicily, leaving a handful of aircraft to continue with general transport duties. During that summer the airfield's personnel were entertained by Bob Hope and Frances Langford, but with no sign of the return of the bulk of the Group to the UK, the 315th was formally assigned to the 9th Air Force in October 1943, moving to Welford on 6 November.

Towards the end of 1942, an area at the south-west end of the main runway was requisitioned for use by the Ministry of Aircraft Production. The self-contained MAP site, linked to the airfield via one of the pan dispersals south of the Padworth Common road, had a single B1 labelled Hangar 5. Vickers took over the site for the final assembly of Spitfires in July 1943, together with numerous former garages in Newbury, Hungerford and Reading for component manufacture. Some 500 Spitfires were built at Aldermaston, the primary variants being the Marks VIII, XI, XIV, XVIII and XIX. All were flight-tested at Aldermaston before delivery by ATA pilots, the last being dispatched in February 1946.

The MAP site closed on 20 July 1946 but the hangar and other buildings survived into the 1960s before the Heath End housing estate took over. Today there is one acknowledgement of the former use of the area in the appropriately named Hangar Road. It is, however, reported that residents of houses in the locality of the former aircraft dispersals occasionally find the remains of the concrete bases when digging in their gardens. A more satisfactory memorial to the work of the Aldermaston MAP factory work is the significant number of surviving Spitfires, mainly Mark XIVs but including one PR XI. Another local link to the time when the area was a Spitfire factory is the former Venture Bus Garage in nearby Baughurst, which was used for stores. Today it is 'Lattice House', its name coming from the 'Belfast' roof trusses of the former bus garage. Which RFC airfield provided these?

The departure of the 315th in November 1943 left Aldermaston in flying-unit limbo for a period, pending a decision on its future use. A temporary solution was the arrival from 12 February of the 370th Fighter Group, straight from its gruelling transatlantic journey. Having trained State-side on the P-47 Thunderbolt, the pilots of the three Squadrons, the 401st, 402nd and 485th, were surprised to learn that they were to fly the twin-tailed P-38 Lightning. A handful of these had arrived and conversion training commenced before the 370th was on the move again. Its destination was RAF Andover, as the 'powers that be' had finally decided that Aldermaston would be a 9th Air Force Troop Carrier Station. In preparation for the new residents, areas on either side of the main runway had PSP laid to facilitate the marshalling of the gliders and towing aircraft.

It was the 434th TCG that had been selected to transfer from its Lincolnshire base of Fulbeck to be nearer its prospective passengers, the 101st Airborne Division, then residing on Salisbury Plain. Immediately after its arrival on 3 March, the Group began intensive training in preparation for the opening of the 'Second Front', which all knew to be imminent although few knew when. The 434th was now part of the 53rd Troop Carrier Wing, which also included the 435th at Welford, the 436th at Membury, the 437th at Ramsbury and the 438th at Greenham Common. The Group's four squadrons were the 71st, coded CJ, the 72nd, coded CU, the 73rd, with CN code letters, and the 74th, whose C-47s carried ID.

From early June 1944 large numbers of airborne troops moved into Aldermaston as tension increased until, on the 3rd, the station was sealed off from the outside world with military police manning every gate. Pat Dufeu (née Wilson) believes it was the night of 4 June that the camp was sealed off, as she and her brother were unable to go to school that week (the only days that they missed during the whole war). The children spent the daytime sitting in the oak tree in their garden noting the numbers of the aircraft as they took off. (Sadly these invaluable records were destroyed after the war.) On the afternoon of 4 June, all the C-47 aircrew and glider pilots were called to a briefing where they were told that they were to have the honour of leading the glider assault on enemy-occupied Europe. Many were rather wary of this somewhat dubious honour and wished that they had been rather less assiduous in their training. The Group's fifty-two gliders were to carry men and equipment of the 101st Airborne Division to Heisville, some 5 miles south-east of St Mere Eglise on the Cherbourg peninsula. Although they had trained with both the American CG-4A Hadrian and the wooden British Horsa gliders, it was decided, to the Group's relief, that it would use its own stronger metal tube design. This was important as the landings were likely to be in the dark, being planned for 4.00am, and the Horsa tended to break up in the almost inevitable heavy landing.

One of the CG-4As destined to take part was aptly named the 'Fighting Falcon', one of four 'purchased' by the children of the Greenville Schools of Michigan, who raised an incredible $72,000 in a War Bond Drive. The Waco was named after their school mascot, and they were told it would be the first to land in France. Publicity photographs were taken of Brigadier General Don Pratt of the 101st Airborne together with his pilot, Lt Col 'Mike' Murphy, in front of the 'Fighting Falcon'. However, men of the 458th Service Squadron had been working on a CG-4A during the morning and afternoon of 5 June, fitting a reinforced 'Griswold' nose and other armour-plating. It was this glider that took pole position, and the 'Fighting Falcon' was moved down to number 45.

From 12.10am on 6 June, the 434th launched its 104 tugs and gliders, all carrying the newly applied black and white 'invasion' bands around the wings and fuselages. As they formed up, one glider detached from its tow and landed near Reading, without injury to the occupants, but the remainder set off on the 3½-hour flight to France. They lost one combination to flak over the French coast and another glider was released prematurely, but forty-nine gliders were released over the LZ, most making successful landings. Sadly, the 'armoured' glider landed down-wind and, with its extra weight on wet grass, could not be stopped before it hit a tree. The jeep on board broke loose, killing General Pratt and his aide, also breaking the pilot's legs. Ironically, the 'Fighting Falcon' landed safely. Reference was made to the 'Armoured Plated' glider and to the sad loss of life in the movie *Saving Private Ryan*.

For their spearhead role on D-Day and for further lifts undertaken on both 6 and 7 June using both Horsa and Waco gliders, the Group was awarded the highly coveted Distinguished Unit Citation. It also received the French Croix de Guerre with Palm. The 434th spent the rest of the summer carrying supplies and further troops into the new temporary landing fields and evacuating the wounded. Training flights in preparation for its next assault operation also continued, one of which had a sad outcome. On 7 July the medical personnel of the B-17 base at Podington in Northamptonshire were called to a crash of a 74th TCS CG-4A glider at Tiffield. There was nothing that they could do as both glider pilots had been killed instantly, their bodies being brought back to the Podington mortuary.

The next operation for the airborne forces was planned during the late summer of 1944, under the code name of 'Market Garden'. The combined ground and airborne charge through the German front line in Holland to Arnhem was conceived by Britain's General Montgomery, the ground thrust by a British armoured column being the 'Garden' part of the operation. The lightly armed airborne troops had the task of securing bridges and other strategic positions in advance of the ground forces. The 434th was to deliver troops of the 101st Airborne to the Veghel Sector, north of Eindhoven. On Sunday 17 September two serials (formations), each of forty-five C-47s, flew some 30 miles behind enemy lines to drop their paratroopers. At a maximum of 800 feet, these were hazardous ops and the Group lost five aircraft to flak, with another nineteen damaged.

The following day it was the turn of the gliders, but this time the towing altitude was a maximum of 500 feet. A total of 160 C-47 and CG-4A aircraft were dispatched to reinforce the paratroops. The formation left mid-morning and after nearly 4 hours the release point was reached. With a further glider operation planned for the next day, most gliders flew with a single pilot, so all were extremely tired on arrival. Two C-47s failed to return, and a further thirty-three came back with flak damage. A total of seven gliders were released prematurely, two over the sea. Another maximum effort on 19 September saw some eighty-two C-47s dispatched towing Waco gliders, again with a single glider pilot. This time twenty CG-4As failed to reach their objective, mainly due to adverse weather, but only one tug was lost, although in unusual circumstances. The pilots of the 74th Squadron heard a radio call 'N-Nan, your engine is on fire'. Flying at low altitude, the pilot of N-Nan ordered his crew to bale out but lost control and crashed before the pilots could escape. Sadly the call was for another aircraft in a different squadron! The Group carried out resupply operations for a couple more days but the situation on the ground at the final objective of 'Market Garden', Arnhem, was lost and the operation was eventually wound down.

The remainder of the 434th's time at Aldermaston was spent in supply and casualty evacuation duties until 12 February 1945, when it moved to Mourmelon-le-Grand in France to be closer to the front line. It was followed by the other groups of the 53rd TCW, although IX Troop Carrier Command retained the use of Aldermaston as a transit base until 15 June 1945. The handing back of the station to the RAF bought a momentous era to a close. After the Americans had left, Pat Dufeu saw a Miles Master tow in a small tailless dual-control glider in which she and her brother played when no one was looking. (This is believed to be the General Aircraft GAL.56 TS510, which first flew at Aldermaston on 27 February 1946.) Then No 25 (RCAF) Aircrew Holding Unit arrived, tasked to select men for further service against Japan or for demobilisation, but its work came to an end in December 1945 when the station was placed in Care and Maintenance.

The General Aircraft GAL.56 TS510, which first flew at Aldermaston on 27 February 1946. (RTP via P. Butler)

When the station reopened on 9 May 1946 it was almost as though nothing had changed, since some of the first aircraft to arrive were DC-3s. However, these were joined by Oxfords and Yorks as BOAC took over Aldermaston as its Training HQ, retraining RAF aircrew to fly the civil types operated by the Corporation. The fleet was expanded by the addition of Haltons and eventually the Viking when, on 30 April, BEA and BOAC merged their training operations into Airways Training Limited. Just prior to that, on 1 January 1947, the base had become a temporary civil airport under the Ministry of Civil Aviation. It was a busy place as the total movements for 1947 were almost 37,000 at a time when Heathrow handled fewer than 30,000, Croydon just over 30,000 and Northolt a little over 31,000. Thus Aldermaston was, for a brief period, London's busiest airport! Eventually more than 1,000 ex-RAF pilots were retrained as civil Captains and Co-pilots.

ATL not only trained aircrew but also cabin crew in a ten-week Stewards and Stewardesses course in which they learned all about cutlery, crockery and glassware, basic first aid, and the ethos of 'personal service' to their passengers, an era far removed from today's strategy of cramming in the 'self-loading freight' as closely as possible! Sadly a change in policy and sufficient aircrew led to the closure of ATL in November 1948. The next major occupant of Aldermaston was Eagle Aviation, which transferred its HQ there following its withdrawal from the Berlin Airlift in August 1949. Other site users included the Reading Aero Club and the Fighting Vehicle Development Establishment, based at nearby Chertsey. All were given notice to leave by April 1950, for the future of Aldermaston was to take a dramatically different direction. In the eighteen years of its existence, Aldermaston had played an important role in defeating the threat of Nazi Germany, then in starting to build the peace. But the threat now facing Britain, its Commonwealth and the free world equalled, if not exceeded, that of Hitler.

To understand how this threat arose, it is necessary to go back to 1940. At Birmingham University, two German refugee scientists wrote a paper that was to change the world for ever. In this historic document, Otto Frisch and Rudolf Peirerls outlined how to manufacture a uranium-fuelled 'super-bomb'. As part of the effort to enlist the support of the USA, Britain revealed this and other of her secrets including the jet engine and the cavity magnetron – centimetric radar. Consolidating her lead in this new technology, the UK formed, in 1941, the world's first atomic weapons research programme under the code name of Tube Alloys. The Americans also initiated the Manhattan Project, which finally led to the creation of the atomic bomb. Following the attack on Pearl Harbor, Britain joined the Manhattan Project, albeit as a junior partner. The weapon successfully brought the Second World War to an abrupt end, at the cost of many lives, but the saving of multitudes more had conventional warfare been used in an invasion of Japan.

Post-war, the Americans, fearing a proliferation of atomic weapons, refused to continue the wartime collaboration with Britain. The then Labour Government decided that Britain should have its own weapon. Also, despite the American attempt to control the secret, it was not too long before the facts were in the hands of the Soviet Government. Under the code name of 'High Explosive Research', a British weapon programme was initiated, but it was soon realised that all such research should be brought together in one location. It was this decision and the choice of Aldermaston that brought about the abrupt eviction of Eagle Aviation in April 1950.

W. E. Chivers & Sons was the contractor tasked with building the Atomic Weapons Research Establishment, and its work to transform the old airfield officially began on 1 April 1950. Work went ahead day and night with the workforce growing to some 3,600 labourers accommodated in temporary camps. In parallel with the work on the former airfield, the area around the village of Tadley, which the media soon labelled 'Atom Town', was also transformed as hundreds of houses were built for the future staff of AWRE. The first of many buildings on the site was formally handed over in the spring of 1952. The now characteristic Aldermaston skyline began to emerge. Numerous two- and three-storey laboratory and office blocks were joined by the jagged roofs of assembly and production buildings. Tall towers housed the accelerators necessary for nuclear research and elsewhere the hulking mass of the bomb chambers squatted on the old airfield. Amidst all this new construction, many of the original buildings were retained, including the four T2 hangars, but for very different uses.

Even as building work continued all around them, the AWRE scientists had been working towards their goal, a British atomic weapon. Under the code name of Hurricane, the first British nuclear test was scheduled to take place off the north-west coast of Australia. An old surplus frigate, HMS *Plym*, carried the device to the Monte Bello Islands, less its plutonium core, which was delivered separately by air. The decision to test the bomb in a ship rather than the easier solution of a tower on land reflected the fear that any nuclear attack on Britain would be by a weapon smuggled into a harbour or docks. The offshore test would give maximum information for future civil defence. At the time the size of the device, and the USSR's lack of a suitable aircraft to carry it, precluded delivery by air. Ironically, the same situation exists today, but now it is a terrorist threat of a so-called 'dirty bomb' being carried into a major city by ship. When, just before 9.30am local time, on 3 October 1952, the bomb was detonated, Britain became a nuclear power. Just over a year later, in December 1953, William Penney, who had been one of the Manhattan team and, together with Group Captain Leonard Cheshire, had witnessed the Nagasaki bomb, formally took over as AWRE's first Director.

The successful test design was adopted to become Britain's first operational nuclear weapon, called 'Blue Danube' with a 10KT yield (equivalent to 10,000lb of TNT). It was in service from 1953 to 1961 and was capable of being carried by all three of the RAF's V-Bombers, albeit a single weapon weighing 10,000lb only just fitting in their bomb bays with the tail fins retracted until released. The replacement bomb, code named 'Yellow Sun' Mk 1, was significantly smaller, weighing only 7,000lb, but had a yield in the megaton range, ie 1 million tons of TNT, and served from 1959 to 1962.

The USA having demonstrated the awesome power of the hydrogen or 'H' bomb, the British Government decided, in July 1954, that Aldermaston should develop a thermonuclear weapon. It took the other nuclear powers, the USA, the USSR and France, between six and seven years from making a decision to the first deliverable test. The scientists and engineers at Aldermaston achieved that landmark in just four years. A Valiant bomber dropped a prototype thermonuclear bomb in May 1957 and a further test off the south-west coast of Christmas Island in November 1957 achieved a yield of 1.8 megatons. The fact that the United Kingdom had now achieved parity with the USA in nuclear technology was the final link in a process that saw the reinstatement of nuclear co-operation between the two nations. The signing of the 1958 agreement led to an AWRE warhead design codenamed 'Red Snow'. When installed in the 'Yellow Sun' bomb casing, it became the Mark 2 version, which was to serve with the RAF until 1972. The 'Red Snow' megaton warhead was also installed in the 'Blue Steel' stand-off bomb, which today would be called a cruise missile. This advanced, supersonic weapon was carried by the RAF's Mark 2 versions of the Vulcan and Victor bombers from 1962 until the end of the decade.

The 1950s had been an incredibly busy period for Aldermaston, as not only were new devices conceived and tested but also a stockpile of service warheads was built for the RAF with ever-increasing destructive powers. The work required new techniques, advanced equipment and a wide diversity of skills. Areas of research included experimental nuclear physics, mass spectrometry and reactor physics. The AWRE led in developing high-speed imaging techniques necessary to record an atmospheric test. Initially they used a massive cine-camera with an electronically activated 'shutter' with an exposure time as short as one-tenth of a microsecond. As these machines demanded high light levels, Aldermaston developed charge coupled device (CCD) imaging technology capable of capturing detailed images of events of nanosecond duration. Neutron radiography, developed at the AWRE for inspection purposes, proved capable of recording images through 2 inches of lead shielding.

Smaller, tactical nuclear weapons were also being developed at this time. 'Red Beard' was a kiloton bomb that, although based on the 'Blue Danube' warhead, weighed just 2,000lb and was to serve with both the RAF and the Royal Navy for a decade from 1961. However, a new generation of air-dropped weapon was being developed for the planned TSR-2 strike bomber under the designation of WE 177. Although the TSR-2 was cancelled in 1965, the lightweight, versatile bomb went ahead and the first was delivered to RAF Cottesmore in September 1966. When the weapon was finally withdrawn in 1998, it had been carried by the Vulcan, Jaguar and Tornado in the RAF and in the Navy by the Scimitar, Buccaneer, Sea Harrier and, as an anti-submarine weapon, by the Sea King helicopter.

Although the RAF got its advanced tactical nuclear bomb, its role as Britain's Independent Nuclear Deterrent did not long survive the cancellation of the joint US/UK 'Skybolt' air-launched ballistic missile. Britain decided to adopt the nuclear submarine-launched 'Polaris' missile under the 1962 Anglo-American Nassau Agreement, which meant more work for the team at Aldermaston. The challenge facing the AWRE scientists was to design three warheads to fit onto a missile just 54 inches (1.372m) in diameter, much smaller than anything previously attempted. The solution utilised the first stage of the WE 177 weapon, and by 1965 Britain's first Polaris submarine – HMS *Resolution* – was on patrol carrying sixteen missiles each with three warheads in the kiloton yield range.

However, the hectic pace of nuclear development was not sustained far in the 1960s due to the cancellation of weapons like the 'Blue Streak' ballistic missile and the completion of design work on WE 177 and Polaris. To retain the design skills of its employees, Aldermaston diversified. Its alternative tasks included the detection of cosmic radiation likely to affect the crew and passengers on Concorde, and medical research. The latter's many varied subjects included electrically powered artificial limbs, titanium alloy hip joints, thermal imaging, corrosion of medical implants, dental fillings and kidney dialysis machines. The AWRE was also in the forefront of the application of computers to engineering, in particular techniques such as numerically controlled machine tools and computer-aided design (CAD). Amongst other research tasks investigated at Aldermaston were the design and fatigue testing of bridges, tunnelling machines, heat-resistant paints and multilayer thick films that led to the miniaturisation of electronic circuits. A less successful project involved women's lingerie. Marks & Spencer wished to improve its manufacturing techniques but was unwilling to adopt AWRE's suggestion that the underwear be glued not sewn together!

Improvements in the Soviet anti-ballistic missile defences led the USA to develop the new 'Poseidon' missile, but an alternate path was chosen for the UK. AWRE's scientists and engineers, together with teams at RAE Farnborough and Hunting Engineering, built the unique 'Chevaline' system. Although reduced to two warheads, which were now 'hardened' against nuclear attack, the new system incorporated a complex variety of chaff and decoys. The missile's 'Improved Front End' was capable of manoeuvring in space to launch its warheads and decoys. 'Chevaline', which entered service with the Royal Navy in 1980, maintained the viability of the Polaris submarine fleet until 1996, by which time its successor had joined the Navy.

The 'Trident' missile was the chosen missile system to be carried by the larger 'Vanguard' class nuclear submarine. The missile itself was built by Lockheed Martin, but the design, testing and manufacture of the warhead was the responsibility of the AWE (the name was changed in 1987). HMS *Vanguard* entered service in 1994 and now, like the rest of the operational fleet, carries up to sixteen Trident D-5 missiles, a total of forty-eight warheads. Today AWE's primary role is to maintain the Trident system for its full operational life of some twenty-five to thirty years. This has become more complex since the ban on any nuclear testing and has led to a range of Above Ground Experiments known as 'AGEX'. This is defined as a 'science-based stockpile stewardship programme in order to re-certify design, materials and process changes without nuclear testing.'

Over the years, Aldermaston had been part of various government bodies from the United Kingdom Atomic Energy Authority, through the Ministry of Technology to the Ministry of Defence. But following a report in the late 1980s by Sir Francis Tombs, then chairman of Rolls-Royce, a major change was proposed to assist in overcoming skill shortages then being experienced in the production of the Trident warheads. The chosen solution was popular in the USA for running similar facilities to Aldermaston. Although the American term was 'contractorisation', it has now become known as GOCO – Government Owned Contractor Operated. Thus on 1 April 1993 Aldermaston came under commercial management, Hunting-BRAE being awarded a seven-year contract. Under this new structure, Aldermaston soon achieved registration under the industry quality standard ISO 9001. A major rationalisation of the site facilities and personnel saw the number of employees fall from 6,000 to about 4,500 by 1999.

Surprisingly, when the contract was retendered during 1999, for an initial ten-year period, it was a new team that won. AWE Management Ltd raised its new flag in front of the main administrative block on 1 April 2000, the 50th anniversary of Aldermaston's nuclear role. AWEML is an equal partnership of three companies, British Nuclear Fuels Ltd (BNFL), Lockheed Martin and SERCO. Today the AWE is acknowledged as a safe and good neighbour complying with or exceeding every safety and environmental standard. This was recognised by two annual gold awards for occupational safety from the Royal Society for the Prevention of Accidents and, more recently, RoSPA's top safety prize, the Earl Award. The AWE Management team recently achieved a twenty-five-year contract, which will permit a significant reorganisation of the site's facilities, most of which date from the 1950s.

Despite the age of most of its buildings, Aldermaston has many of Britain's most advanced facilities including the UK's largest laser, largest centrifuge and the largest single computer. AWE's HELEN laser was opened in 1979 and, by generating temperatures of up to 3 million degrees and extreme pressures, can simulate the conditions within a nuclear explosion. Its replacement, called ORION, is now being planned. AWRE's first Ferranti computer, installed in 1955, would be totally outclassed by today's most basic home PC, but the present IBM RS6000 is capable of 'numerical simulations of dynamic processes in three dimensions' – whatever that means – but is apparently essential for supporting Trident. The

AWE's employees number some 4,000 plus around 1,000 contractors, although there are now more computers than people on the site. In March 2000 AWE's care of its staff was recognised by the 'Investor in People' award. As well as maintaining and certifying Trident, other significant skills retained by AWE include the capability of producing a future nuclear weapon, decontaminating redundant weapons and verifying compliance with nuclear treaty agreements.

Casual visitors to Aldermaston are naturally not encouraged. It is one of the most secure sites in the UK and even a prearranged official visitor with a valid reason has to go through many hoops before finally being allowed in. After the somewhat chilling introductory video with its range of different warning sirens for different emergency scenarios, I was in the hands of my host, who would never leave me alone. For what is believed to be a first-ever, one-off opportunity, I was allowed access to Aldermaston to see what remains of its wartime infrastructure and to be briefed on the work of AWRE and AWE since 1950.

Passing the armed police on the main gate, after a very short walk up to a T-junction with an unusually wide service road complete with all the standard roadside furniture of a public highway, I entered what appeared to be a rather dated industrial estate. Although I knew that we were now on a former Second World War airfield, my eyes said that this was nothing like any other wartime airfield, in use or disused, I had ever seen. This disorientation was eased somewhat when I began to comprehend, confirmed by my host, that this wide service road was in fact the southern taxiway, and the T-junction with traffic lights was the intersection of a 'frying-pan' dispersal. Crossing the road/taxiway, we headed towards what I realised, from the flag pole with its AWE flag and a modest memorial stone, was Aldermaston's equivalent of a Station Headquarters. Entering, one of the first things I noticed was the steady tick, tick, tick of a radiation monitor. Although initially slightly disconcerting, after a very short time it became reassuring, then, although audible everywhere, no longer noticeable.

After an excellent briefing on the history of the AWRE/AWE, I was joined by more hosts with specialist knowledge of the wartime history of Aldermaston. Leaving me with no excuse for getting my facts wrong, I was deluged with information, documentation and other reference sources. After further orientation to help me understand how AWE today related to the wartime layout, we all embarked on a minibus, together with an AWE photographer, for a tour of the site concentrating on the surviving wartime infrastructure. It was made very clear that, although my hosts would be as helpful as possible, it was likely that some of my questions may not get an answer.

The wartime runways and taxiways provide the transport arteries for the Atomic Weapons Establishment. (AWE)

Beneath the many additions, the Control Tower is still just recognisable. (AWE)

I wonder how many parachutes were dried and packed in this building. (AWE)

The first destination was the former Technical area adjacent to the Falcon Gate where, in wartime, virtually all the support buildings had been concentrated. Of the original four 'Transportable Sheds', more commonly known as T2 hangars, all but the most easterly survive, but one, surrounded by additional security fencing, cannot be photographed. Close to T2 No 1, the most easterly, is the site of the old machine-gun range, the rear wall of which just survives, although condemned for demolition. In the woods to the south of this hangar is the last of the dozens of blast shelters that had dotted the site. Adjacent to No 3 hangar is a former maintenance block and a small Nissen hut, which, as it does not appear on the 1945 Record Site Plan, is likely to be a post-war addition. A number of other original buildings remain including the parachute store, dinghy shed and armoury, all built in temporary brick. Unlike these, which are recognisably wartime structures, across the taxiway and surrounded by other buildings, the most evocative of all airfield buildings, the watch office or control tower, is virtually unrecognisable. The purpose of the various external adaptations was not explained. To the east, the base of the sleeve streamer (windsock) mast could be seen, when I was told what to look for.

The layout of all three runways is clearly visible, especially from the air, but all have been built on to a greater or lesser extent. The southern and part of the northern taxiways are still in use as service roads, but that to the east is now part of the very large explosives area, with the service road diverted to the boundary of the site. Within the explosives area are a pair of structures that would appear to be environmental test laboratories similar to those now part of the National Trust site on Orford Ness, where they are known as 'pagodas'. To the south of the explosives area is one of the many wildlife havens to be found at AWE. The Decoy Pool was a feature of the original Aldermaston Court, where it served to attract and trap wildfowl for the table. Today it provides a relaxing venue for members of the AWE Angling Society.

From the rural idyll of the Decoy Pool, the final visit of the day was a reminder of the true role of the site. Housed in one of the post-war Aldermaston's most historic buildings, originally erected to assemble the centre section of the 'Blue Danube' bomb, is the AWE Historic Collection, officially opened in December 2000. With some 400 items on display, many more in store, some 6,000 documents, an extensive collection of personal memorabilia, ephemera and more than 2,000 cans of cine film, as well as video and still photographs, the collection is without doubt the most comprehensive record of Britain's nuclear weapons programme. Among the fascinating exhibits is, of course, an example of the 'Blue Danube' with its 5ft (1.52m) diameter single-stage atom bomb on view, displaying the numerous detonators that would have detonated the high explosive surrounding its plutonium core. Examples of many of the other weapons developed at Aldermaston are also present, including the 'Red Beard', 'Yellow Sun' Marks 1 and 2, 'Blue Steel', 'Chevaline' and the WE 177.

Perhaps the most chilling exhibit was one the existence of which was, until very recently, a closely guarded secret. The 'Blue Peacock' looks a most unlikely nuclear weapon. The massive dark green cylinder, weighing some 16,000lb (more than 7 tonnes), some 7 feet (2 metres) in diameter, mounted on agricultural cart springs, would appear to be some sort of industrial boiler. Only when the end of the 'boiler' is opened, revealing a 'Blue Danube'-type atomic bomb, is the illusion broken. Even then the sinister true purpose is not obvious. The 'Blue Peacock' was a British Army atomic demolition mine conceived in the early days of the Cold War. Possible targets included oil refineries, irrigation and hydroelectric systems, canals and railway junctions. The plan was for the British Army of the Rhine to have ten 'Blue Peacocks', which would be deployed should a Soviet invasion appear imminent. By 1957 the design was virtually finished but the Army was having second thoughts. The weight and size of the weapon, together with the need for suitable environmental storage, meant that it would have to be kept well back from the front line, giving rise to almost insurmountable deployment problems. It was recognised that the political 'fall out', let alone the actual irradiation hazard following its use, would be hard to justify even in the most desperate of situations, so finally only two inert prototypes were built, the AWE example being the sole survivor of this flawed Cold War weapon.

For decades, the secret nature of the work at Aldermaston meant that the former role of the airfield was virtually ignored. Only the most knowledgeable would have found any evidence of the original wartime occupants. Visitors to Aldermaston Court who paused at the entrance gates may have noticed the graffiti inscribed into the brickwork of the boundary walls by the bored young GIs who manned the picket post. Other graffiti could be found carved into the bark of mature beech trees on the north side of the airfield, some of which was still legible. But with the ending of the Cold War and the approaching 50th anniversary of D-Day, it was agreed to formally acknowledge the

Unveiled on 6 June 1994, the Aldermaston memorial is in front of the main administrative building. (AWE)

debt owed to the wartime American airborne personnel by placing a memorial in front of the main administrative building. The chosen design was based on a painting called 'Dawn over England' by Dale Oliver, a very talented former glider pilot of the 73rd Troop Carrier Squadron. The original work evolved from sketches made by Dale at dawn on 7 June 1944, as his squadron formed up for the flight to Normandy. Aldermaston's unofficial historian of the American period, Gordon Timmins, designed and donated the black granite plaque, with AWE paying for the base. The memorial was unveiled on 6 June 1994 by Mr Tom Grievson, then Executive Chairman of the AWE, and dedicated by the AWE chaplain, the Rev Barry Norris, in the presence of AWE personnel, local councillors, MOD representatives and members of the West Berks Parachute Regiment Association representing their American colleagues. In his introduction Mr Grievson said:

> '100 gliders left Aldermaston on D-Day bound for the Omaha area of Normandy. The men on board contributed in no small manner to the winning of peace and this plaque is dedicated to the brave men who returned and those who did not. As they fought for peace then so AWE continues the business of keeping the peace today.'

Sadly, like most aspects of AWE Aldermaston's fascinating history, the memorial is not available for public viewing.

Main features:
Runways: 060° 6,000ft x 150ft, 170° 4,200ft x 150ft, 350° 4,200ft x 150ft, concrete with wood chippings. *Hangars:* four T2, one MAP. *Hardstandings:* fifty-two concrete loop type. *Accommodation:* USAAF: 537 Officers, 2,280 enlisted men.

ANDOVER, Hampshire

51°12N/01°31W 260ft asl; SU328458. 2.5 miles W of Andover on A303

In 1984 it was possible to begin this section with 'Andover has the distinction of remaining almost unchanged after nearly sixty years of active RFC/RAF use'. Sadly, in 2004 very few of the RFC buildings remain and the handful that just survive are totally derelict, forlornly awaiting the allocation of money for their demolition. In less than twenty years, the evidence of an aviation history that began in the middle of the First World War has been virtually obliterated.

Built on a triangular-shaped 400 acres of gently sloping pasture bordered by three roads, the Royal Flying Corps station was officially opened in August 1917. Accommodation for aircraft and personnel was located either side of the western boundary road, but typically many buildings, including the standard three double- and one single-bay General Service Sheds with their graceful Belfast Truss roofs, were far from complete. The first squadron, No 104 with its DH.9s, arrived from Wyton on 16 September, being joined by No 106, which was formed at Andover with the RE.8 on 30 September. The next unit, No 105 Squadron, arrived on 3 October from Waddington.

All their aircraft were housed in a row of canvas-covered Bessonneau hangars alongside the northern (now A303) road, while bell tents provided the accommodation for many of the RFC personnel. All three units began to work up on the training ranges of the nearby Salisbury Plain in their daylight bomber or reconnaissance roles. A further squadron, No 148, was formed on 10 February as an FE.2 night bomber unit before moving to Ford in early March and on to France by the end of April. With the Allies being hard-pressed by the German 1918 offensive, France was also the destination of 104 on 19 May. But in the same month the other two resident squadrons went in the opposite direction to support the Army in Ireland.

The next Andover residents were both former RNAS squadrons originally formed in France as No 7 and No 15 night-bomber squadrons. With the creation of the RAF on 1 April 1918, they were renumbered 207 and 215 and both arrived in mid-May to exchange their Handley Page 0/100s for the improved 0/400. In June No 207 left for France to join the newly formed Independent Force tasked with strategic bombing of German industrial targets, followed, in July, by 215 Squadron. For a few weeks Andover was quiet, but on 23 June a new unit came into being when No 2 School of (Aerial) Navigation & Bomb-Dropping was formed (the 'Aerial' was later dropped). The school was equipped with a variety of aircraft including the DH.4, DH.6, DH.9 and 9A, as well as the mighty HP.0/400. The latter was used solely for night training, which included a specialised navigation course for the planned bombing assault on the German capital city. The Armistice in November 1918 meant that this attack was postponed for a generation, although general training continued into 1919.

In September 1919 Nos 1 & 2 Schools of N&BD were merged into the School of Air Pilotage, renamed the Air Pilotage School on 23 December 1919 under No 7 Group, the headquarters of which had arrived at Andover on 4 December. The limited requirement for the APS led to its reduction to a cadre on 1 April 1920 and eventually to its disbandment in January 1923. The personnel of the school became the re-formed No 11 Squadron and for a time looked after No 7 Group's communications aircraft before being posted to Bircham Newton in mid-September 1923, where they received DH.9As.

The long-serving Bristol F2B Fighter was the next Andover resident at the end of September when No 2 Squadron was posted in from Farnborough, remaining until 31 March 1924. It overlapped with No 12 Squadron, which arrived on 23 March with its newly acquired but very inelegant Fairey Fawn day-bombers. Thus began 12 Squadron's association with Andover, which was to last for more than eleven years. With the arrival of No 13 Squadron with its Bristol Fighters at the end of June, Andover settled into a period of relative stability.

No 7 Group was disbanded on 12 April 1926 and immediately re-formed at Andover as the Wessex Bombing Area responsible for all RAF bomber squadrons with the exception of two units at Martlesham Heath. From June 1926 for the rest of the year No 12 Squadron gradually replaced its unlamented Fawns with the much more acceptable Fairey Fox, its streamlined Curtiss engine giving a top speed some 50mph more than its predecessor. Although the Fox only equipped one squadron, it was to influence the design of RAF aircraft, especially the Hawker line, examples of which were to equip No 12 at Andover almost up to the outbreak of war. In April 1927 the Andover Communications Flight was created by the amalgamation of the communication aircraft of the Wessex Bombing Area and those of the RAF Staff College near Weyhill. In August No 13 Squadron swapped its long-serving F2Bs for the Armstrong Whitworth Atlas, the first RAF aircraft to be designed specifically for the Army Co-operation role. However, after five years at Andover, in September 1929 they were transferred to Netheravon and their replacement at long last gave Andover its planned two-bomber-squadron establishment.

The newcomers, No 101 Squadron, which arrived in October 1929, brought a machine that could not have been visually more different than the sleek mounts of No 12. The bulky twin-engined Sidestrand with its three- or four-man crew was named, like its successor the Overstrand, after a small north Norfolk coastal village. Although No 101 was the only RAF unit to operate the type, the medium bomber Sidestrand was able to match the range and bomb-load of the then night-bombers with the speed and agility of the single-engined day-bomber. It was therefore logical to bring these two apparently very different solutions to the day-bomber together on one base. The importance of the Fox to the squadron's history was acknowledged when it was chosen as the centrepiece of the 'Shiny 12' Squadron badge. The aircraft served until January 1931 before being replaced by an even more remarkable machine. The Hawker Hart retained the elegance of the Fox and in the annual exercises of the early 1930s proved faster than the defending fighters!

The aeroplanes of the HQ Wessex Bombing Area in 1926/27 included (from left to right) a Fairey Fox, Avro 504K and Bristol F2B. (J. Hayward via P. H. T. Green collection)

No 101 Squadron operated the Boulton Paul Sidestrand III at Andover from 1929 to 1934. (Fordyce via P. H. T. Green collection)

On 1 October 1933 the Wessex Bombing Area was renamed Western Area, being responsible for Boscombe Down and Worthy Down in addition to Andover. The Air Pilotage School had been re-formed at Andover in May 1933, being redesignated the Air Navigation School in January 1935. It operated various types including the Vickers Victoria transport and Saro Cloud amphibian, before moving to Manston in January 1936. Just prior to the redesignation, 101 left for Bicester in December 1934, its hangars being soon occupied by the Harts of No 142 Squadron. Following the invasion of Abyssinia by Mussolini's Italy, both 12 and 142 left for the Middle East in October 1935, being replaced immediately by the majestic dark green Virginia Mk Xs heavy bombers of Nos 9 and 214 squadrons. No 9 only stayed until January 1936, although 214 remained until the following October. They overlapped with two new squadrons, Nos 103 and 107, which were re-formed at Andover with the Hind day-bomber during August 1936. Just prior to its formation, on 1 May, Western Area had been officially renamed No 3 (Bomber) Group and was allocated to Bomber Command on its formation on 14 July 1936. Andover's day-bomber role was re-confirmed when two familiar units in the shape of 12 and 142 returned from overseas in August and December respectively.

No 3 Group headquarters moved north to Mildenhall in January 1937, being replaced by No 2 Group, which, having responsibility for all light bomber units, meant a more sensible administrative arrangement. Andover saw a succession of Hind squadrons over the next year or so as they were formed, worked up to full strength, then moved on. During February and March 1938 the two resident squadrons, Nos 12 and 142, were both re-equipped with the new monoplane Fairey Battle. Capable of carrying twice the bomb load of the old Harts and Hinds, with its retractable undercarriage, flaps and variable-pitch propellers, it was a quantum leap forward. Sadly, despite a 1,000hp Merlin engine, it was to prove to be underpowered and poorly armed when war came.

During 1938, ever-increasing international tensions led the Air Ministry to issue orders placing the RAF on a war footing. Each station was to prepare full defence and dispersal plans including digging slit trenches and gun pits, not the most popular task for any soldier, let alone an RAF airman. No 2 Group HQ left for Wyton and its accommodation was taken over on 7 August 1938 by Maintenance Command, an association with Andover that, through many changes of title, continues to this day. War fever reached a peak in late September during the Munich Crisis over Czechoslovakia; the removal of all peacetime markings led to the application of camouflage and code letters to all the aircraft.

Although the immediate crisis passed, preparation for war continued throughout the coming months. Maintenance Command was expanding rapidly with No 40 (Equipment Maintenance), No 41 (Aircraft Maintenance) and No 42 (Ammunition & Fuel) Groups forming at No 81 Weyhill Road, Andover, the former Kelly's Directories HQ, on 1 January 1939. In May the Battles left for Bicester as the station became part of Fighter Command under No 22 (Army Co-operation) Group, with No 59 Squadron arriving with its Hectors. Although these biplanes soldiered on until September 1939, deliveries of their replacement Blenheim IV began as the squadron got used to its new quarters.

The day after war was declared, No 42 Group, which was by then responsible for all Air Ammunition Parks (renamed MUs in October 1939), moved to 'Highwoods', Burghfield Common, near Reading (see Theale). The Blenheims of 59 Squadron, as part of 51 Wing, left for France in early October. The lack of flying units was short-lived as No 2 School of Army Co-operation was created on 20 October to train crews on the Blenheim and Lysander; Ansons and Magisters were also on strength for support duties. Andover spent the winter period known the 'Phoney War' training hard and preparing for the time when the inevitable onslaught would be unleashed. This came on 10 May 1940 as the German Blitzkrieg swept through the Low Countries and on into France. After the evacuation of the Allied troops from Dunkirk, the aerial attack on Britain began in July 1940.

Andover's first experience of the horrors of warfare came on the Luftwaffe's 'Adler Tag', or 'Eagle Day'. During the afternoon of Tuesday 13 August, five Ju 88s from Lehr Geschwader 1 (LG 1) attacked, hitting the airfield, parade ground, SHQ and Officers' quarters. A total of three men were killed and six aircraft damaged. The next day a single raider dropped anti-personnel bombs, killing a further airman and a civilian. The Luftwaffe in the shape of LG 1 claimed to have bombed Andover on 15 August, but in fact hit Odiham, a more important target at the time. The next time Andover was attacked was not until January 1941 when a single HE bomb and a number of incendiaries caused little damage.

Further attacks ensued in March when a Ju 88 attacked dispersed aircraft but at such a low level that the bombs failed to explode; the defences got hits on the aircraft, which crashed 2 miles away with the loss of all its crew. The Luftwaffe got its revenge on 7 April when an attack at 22.45 by a single raider killed an officer and caused other injuries. Bombs wrecked the most northerly double-bay GS hangar, leading to its demolition; other buildings hit included the offices of No 2 School of Army Co-op, the squash court and garages.

During this time No 2 SoAC had continued its valuable work, but at the end of May 1941 it was disbanded, being re-formed on 1 June as No 6 (Coastal) OTU within 17 Group. This reincarnation only lasted until 18 July, when it reverted to its Army Co-operation role as No 42 OTU. Its primary task was the retraining of Lysander pilots to the Blenheim in anticipation of the use of the Bisley in the Army ground support role. By January 1942 the unit had twenty-seven Blenheims plus nine reserves on strength and ten Anson/Oxfords including three reserves. The casualty rate was high throughout this period, but beginning on 15 October the OTU was transferred to Ashbourne in Derbyshire as Andover's flying role changed yet again.

The first new arrival on 20 October was 170 Squadron with its Mustang 1, operating in a tactical reconnaissance role. It was followed by No 296 Squadron with Whitleys on 25 October 1942, which immediately began leaflet-dropping over France but only stayed until 19 December. The next unit was No 15 (Pilots) Advanced Flying Unit, (P)AFU, which arrived in mid-December with a large fleet of Oxfords plus a mixed bag of support aircraft including such rarities as the Audax, Moth, Tipsy B and Tutor. They spread out to many local RLGs including Greenham

Common, Ramsbury and Thruxton. By May 1943 the establishment totalled no fewer than 124 Oxfords plus a further sixty-one in reserve! On 2 January No 16 Squadron increased the incredible mix of aircraft at Andover with its Lysanders and Mustangs, the latter, like those of 170 Squadron, used for tactical reconnaissance. They stayed until June, although 170 Squadron had moved on by the end of March. This succession of Army Co-op squadrons continued through 1943, and during June/July they were joined by No 4 Naval Fighter Wing. Nos 808, 809 and 879 Squadrons, with a total of sixty Seafires, were trained in Army Co-operation work. Nos 809 and 879 returned in October for more training until early December, while 808 remained at Burscough. Another resident for six weeks during the autumn of 1943 was No 660 Squadron with its Auster IIIs. As No 15 (P)AFU had moved on to Babdown Farm at the end of October, the departure of the naval Seafires left Andover without any flying residents. Something was in the offing!

That something proved to be the Lockheed P-38 Lightning flown by the three squadrons of the IXth Air Force's 370th Fighter Group. Their first brief UK home had been Aldermaston, but they arrived at Andover on 29 February in the leap year of 1944, followed the next day by the HQ of their 71st Fighter Wing. On 3 March the station officially became Base 406 of the 9th Air Force functioning as a forward operating base for the impending invasion of Europe. The Lightnings of the 401st, 402nd and 485th Squadrons overflowed the surviving GS hangars and the five Blisters around the perimeter. The somewhat undulating grass field with its maximum run of just 3,900 feet (1,189 metres) was also marginal at times. However, needs must in wartime and the 370th soon settled in and trained hard for what was to come. Declared operational on 1 May, its assigned tasks soon included the dive-bombing of radar sites, flak positions, bridges and marshalling yards.

On D-Day the Group provided top cover over the Channel for the massive Allied sea and air armada before reverting to its armed recce role, concentrating on the area of the Cotentin peninsula for the remainder of June. At times its losses were very heavy in the fighter-bomber role. On 22 June it lost five of the thirty-seven aircraft committed during attacks on gun positions and strong points. Three days later the losses were even worse, with seven Lightnings failing to return. In total the Group lost thirty-one aircraft during its stay in England. During July the whole Group moved to France, becoming operational towards the end of the month at its new temporary airfield coded A-3 near Cardonville. Andover's brief flirtation with the excitements of wartime operational flying was over and the station was handed back to the RAF on 29 July.

Throughout the American period, Andover had retained its RAF links as the HQs of Maintenance Command and 41 Group were still in residence, together with their Communication Squadron with an eclectic mix of exotic aircraft. The first training unit to return was No 43 OTU, which brought in its thirty-six Austers from Oatlands Hill on 10 August 1944. It was to become a long-term resident through to June 1945, although visited by a succession of other newly formed AOP squadrons. Although Andover had seen a wide variety of aircraft types in its long history, the type that entered service in early 1945 was justifiably described as unique. It was the RAF's first helicopter. Formed on 6 February, the Helicopter Training Flight, with nine Hoverfly Mk 1s, converted AOP pilots to the helicopter during a five-week course. Its job done, the Flight was disbanded in January 1946. Its parent unit was redesignated No 227 OCU on 7 May 1947, still tasked with operational training of Auster pilots with an establishment of some twenty Auster VIs. In January 1948 No 227 moved to Middle Wallop and Andover finally lost its training role.

The RAF Staff College returned to Andover in February 1948 and transferred its Communication Flight from White Waltham. In August 1949 Maintenance Command Communications Flight absorbed that of the Staff College and reverted to squadron status. In 1960 the Squadron became Maintenance Command Communications & Ferry Squadron before disbanding into the Western Communications Squadron on 31 March 1964, of which more anon.

The Joint Experimental Helicopter Unit from Middle Wallop was posted to Andover as 225 Squadron on 1 January 1960. For a second time in its history, the old station reverberated to rotary wings, specifically those of the Sycamore and Whirlwind. This was to be a brief reunion as 225 moved to Odiham after four months, leaving Andover to its HQ and communications role.

The Western Communications Squadron operated the Pembroke and Basset aircraft, but it was soon found that Andover's undulating grass surface was causing the long propeller blades of the Basset to mar that sacred turf. The Basset had to go. The RAF continued to contract, with many units being renumbered to keep more historic squadrons in being. Thus in February 1969 the Communications Squadron, by then equipped with the Devon, was redesignated 21 Squadron. The RAF Staff College moved to Bracknell at the end of 1969 and Support Command was created in September 1973 by the merging of the Maintenance Command and the former 90 Group ex-Signals Command. Still headquartered at Andover in the new office block built for Maintenance Command in 1961, it was the main customer of 21 Squadron. Sadly the 1975 Defence Review identified the Squadron as an unnecessary luxury and, with its disbandment on 31 March 1976, the airfield finally closed.

The further contraction of the RAF led in June 1977 to the merging of Training Command into Support Command and the departure of the expanded Support Command to RAF Brampton and RAF Wyton in Cambridgeshire. The link with Maintenance Command, which had begun thirty-nine years earlier, was apparently broken. However, it was to prove to be stretched but not completely severed. The facilities at Andover were snapped up, as with so many former Air Force installations, by the British Army as the Headquarters of the Army Logistics Executive. RAF Support Command was to survive until April 1994 when its training elements became RAF Personnel and Training Command and the maintenance role became … RAF Logistics Command! The wheel came round full circle in April 2000 when the Defence Logistics Organisation (DLO) was created. The DLO now covers every aspect of military logistics from munitions and mail delivery to storage depots and engineering workshops. With more than 30,000 employees, military and civilian, it is the largest single organisation within the MOD. From its HQ in Bath, the DLO has a presence on more than eighty sites throughout the UK, plus a number of overseas locations. These UK sites include Equipment Support (Air) at RAF Wyton and Equipment Support (Land) at Andover. Thus the maintenance support duty that Andover has faithfully provided since August 1938 continues into the 21st century, albeit supporting the Army rather than the Air Force.

The effect on Andover of this major rationalisation has been disastrous to the stock of historic RFC buildings. The Belfast hangars went many years ago, only the bases of the most southerly double hangar and the ARS surviving at the end of 2003. As recently as 2001, the Officers' Mess and barrack blocks joined the list of buildings demolished to make way for gleaming new office blocks or, in the case of the Mess, an ornamental lake. By the end of 2003 only the most southerly buildings adjacent to the road hung on to a tenuous existence, albeit totally derelict. These include the MT sheds, the 25-yard rifle range and other smaller buildings. Some of these can be glimpsed through the security fence among the trees, but over-obvious interest will be noted on the CCTV coverage and bring a speedy response from the MOD Police, as the author can personally testify.

A complete set of RFC GS Sheds (Belfast hangars) were to be seen in April 1988. (DWL collection)

By December 2003 the GS sheds were all gone and the MT area was scheduled for demolition. (DWL collection)

However, it is possible to have a view over the former airfield from the old No 1 Crash Gate on the minor road to the west. It is still an open space and the frequent presence overhead of Lynx helicopters from Middle Wallop provides a tenuous aviation link for the visitor. At the end of 2003 it was reported that the link was to be strengthened with HS Andover XS 641 earmarked to become the station's future gate guardian. Although the type had never been resident at Andover, the name provides an appropriate linkage.

Main features:
Landing surface: grass, ENE-WSW 3,900ft, NE-SW 3,000ft, SE-NW 2,700ft, N-S 2,490ft. *Hangars:* five Blister, four GS, seven Old Belfast Truss. *Hardstandings:* four 'frying-pan' (100ft diameter), twenty-one temporary type. *Accommodation:* RAF: 225 Officers, 148 SNCOs, 1,284 ORs; WAAF: 18 Officers, 4 SNCOs, 385 ORs.

APPLEDRAM, West Sussex

50°48N/00°48W 22ft asl; SU839018. 2.5 miles SW of Chichester alongside A286

Like most of the sites identified as a potential ALG during 1942, the open grass fields between the Chichester to West Wittering road and the Chichester Channel attracted strong objections from the Ministry of Agriculture to the loss of valuable farmland. Controversial from the outset, the name of the airfield remains a source of argument sixty years after its purpose was over. The small hamlet to the north is called Apuldram, but the Ordnance Survey records the airfield area as Appledram. As the latter name was that used by the RAF, Appledram it is.

Approval to requisition the site was given on 10 December, the RAF Airfield Construction Unit moving in during February 1943. As with other ALGs, fences and hedges were removed and a pair of Sommerfeld tracking runways laid down, the work being completed by the end of May. The first occupants in early June were the three squadrons of the recently created No 124 Airfield, posted into Appledram to gain valuable experience of operations from virtually unprepared strips. The Typhoon fighter-bombers of the three squadrons, Nos 175, 181 and 182, were dispersed around the edges of the grass field while the Squadrons' personnel pitched their tents under whatever tree cover they could find.

Although Nos 181 and 182 had been operating the Typhoon since September 1942, 175 Squadron had just a few weeks' experience of its powerful twenty-four-cylinder mount. The rest of the Wing started operations on 4 June against ground targets including airfields; that at Abbeville was the destination of 175 Squadron when it flew its first operational sortie on 12 June. Despite the primitive conditions, the stay was very successful, marred by one serious flying accident but no combat losses. The Squadrons left in early July, No 175 to Lydd and Nos 181 and 182 to the ALG at New Romney. Local farmers were then allowed to graze their livestock on the airfield pending the arrival of the next squadrons. It was to be a long nine months before the animals had to leave.

Meanwhile, a single Extra Over Blister hangar was erected and metal mesh hardstandings provided for the aircraft. Thus, when the animals were displaced from 3 April by the Spitfire LF IXs of 134 Airfield, the aircraft of the three Czech squadrons, Nos 310, 312 and 313, had a few facilities, unlike the men themselves, who were still expected to live under canvas. The Czechs, who had expected to move to the comforts of Tangmere's permanent station, requisitioned a number of local farm cottages instead, before embarking on the task in hand. The round of daily sweeps, *Noball* site attacks and bomber escorts was all in preparation for Operation 'Overlord', the landings in Normandy. Dawn on 6 June saw the Wing patrolling over the beaches without meeting the Luftwaffe, but on D+2 No 312 Squadron tangled with a group of Fw 190s, two being destroyed by Fg Off Ota Smik.

The Wing got its wish on 22 June when the squadrons moved to Tangmere to counter the threat of Hitler's first retaliation weapon, the V-1 or 'Doodlebug'. Its replacement at Appledram was another Wing manned by escapees from Europe, this time Poles. Nos 302, 308 and 317 Squadrons of No 131 Wing and their Spitfire IX fighter-bombers were immediately into action over the battlefield. After a couple of weeks they were again on the move, this time to Ford in preparation for transfer to France. This was the last operational use of Appledram. By November 1944 the land and cottages were released back to the farmers, and in January 1945 two Flights of 5027 Works Squadron removed the mesh runways, dispersals and hangar. Today the fields beside the Chichester Channel display no evidence that war ever touched this quiet corner of Sussex.

Main features:
Runways: 051° 5,200ft, 143° 4,200ft, steel matting (Sommerfeld track). *Hangars:* one EO Blister. *Hardstandings:* Temporary Sommerfeld track. *Accommodation:* Tented camp.

ASHFORD (Great Chart), Kent

51°07N/00°49E 130ft asl; TQ972402. 2.5 miles SW of Ashford off A28

In early October 1943 two RAF Spitfire squadrons lost three of their aircraft. Not an unusual occurrence in wartime, but the culprits were their Allies and it was not a case of so-called 'friendly fire'. As part of an 'escape and evade' exercise, the pilots of No 126 (RCAF) Airfield were deposited in Kent with instructions to get back to their Staplehurst home by whatever means possible. Two unguarded Spits and a Tiger Moth on Ashford were a legitimate means as far as the Canadians were concerned, and three of their number returned home in style to the considerable embarrassment of the RAF.

The creation of an ALG on the triangle of grassland between the A28 and the road to Stubb's Cross, just to the west of Chilmington Green, was approved in September 1942. The 400 acres were requisitioned during January 1943, with Chilmington Farm earmarked for stores and equipment. Preparation work was limited to laying a partial taxiway and two Sommerfeld track runways in a 'V' layout running parallel to the existing roads.

Known locally as Great Chart, the first RAF occupant was 2875 AA Squadron of the RAF Regiment, which arrived on 11 August 1943 to set up defensive gun posts. Aircraft followed two days later when the Mustangs of No 129 Airfield (Nos 414 and 430 Squadrons) flew in from Gatwick for armed reconnaissance *Rangers* over France. During their occupation an impregnated-hessian landing strip was experimentally laid by the Royal Canadian Engineers but, like a similar installation at Dunsfold, the trial was unacceptable. The soon to be embarrassed Nos 65 and 122 Squadrons replaced the Canadians on 5 October, flying diversionary fighter sweeps and top cover operations before moving on ten days later to Gatwick (No 65) and Weston Zoyland (No 122).

The next occupant was scheduled to be a IXth Air Force fighter-bomber unit, which necessitated significant improvements. Over the winter of 1943/44 the taxi track was completed; hardstandings increased to a total of seventy and the main runway was extended. Little Chilmington house was requisitioned as the HQ, and staff of the 303rd FW arrived on 8 March, followed a month later by the 406th FBG (512th, 513th and 514th FS) with its new Republic P-47Ds. After training and acclimatisation, the Group was declared operational on 9 May as the 406th Fighter

USAAF officers in front of Little Chilmington House, the 406th FG HQ. (via A. Moor)

Fitted with long-range drop tanks, a 406th FG P-47 awaits its next mission. (via A. Moor)

Group. Ashford was still very much in the front line, as it found out later in May 1944. The Operations Record Book of No 5003 Airfield Construction Squadron recorded:

'RAF Ashford, (Kent). Bomb Damage: On the night of 21-22 May 1944, at 0035hrs (12.35am), a 1,000lb HE bomb was dropped on the tented site, accommodating the reserve flights, M&E, MT, and Plant flights. Total casualties were thirty, fourteen proving fatal. Twenty tents were damaged beyond repair, and a further fourteen rendered unserviceable. The camp field kitchens were demolished and two water bowsers and two items of MT were damaged. Primary Conclusions: the vital necessity of a medical orderly and first aid staff complete with medical supplies, stretchers etc on each site not covered by, or within reach of RAF Station or USAAF Station medical facilities.'

It is obvious that the provision of medical services at Ashford was not capable of handling thirty casualties at one time.

On D-Day, the Group provided top cover over the hard-fought Utah beach, losing five of its number. Once the beachhead was secured, the Thunderbolts undertook armed reconnaissance, equipping with the devastating high-velocity 5in (127mm) rockets, which were particularly effective against armoured vehicles, especially during the breakthrough at St Lô on 25 July. Two days later the Group moved to France followed by the 303rd FW HQ in early August. The site was officially released on 15 September 1944. Work commenced on its clearance and reinstatement, which was completed in early 1945 before being handed back to civilian ownership. Although American veterans returned to their former base during reunions in the late 1980s, only an unmetalled track parallel to the A28 survived to remind them of four hectic months of 1944.

Main features:
Runways: 150° 4,800ft, 040° 3,750ft, steel matting (Sommerfeld track) and steel planking. *Hangars:* none. *Hardstandings:* seventy temporary Sommerfeld track. *Accommodation:* Tented camp.

ASHFORD, Kent – see LYMPNE

BEKESBOURNE, Kent

51°15N/01°09E, 150ft asl; TR205553. 4 miles SE of Canterbury on minor road

In late 1995 a battle broke out over Bekesbourne, which, unlike the earlier 20th-century conflicts in which the historic aerodrome participated, did not have a happy ending, at least not for future historians. The battle was over the future of Kent's last surviving First World War GS shed (Belfast hangar), built in 1918, but the aerodrome's story had started even earlier.

The large triangular field, sloping down to the north-west, was bounded on the north by the Canterbury to Dover railway line and to the south by the Bekesbourne to Adisham road. Requisitioned as an ELG in 1916, the first occupant was 'B' Flight of No 50 (HD) Squadron, which arrived in October with a mix of aircraft including BE.2C, BE.12 and Vickers FB.19s. With other Flights at Detling, Harrietsham and Throwley, the Squadron was tasked to provide defensive patrols to counter the aerial threat to London. Two BE.12s were dispatched on 28 November when it was reported that a single LVG C.IV was dropping bombs on London. Not unnaturally, the pilots failed to intercept with their outmoded machines. Following the public outrage in 1917 after further daylight attacks by Gothas of Kagohl 3, the War Office decided that more modern aircraft must be deployed in the country's defence.

The SE.5s of No 56 Squadron were temporarily withdrawn from the Western Front, 'B' and 'C' Flights joining 50 Squadron at Bekesbourne on 21 June 1917. However, in the couple of weeks they were there the only daylight raid was on 4 July, when thirteen unsuccessful sorties were flown before 09.30 as the Gothas attacked Harwich and Felixstowe. No 50 had begun to receive new equipment in May and June in the shape of the Vickers ES.1, FK.8 and the potent Sopwith Pup. Both ES.1s and Pups were flown on 7 July to intercept a raid of twenty-four Gothas on London without success. Sadly this was the pattern for subsequent raids, although other squadrons had more success forcing the Gothas to change to night-bombing from September 1917, posing yet another problem for the defenders.

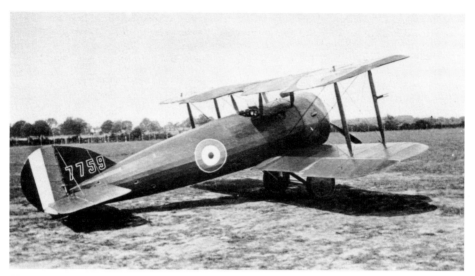

*Vickers ES.1 Mk II No 7759 of No 50 (Home Defence) Squadron during 1916/17.
(JMB/GSL collection)*

*SE.5 A8913 of No 56 Squadron was Lt Keith Muspratt's aircraft at Bekesbourne in June 1917.
(JMB/GSL collection)*

The importance of Bekesbourne was recognised by the decision to build more permanent structures. Two large General Service Sheds and associated buildings were erected in the north-western corner of the aerodrome and a wooden-hutted domestic site positioned adjacent to Chalkpit Farm. Construction work was still in progress on 8 February 1918 when the rest of No 50 Squadron joined 'B' Flight at Bekesbourne. Five Staaken Giants raided London on the night of 16/17 February, and 50 Squadron dispatched six BE.12s, two of which intercepted and fired on a Giant R.12, but failed to destroy the target. During April 1918 No 50 Squadron began to receive the SE.5a, seven of which were dispatched on the night of 19/20 May as a large force of Gothas and Giants raided London. Although a number of raiders were shot down by other squadrons, only one 50 Squadron aircraft intercepted, without success. Apart from a Zeppelin raid in August, this proved to be the last attack on Britain in the First World War.

During May Camels began to replace the SE.5as, which were all gone by June; however, the Camel era was short-lived as its replacement arrived in November. No 50 Squadron's 'new' equipment was the very familiar SE.5a. The construction work on the 98-acre site was finally completed in September, just in time for the cutbacks that followed the November Armistice. Just before Christmas 1918, No 50 received a new CO, who was to play a significant role in the new RAF. Major 'Bert' Harris was later to become Air Chief Marshal Sir Arthur Harris and the wartime commander of Bomber Command. It was during his service at Bekesbourne that Harris decided not to return to his home in Rhodesia but accept a permanent RAF commission. Under his leadership, No 50 survived until June 1919 when it was disbanded, the aerodrome being released during 1920.

Unlike so many aerodromes, Bekesbourne did not revert to farmland, but became Canterbury Aerodrome. Charles Lowe-Wylde, the founder of the British Aircraft Co Ltd at Maidstone, also set up the Kent Flying Club at Bekesbourne in January 1930. Although Lowe-Wylde was killed in one of his powered gliders in 1933, the Flying Club survived him. When, in July 1938, the Civil Air Guard was announced with Government-subsidised pilot training, a section was quickly established at Bekesbourne.

The aerodrome was shut down following the declaration of war, but in May 1940, with the BEF about to be thrown out of France, it was resurrected as a 'Black Violet' aerodrome. This was an Air Ministry plan that based squadrons on South East airfields while operating from ALGs in France.

No 2 arrived with Lysanders from Abbeville/Drucat via Lympne on 20 May, being joined on 29 May by 13 Squadron, also with Lysanders. Although the latter only stayed one day before moving on to Hooton Park, No 13 made a number of tactical recces over France. Remarkably it only lost one aircraft at Bekesbourne when a hung-up bomb fell off on landing. After Dunkirk, No 2 moved to Hatfield on 8 June, abandoning Bekesbourne to be obstructed to prevent enemy use.

After 1945 the site was returned to its former owner and the remaining Belfast hangar was used for storage. Other technical buildings on Aerodrome Road were converted into bungalows, and for forty years the former RFC field was quietly forgotten. Then in September 1995 East Kent Packers, the owner of the hangar and two adjacent warehouses, sought planning permission to demolish its buildings and build up to fifteen houses on the site. Sadly the hangar was unlisted and, despite many protests, the developers got their way.

Bekesbourne's last GS shed (Belfast hangar), photographed in September 1987. (DWL collection)

Visitors approaching Bekesbourne from the south-east have an elevated view over the former landing ground. The unmade Aerodrome Road forks off to the right to where it crosses a new road leading to where the hangar stood. The new houses are on a cul-de-sac called, for no obvious reason, 'de Havillands'. Further down Aerodrome Road, near the railway line, is the more appropriately named Lysander Close.

On the hangar site is a commemorative stone with the outline of an RFC GS shed surmounting the text:

'This monument was erected to commemorate the part played by the Royal Flying Corps and the Royal Air Force squadrons who were based at Bekesbourne Aerodrome during the defence of Great Britain 1914-1918 and 1939-1945.'

A quote from Winston Churchill is also recorded:

'History with its flickering lamp stumbles along the trail of the past, trying to reconstruct its scenes to revive its echoes, and kindle with pale gleams the passion of former days.'

A further memorial was erected by the Airfields of Britain Conservation Trust in February 2009.

Main features in 1918:
Landing ground: grass. *Hangars:* two General Service Sheds (Belfast Truss). *Accommodation:* wooden huts.

Short 310-A4 N1393, powered by a 320hp Sunbeam Cossack, was based at Bembridge in January 1918. (JMB/GSL collection)

BEMBRIDGE, Isle of Wight (Marine)

50°41N/01°05W 5ft asl; SZ642887. 3.5 miles SE of Ryde off B3395

With no connection to the later civilian airport of the same name, Bembridge was chosen as the location for a harbour sub-station of Calshot during 1915. Part of the Solent defence scheme, the minimal facilities consisted of a hardstanding and slipway for the temporary operation of seaplanes. The first aircraft to be based at the sub-station were four Short 184s, which arrived in November 1916. By January 1917, when Bembridge became part of the reorganised Portsmouth Group under the Naval C-in-C, the base consisted of two seaplane sheds and other hutting on the hardstanding. Accommodation was the Spithead Hotel for officers, and the ratings used a former coastguard station.

The location was not ideal, as the marginally seaworthy floatplanes had to taxi to and from the harbour to the take-off and alighting area in the open sea to the north-west of St Helen's Fort. The weather was a constant hazard but boredom was the biggest problem. The monotony of constant patrols was only occasionally enlivened by the sight of the enemy. However, it was a Bembridge-based Short that came closest to achieving a 'kill'. The unit CO, Flight Commander McLaurin, and his Observer attacked a surfaced U-boat with a 100lb (45kg) bomb. Although the submarine submerged with a distinct list to port, its destruction could not be confirmed.

With the creation of the RAF on 1 April 1918, the Portsmouth Group at Calshot became No 10 Group in the South Western Area. On 7 June No 253 Squadron was formed as a coastal patrol unit. The Bembridge Harbour Flights were numbered 412 and 413 with other Flights at nearby Foreland. The Short 184s were supplemented, from August 1918, by the Fairey Campania, when the official establishment was 190 officers and men. Following the November Armistice, the Squadron was disbanded 21 June 1919, and the station closed in September before final disposal in 1920.

Main features in 1918:
Take-off and alighting area: open sea off St Helen's Fort. *Hangars:* two seaplane sheds. Facilities: Slipway and hardstanding. *Accommodation:* requisitioned local hotel and other buildings.

BLACKBUSHE (Hartford Bridge), Hampshire

51°19N/00°05W 329ft asl; SU805595. 5 miles W of Camberley, on A30

In September 1970 two Rolls-Royce Hucknall engineers concluded their regular pilgrimage to the SBAC Farnborough Air Show by an informal visit to Blackbushe on their way home. They entered the terminal building to seek permission for access to the airfield and met an RAF legend. As the younger of the pair, I was not initially aware of this, but Herbert Watson had been a wartime ATC cadet and served with the RAF post-war; he had immediately recognised Air Vice-Marshal D. C. T. Bennett, the founder of the renowned Pathfinder Force. Don Bennett was then the owner and manager of Blackbushe airport and this brief meeting will, for me, be forever a highlight of the airfield's history.

In October 1941 the site was requisitioned for a standard class A three-runway bomber aerodrome together with twelve dispersed domestic sites to the north-east of the flying field. Even before this, the land known as Hartford Bridge Flats was used for a demonstration of the embryo airborne forces. Poor weather prevented the Kirby Kite glider trainers from RAF Haddenham (Thame) participating, but Farnborough provided a prototype Hotspur glider towed by a Handley Page Heyford. The Hotspur was not released but a Whitley dropped a stick of eight parachutists to demonstrate to the visitors from London the other means of delivering troops by air. The Royal Aircraft Establishment continued to use the area for glider trials, even after McAlpine arrived at the beginning of 1942 to build the aerodrome.

The official opening of RAF Hartford Bridge took place on 1 November 1942, the airfield coming under No 70 (Army Co-operation Training & Development) Group. As usual, the airfield was still far from complete and, with the RAE still occupying the most complete sites, No 171 (AC) Squadron delayed its arrival until 7 December. After just three weeks of reconnaissance operations along the French coast, the Squadron disbanded, its Tomahawks and Mustangs going to the newly formed No 430 (RCAF) Squadron, which left for Dunsfold on 11 January 1943. No 140 Squadron arrived from Mount Farm on 13 March 1943 with its PR Spitfires and Blenheims, the latter being gradually replaced by Venturas from February. It was joined on 29 June by the Mustang Mk 1s of No 16 Squadron to form No 34 (Strategic Reconnaissance) Wing attached to HQ TAF, later the 2TAF.

In June 1943 Hartford Bridge was earmarked as a diversion aerodrome for Bomber Command and chosen to be the third airfield to be equipped with FIDO. Unannounced visitors became common; 4 July was a typical night when two Wellingtons from No 196 Squadron dropped in, plus a Halifax from each of Nos 76 and 158 Squadrons. An unusual visitor flew in on 13 July causing some initial consternation, until it was realised that the Ju 88 from Farnborough was there to carry out night-flying tests with a Mosquito. The RAE continued with trials of both the Horsa and Hamilcar gliders, including an overweight Hamilcar trying rocket-assisted take-offs and towed by a pair of Halifaxes.

Although the London to Basingstoke road closed briefly whenever an aircraft crossed over from the southern dispersals, it closed completely for a month from 16 August for Operation 'Starkey'.

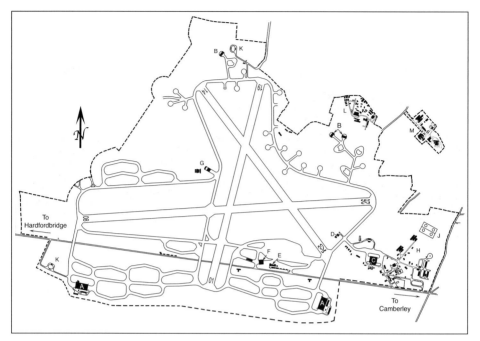

BLACKBUSHE, 1952

A   T2 hangar (23-bay)
B   Blister hangar
C   T2 hangar (14-bay)
D   Flying Control
E   Airport Terminal Building
F   Airport Freight Shed
G   Machine Gun and Cannon Butts
H   Technical Site
J   FIDO Tanks
K   Bulk Petrol Installation
L   Airport Club and Offices complex
M   MCA Offices and Stores complex

*From 15 February 1947 Blackbushe was a civil airport operated by the Ministry of Civil
Aviation although most of the wartime features remained. What was then called a Passenger
Control Building was designed by the Superintending Engineer, No 13 Works Area HQ, and
built alongside the A30. It consisted of two linked Nissen huts with end extensions. The Nissen
nearest the airport provided Arrivals and Departure Waiting Rooms, Toilets, Customs and
Baggage Room. That nearest the road had a Waiting Room, Toilets, Restaurant, Kitchen,
heating plant and staff facilities.*

*On the airfield in 1952 the most northerly Blister hangar was used as a Stores; Dispersed Site
No 4, which had been the WAAF Quarters and Communal site, became the Airport Club and
Stores complex. Communal Site No 2 was also used as the MCA Offices and Stores complex.*

*The A30 continued to bisect the airfield, and traffic lights were used to control vehicles when it
was necessary to use runway 01/16 or when access to or from the southerly T2s was required.*

*The last FIDO demonstration was on 11 November 1952 when a BEA Elizabethan took off, but
the system was not shut down until May 1958.*

A Farnborough-based Army Co-operation Command Gladiator visited Hartford Bridge in early 1943. (140 Sqn records via P. H. T. Green collection)

Bostons of Nos 88 and 107 Squadrons, together with No 21 Squadron's Venturas, operated from the western end of the airfield as a Wing of No 2 Group, bombing marshalling yards, ammunition dumps and airfields. In a particular attack on a power station, No 107 lost three of its aircraft. Amongst all this activity, the FIDO installation went ahead alongside the east-west runway (08-26) with the pump house and storage tanks to the east of the 26 threshold.

No 342 (Free French) Squadron replaced 21 Squadron on 27 September, making the Wing wholly Boston-equipped. The previous power station raid was followed up in early October by further attacks on French power supplies. No 88 attacked the Distre electricity distribution centre while No 107 bombed a transformer station at Orleans, and eleven French Bostons hit another transformer target at Chevilly. On 14 November the three Boston squadrons became No 137 Airfield, their targets becoming the *Noball* V-1 missile sites as these were identified by photo-reconnaissance. The first FIDO trials took place on 19 and 20 November and a pilot of the Free French squadron recalled that the heat from the pipes was a good way to keep warm. During the summer, 140 Squadron had begun to receive PR Spitfires, the Mosquito PR.IX and, from December, the Mosquito PR.XVI. At around the same time No 16 completed the replacement of its Mustangs with the Spitfire PR.XI. The disbandment of RAF Fighter Command and the creation of the 2nd Tactical Air Force on 15 November 1943 saw all the Hartford Bridge squadrons transfer to the new organisation, but their duties continued as before.

In the middle of February 1944 No 107 Squadron was replaced by Mitchells of No 226 from Swanton Morley, which mainly operated with their fellow Mitchell squadrons at Dunsfold. By February No 140's long-range Mosquito PR.XVIs, equipped with *Gee* and *Rebecca* radar-navigation aids, were able to roam over much of the continent at night and in virtually any weather conditions on their photographic sorties. On 24 February 1944 the first major use of FIDO was recorded. Eighteen Bostons from Nos 88 and 342 had attacked V-1 sites at Bois de la Justice while Mitchells from Nos 226 and 320 (Dutch) Squadrons had been to Le Groseiller. Both formations had the benefit of Spitfire escorts and No 140's Mosquitoes were also active. As aircraft began to return, the hazy conditions made finding the runway difficult and for 5 hours the FIDO burn enabled seventy-nine aircraft, from a number of bases, to land safely at Hartford Bridge.

On 7 April 1944 No 34 (PR) wing moved to Northolt, missing the visit on 18 April of General Eisenhower and other senior officers. The personnel of No 137 Airfield were congratulated on their success against the V-1 sites and given an outline of their likely role in the coming invasion. The General was also given a demonstration of FIDO, but when told that it burned around 80,000 gallons an hour, he promptly ordered it to be shut down. As the build-up in the South of England continued, No 322 (Dutch) Squadron's Spitfire XIVs arrived with night-fighter Mosquitoes of 264 Squadron to prevent high-flying Luftwaffe reconnaissance. They were soon in action; Flt Lt C. M. Ramsey DFC destroyed a Ju 88 near Alton but became disorientated; both he and his navigator bailed out, but sadly the latter was killed.

The bomber squadrons were also busy, hitting gun batteries and the French transport system. In early June the aircraft were equipped with special tanks and smoke-laying apparatus in the bomb bays. With all squadron personnel confined to camp on the afternoon of 5 June, the aircrew were briefed on their D-Day task. From first light the Bostons laid a smoke screen over the beaches as the ground forces stormed ashore. The mission was judged a success although one Boston was lost to flak and another, from No 88 Squadron, flew into the sea; the pilot, W/O Alan John Boyle, and his navigator are both commemorated on the Runnymede Memorial. On 12 June a daylight attack on the Foret de Chambecq caused significant damage to the concealed 21st Panzer Division. Another successful attack on 22 June by a force of seventy-two Mitchells and Bostons on the Moneville steelworks brought a special commendation from the 51st Highland Division, whose advance had been stalled for twelve days.

On 20 June 1944 No 322 Squadron departed for West Malling and No 141 Wing then disbanded, leaving No 264 to carry on flying night patrols until it also left on 26 July for Hunsdon. However, before it moved on Hartford Bridge was honoured by a visit by HM King George VI and Queen Elizabeth, who presented eighty awards to station personnel. No 2 Group then supported Operation 'Market', the airborne element of the operation to capture the bridges up to Arnhem. A daylight attack on the Ede barracks on 17 September was led by No 137 Wing accompanied by 139 Wing's Mitchells. Sadly, poor weather resulted in scattered bombing and little success was had until 26 September when the Bostons successfully attacked a road/rail bridge at Cleve – the first attack on Germany.

From early October all 2TAF light-bomber units moved to the continent; No 137 Wing left for B50 (Vitry en Artois) on 17 October. Their successors were the fighter-bomber Mosquito squadrons of No 138 Wing (Nos 107, 305 and 613 Squadrons), which arrived from Lasham but moved to France in mid-November. On 21 November Nos 418 and 605 Squadrons brought their Mosquito FB.VIs and became the third 2TAF Mosquito Wing. Shortly after their arrival Hartford Bridge was no more, the station being renamed Blackbushe on 2 December. Apparently there was confusion with a Hartford near RAF Wyton and the new name was taken from the Blackbushe Road to Fleet and Blackbushe Farm south of the airfield.

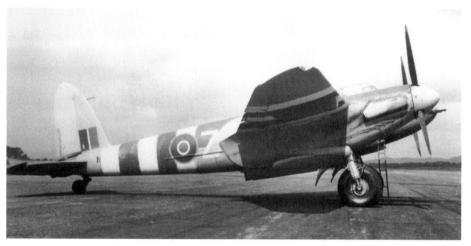

A Mosquito Mk VI of No 613 Squadron, which flew from Hartford Bridge during November 1944. (via S. Marshall)

No 136 Wing's first operation was on New Year's Eve when nineteen Mosquitoes bombed and strafed targets in the Ardennes. On 22 February 1945 the Wing participated in Operation 'Clarion', a major offensive involving some 9,000 aircraft targeting the German communications and transport system. No 136 Wing flew thirty-nine sorties dropping fifty-six 500lb (227kg) bombs on targets of opportunity in north-eastern Holland and north-west Germany. The cost was high; eight aircraft and crews including the CO of No 418 Squadron, Wg Cdr J. Wickett, were lost to flak.

Finally, on 15 March No 136 Wing became the last 2TAF operational unit to move to the continent, its destination being B71 (Coxyde) in Belgium. Interestingly, an ATA ferry pilot, Peter George, delivered a Mosquito FB.VI to Blackbushe from Shawbury on 3 April; perhaps someone had not told the ATA that 136 Wing had moved.

Blackbushe transferred to No 46 Group, Transport Command, on 27 March 1945, as Warwicks of No 167 Squadron arrived. Part of 110 Wing, they carried freight and passengers to the continent. No 301 Squadron re-formed at Blackbushe on 4 April, received its Warwicks during May, before moving to North Weald on 2 July. An express delivery service to the continent was instigated after 6 July when 162 Squadron appeared from Bourn. From early July No 162 Squadron used Mosquito Mk XX and Mk 25s to free-drop mail and newspapers to airfields as far apart as Cairo, Rome, Naples and Athens, often before breakfast! 167 Squadron extended its routes to include daily services to Prague, Vienna and Naples, as well as Paris and Brussels, together with Malta three times a week and Gibraltar twice weekly. However, problems with the Warwicks meant that they were supplemented by Dakotas from June 1945.

Blackbushe was chosen as the southern destination of an experimental all-weather transport service by No 24 Squadron Dakotas based at Hendon. The 385-mile (620km) service began on 16 September 1945 between Blackbushe and Prestwick, providing links to London and to the transatlantic terminal. A manor house near Hartley Wintney was used as a restful transit hotel. When the service finally closed, only two of the 728 planned flights had had to be cancelled, although the FIDO installation at Blackbushe was used to facilitate five landings. A tragic accident occurred on 4 October when a No 311 (Czech) Squadron Liberator, then based in Prague for repatriation flights, crashed after take-off with twenty-three fatalities.

In January 1946 the UK end of the Air Delivery Service transferred from Northolt but disbanded on 20 April. No 167 also disbanded on 1 February 1946, its services being taken over by BEA. No 160 Staging Post arrived in March, starting operations on 5 May. It was responsible for handling ferry and special VIP flights, including many visits by Field Marshal Montgomery en route to Camberley Staff College. The crew of *Aries*, the famous Lancastrian of the Empire Air Navigation School, departed from Blackbushe on 21 August 1946 on their record-breaking flight to Darwin, Australia.

No 162 Squadron disbanded on 14 July leaving Blackbushe with no resident aircraft, although the station staged an excellent Battle of Britain display in September 1946. No 160 Staging Post disbanded on 15 November and this signalled the closure of Blackbushe. Since the station had come under the control of Transport Command in March 1945, a very impressive 11,444 aircraft and 63,934 passengers had used the station. Although the last wartime use of the FIDO installation had been on 25 December 1944 to assist a 305th Bomb Group B-17 to land, a further twenty-eight landings were recorded post-war. It was therefore estimated that during RAF occupation, assisted landings had totalled 294 plus some seventy-three take-offs.

For a few months the station was under Care and Maintenance before its transfer to the Ministry of Civil Aviation on 15 February 1947 as Blackbushe Airport. The MCA invested substantially in improvements, including a new terminal building alongside the A30. In front of the terminal, a large apron was created by filling in the grass centres of two Special Loop dispersals. The FIDO system was upgraded to provide a quicker and more economical start-up. The former WAAF communal area in the north-east corner of the airfield became a domestic area for airport workers with provision for an airport club, industrial canteen, stores and a female hostel. The adjacent No 2 communal site was converted into MCA MT offices, stores, workshops and garages.

British Aviation Services was established at Blackbushe in 1946 and was later joined by its associated charter operators, Silver City, Airwork and Air Contractors. Many interesting aircraft were ferried through Blackbushe, such as Hawker Furies for Pakistan and Mosquitoes destined for Israel. On 22 March 1948 a former ATA pilot, First Officer Joan M. Allen, left Blackbushe on a twenty-six-day flight to Singapore in Fairchild Argus VR-RBE. It was not a record, but it was the first solo flight by a Malaysian woman from England to Singapore, a now forgotten achievement. Blackbushe was a popular departure point for such flights, as another left on 15 April 1948. New Zealand pilot Captain A. A. Mansfield flew a Proctor 'Windmill Girl' on an around-the-world record attempt with a return to Blackbushe planned for 26 April. Sadly it would appear that his attempt failed.

The improved FIDO had its first (and, as it turned out, its only) operational burn on 30 November 1948. It increased visibility from some 90 feet (27 metres) to nearly 2,400 feet (732 metres) to enable an Airwork Viking G-AJFS to depart to East Africa on charter to the Crown

Agents carrying urgently needed currency. A BEA Elizabethan (Ambassador) took off during a FIDO demonstration on 11 November 1952 but the installation was finally shut down in May 1958 and dismantled in 1960. From August 1948 the Berlin Airlift provided much valuable, albeit temporary, income for several Blackbushe companies including Airwork, Silver City and Westminster. Airflight arrived from Langley in August 1949; led by the charismatic but volatile Air Vice-Marshal D. C. T. Bennett of wartime Pathfinders fame, the company specialised in immigration and pilgrim flights under the name of Fairflight.

When No 622 Squadron, the sole transport unit of the post-war Royal Auxiliary Air Force, re-formed at Blackbushe with Valettas on 15 December 1950, many of the new recruits were airline staff with a nucleus of regular RAF personnel. However, the often conflicting needs of the airlines and the RAuxAF proved insoluble and the unit was disbanded at the end of September 1953. Airwork undertook MOD contracts to fly troops and service families to the Canal Zone and Kenya. In 1952 it bought four Handley Page Hermes, which, although civilian-registered, operated with full RAF identities when flying to Egypt. From June Airwork also began safari services to Nairobi using Vikings. The journey took in Nice, Malta, El Adem, Wadi Halfa, Khartoum, Juba and Entebbe, with two overnight stops. In November the Blackbushe-based Aviation Services was acquired by Mr Harold Bamberg, whose Eagle Aviation began scheduled Viking services to Belgrade in June 1953. As Eagle Airways, it was one of the first of the charter companies in the new package tour industry.

Although each September saw Blackbushe filled to capacity by an incredible collection of visiting aircraft in association with the then annual SBAC Farnborough Air Show, the airport was an all-year-round Mecca for the aviation enthusiast. In addition to the civil residents, military visitors included RAF Hastings and Beverleys, which collected their paratrooper passengers for training over the local Frensham DZ. US Navy R5D Skymasters of VR-24 made a twice-weekly appearance as they carried passengers and mail around Navy bases in Europe. Other US Navy visitors included R6D Liftmasters of VR-1 and VR-22 plus Martin Mercators and P2V Neptunes. During 1955, FASRON (Fleet Aircraft Service Squadron) 200 moved into a new hangar built on Yately Common to the east to the airfield. As the only operational US Navy Squadron based in the UK, it operated R4D-8 (C-117D Super Dakotas) and SNB-5 (Expeditor) aircraft, and, from August 1958, a VIP R4Y-1 (C-131) on communication services. In the mid-1950s military Constellations also frequently visited Blackbushe, and their wingspan caused some problems at the eastern end of the main runway. A sign appeared on what is now Vigo Lane that read 'DANGER. For the next 100 yards, wings of taxiing aircraft may overhang the road'. It must have worked, as no collisions are recorded!

Although a number of smaller companies were set up and faded away during the 1950s, Eagle Airways continued to expand its European services, to Gothenburg, for example. On 18 December 1955 Airwork suspended its North Atlantic cargo service, but from April 1956 Eagle used DC-3s to operate BEA's London-Amsterdam-Copenhagen-Hamburg-Berlin night freight service. This increased use triggered local opposition, especially in Yately, and at the end of 1959 the Ministry announced that the airport was to close. Most of the residents departed: Eagle to Heathrow, Airwork and Dan Air to Gatwick, and FASRON 200 to West Malling, although the Blackbushe Aero Club hung on as Blackbushe officially closed on 31 May 1960.

That should have been the end of the story but for the indefatigable Don Bennett. Although the northern and eastern parts of the airfield had been built on common land, the privately owned remainder was bought by the former Air Vice-Marshal. The buildings on Yately Common were cleared and fenced off from the rest of the airfield. Despite bitter opposition, Blackbushe reopened

Bristol 170 Freighter G-AILW was recorded at Blackbushe before being sold in Belgium in 1963. (N. Cullingford)

on 6 October 1962 as a club and executive airfield. The available hangars and virtually all the other wartime buildings had been removed in the interim, but the western end of the terminal building was adapted and refurbished for Air Traffic Control, offices and aero club. Planning applications for new hangarage were always refused, leaving the resident aircraft permanently parked in the open. Finally, in 1973, Bennett sold the 354-acre airfield to Mr Douglas Arnold, a wartime fighter pilot and buccaneering millionaire entrepreneur who, with his sons David and Peter, was seeking a base for his growing collection of historic military aircraft.

Although the day-to-day operation of the airfield continued much as before, new ventures appeared, including a regular Sunday market and, in 1978, a major pop festival. However, Doug Arnold had no greater success than Don Bennett in persuading the local authority to allow permanent developments. Under a threat of a compulsory purchase order, he housed his Warbirds of Great Britain collection in temporary structures at the western end of the site while battling with the planners. Finally, in 1980 the planners accepted Arnold's proposals for a permanent museum, and construction of a linked pair of hangars to the north of the main runway was undertaken in the following year.

The new facility housed a number of tasty aircraft in flying condition, including Spitfire IX NH238, which carried its owner's initials 'DA' as a squadron identity, but they rarely appeared in public. There was also no sign of the proposed Warbirds of Great Britain Museum. However, if you were considering acquiring one of the 'exhibits' it was possible to visit and drool over the gems hidden away at Blackbushe. The Imperial War Museum's interest in both a Lancaster and a Liberator gave me a fascinating opportunity in August 1984. As well as the aforementioned pair of wartime bombers, a B-17, a Mosquito and a Lincoln made up an incredible quintet. Fighters were also in abundance: three Spitfires, a Hurricane fuselage, plus a Mustang, a Thunderbolt and a Sea Fury. A pair of Ju 52s was matched by equal gems such as a Lysander, Stearman, Avenger and Pilatus P-2. A unique gathering of warbirds – the collection was well named. Sadly the IWM could not meet the asking price for the B-24, which was sold to the Collings Foundation before the end of 1984, but the Lancaster was eventually secured for the nation. It was May 1986 when the Canadian-built, ex-No 428 (RCAF) Squadron aircraft was finally collected, but not from Blackbushe. By then it and others of the ever-changing collection had moved to Bitteswell in Leicestershire as Doug Arnold continued to buy and sell airfields as well as aircraft. British Car Auctions was the new owner of Blackbushe and began to invest heavily in the site.

The outstanding contents of the Warbirds of Great Britain hangar in 1984, included a Mosquito, Spitfire, Sea Fury and Mustang. (DWL collection)

One of a pair of CASA 352Ls (Ju 52/3m) seen outside the hangar in August 1984.
(DWL collection)

The Sunday markets continued on the large hardstandings north of the east-west runway and now claim to be the biggest in England. The car auction centre shares a separate entrance to the west of the airfield with the market and has an undercover vehicle viewing area capable of holding more than 1,000 vehicles, with customer parking available for 1,100 cars. A major reconstruction of the airport terminal was completed in July 1997; the semi-derelict western end had already been demolished and the remainder was totally renovated. The most obvious change was the construction of a new, substantial Air Traffic Control tower replacing the earlier long-serving temporary structure. To mark the official opening, a number of former members of No 342 (Free French) Squadron were amongst the invited guests.

A Cabair Robinson R22 guarded the entrance to Blackbushe in September 2003.
(DWL collection)

The history of the former Hartford Bridge is not neglected. Inside the tower are a group of badges of the squadrons and other units associated with the airfield, and externally, at the base of the tower, is mounted a brass memorial plaque, originally dedicated on 12 July 1992 by the renowned aviation author, the Rev J. D. R. Rawlings. More informal reminders of the airport's military history can also be found. In the Biggles Bistro, an original 16 Squadron RAF Hartford Bridge nameboard, circa 1944, is displayed, as are photographs of both past and present aircraft residents. Evidence of the FIDO installation remain in the undershoot areas of runway 26 and alongside the runway. The taxiway and the northern ends of both 14/32 and 01/19 runways are in good condition and, being on common land, are easily accessible from a public road. A complete group of 'frying-pan' dispersals in this area are used as a go-kart racetrack.

The former Warbirds of Great Britain hangars are still the only ones available for aviation purposes. They are used by PremiAir (formerly Air Hanson) for hangarage and maintenance of Beechcraft aircraft, and one hangar also houses a Sikorsky S76 helicopter, occasionally used by the Royal Family. Cabair Flying School offers both fixed-wing and helicopter instruction and advertises its services at the entrance to the airport with a retired, pole-mounted Robinson R22. Blackbushe's future as a busy executive and private flying centre looks assured and all visitors can be sure of a warm, friendly welcome.

Main features:
Runways: 080° 6,000ft x 150ft, 140° 4,200ft x 150ft, 190° 4,200ft x 150ft, concrete and wood chippings. *Hangars:* three T2 (one 14-bay, two 23-bay), six Blister, two Bessonneau. *Hardstandings:* eighteen 'frying-pan', fifty Special Loop type. *Accommodation:* RAF: 183 Officers, 414 SNCOs, 1,970 ORs; WAAF: 6 Officers, 18 SNCOs, 389 ORs.

21st-century features:
Runways: two at 080°; the hard surface has 4,379ft and the parallel grass runway offers a usable 1,640ft.

A vertical aerial view shows how much of wartime Hartford Bridge survived into the 21st century. (via S. Marshall)

National Aviation Day Display

Approved by the AIR MINISTRY and supported by
THE ASSOCIATION OF BRITISH CHAMBERS OF
COMMERCE and THE AIR LEAGUE OF THE
BRITISH EMPIRE • *Under the direction of*

SIR ALAN COBHAM, K.B.E., A.F.C.

General Manager :	*Chief Pilot :*	*Director of Publicity :*
D. L. ESKELL	Flight-Lieut. H. C. JOHNSON	E. M. ROSSITER
GRAND BUILDINGS		*Telephone :* Whitehall 7708
TRAFALGAR SQUARE		*Telegrams :* Ayjaycob, Westrand,
LONDON. W.C.2		London

Cobham's National Aviation Day Display visited Bognor in 1934. The title page of that year's souvenir programme is signed by D. L. Eskell. (DWL collection)

BOGNOR, East Sussex

50°47N/00°42W 23ft asl; SU915005. 1.5 miles NW of Bognor Regis on B2166

During his 1929 twenty-one-week tour of 110 towns to publicise his campaign for municipal aerodromes, Alan Cobham visited Bognor Regis in early September. Land at Chalcraft Farm, North Bersted, was identified as potentially suitable and was used for the National Aviation Day display on 9 August 1932. Alan Cobham's Flying Circus returned in the August of 1933, 1934 and 1935 as he negotiated with the burghers of Bognor for the permanent establishment of a municipal aerodrome. Sadly the planned facility never appeared, but it was this history that brought the Air Ministry surveyors to Bognor in 1942 seeking sites for future ALGs. Although the original location was not then available, further to the west an area of prime agricultural land north of Chalcraft Lane was earmarked as ideal.

The usual objections from the Ministry of Agriculture were overruled and the land was requisitioned in early 1943. In favourable weather, work began almost immediately; hedges and isolated trees were removed and the line of the two runways graded. The 4,800ft (1,463m) SW/NE run of Sommerfeld tracking required the closure of the B2166 near Morells Farm. The second 4,200ft (1,280m) runway on a NE/SW heading meant the closure of a number of farm tracks.

The ALG officially opened on 1 June 1943, parented by Tangmere although intended for use by the Tactical Air Force, later 2TAF, which also came into being on 1 June 1943. The same date saw the arrival of the first occupant. No 122 Airfield Headquarters and No 122 Squadron arrived from Eastchurch, being joined by No 602 Squadron from Fairlop, both squadrons flying the Spitfire Mk VB. The squadrons made good use of the experience of settling into a new airfield, a skill that they were to practise frequently over the next eighteen months. They were joined on 26 June by the Spitfire VCs of No 19 from Gravesend, completing 122 Airfield's complement. During their time at Bognor the pilots practised ground-attack techniques on the local ranges and participated in *Ramrods* supporting day-bomber raids. Just a month after No 122 Airfield arrived, it left for Kingsnorth in Kent with both 122 and 602 Squadrons. No 19 left the following day for Newchurch, leaving Bognor deserted.

Experience at Bognor and other early ALGs led to an upgrading programme that began at Bognor in the autumn of 1943. No 4 Works Squadron provided extended hard taxi-tracks, more hardstandings and the doubling of the Extra Over Blister hangars to four. As usual no housing was built for personnel. Like most ALGs, tents were the main accommodation, but Bognor was fortunate in having requisitioned some local property. Morells farmhouse was taken over as the HQ, with the barns used for storage. On the North Bersted side of the airfield the Paymaster's office was in what is now the Old Chapel Forge. The adjacent disused chapel was used as a store and workshops.

A period of intense activity began with the arrival of No 132 (Norwegian) Airfield from North Weald on the last day of March 1944. Part of No 84 Group, the Airfield consisted of Nos 66, 331 and 332, the latter pair being Norwegian squadrons, all three operating the highly successful Mk IX version of the Spitfire in a fighter-bomber role. Their working-up included visits to Armament Practice Camps, and No 66 also paid brief visits to Southend in April and Castletown in mid-May. One of the most successful of its offensive operations was a *Ranger* flown by No 332 on 11 April when six enemy aircraft were destroyed during a strafing attack on Juvincourt airfield near Paris. On 12 May, in common with all Airfields, No 132 was renamed No 132 Wing.

D-Day and the subsequent days saw the Wing operating over the beachhead, although contact with the Luftwaffe was very limited, interspersed with escorting bombers attacking the *Noball* V-1 sites and other targets. On 14 June the Wing joined other Wings in escorting 221 Bomber Command Lancasters on a daylight raid on Le Havre, targeting the port in general and the E-boats in their reinforced concrete pens in particular. The raid, the first in daylight for more than a year, was very successful and only one Lancaster was lost. Before the Wing moved to Tangmere on 21 June, it was honoured by a visit from Crown Prince Olav, who slept under canvas with his fellow countrymen.

The next unit to move into Bognor on 25 June 1944 was a departure from what had become the norm. No 83 Group Support Unit left Redhill hurriedly due to the increased threat of the V-1 to its large holding of reserve aircraft and pilots. With more than 100 aircraft (at least three for each 83 Group squadron), Bognor was overwhelmed by Spitfires, Mustangs and Typhoons, which were dispersed and hidden around the airfield as much as was possible. Also leaving Redhill was No 1310 Transport Flight with the Anson Mk 1. Originally formed to ferry pilots and aircraft for the 2TAF, the Flight's main duty while at Bognor was carrying blood plasma to France. The Flight received Anson Mk Xs, converted to carry stretchers, in early July, but on the 21st the unit was disbanded, its aircraft and role being transferred to No 83 GSU.

Aircraft were constantly coming and going. On 10 August an ATA ferry pilot, Peter George, based at No 6 Ferry Pool at Ratcliffe, arrived from Lichfield in an Anson to collect ATA colleagues, returning them to White Waltham. On 21 August he delivered a Typhoon himself from 51 MU at Lichfield and was back two days later with a second Typhoon. With so much activity, accidents were inevitable. On 9 August a Mustang crash-landed, but a more serious incident on 11 September resulted in the death of a pilot awaiting take-off clearance. His aircraft was hit by a Mustang making an emergency landing with an engine fire.

With the move of No 83 GSU to Thorney Island from 25 September 1944, Bognor's military role was completed. The requisitioned properties were returned to their owners during November and a Canadian Works Flight began to lift the steel matting to reinstate the site prior to its return to agriculture in September 1945. Over the years the West Meads housing estate has gradually encroached on the southern end of the former airfield, but most of the terrain remains open farmland. Home-owners on the former boundaries have found concrete bases in their gardens, possibly former hardstandings or roads. Similarly, pieces of Sommerfeld track or metal pegs have also surfaced in gardens or fields. Although there is virtually no visual evidence of the site's wartime role, the line of the southern end of the NW/SE runway can be found. On Chalcraft Lane there is a large section of the hedge missing just after the entrance to the cemetery. The name of Bognor Airfield was resurrected during the 1980s, but located on the A29 to the north of the town, not on the former ALG site. Used by the LEC company for its executive aircraft, the airfield was still in use in 1981 but closed some time prior to the company's move to a new location.

During 2004 a temporary exhibition in the Jubilee Hall, North Bersted, on the history of the Bognor ALG aroused many local memories highlighted by a visit by a Norwegian veteran who served on the airfield. For those wishing to learn more, a local historian, Sylvia Endacott, published a history of Bognor in 2005 under the title of *It Started With a Map*.

Main features:
Runways: 072° 4,800ft, 151° 4,200ft, steel matting (Sommerfeld track). *Hangars:* four EO Blisters. *Hardstandings:* temporary Sommerfeld track. *Accommodation:* tented camp.

BRENZETT (Ivychurch), Kent

51°01N/00° 52E 9ft asl; TR015280. 3 miles NW of New Romney on minor road off A259

Advanced Landing Grounds generally had a transient existence, hastily created from farmland and, usually within three years, just as quickly returned to agriculture. With virtually no permanent structures to tell the story sixty years on, most have nothing to distinguish them from other farmers' fields. A few have a memorial in the village or on a nearby road and a handful have had their history written by a dedicated local historian. Brenzett is no different in having nothing on the site to tell the tale, but is different in that it has a museum in its name nearby, a memorial and a published history.

It was July 1942 when the Air Ministry approved the use of 300 acres in the triangle between Brenzett, Ivychurch and Snave as an ALG and began the process of requisitioning. Finally, on 10

December No 4 Works Squadron was authorised to begin preliminary work, including demolishing a bungalow, closing two minor roads, burying telegraph wires and infilling ditches. Moat House on the eastern side of the site and its associated buildings were taken over for accommodation. Two Sommerfeld track runways were laid aligned virtually N/S and E/W and a pair of Blister hangars erected. Completed by March 1943, the ALG was handed over for grazing. This state of limbo was interrupted for three days from 14 September 1943 when urgent repairs to Kingsnorth ALG required a temporary home for No 122 Squadron. In common with all the ALGs, Brenzett underwent a programme of upgrading in early 1944. The 5003rd Airfield Construction Squadron (the former Works Squadrons had been renamed during 1943) laid steel mesh taxiways, three more standard Blister hangars and four large hardcore dispersals.

Although not required over the D-Day period, it was the V-1 offensive that brought operational units to Brenzett. The first to arrive were Nos 129 (Mysore) and 306 (Polish) Squadrons on 8 July, followed two days later by the second Polish Squadron, No 315, all transferring from Ford as No 133 Wing, 84 Group. For the next two months the pilots lived, slept and ate in tents beside their Merlin-powered Mustang Mk IIIs, which, with their marginal speed advantage over the V-1, required careful tactical positioning to ensure an interception. The first of these weapons to be destroyed by 133 Wing fell to the guns of Flt Sgt Jankowski of No 315 Squadron on 11 July. The scores mounted up over the following weeks and, by the time the last V-1 patrol was flown on 1 September, the Wing had destroyed 179 'Doodlebugs'. The Mustang's long range was utilised on 30 July when nine 315 Squadron Mustangs positioned to Coltishall to fill up their drop tanks to escort Beaufighters on a shipping strike off Norway where they claimed eight defending fighters without loss.

Other operations included a Wing *Rodeo* on 18 August with thirty-six Mustangs. No 315 tangled with some sixty Fw 190s around Beauvais, claiming sixteen destroyed for the loss of one Mustang, but sadly that was their CO, Sqn Ldr Horbaczewski. With sixteen enemy aircraft destroyed, he was one of Poland's leading fighter aces, having already won the DSO and DFC. Posthumously he was awarded

With its pilot at readiness, a No 315 (Polish) Squadron Mustang III awaits the order to scramble. (via A. Moor)

An armourer checks the guns of a Polish Mustang III at Brenzett in the summer of 1944. (via A. Moor)

The history of Brenzett and other local ALGs can be found in the superb Brenzett Aeronautical Museum. (DWL collection)

Poland's highest combat decoration, the Gold Cross of the Order Virtuti Militari. From 17 to 26 September the Wing flew operations in support of Operation 'Market', escorting transports and glider combinations to the Grave and Arnhem area. Before moving to Andrews Field over 10 and 11 October, the Wing escorted thirteen Lancasters of No 617 Squadron on 7 October on a successful daylight raid on a dam near the Swiss border with the loss of one Lancaster.

The ALG was released in December 1944 and work began on returning the site to its former condition. This was completed in 1945 and the roads reinstated, virtually eliminating all evidence of the former airfield. A few gaps in hedges now indicate the line of former taxiways or runways, and a substantial concrete bridge over a ditch on the road to Ivychurch is a more permanent relic, but of course the best monument to RAF Brenzett is the superb Aeronautical Museum (see below). An excellent history, *Mustang Wing: RAF Brenzett Advanced Landing Ground*, was written by Tony Moor, a member of the Brenzett Aeronautical Museum Trust. All this will go a long way to ensure that, of all the temporary airfields of the Second World War, Brenzett will always be one that is remembered.

Main features:
Runways: N-S 4,800ft, E-W 4,200ft, steel matting (Sommerfeld track). *Hangars:* five Blister. *Hardstandings:* four hardcore surface. *Accommodation:* tented camp.

Place of interest nearby:
The Brenzett Aeronautical Museum opened in 1972, just down the road from the ALG's location in what, at first sight, appear to be airfield buildings but were in fact a wartime Land Army hostel. As well as telling the story of Brenzett ALG and other local airfields, the extensive exhibition includes many historic artefacts recovered from crash sites. Aircraft on display comprise the cockpit of a Hurricane Mk 1, the nose of a Dakota and more modern machines. The impressive memorial commemorates the 50th Anniversary of D-Day and all the squadrons based on Kent's ALGs. Any aeronautical visitors to the Romney Marshes should include Brenzett in their itinerary.

CAPEL (Folkestone), Kent

51°06N/01°13E; TR0260389. 2 miles NE of Folkestone alongside B2011

The name Capel or Capel le Ferne is now associated with the location of the superb Battle of Britain Memorial. However, it was the Great War nearly ninety years earlier that brought the Capel airship station into existence, sited to the north of the then main road from Folkestone to Dover. The German declaration of unrestricted submarine warfare from February 1915 stimulated the establishment of RNAS airship stations around the coast, especially where shipping was concentrated. The English Channel and particularly the Dover Straits were of special concern to the Admiralty. The open fields to the east of Capel le Ferne were selected as a suitable location and work began in April 1915. The urgency was such that, although still under construction, the station was commissioned on 8 May 1915. The naval ratings were billeted in four houses on the outskirts of the village and the Officers' Wardroom was established in Abbots Cliff House.

It was planned that RNAS Capel would operate the new Sea Scout class of non-rigid airship. The first, SS-1, was built at Kingsnorth with a BE.2C fuselage suspended below the envelope of a Willows airship. On its delivery flight to Capel on 7 May 1915, with a young Sub Lt R. S. Booth in command, it was destroyed by fire, when Booth mistook the wind direction, attempted to land down-wind and collided with telegraph wires. An inauspicious start, but Booth was later to command the successful R.100 rigid airship. It is possible that SS-2 had arrived at Capel earlier, as the RAeS library holds a photograph captioned 'SS-2 in shed at Dover, 9 April 1915', ie at Capel/Folkestone, but other sources put the SS-2's first flight as 5 May 1915. Whichever is correct, the number of Sea Scouts at Capel increased rapidly, with SS-4 arriving on 8 May followed by SS-5, which then moved on to Polegate. May 1916 also saw the arrival of SS-10, followed by others including SS-8, SS-11 and SS-12.

The SS-12 airship being walked into its shed at Capel in August 1915.
(Ces Mowthorpe collection)

The SS airships provided very basic accommodation for their crews, but gave air cover for Channel shipping when nothing else was available. They were also simple to fly, thus giving new airshipmen invaluable experience when more advanced airships followed. Capel undertook the rebuild of SS-10, which was wrecked in the Channel on 10 September when operating from France. It reappeared as SS-10A, and around the same time Folkestone took over the production of the SS series from Kingsnorth. Many of the Capel airships were fitted with modified Maurice Farman cars, which, with their 'pusher' engine configuration, provided a much more comfortable environment. However, by early 1916 production of the SS was moved to Barrow and Wormwood Scrubs.

The term 'Blimp' often applied to non-rigid airships is believed to have originated at Capel. It is recorded that Cdr (later Air Commodore) A. D. Cunningham, as Station Commander, made his weekly inspection during December 1915 and flicked the fabric of SS-12 with his finger and thumb, verbally imitating the resulting reverberation as 'blimp'. This humorous interlude was reported in the Wardroom by the young midshipman who had delivered SS-12 to Capel, later Air Marshal Sir Victor Goddard. Thus it is believed the term passed into general usage.

In the summer of 1915, the BE.2c control car of SS-4 was fitted with a supplementary instructor's seat behind the pilot. (JMB/GSL collection)

From early January 1916 the Germans began to take an interest in the aerial activities around Dover and Folkestone. Over lunchtime on Sunday 23 January two floatplanes overflew Dover and one proceeded to drop five bombs close to Capel without damage, although the Germans claimed to have set an airship shed on fire with seventeen bombs. The following day another flight was made over the station, apparently a photo-reconnaissance to assess the results of the earlier raid. Aircraft of the RFC attempted an interception without success.

The continuing search for improvements in the performance of the SS airship led the engineering section at Capel to evolve the SSZ. A new streamlined ash-framed car covered in aluminium, designed to be watertight to permit water landings, was fitted with a superb 75hp Rolls-Royce Hawk aero engine, the only engine to be designed specially for airships. The three-man crew consisted of the pilot in the centre, his W/T operator forward and engineer aft. The car was fitted to a 70,000cu ft (1,982cu m) envelope. Built between June and August 1916, the prototype was initially designated SS.0, referred to as the SS Zero, which became the SS.Z1. After successful trials were completed during September 1916, the Admiralty was informed. After censuring Cdr Cunningham and his team for unauthorised modification of Naval equipment, Their Lordships ordered the new design into full production. The next four 'Zeros' were built at Folkestone, but in April 1917 Z1 was sent to Messrs Sage & Co of Peterborough to act as a pattern for the manufacture of the SSZ car. It was estimated that a new 'Zero' then cost £5,000.

The garage and men's quarters at Capel in July 1916. (GSL collection)

Capel settled into the routine of escorting Channel shipping, especially on the Folkestone-Boulogne service, enlivened with the very occasional sighting of a U-boat. After service in Dunkirk, the original 'Zero' returned, its identity having undergone a minor change to SSZ.1. On the creation of the RAF in April 1918, the station became officially Folkestone as part of No 5 Group, with its HQ in Dover. By then it had grown to include three large airship sheds with wind-breaks at each end, and had two sub-stations at Godmersham Park and Wittersham. Its personnel were accommodated in a small town of wooden hutting adjacent to the Royal Oak Inn. By November 1918 seven SSZ airships were on strength, plus two twin-engined SSTs with a 100,000cu ft (2,832cu m) envelope. SST-1, the first of her class, had arrived from Wormwood Scrubs on 26 June 1918. The second, SST-8, arrived in mid-October. A month earlier, on 16 September 1918, SSZ.1, under the command of Ensign N. J. Learned of the US Navy, depth-charged and sank a German submarine, UB-103. This historic airship operated from Capel until deflated on 14 January 1919, when it had flown 960 hours. That was to be the fate of all non-rigid coastal patrol airships as the service was rapidly run down following the Armistice.

Capel/Folkestone closed in 1919, the land and buildings being passed to the Disposal Board in August 1920. For many years one airship shed survived, and the airfield was used for an airshow in 1933. Deemed unsuitable for airfield use in the Second World War, the site was a part of the Y Service, monitoring German radio traffic. A large caravan park now covers part of the airfield and the site of the wooden hutting. In September 1987 one of the hangar bases was in use for the storage of caravans, but this feature could not be located during a visit in 2004. The Royal Oak Inn remains but sadly, despite my thirst, was closed at the time of my visit, so may contain mementoes of Capel's history. As most readers will want to visit Capel le Ferne to see the stunning Battle of Britain Memorial (see below), a nostalgic glance along the road at a historic former airship station will not be time wasted.

Main features:
Runways: grass landing and take-off area. *Hangars:* three airship sheds. *Accommodation:* wooden huts.

Place of interest nearby:
Capel le Ferne is now associated with the location of the superb Battle of Britain Memorial, situated on the site of the former Second World War Capel Battery. Conceived by the late Wg Cdr Geoffrey Page, the memorial was unveiled by Her Majesty the Queen Mother on 9 July 1993. It is in the shape of a large propeller, with a pilot sitting at the centre. Also on the site are replicas of a Hawker Hurricane and Supermarine Spitfire, and the Christopher Foxley-Norris Memorial Wall, on which appear the names of the almost 3,000 aircrew who flew in the Battle.

A seated figure of an airman at the centre of a three-bladed propeller commemorates the Battle of Britain. (DWL collection)

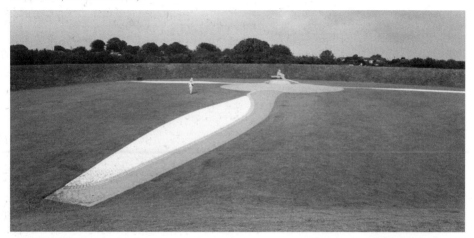

CHAILEY, East Sussex

50°57N/00°02W 105ft asl; TQ370192. 3.5 miles E of Burgess Hill on minor road

The sleepy mid-Sussex countryside, and specifically Bower Farm, had seen nothing like it for sixty years! Over a glorious summer weekend of 7-8 August 2004, Chailey celebrated its historic role during the momentous summer of 1944. The broad valley again reverberated to the sound of Rolls-Royce Merlins as Spitfires, Hurricanes and Mustangs competed with radial-engined warbirds to see which could make the best music. Nostalgia was heavy in the air with the attendance of Dame Vera Lynn and four veterans of No 131 (Polish) Wing. In addition, an excellent history of the ALG was published on the day with the appropriate punning title of *Spit and Polish*. The author, Richard Whittle, and Dame Vera were on hand to autograph copies for the long queues of eager purchasers – a wonderful celebration of Chailey's notable past.

The future ALG was originally surveyed in June 1942, with the final plans, which included a lengthened main runway, being accepted by the Air Ministry in October, subject to Fighter Command agreement on dispersal arrangements. Notice was given to the occupants of Bower and Great Homewood farms, on whose land the airfield was to be built. As usual for an ALG, the two runways were aligned virtually at right angles to each other, the intersection being virtually on Bower Road, the closure of which meant of long diversion for local residents via Wivelsfield Green. That inconvenience was as nothing compared with the loss of The Plough Inn on South Road, which was directly under the approach to the main east-west runway. It, together with the adjacent Lambourne Cottages, was demolished, as was Great Homewood farmhouse, which was on the line of the north-south runway. Bower Farm and buildings at Gurr's Farm were taken over for accommodation and storage.

The preparation of Chailey was far from straightforward as it was a heavily wooded area with many fully mature oaks to be removed. HT cables had to be buried and rubble from blitzed London houses brought in for tracks and three large hardstandings. Although it was planned to have the airfield ready by 1 June, it was not until early July that personnel from No 5004 Airfield Construction Squadron arrived to complete the preparation and to lay the Sommerfeld track runways. On 27 August, while work was still in progress, a severely damaged Marauder of the 322nd BG made an emergency landing on the north-south runway. The final work was the erection of four Extra Over Blister hangars during November 1943. In time for Christmas a 'new' Plough Inn was opened for business in a wooden former Army hut, which was in use as a chicken house before being moved to a new site; the structure survived in its new role until 1956.

It had been decided that Chailey was to be the home of No 131 (Polish) Airfield. But before the 'permanent' Spitfire residents arrived, Chailey received temporary visitors in the shape of a 367th FG Thunderbolt on New Year's Eve, and on 25 February 1944 a B-17 from Glatton made a precautionary landing, departing after repairs on 13 March. Six days later a party of Polish officers from Northolt inspected their future home, which was not due to be commissioned until late April. In the interim, the three Polish squadrons, Nos 302 (Poznan), 308 (Krakow) and 317 (Wilno), transferred to Deanland, moving to Chailey on 26 April 1944. The following morning the Wing, led by Gp Capt Gabszewicz, escorted Bostons on a *Ramrod* operation, followed in the afternoon by another *Ramrod* with USAAF Marauders. This tempo of operations continued into May with the exception of the 3rd, the Polish National Day, when there was no operational flying.

From the second week of May, the change of name to No 131 Wing saw a high proportion of its Spitfires operating with 500lb (227kg) bombs on *Rangers* seeking communication, V-1 and airfield targets. Generally, opposition was limited and casualties were few with the exception of 21 May, when No 308 lost two aircraft and one pilot to heavy flak. The cadence of operations grew as the month ended. The Wing knew that the longed-for invasion of Europe was close, confirmed by the attendance of Gp Capt Gabszewicz and two of his Wing Commanders at a top secret conference on 2 June, followed by the confinement to camp of all personnel and the painting of 'invasion stripes' on the aircraft.

On 6 June the Wing flew its first operation over the beachhead from 0500 hours. With total air superiority, the biggest hazard was a mid-air collision with another Allied aircraft. A further three ops were flown, the last landing at 2100 hours, after a very busy but uneventful day. This pattern, interspersed with *Ramrods*, continued for much of the rest of the month except for 20 June, when two Fw 190s were destroyed and another damaged. The previous day a 302 Squadron Spitfire and its pilot had been lost to flak. On 25 June a Halifax of 433 Squadron chose Chailey as its emergency landing ground, departing for Skipton-on-Swale three days later. No 131 Wing transferred to Appledram over 28/29 June, leaving Chailey in the hands of a small RAF contingent.

Spitfire IXc MK984 was Sqn Ldr Witold Rettinger's usual aircraft when CO of 308 (Krakow) Squadron. (MAP via P. H. T. Green collection)

The now abandoned airstrip was host to another bomber in distress on 3 August. The 384th BG B-17 crash-landed on fire with its bombs aboard; they exploded almost immediately, but fortunately after the crew had escaped. Probably the last wartime visitor was a No 161 Squadron Lysander, which was written off in a forced-landing on 18 October 1944. Chailey was officially released on 20 January 1945, but it was not until 11 April that personnel from 5027 Airfield Construction squadron arrived to return the site to agriculture. The Sommerfeld tracking was lifted, but was left rolled up on the farm for many years. Its work completed, the team moved on to Swingfield on 15 June and Chailey reverted to its pre-war slumbers.

A painting in the Plough Inn illustrates a section of four Chailey Spitfires over-flying their home base during 1944. (DWL collection)

At the 2004 Chailey Air Display, Ray Hanna displayed his Spitfire Mk IX, MH434, resplendent in the personal markings of Chailey's wing leader, Group Captain Gabszewicz. (DWL collection)

By the 21st century the only surviving wartime building was the bulk fuel store pump house, but both Bower farmhouse, the 131 Wing HQ and Westland Cottage, the Operations Room and 18 Sector HQ remain as private houses.

Main features:
Runways: E-W 4,500ft, NW-SE 3,600ft, steel matting (Sommerfeld track). *Hangars:* four EO Blisters. *Hardstandings:* three hardcore and ash surface. *Accommodation:* tented camp.

Place of interest nearby:
The wartime temporary Plough Inn at Plumpton was replaced by a new building in the mid-1950s and its grounds were chosen as the location of a spectacular memorial to the former ALG and its Polish airmen. Unveiled on 8 August 2000 by Dame Vera Lynn and Lady Joan Bader, it alone makes a visit to the area worthwhile. The Plough has many photographs and other memorabilia of Chailey if the reader needs an excuse to call in for a pint.

The bulk fuel store pump house is Chailey's last wartime building. (DWL collection)

CHATTIS HILL, Hampshire

51°07N/01°31W 250ft asl; SU335355/SU325355. 2.5 miles W of Stockbridge on A30

A mile south of the 4th-century BC Danebury Ring hill fort lies Chattis Hill, on whose slopes mid-20th-century aeronautical archaeological remains may be found, although the first aviation use of the site was a couple of decades earlier. The proximity of Houghton Downs (south-east of Chattis Hill) to the nearby Army ranges on Salisbury Plain first attracted the RFC. Avoiding a pair of ancient tumuli, a 120-acre airfield (SU335355) was created in the summer of 1917. A line of Bessonneau hangars was erected near Chattis Hill House along the main road to Stockbridge. Although a tented camp was established, many personnel managed to find more comfortable billets in Stockbridge. The officers selected The Grosvenor Arms to be their Mess.

The first two squadrons arrived on 14 September. No 91 came from Spitalgate for wireless telegraphy training with a variety of machines including the RE.8 and BE.2C. Its partner, No 92, a fighter trainer unit, moved in from London Colney bringing Spad S.7s, Pups and Avro 504s. Another potential fighter squadron, No 93, joined the first pair in early October. As winter deepened, the sloping land channelled the rain towards the camp at the bottom of the hill, producing a morass. The squadrons' misery was not relieved until mid-March 1918, when all three departed to Tangmere, thus making way for Nos 34 and 43 Training Squadrons. Both flew a wide variety of aircraft including the ubiquitous Avro 504 and relative rarities such as the Scout D, 1½ Strutter, DH.5 and Morane Parasol.

By early April improved weather allowed increased flying training. The two squadrons were on 14 April joined by the Wireless Telephony School from Biggin Hill. Chattis Hill became very busy. Short flying courses for pilots and observers and longer sessions for W/T officers and technicians being available. Originally known as Reserve Squadrons, the pair became Training Squadrons in May 1917, but by mid-July 1918 merged, as Chattis Hill became No 43 Training Depot Station. When the TDS entered 8 Group on 12 October, the establishment then included thirty-six Avro 504Ks, thirty-six Camels and a few Pups. The latter were obsolete but were used by the instructors for 'personal' travel!

The two training roles of the station were not wholly compatible, for while TDS pilots and observers learned their flying skills constantly buzzing around the circuit, the Wireless School machines had a habit of trailing virtually invisible lengths of wire aerial. Somehow the worst never happened.

Summer 1918 saw an American Construction Unit arrive to build a permanent station consisting of three pairs of GS sheds (Belfast hangars) and a single-bay ARS. Messes and quarters were located to the east of the airfield, the WRAF being accommodated at Houghton Down Farm near Stockbridge. The hutted accommodation was occupied but the technical area, including the hangars, was incomplete when the November Armistice was signed. Building work ended abruptly. The clash of interests between the TDS and Wireless School was resolved by the latter's departure to Winton on 21 November.

In early 1919 Chattis Hill became a store for aircraft from other local airfields. Many served with 34 TDS until they became unserviceable and were discarded. On 15 May 1919 the TDS was disbanded and Chattis Hill began a rapid wind-down. Closure came in early 1920, the incomplete hangars were dismantled and huts auctioned off for civilian use. Their concrete bases survived for a while and part of the MT garage was converted into a private house. The historic landscape reverted to its normal peaceful way of life with much of Chattis Hill being used for racehorse gallops.

It was the 1940 bombing of the Supermarine factories in Southampton that shattered the peace. The company's tentative plans for the dispersal of the vital Spitfire production were rapidly implemented. Chattis Hill was again requisitioned, final assembly hangars being erected in the woods to the north of the former First World War airfield. The new test and delivery airfield (SU325355) was prepared on the racehorse gallops of Atte Persee, the racehorse trainer, with the combination of woodland and horse tracks disguising the new facilities.

Completed by December 1940, just three months later Spitfires were rolling off the assembly lines. After flight testing, they were flown out by ATA pilots of the Hamble sub-pool of No 1 Ferry Pilot's Pool, White Waltham, which, in July 1941, became No 15 FPP, staffed wholly by women pilots using Anson and Argus crew ferry aircraft. Chattis Hill was also the designated emergency base for the FPP in the event of a German invasion. From mid-1944 production was a mix of Merlin-engined PR.XIs and Griffon-engined F.XIVs and PR.XIXs. The photo-reconnaissance aircraft were a batch of

600 ordered from Vickers-Armstrong, their construction being divided between Chattis Hill and Aldermaston. The Mark XIVs were the last Spitfires to be delivered before production ceased in mid-1945. Although the airfield was closed, Vickers-Armstrong retained the site until 31 May 1948.

The assembly hangars were removed and their bases served the County Council for road stone storage. Open spaces within the woodland indicate where three of these deteriorating foundations survive. An EWS (Emergency Water Supply) tank full of old tyres together with a number of brick-built structures may also be found. A circular concrete base is possibly the compass swinging platform. Although there is no formal memorial to the site's military use, the former service road does acknowledge the Supermarine connection by its name of Spitfire Lane. A more lasting memorial to the work of Chattis Hill is the significant number of surviving Spitfires that originated from this forgotten airfield. These are mainly PR.XIXs, but perhaps the most famous survivor is Mk XIV RM689; delivered on 3 July 1944, it served with No 350 (Belgian) Squadron among others. In 1949 it was acquired by Rolls-Royce as G-ALGT based at Hucknall on flight-test duties and display work. It is currently being rebuilt after an accident in 1992.

Old hangar bases and this overgrown building were to be found at Chattis Hill in 2003. (DWL collection)

Main features:
Runways: grass strips. *Hangars:* MAP aircraft assembly hangars. *Accommodation:* not known.

CHILBOLTON, Hampshire

51°08N/01°26W 300ft asl; SU393385. 1 mile S of Chilbolton village off A3057

Located on a plateau some 40 metres (130 feet) above the River Test and the charming Chilbolton village lay Manor Farm, part of which was occasionally used during the 1930s by private light aircraft. This use was noted in 1936 by the Air Ministry, which earmarked the site as a prospective military airfield. This interest was confirmed in 1939 when 145 acres of land was requisitioned from Manor Farm and construction work commenced. The work consisted of merely the removal of hedges and some levelling to give an excellent freely draining grass landing surface. However, two sunken forts, believed to be the Pickett-Hamilton type, were also installed on the airfield.

The planned use for Chilbolton was as a dispersed site for aircraft from Middle Wallop, then under construction as a bomber station, but before both airfields were ready Fighter Command had a greater priority. Middle Wallop became a Sector Station of 10 Group, building up to four squadrons by the start of the Battle of Britain. Although Chilbolton's first visiting aircraft, a Harvard, landed on 3 May 1940, the station had no resident unit until No 238 Squadron dispersed from Middle Wallop on 30 September.

The Squadron's Hurricanes were immediately in action from their new base. Just after 11.00am on 1 October in a mêlée over the Isle of Purbeck the Squadron lost two Hurricanes, with one pilot, PO Covington, bailing out over Sherborne. The Squadron claimed one Bf 110D, believed to be from 1/ZG 26, which was brought down into the Channel off Swanage. Another Hurricane was lost on 5 October, when Sqn Ldr J. R. MacLachlan bailed out with burns. Two days later, on 7 October, the Luftwaffe attacked Westland's Yeovil factory. No 238 intercepted, destroying a Bf 110 from II/ZG26 plus a Ju 88 of II/KG 51 for the loss of another Hurricane shot down by Bf 109s, the pilot bailing out safely.

The Squadron then had time to catch its breath as Luftwaffe attacks moved elsewhere, and by November, with the Germans concentrating on night raids, No 238 settled down to a relatively quiet winter. The only diversion from the routine was a squadron detachment to Pembrey on 1 April 1941, returning on 16 April. The Squadron was stood down in early May in preparation for a move to Malta, the Hurricanes embarking on HMS *Victorious* on 16 May. After a voyage up the Mediterranean, they flew off, arriving at Takali on 14 June. Their brief replacement during most of June was No 308 (Polish) Squadron with Spitfire Mk IIAs. The day after the Poles left, 501 (County of Gloucester) Squadron arrived, also with Spitfire IIAs, and set about convoy escort patrols and night interception using the pilot's Mark One Eyeball night sights. The normal success rate for day-fighters on night patrols was usually very low, but almost immediately the CO, Sqn Ldr A. H. Boyd, scored the Squadron's first night victory over Portsmouth. The Squadron was accorded another honour when it was chosen to provide the flying sequences for the movie *The First of the Few*, the story of the Spitfire's designer, Reginald Mitchell. One of No 501's flight-commanders at this time was 'Ginger' Lacey, the top-scoring RAF ace of the Battle of Britain with twenty victories.

No 501 left for Ibsley in early August to make way for another Auxiliary Air Force Squadron, No 504 (County of Nottingham), which was rebuilding after losing 'A' Flight to the re-forming 81 Squadron. By the end of August No 504 departed for Northern Ireland, changing places with No 245, which arrived on 1 September 1941. The new residents relished in the opportunity for offensive action, taking their Hurricane IIBs on *Roadstead* anti-shipping sorties over the French coast. A brief sojourn at Warmwell in mid-October was followed by a transfer to Middle Wallop just before Christmas for a spell of night-flying.

After some eighteen months of use, the rather basic airfield was scheduled for some upgrading; although a concrete perimeter track was laid, the grass flying field was retained. Around the new taxi-way, fighter hardstandings were built, some with double blast pens. Additional technical accommodation was provided including three Blister hangars. More land was acquired to provide space for semi-permanent domestic sites.

As usual, while all this work was under way the airfield continued to be used, but only as an RLG for the Army Co-op Tomahawks of No 41 OTU from Old Sarum, a role that continued until December 1942, although the airfield was still a full satellite station of 10 Group. It was obvious that 10 Group really had no requirement for Chilbolton, and on 7 December it became a satellite of Netheravon as part of 38 Group. The Night Flying Flight of the Glider Pilots' Exercise Unit brought in its Tiger Moths on 18 December, followed by the rest of the unit on 8 January 1943. Tasked to provide refresher and flying practice facilities for the pilots of the Army Glider Pilot Regiment, the

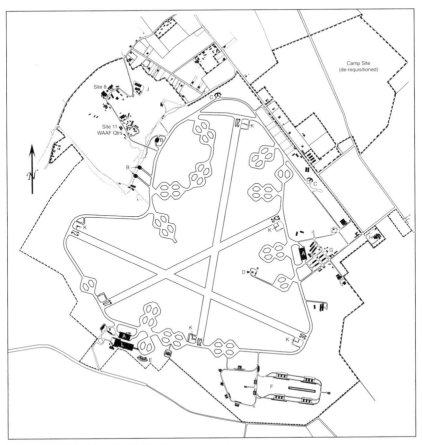

CHILBOLTON, 1953

A T2 hangar
B Blister hangar
C Aircraft pen
D Flying Control
E Shooting-in Butt
F Bomb Store
G Technical Site
H Administrative Area
J Sewage Disposal Site
K Floodlight
L B1 hangar; Vickers-Supermarine Assembly Building

When Vickers-Supermarine took over Chilbolton in 1947, it erected a B1 hangar south of the southern T2 for use as an assembly building, but allowed most of the rest of the airfield to become derelict. By 1953, the date of the plan, the off-airfield dispersed sites Nos 3, 4, 5, 6 and 12 (the sick quarters) had been derequisitioned. Communal Site 2 and Sites 6 and 11 (the WAAF site) were retained.

Chilbolton had a number of interesting features that reflect its original role as a fighter aerodrome. The two aircraft pens (labelled C) were double blast pens built towards the end of 1941, and at least two 'sunken forts', believed to be Pickett-Hamilton elevating forts, had been located on the grass aerodrome in 1940.

unit's establishment by April 1943 consisted of ten Tiger Moths, thirty Masters (including reserves) and sixty Hotspurs. Chilbolton reverberated to the roar of the overworked Bristol Mercury radial engines of the Masters as they aero-towed an endless succession of Hotspurs.

Chilbolton played a significant role in the *Spartan* exercise, which took place during February and March of 1943. The largest military exercise of the war, it involved all home-based Army Co-op and ground attack units and involved both mobility exercises and field operations. In that context Nos 174 and 184 Squadrons brought in their Hurricane IIBs from 1 to 11 March, all personnel living under canvas. On 10 May the Tigers, Masters and Hotspurs returned to Netheravon as Chilbolton was prepared for yet another new role.

For the planned occupation by the USAAF, the airfield needed a total rebuild. First more land to the south-west was requisitioned, bringing the total to 345 acres, sufficient for a standard Class One three-runway airfield. The first USAAF personnel arrived at Station 404 during December 1943 as the 5th Tactical Air Depot, with its constituent 10th and 86th Air Depot Groups. However, as the construction of the depot was still in progress, the transfer from Zeals took some weeks. The mighty P-47 Thunderbolt became a common sight over Chilbolton as the 5th TAD carried out major maintenance, modifications and prepared new aircraft for issuing to 9th Air Force Fighter Groups. In March the TAD was briefly joined by the 12th and 15th Tactical Reconnaissance Squadrons with their Spitfires and Mustangs, their two-week stay being terminated in favour of another IXth Air Force Fighter Group.

With a bomb under its fuselage, P-47 Thunderbolt Peg of my Heart frames another 395th FS P-47 42 0081 and visiting C-47s from Ramsbury prior to D-Day. (J. Antrim via R. Day)

The 368th FG led by Col Gil Meyers brought its Thunderbolts over from Greenham Common on 15 March 1944. When the seventy 'Jugs' of the three squadrons (395th, 396th and 397th) were added to those in the care of the TAD, the number of P-47s at Chilbolton frequently totalled 150! The Group had flown just one mission at Greenham and was soon committed to escort and fighter-bomber sorties over France, the workload intensifying in support of Operation 'Overlord', launched on 6 June. Typical of its missions was that on D+1, when it concentrated on five German gun positions that were pinning down V Corps on the beach. All were destroyed with a combination of 1,000lb (454kg) and cluster bombs. Although its work was primarily ground attack, the Group shot down eighteen enemy aircraft for the loss of twelve Thunderbolts during its stay at Chilbolton, a loss rate significantly less than many similar Groups. Perhaps the most remarkable air-to-air combat was that of Major Randall Hendricks of the 379th FS, who shot down four Fw 190s in rapid succession on 12 June.

Being among the most distant from the front line meant that the 368th was the first Fighter Group to move to the continent. On 16 June the 397th began to use the A-3 Cardonville ALG carved out of Normandy farmland. By 20 June the rest of the Group had followed it. The 5th TAD remained at Chilbolton, but its 10th ADG moved to France in late July, followed by the 86th ADG in September. Meanwhile, Chilbolton became an air evacuation centre with C-47s bringing in casualties from the battle front for treatment at a large temporary hospital near Stockbridge, and returning to France with urgent supplies. This was to continue for many months.

A more permanent association with the C-47 began on 11 September when the three squadrons of the 442nd TCG were transferred from Boreham. Their ground personnel had arrived earlier, and on the very next day the Group's aircraft were dropping supplies over Normandy. However, the move was in preparation for what was to become Operation 'Market', the aerial part of the 'Market Garden' charge through the Netherlands to outflank the German defences. The base was sealed off from the outside world on 14 September as paratroopers of the 501st and 506th Parachute Infantry Regiments set up encampments on the airfield.

A little after 10.00 hours on 17 September, the forty-five C-47s of the 303rd, 304th and 305th TCS took off carrying the 501st PIR to a drop zone near Veghel to secure the critical river and canal bridges. The drop was successful but shortly afterwards the flak defences brought down two C-47s. The second serial was launched, successfully carrying the 505th to another bridge over the River Dommel at Son en Breugel, again losing two aircraft with another seven damaged. The following day saw two serials, each of forty C-47s towing CG-4A gliders, reinforce the paratroops with fresh troops carrying slightly heavier weapons. Only one aircraft was lost, but on 19 September bad weather meant that only twenty-eight of forty gliders of the first serial reached the drop zones, seven Hadrians fell into the sea and two tug aircraft were lost. The second serial that day of forty-one C-47s experienced even worse problems, none of the gliders reaching the DZ at Son and flak claiming two C-47s. With the failure of the armoured thrust to reach Arnhem, the tempo of missions reduced and in October the Group moved to the continent.

Fairly frequent casualty evacuation flights continued to arrive, but without warning, on Christmas Day 1944, the airfield was deluged with C-47s. With the Battle of the Bulge at a critical phase, the aircraft had arrived to collect the 17th Airborne Division to stem Von Rundstedt's advance through the Ardennes. The mission had been so unexpected that the road from the troops' camp at Barton Stacey to the airfield was littered with discarded turkey bones as the paras finished off their interrupted Christmas dinner! The USAAF retained Chilbolton for cargo use until March 1945, when it was handed back to the RAF.

After its RLG use of Chilbolton in 1942, 41 OTU returned in strength towards the end of March with its forty-four-strong fleet of Hurricanes, Spitfires, Masters and Martinets, plus a single Proctor. Its tenure was brief, the fighter reconnaissance training role being transferred to 61 OTU at Keevil when No 41 disbanded on 26 June. The station reverted to its original 'owners' in the form of the Middle Wallop Sector of what was now 11 Group, acting as a forward airfield. No 26 Squadron passed through on its way to Brussels, but on 17 June No 183 arrived with Spitfire IXs before converting to the Tempest II in August. It was joined on 20 August by 247 Squadron, which exchanged its Typhoons for the Tempest. The intention was that this, the first Tempest II Wing, led by Wg Cdr R. P. Beamont, would join the Tiger Force for operations against Japan, but the atom bomb ended that plan. No 183 was renumbered 54 Squadron during a brief visit to Fairwood Common in early October, and 247 Squadron also visited South Wales for a month from early January 1946. While No 54 busied itself converting pilots destined for the Middle East to the Tempest, No 247 had been earmarked to be the RAF's first Vampire squadron. The pilots' first sight of the Vampire was when Geoffrey de Havilland gave a superb display during March, with deliveries following shortly after.

No 54 took part in an unusual presentation ceremony around this time. Back in May 1941 a member of the RCAF had created a fund to purchase an aircraft based on the sixpence a day granted to Canadian holders of the DFM. The fund had eventually reached its target and No 54 was chosen to be the lucky recipient of a new Tempest named *Canadian DCMs*. In late June both 54 and 247 Squadrons left for Odiham, leaving Chilbolton to a C&M party until November 1946, when the station closed.

Unlike the majority of wartime airfields, this was not the end for Chilbolton, because in February 1947 Vickers-Supermarine saw it as a much more suitable base for its Flight Test Centre than High Post. A B1 assembly hangar was erected on the site of the former gas clothing and

A No 54 Squadron Hawker Tempest II taxies past the photographer during 1946.
(MAP via P. H. T. Green collection)

respirator store alongside the southern T2, but most of the rest of the airfield was allowed to become derelict except for a few huts that were taken over by Vickers technicians pending more suitable accommodation. Initially much of the test work involved the Attacker, but the Supermarine 510, Britain's first design with swept wings and tail, moved to Chilbolton after its initial flight from Boscombe Down on 29 December 1949. The design evolved via the Type 535 into the Swift, the development of which proved to be protracted and difficult. On 3 August 1951 the first production example suffered engine failure in the hands of Mike Lithgow but managed to make an emergency landing at Chilbolton. A month later his deputy, Dave Morgan, while practising for the Farnborough show, also lost his engine, making a forced landing on the approach to the airfield. It was not until 26 February 1953 that a Supermarine aircraft exceed Mach 1 for the first time in a dive. The flight test team at Chilbolton were delighted to have a sonic bang planted on their airfield.

The facilities at Chilbolton attracted a second manufacturer during 1953 when Folland took over the eastern T2. After its first flight on 11 August 1954 the diminutive Midge jet fighter transferred to Chilbolton. Sadly, on 26 September it crashed on take-off. However, its more powerful derivative, the Gnat, flew in July 1955 before also moving to Chilbolton. Although Folland continue to use the airfield for development of the Gnat, especially in its two-seat trainer version for the RAF, until 1961, when it moved to Dunsfold, Vickers-Supermarine had left in 1957.

A trio of Folland Gnat F1s await the day's test flying. In the centre is XN724, which first flew on 26 May 1956. (MOS via P. H. T. Green collection)

The Space Research Council saw the open spaces in the centre of the disused airfield as an ideal location for a radio telescope. Work started in 1963, locating the giant 'dish' on the runway intersection. The facility opened on 14 April 1967 and cost just over £500,000. The 'dish', officially a 25-metre 3GHz Doppler-Polarisation antenna, is the world's largest fully steerable meteorological radar. The site has gone through various name changes over the years, today being known as the CCLRC Chilbolton Observatory. It is one of three sites of the CCLRC (Council for the Central Laboratory of the Research Council) – a snappy title, so no wonder they use an abbreviation! And there are more! The Observatory is home to the CFARR, the Chilbolton Facilities for Atmospheric & Radio Research, and is operated by the Radio Communications Research Unit (RCRU) of the world-famous Rutherford Appleton Laboratory in Oxfordshire. More usefully, it is possible to get live weather reports on the Chilbolton Weather Web – go to www.rcru.rl.ac.uk/weather.

Although the radio dish dominates the landscape, there is still much of Chilbolton's aeronautical history to be found. A pillbox crouches at the edge of the woodland, still defending the southern approach to the airfield including the Supermarine B1 hangar. This was subsequently converted into a grain store and survives today as part of a farm complex together with other original buildings. The central strip of much of the runways remains to service the farmer's fields and give access to a new industrial facility, Tunnel Tech Ltd, not far from the B1.

On the western side of the airfield there are original buildings in three separate locations. Beside the service road opposite the private housing is a pair of Romney huts – former maintenance and repair huts. At the entrance to the airfield beside the water tower the old operations block and the crew briefing room annexe are in use as a garage and a bottled gas store. Adjacent former RAF and WAAF latrines are in poor condition and are to be demolished. By far the best site can be found on the left of the access road from the A30. This is a small industrial estate called Stonefield Park, which is the virtually complete Communal Site No 2. Externally the buildings look totally original, but internally they are modern office and business facilities. Perhaps the best example is what used to be the Airmen's Dining Room, now a complex of offices of Flying Pictures, which provides aerial marketing and advertising using hot air balloons and lightships, as well as aerial filming and live outside broadcasts from airships. In part of the former NAAFI and Institute, Cliff Lovell's Hants Light Plane Services continues to work restoration miracles on historic aircraft, especially 'Ah de Havilland'. Other former buildings having found new uses are the Sergeants' and Officers' Messes, the Gymnasium and numerous air raid shelters. The 1,350ft (411m) grass strip aligned 06/24 adjacent to Stonefield Park is used by Hants Light Plane Services and the Chilbolton Flying Club's microlights.

The former Officers' Mess is in immaculate condition on the Stonefield Park Industrial Estate. (DWL collection)

Awaiting its turn for refurbishment is the old gymnasium on the Communal Site No 2. (DWL collection)

In part of the former NAAFI and Institute, Cliff Lovell's Hants Light Plane Services recreates everything de Havilland. (DWL collection)

Where else to put a memorial than in this evocative setting? On 12 June 1994 a memorial tablet on a brick and flint base was formally dedicated. Funded through the generosity of Gordon Timmins, a IXth Air Force historian who works at Aldermaston, under an engraving of a Hadrian glider the memorial reads:

'Dedicated to the memory of those members of the Airborne Forces who gave their lives in World War II erected as a token of thanks'

Main features:
Runways: 200° 5,400ft x 150ft, 300° 4,800ft x 150ft, 250° 4,200ft x 150ft, concrete, tarmac and wood chippings. *Hangars:* two T2, three Blisters. *Hardstandings:* forty-eight loop type. *Accommodation:* RAF: 225 Officers, 638 SNCOs, 1,937 ORs.

COLDHARBOUR, Kent – see HEADCORN

COLEY, Berkshire – see READING

COOLHAM, West Sussex

50°59N/00°23W 60ft asl; TQ125224. 4 miles SE of Billingshurst on B2139

Fifty years on from the frenetic days of June 1944, men and women from all over the world joined the residents of a peaceful West Sussex village for a weekend of commemoration marking the wartime use of the Coolham ALG. Midday on Saturday 11 June saw the unveiling of an impressive memorial in the garden of the Selsey Arms honouring the airmen of many nations who flew from Coolham in the defence of Britain, especially those who made the ultimate sacrifice. The final notes of the 'Last Post' merged into the roar of a Merlin as a Spitfire dipped a wing in its own tribute to the fallen. The afternoon saw the airfield reopened with a 1350ft (410m) E-W grass strip on the line of the old runway, receiving twenty-two historic aircraft. On the Sunday an open-air Service of Remembrance on the old airfield was attended by some 1,500 people. The originator of this historic gathering, a local PC, Paul Hamlin, subsequently published a superb book of the history of the ALG and of the memorial weekend.

One of more than seventy potential sites surveyed during 1942, and after severe opposition from the War Agricultural Executive Committee, Coolham was one of twenty-three that were eventually built. The 113 acres of farm and woodland requisitioned came under the control of 5004 Airfield Construction Squadron in August 1943 under the command of Sqn Ldr J. K. Lancaster. One property was demolished and another had the roof removed to reduce its height as two Sommerfeld tracking runways were prepared. Part of Farley's farmhouse was used for administration, but all other accommodation was to be under canvas.

Photographed shortly after the 2004 Remembrance Service, the impressive Coolham Memorial is a worthy tribute to the men who served there and those who died flying from this Sussex airfield. (DWL Collection)

As work was nearing completion in mid-February 1944, Coolham had it first aerial visitor and suffered its first fatality. A 323rd BG Marauder from Earls Colne, returning from Cherbourg on one engine, attempted an emergency landing as the second engine cut out. The uncontrollable bomber killed a Sergeant of the No 5016 ACS, although the crew escaped from the wrecked machine with just minor injuries.

The ALG opened on 1 April when Nos 306 and 315 (Polish) Squadrons flew in from Heston, joined two days later by No 129, also from Heston via Llanbedr. All three squadrons, which made up No 133 Airfield, were in the course of converting from the Spitfire IX to the Mustang III. Over the following weeks the process was marred by three fatal accidents. In the first, on 4 April, a 306 Squadron pilot crashed on take-off while ferrying a Mustang from Aston Down to Coolham. More worrying, on 19 April a No 315 Mustang broke up in mid-air after a high-speed dive, and two days later No 306 lost its second pilot as he undershot on landing.

Finally, on 26 April Coolham was officially operational as four Mustangs of 129 (Mysore) Squadron carried out a *Ranger* over airfields in the Cambrai area. Sadly one aircraft was hit by flak and the pilot killed. All three squadrons were fully committed to *Ramrods* and *Rangers* for the rest of April and through May. Redesignated No 133 Wing from 15 May, the airfield was visited on 29 May by the Polish C-in-C, General Sosnkowski, and Air Marshal Sir Arthur Coningham. On the evening of D-Day, thirty-six Mustangs of No 133 Wing escorted the second wave of the Airborne Forces, destroying one Fw 190 in the process.

If D-Day was relatively quiet, 7 June was quite the opposite. The first *Ramrod* began at 06.00 hours and, after the fourth operation finished at 21.37, the Wing claimed sixteen enemy aircraft, plus three possibles and two damaged. No 306 lost two aircraft, including that of the CO, who bailed out safely. The hectic tempo of low-level *Ramrods* continued with losses due to accurate flak and the hazards of low flying balanced against a number of combat victories until a remarkable act of bravery took place on 22 June. While strafing German Panzers, No 315's 'A' flight commander and his wingman, Warrant Officer T. Tamowicz, were both shot down. His leader was killed, but the WO was seen to crash-land into a marsh. His CO, Sqn Ldr E. Horbaczewski, landed at a nearby airstrip and rescued his injured pilot. Both men squeezed into the cockpit of the Mustang and returned to Coolham to the amazement of their groundcrew.

At the end of an eventful day, No 133 Wing transferred to RAF Holmsley South after fifty-seven days of operations from Coolham in which they had destroyed twenty-eight enemy aircraft in combat for the loss of twenty-one P-51s in action and three during training. Its replacement was 135 Wing, consisting of Nos 222 (Natal), 349 (Belgium) and 485 (New Zealand) Squadrons with Spitfire IX fighter-bombers, which arrived from Selsey on 30 June but only stayed until 4 July, when Funtington was its destination. The Wing's departure brought the short but hectic career of Coolham ALG to a close, although a local contractor continued to cut the grass.

As an American aircraft was the first to use Coolham, it is fitting that another USAAF Liberator from the North Pickenham 491st BG was the last. After an emergency landing on 19 January 1945, the repaired and lightened bomber left seven days later. In September 1945 personnel from the 5027 ACS, assisted from October by men of 5003 ACS, began the process of returning Coolham to agriculture, which was completed on 11 November 1945.

In May 1992, following an initiative by Paul Hamlin, a Coolham Airfield Memorial Fund Committee was set up. In April 1994 fifteen sapling oak trees were planted along the public bridleway that follows the route of the northern perimeter track. Each tree has a plaque bearing the name of an airman who died serving at Coolham. The wonderful commemorative weekend of 11/12 June followed, and a year later a sign was placed at the airfield's northern entrance off the B2139 reading: 'Historic site, Coolham ALG, D-Day airfield'. The only surviving building, the former pump house of the bulk fuel installation, was considered to be worth preservation and was recommended for listing.

During my visit in mid-November 2004, the impressive memorial, airfield sign and line of poignant memorial trees were located and recorded, but due to failing daylight the continued survival of the pump house could not be confirmed.

Main features:
Runways: 050° 3,600ft, 120° 4,500ft, steel matting (Sommerfeld track). *Hangars:* five EO Blisters. *Hardstandings:* fifty Sommerfeld track, five hardcore. *Accommodation:* tented camp.

With folded wings, the Albacore will fit into one of Cowdray Park's Dutch Barn hangars. (via J. Moffat)

COWDRAY PARK (Midhurst), West Sussex

50°58N/00°41W 85ft asl; SU925203. 2.5 miles E of Midhurst on minor road

Pre-war, Lord Cowdray occasionally used the polo field of his lovely Cowdray Park estate as an aerodrome. Known as Midhurst or South Amersham, the flying field was on land gently sloping down from the Pulborough to Petersfield railway to the minor road from South Amersham to Selham and provided landing runs of some 2,250ft (686m) E/W and 1,650ft (503m) N/S.

When the Admiralty decided to disperse its ever-increasing aircraft stocks held at Lee-on-Solent, the former polo field together with land to the north between the road and the River Rother was requisitioned and commissioned in June 1941 as RNAS Cowdray Park, part of HMS *Daedalus*. Twenty-nine 20ft (6m) by 40ft (12m) Dutch barn hangars, widely dispersed throughout the site, were erected, capable of holding a single aircraft with folded wings. Local properties, including the polo pony stables and farm buildings, were requisitioned for domestic accommodation and workshops, while the big hay shed became the dining hall and theatre. The HQ was a small brick building on the airfield.

In addition to the storage role, aircraft repaired at Lee-on-Solent were sent to Cowdray Park for testing prior to being dispatched to ships and squadrons. After wartime service, which began in 1939, Lieutenant John Moffat RN, flying Swordfish and Albacores from four Royal Navy carriers, including participation in the attack on the *Bismarck*, during which his torpedo crippled the ship, was posted to Cowdray Park in the summer of 1943. As the station's only Flying Officer, John Moffat was also its test pilot, flying Seafires and Walruses in addition to the Swordfish and Albacores with which he was already familiar. It was an Albacore that earned Lt Moffat a Green Recommend endorsement in his logbook. He takes up the story:

'I had just taken off from Ambersham and was climbing out westwards towards Petersfield. Just as I was passing over Midhurst, at about 500 feet, the engine blew up. There was a loud bang from the cowling and clouds of black smoke came pouring out of the engine. The cockpit filled up with smoke and I opened the canopy. On opening the canopy the engine cut out. I got her down in one piece on the airfield. I thought nothing more of it. Later I discovered that a high-ranking officer had been flying in the vicinity and had witnessed the whole incident.'

The only aircraft that was permanently based at Cowdray Park was a Stinson Reliant, which John Moffat used for communications duties in connection with aircraft deliveries and collection. It occasionally also flew to Glasgow, the home of his then fiancée Marjory, whom he later married in nearby Selham parish church. When not in use for flying, the airfield was obstructed by a series of wire trestles, each 10ft (3m) in length. After D-Day the demands on Cowdray Park diminished,

The personnel of Cowdray Park with (inset) its CO, Lt J. Moffat. In May 1941 he had flown the Swordfish that crippled the Bismarck. (via J. Moffat)

During 1944/45 Proctors were used for R/T training. (via J. Moffat)

although it continued to be used for the rest of the war including possible use by Proctors for R/T training during 1944/45 and by Ansons of the RN School of Photography from April to October 1944, when its Ford base was fully committed to invasion preparations.

The RN Storage Section was put into Care and Maintenance on 30 September 1945, and by 15 November the site had been derequisitioned, cleared and subsequently released back to the Estate.

In 2004 John Moffat flew into Cowdray Park again, this time in his trusty Piper Colt as a guest of Lord Cowdray. Although most of the wartime buildings had been cleared away, in the case of his Flight Offices within the previous two years, he was able to confirm that at least two of the Dutch barn hangars survived, one of which was the MT section.

One of the two remaining Dutch Barn hangars at Cowdray Park. (DWL collection)

Main features:
Landing surface: grass, N-S 1,650ft, E-W 2,250ft. *Hangars:* twenty-five Dutch Barns 20ft x 40ft. *Hardstandings:* none. *Accommodation:* 1 RN Officer, 53 CPO/PO/Ratings.

DEANLAND, East Sussex

50°53N/00°10E 77ft asl; TQ523118. 4.5 miles NW of Hailsham off B2124

With very few exceptions, the wartime ALGs that were created from farmland have returned to that status, leaving little or nothing behind to tell their story. Deanland is one of those exceptions, being now an active and welcoming general aviation airfield that is proud of its wartime service.

Deanland was originally surveyed in 1942 and the plans were approved by December, leading to requisition in early 1943. The site, which included a dispersed gun emplacement, included pasture land on either side of the Golden Cross to Ripe road, leading to the road's closure on 2 March 1943. After the initial grading and the removal of hedges and trees, the ALG was released for grazing until 2 July when No 16 Airfield Construction Group RE arrived to upgrade the airfield.

Two Sommerfeld tracking runways were laid in the usual form of a cross, with Blister hangars and hardstandings. Although the ALG remained closed until 1 April 1944, a B-17F from the 306th BG was an early arrival on 6 September 1943. The official residents in April were Poles of Nos 302, 308 and 317 Squadrons, which made up No 131 Airfield of 84 Group, 2TAF. Operating their Spitfire IXs in a fighter-bomber role, they stayed until 26 April when Chailey was their destination.

No 149 Airfield HQ moved down from Castle Camps, with Nos 64 and 611 Squadrons arriving from Coltishall and No 234 from Bolt Head. Despite the growing obsolescence of their Spitfire Vs, the Airfield was fully employed escorting No 2 Group Bostons, Mitchells and Marauders of the IXth Air Force. Redesignated No 149 Wing from 15 May, D-Day saw No 611 airborne at 03.00 hours, claiming to be the first British fighter unit over Gold and Omaha beaches, as the remainder of the Wing escorted tug and glider formations. No contact was made with the Luftwaffe until 10 June when a Ju 88 was destroyed. The Wing transferred to Zeals at the end of June as Deanland awaited its next residents.

After almost a month, Nos 91 and 322 (Dutch) Squadrons brought their Griffon-powered Spitfire XIVs from West Malling to continue their successful war against the V-1. This task afforded Deanland a longer existence than most ALGs and even brought some Nissen huts as accommodation and messes within Deanland Wood. The third squadron, No 345 (Free French),

The present-day entrance to Deanland airfield. (DWL collection)

The nearby Ripe Church commemorates the wartime role of Deanland, its squadrons and those who never returned. (DWL collection)

flew in on 16 August from Shoreham, but the worst of the 'Buzz Bomb' menace was over, and in October all three units moved to Biggin Hill in preparation for a transfer to the continent.

The ALG closed a month later and the process of lifting the Sommerfeld track and dismantling the hangars began shortly afterwards. Although the land was returned to the farmers in January 1945, the road closure was not revoked until August 1947. Deanland Wood Park uses many of the roads laid for the Nissen huts to service the residential caravan homes.

At the entrance to the present Deanland Airfield, a tree was planted on 6 June 1994 by Wing Commander B. Carroll GM to commemorate Nos 64, 91, 234, 302, 317, 322, 345 and 611 Squadrons, and in special remembrance of the eight pilots who lost their lives operating from the ALG.

Main features:
Runways: WSW-ENE 4,800ft, SSW-NNE 4,200ft, steel matting (Sommerfeld track). *Hangars:* none. *Hardstandings:* four 200ft x 100ft, concrete refuelling. *Accommodation:* tented camp and Nissen huts.

21st-century features:
Runway: 06/24 1,640ft x 90ft, grass airstrip. *Hangars:* two modern types.

Places of interest nearby:
In Ripe Parish Church the badges of Deanland's squadrons are illustrated and a plaque notes their identities:

> 'This plaque was presented to Ripe Parish Church on 6 June 1994, the 50th Anniversary of D-Day, to commemorate the airmen who flew from Deanland airfield, Ripe, and made the ultimate sacrifice.'

DOVER (Guston Road), Kent

51°08N/01°19E 407ft asl; TR325430. 1.25 miles NE of Dover adjacent to A2

When the Admiralty was looking for a suitable site for an aerodrome to protect its naval base in the harbour at Dover, Government-owned land between the old Fort Burgoyne and the Duke of York's Military School was the obvious choice. Although earmarked in June 1913, the 55-acre site some 400 feet (130 metres) above the town was still incomplete when the Great War started in August 1914. The impetus of war and the RNAS acceptance of the UK air-defence role in early September saw a Defence Flight of No 2 Sqn RNAS consisting of two Bristol TB.8s arrive on 24 December 1914. It was relieved by B Flight of No 1 Sqn RNAS on 2 January 1915. En route to the Dardanelles, No 3 Sqn RNAS trained at Dover from late February until it sailed on 11 March 1915.

In 1917 this Sopwith Pup was part of the RNAS Dover Defence Flight. (JMB/GSL collection)

The Dover Defence Flight was the basis of No 4 Sqn RNAS, which was formed at the Station on 23 March 1915 under the command of Sqn/Cdr C. L. Courtney. To replace the Defence Flight, a No 2 Squadron detachment of four Blériot Parasols arrived circa March 1915, staying until June. On 16 April 1915 a single Albatross B.II dropped small bombs and incendiaries on Sittingbourne and Faversham. Although two Blériot Parasols and a Vickers FB.5 were ordered up from Dover at 12.30pm, nothing was seen. A similar inconclusive sortie was carried out on 3 July by a BE.2c and an FB.5. When No 4 left for Eastchurch in early August it left behind a nucleus of personnel that became No 5 Squadron on 2 August 1915.

To cater for this hectic expansion, the station also expanded. From the original four canvas-covered hangars, a group of permanent aeroplane sheds was erected on the western side of the aerodrome adjacent to the Dover to Guston road. By October 1915 the busy Royal Naval Air Station housed seven BE.2cs, three Bristol Scouts, four Curtiss JN3s, a couple of Avro 504s and eight dismantled Morane Parasols. Over the road a large camp of wooden hutting provided accommodation and wardrooms.

On 9 January 1916 an unidentified German reconnaissance machine flew over the harbour and the Air Station. Four of the defending Nieuport 10s and Bristol Scouts took off but failed to intercept. Again on 20 February Dover launched defenders without success. This pattern of hit-and-run raids continued through the spring and the summer. Over two days in July 1916 RNAS Dover joined with RNAS Dunkerque in providing fighting patrols protecting spotter aircraft recording the fall of shot from a 12-inch (30.5cm) Dominion gun, which was trying (unsuccessfully) to silence the Tirpitz Battery. RNAS Guston Road was itself the target on 12 August when a single daylight raider dropped four bombs on Dover, one of which landed on the aerodrome. Again none of the defenders was able to intercept.

The nucleus of the new 6 Squadron RNAS assembled at Dover on 1 November 1916 before taking its Nieuport Scouts to France just over a month later. Before it left one Scout was scrambled on 28 November as part of the widespread but unsuccessful response to an audacious daylight raid by a single LVG C.IV over central London.

The early part of 1917 was relatively quiet, but in the late afternoon of 25 May a force of twenty-three Gothas, frustrated in their plan to bomb London, attacked Folkestone as they withdrew, killing and injuring nearly 300. The defensive response was widespread but virtually futile. The only home success came from Dover, which sent up three Sopwith Pups and a single Camel. A RNAS ferry pilot, Flt Sub-Lt Reginald Leslie, was waiting to leave for France in a DH.4 when the alarm sounded. He took a Pup of the Dover Defence Flight and caught up with the raiders over the Channel, forcing one machine into a steep dive but was unable to confirm his victory. As the formation was also intercepted by RNAS Pups from Dunkirk, who also claimed a victory, it is uncertain who destroyed the single Gotha, which the Germans admitted losing. Dover provided defensive sorties against subsequent daylight raids by the Gothas during the rest of 1917 until the autumn when the Germans turned to a night offensive and the station's defensive role diminished.

After a long gap, a new squadron was created at Dover on 24 April 1918 when No 218 Squadron RAF formed with DH.9s, moving on to Petite Synthe in France a month later. Also equipped with the DH.9, No 491 Flight was formed on 25 May as a maritime patrol unit. At the end of August, it and two other Flights, No 407 from Dover (Marine Parade) and No 471 at Walmer, became the new No 233 Squadron. Tasked with anti-submarine duties over the Straits of Dover, the unit was very successful in denying the U-boats access to this vital shipping artery.

Following the November Armistice the three Flights lost their separate identities and on 15 May 1919 No 233 Squadron disbanded, leaving Dover virtually abandoned until closure in 1920. All physical signs of the camp were soon swept away and in the late 1970s the site was buried under housing for military personnel, leaving nothing behind to remind today's historians of the role of RNAS Dover (Guston Road).

Main features in 1918:
Landing ground: grass. *Hangars:* a number of permanent aeroplane sheds.
Accommodation: wooden huts.

DOVER (Marine Parade), Kent

51°07N/01°20E; TR326414. 1.5 miles from Dover town centre

Nestling under the Castle, Dover's Great War seaplane base covered almost 2 acres of land of the harbour seafront, but now its approximate location can be found from the statue of the Hon Charles S. Rolls, the joint founder of Rolls-Royce. It commemorates the first non-stop double crossing of the Channel on 2 June 1910, achieved in a Wright pusher biplane on 2 June 1910. Sadly, a few weeks later he was killed in the same aircraft at Bournemouth.

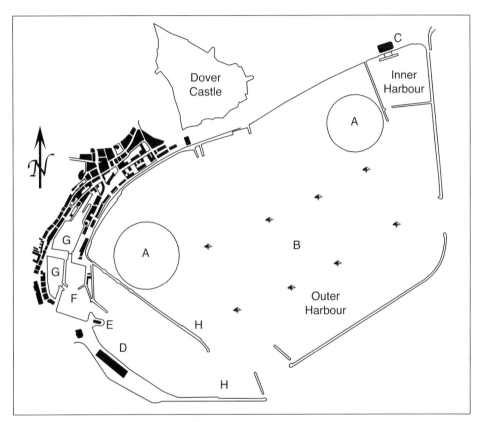

DOVER (MARINE PARADE)

A	Sheltered Area
B	Alighting Area
C	Petrol and Oil Stores
D	Marine Station
E	Customs
F	Tidal Harbour
G	Docks
H	Piers

The plan is based on the 3rd Edition of the Air Ministry's The Air Pilot publication, which was published towards the end of 1934. It shows the joint RAF and civil seaplane Alighting Area although the use of Dover as a public seaplane port ceased shortly after 1934. The RAF continued to use Dover until the declaration of war.

Just two years on, the first recorded use of Dover by a seaplane occurred on 13 July 1912. Returning to Harwich from the Portsmouth Naval Review, one of the pioneers of naval aviation, Commander Charles Samson, moored his Short S.41 100hp seaplane HMS *Amphibian* in the harbour overnight. Selected as a Hydro-Aeroplane Station during 1913, it wasn't until the torpedo-gunboat HMS *Niger* was sunk by U12 on 11 November 1914 that the Admiralty took action to establish the Dover seaplane base. The skating rink on Marine Parade was requisitioned as cover for the two large, 63ft (19.2m)-wingspan Wight pusher seaplanes and a slipway built to allow the machines to be manhandled up the beach and across the road to their shed.

During December 1914, under the command of Sqn Cdr Bromet, the station was charged to keep both aeroplanes at readiness to defend the local towns from attack by German floatplanes. Since the small harbour inside the breakwater was too small and overcrowded for take-off or alighting, all flights had to be made from open water. The usefulness of the Wights was thus strictly limited, but fortunately they were soon replaced by more effective machines. When, on 20 March 1915, four German seaplanes attacked coastal shipping off Dover, two flying boats, a White & Thompson and a Curtiss, were launched but failed to sight the enemy. On the night of 16/17 May 1915 it was Army Zeppelin LZ38 that was the intended target of a Sopwith 860 seaplane, which took off at 03.30 but returned empty-handed.

In addition to its defensive task, the station was allocated a training and repair role. To cater for this extra work two additional standard 100ft (30.4m) by 90ft (27.4m) Admiralty sheds were erected beside the skating rink. An extra slipway was also built. By October 1915 RNAS Dover had on strength four Shorts 184s, one FBA flying boat, two Sopwith Schneiders, seven Sopwith Babies and a single White & Thompson floatplane. The 'Dover type' 184 was an improved version of the Short, which originated at the station and featured a car-type radiator behind the airscrew.

By early March 1917 the defences of Dover were 'strengthened' by the addition of a rather unlikely fighter, the Short 830 floatplane, with a maximum speed of 61mph. During the major attack on Folkestone in the early evening of 25 May, two Short 830s were among the many defending aeroplanes in the air. Most never even saw the raiders, but a Short 830 flown by Flt Sub-Lt L. C. Pincott attempted an interception but, being some 25mph slower than its prey, was soon left far behind.

One of the mixed fleet of Seaplanes at Marine Parade in October 1915 was this Sopwith Schneider, No 3739. (JMB/GSL collection)

With the formation of the RAF on 1 April 1918, the Dover seaplanes became part of No 5 Group and participated in the naval attack on Zeebrugge during 22/23 April. On 20 May the unit at Dover Marine Parade became No 407 Flight with Short 184s and Sopwith Babies, employed on anti-submarine patrol duties. Together with other Flights at Guston Road and Walmer, it joined No 233 Squadron on its formation in August 1918, the HQ being on Marine Parade. The Squadron was only to survive until 15 May 1919 and the base closed in 1920, the Admiralty sheds being removed soon after.

Dover Harbour continued as an official RAF flying boat alighting area up through to the end of the 1930s with two, later increased to six, RAF flying boat moorings in the north-west corner of the Outer Harbour. It was also a public seaplane port until after 1934 under the control of the Harbour Master. However passengers embarking or disembarking were liable to a poll tax of 2 shillings! The RAF use of the Harbour ceased with the outbreak of the Second World War. The original former ice-skating rink was finally swept away in a road improvement scheme in the late 1970s, leaving nothing for future historians except photographs and written memories.

Main features:
Take-off and alighting area in 1930s: Outer Harbour of 6,600ft by 3,900 ft. *Hangars:* two Admiralty seaplane sheds and requisitioned skating rink. *Facilities:* Slipway and hardstanding. *Accommodation:* requisitioned local accommodation.

DOVER (St Margaret's/Swingate Down), Kent

51°08N/01°20E 400ft asl; TR338432. 2 miles NE of Dover off minor road

The growing militaristic stance of Germany during the early summer of 1914 led the War Office to look for a suitable site from which the small RFC might fly to France as required under the Entente Cordiale. The need for as short a flight as possible led to the obvious choice of Dover, where just five years earlier Louis Blériot had landed after achieving the first powered crossing of the English Channel. The sloping field on which Blériot had arrived was unsuitable, but close-by Swingate Downs was eminently suitable.

Eight days after the 4 August declaration of war, the aeroplanes of Nos 2, 3 and 4 Squadrons RFC arrived at Swingate Down. All three, with the exception of C Flight No 4 Squadron, which stayed behind for patrol duties, departed for France the following day. The first to arrive was a BE.2a of 2 Squadron flown by Lt H. D. Harvey-Kelly, who had left Dover at 06.25 and reached Amiens 2 hours later, followed safely by the rest of the initial batch of RFC machines. On 14 August No 5 arrived from Gosport with its Avro 504s and BE.8s, leaving for Amiens the next day. When C Flight left in mid-September the Dover Landing Ground was left deserted because the RFC had no more serviceable aeroplanes to send. Finally No 6 Squadron with its BE.2 and Henry Farman F.20 machines staged through on 6/7 October for Bruges. The first emergency role of Swingate Down was over.

Conversion of the temporary LG to an RFC aerodrome provided a long row of wooden sheds along its southern boundary as the station officially became Dover (St Margaret's). The first occupant was No 15 Squadron, which arrived on 11 May 1915 with its eclectic mix of F20s, Longhorns, Shorthorns, Avro 504s, Blériot XIs and BE.2cs. Although officially preparing for overseas service, the Squadron became an informal training unit as its pilots were regularly posted to other front-line squadrons. However, one BE.2c and its crew were on standby for anti-Zeppelin duties. No 9 Squadron arrived towards the end of July with its Blériots and Longhorns in a training and coastal defence role. More aeroplanes in the shape of Avro 504s, Martinsyde S1s, BE.8s, BE.2cs and RE.7s added to the camp's growing problems of maintenance. Fortunately, in December 1915, when both squadrons moved to St Omer, they were fully equipped with the BE.2c.

Before they left, the training role and much of the equipment became the responsibility of two Reserve Squadrons, No 12, formed on 15 November, and No 13, created twelve days later. No 12 was immediately transferred to Thetford, and it was 13 RS in No 6 Wing that became Dover's resident training unit with a secondary home defence role. Accidents were frequent and the cliff-top location even saw aeroplanes overshooting their landings and ending up on the beach below. A second training unit, No 20 RS, was formed at Dover on 1 February 1916 from a nucleus of No 27 Squadron, which had arrived in December from Hounslow to equip with the Martinsyde G.100,before moving to St Omer in March. No 13 RS provided personnel, BE.2cs and Avro 504s for the formation of No 49 Squadron on 15 April in an advanced training role as the casualty rate on the Western Front mounted ever higher.

No 13 Reserve Squadron with Avro 504As was Dover's training unit in November 1915.
(JMB/GSL collection)

Although there had been some successes against the Zeppelin threat, the War Office finally admitted that specialist RFC home defence squadrons should be formed. At Dover it was the turn of No 20 RS to provide a nucleus of personnel when No 50 Squadron was formed in mid-May 1916 with the marginally useful BE.2 variants. Although immediately supplemented by the BE.12 and by the Vickers ES.1 from June 1916. it was a BE.2c flown by Capt J. W. Woodhouse that came closest to success. Four Zeppelins attacked London on the night of 24/25 August with L32 being illuminated by the Dover searchlights shortly after Woodhouse had taken off at 02.15. At 7,000 feet (2,130 metres) he fired his Pomeroy ammunition but they fell short of the giant airship some 200 feet (61 metres) above. He pursued his prey up to 11,000 feet (3,350 metres) but had to break off and let the searchlights over Dover lead him home. Before the end of October No 50 moved to Harrietsham with detachments at Detling, Bekesbourne and Throwley, leaving Dover to its training role.

After assisting in the creation of 50 Squadron, No 20 RS left for Wye in June 1916. No 49 received the RE.7 during December as it changed to a bombing training role. Again it was No 13 that donated personnel for the creation of a new unit, No 64 RS being formed in early April 1917, moving to Narborough on 14 April. Recognising their true role, the Reserve Squadrons were redesignated Training Squadrons and on 1 June the long-serving 13 TS took its eighteen-strong fleet of 504s, RE.8s and BE.2cs to Yatesbury, swapping places with 62 TS.

The Martinsyde G.100 had joined the Avro 504s and the RE.7s in No 49 Squadron, but by 12 November 1917 all had been replaced by the superb DH.4 when the Squadron transferred to La Bellevue as a day-bomber unit. On the same day No 110 arrived from Rendcombe where it had been formed from a cadre of No 38 TS on 1 November, but before the end of the month it had moved on to Sedgeford. No 65 TS arrived from Sedgeford on 25 November 1917 to join 62 TS. Dover's training role was confirmed with a major upgrading of the station, the original wooden sheds being replaced by permanent GS sheds and substantially more domestic accommodation being provided. The camp now covered 219 acres.

A month after the creation of the RAF on 1 April 1918 No 62 TS moved to Hounslow and No 65 was expanded by mid-July to become the No 53 Training Depot Station with forty-eight Camels and Avro 504s. The new TDS was to last until 15 October 1918 when it was disbanded into the School of Marine Operational Pilots operating the DH.9 to give specialist training in anti-submarine and convoy duties. Following the Armistice the tempo of work slackened and on 1 February 1919 the School closed. Dover saw other squadrons pass through as part of the run-down. No 3 came as a cadre via Wye in early May 1919 before moving to Croydon in mid-October. No 212 Squadron came from Great Yarmouth on 7 March with DH.4s, 9s and 9As for maritime duties, but following its disbandment on 9 February 1920 Dover (St Margaret's) closed.

This memorial commemorates the RFC squadrons that flew to France from Swingate Downs in mid-August 1914. (DWL collection)

The site was derequisitioned, the buildings auctioned off and removed. Swingate Downs largely reverted to farmland until 1938, when it was again acquired for military purposes, but not for flying. The site became one of the first five locations for Britain's Chain Home RDF early warning system. Four steel transmitter masts 350 feet (107 metres) high and four smaller wooden receiving towers were erected. Later a Chain Home Low station was built at nearby Fan Bay.

By the 1970s all but three of the Chain Home masts had been removed, the survivors being used for the then Eurovision TV network. Around this time the towers were also used by the USAF for microwave transmissions over southern England. Although the 'Three Sisters', as the masts are known locally, survive into the 21st century, the communication dishes had been removed by 2004. The A2(T) now crosses over part of the site, giving a view of the towers, although in a cutting. Better views can be had from local minor roads and tracks, where visible remnants include the concrete base of a receiving tower, the bases of some of the hangars and former ammunition stores. Part of the site is still a secure MOD communications facility and other 'Keep Out' signs from the USAF period remain.

On the Dover to St Margaret's at Cliffe road, to the left of a gate into the site, a simple memorial stone was erected with the inscription 'The ROYAL FLYING CORPS contingent of the 1914 BRITISH EXPEDITIONARY FORCE consisting of Nos 2, 3, 4 and 5 Squadrons flew from this field to AMIENS between 13 and 15 August 1914'. On 15 August 1986 a matching stone was dedicated in memory of all ranks of the Royal Regiment of Artillery and the 127 AAA Gun Battalion US Army, which served in the Dover area. With the Chain Home masts in the background, these two memorials are an evocative reminder of the sacrifices made in both 20th-century World Wars.

Main features in 1918:
Landing ground: grass. *Hangars:* a number of General Service sheds (Belfast Truss). *Accommodation:* wooden huts.

Places of interest nearby:
A century ago on 25 July 1909 Louis Blériot achieved the first aeroplane crossing of the English Channel. His landing, in what was then an open field called Northfall Meadow behind Dover Castle (TR3277421), was subsequently commemorated by a memorial in the shape of his aeroplane. After years of neglect, a programme of tree clearance and improvements began in early 2009 to mark the centenary.

DUNSFOLD, Surrey

51°07N/00°32W 168ft asl; SQ027561. 6 miles SE of Godalming on A281

Initial contacts between the then British Aerospace and the Rutland Group in late 1999 gave a glimmer of hope for the future of Dunsfold airfield. This had been very much in the balance since BAe announced in mid-1999 that the airfield would close before the end of 2000. After more than two years of negotiation, the Rutland Group, in a joint venture with the Royal Bank of Scotland, acquired 2,000 acres (810 hectares) of land, which included the 550-acre (223-hectare) airfield. Although discussions with planners and local residents were to continue for some time, the short- to medium-term future of Dunsfold Park, as it was to be known, was assured.

The possibilities of the heavily wooded land to the east of Dunsfold village were first identified by the team of surveyors seeking sites for future ALGs. However, the needs of Army Co-operation Command took precedence and the site was requisitioned in April 1942 for development into a standard three-runway aerodrome, although it necessitated a major diversion of the A281 Guildford to Horsham road. The Canadian Forestry Corps was given the task of clearing the site for the Royal Canadian Engineers who, assisted by the Royal Canadian Army Service Corps and Ordnance Corps were to build the new aerodrome. An unusual solution was adopted to solve the problem of Broadmeads Cottage, which obstructed a planned runway. Listening to the pleas of its lady owner not to bulldoze it, the engineers positioned many of the readily available beech logs under the historic building. Five giant Caterpillar tractors pulled the house a quarter of a mile to the west, close to the airfield's southern boundary. The main runway of 6,000ft (1,829m) was aligned WSW-ENE with two secondary runways both of 4,200ft (1,280m). A total of thirty-eight 'frying-pan' aircraft dispersals were provided together with two T2 and eleven Blister hangars.

After a remarkably short construction period, Dunsfold was officially opened on 16 October 1942 by Lt General McNaughton, COC in C, First Canadian Army, and handed over to Air Marshal H. Edwards, AOC in C RCAF Overseas. The first occupant was No 39 (Reconnaissance) Wing RCAF, which was formed at Dunsfold in Army Co-op Command on 3 December 1942, comprising Nos 400, 414 and 430 Squadrons operating Mustang Mk 1s. Despite October's official opening, construction of the dispersed accommodation to the north of the aerodrome continued well into the winter.

The Wing took part in the *Spartan* exercise during early March, operating from a tented encampment in the adjacent woods. In May 1943 the Royal Canadian Engineers laid down an experimental runway known as Prefabricated Bituminous Surfacing (PBS), which consisted of bituminised jute hessian similar to heavy-duty roofing felt laid over a prepared rolled surface. Much lighter than metal alternatives, a successful trial of the surface, which was 3,660ft (1,097m) long and 150ft (46m) wide, was carried out on 23 June with numerous take-offs and landings by aircraft up to the size of a Wellington. After an explosive charge made a deliberate crater in the surface, it was filled with hardcore, re-covered and in use again within an hour. The system was used extensively in France, with nearly 20% of the post-D-Day temporary airfields having PBS runways, although the waterproof surface was liable to waterlogging.

Army Co-operation Command disbanded on 1 June 1943 and the creation of the Tactical Air Force saw Dunsfold's transfer to the 2nd TAF as a fighter station. On 4 July No 128 Airfield was formed at Dunsfold initially with just No 400 Squadron, as Nos 414 and 430 Squadrons were posted to Gatwick the following day. Its replacement on 6 July was No 231 from Clifton near York. The two Squadrons were immediately ranging over France, and on 8 July two 400 Squadron Mustangs destroyed a Fieseler Storch. Also during July No 403 Repair & Salvage Unit arrived to undertake repairs that were beyond the capability of the squadrons. Attached to the R&SU was the similarly numbered Aircraft Reception Flight, which held replacement aircraft ready for issue to the squadrons. When 128 Airfield moved to Woodchurch on 28 July, the R&SU with its ARF was briefly left in sole occupation, until it too left during September 1943.

Two Mitchell Squadrons, Nos 98 and 180, had arrived on 18 August, No 98 Squadron taking over Broadmeads Cottage, which it renamed Rose Cottage, as its HQ, together with its surrounding Nissen huts. Other crews moved into the requisitioned Hall Place and Stovold's Hill Farm. The unit's first operation took place on 24 August 1943 when twenty-four Mitchells bombed the railway marshalling yards at St Omer. Initially Dunsfold's Mitchells concentrated on Boulogne docks, but by late October the target changed to the V-1 missile launch sites in Northern France known as 'ski' sites. Operation 'Crossbow', the first attack of the long campaign against the V-1, took place on 5 November, the target being the major installation at Mimoyecques near Calais. The two Squadrons became 139 Airfield on 17 November 1943.

On 7 January 1944 two Mitchells, one from each squadron, collided over the airfield in bad weather; there were no survivors. On 18 February the Airfield's third Squadron, No 320 (Netherlands), moved in from Lasham, and on 12 May No 139 Airfield was redesignated No 139 Wing. Night attacks on communication centres and airfields became more frequent, and on the night of 6/7 June the Wing sent sixty Mitchells to bomb communication bottlenecks.

Dunsfold participated in a spectacular operation on 10 June; the target was a concentration of Panzer tanks and its Chateau de la Gaine HQ. No fewer than forty Typhoons plus seventy-one

The North American Mitchell was flown by No 98 Squadron at Dunsfold from August 1943 to October 1944. (MAP via P. H. T. Green collection)

Mitchells with a strong Spitfire escort virtually destroyed their targets with rockets and more than 400 500lb (227kg) bombs. It was later learned that General Von Dawans and most of his HQ staff had been killed. Two days later a visit by Queen Wilhelmina and Prince Bernhard saw many of their Dutch compatriots receive gallantry decorations.

The Wing's targets tended to have strong flak defences, with consequent losses, but one particularly distressing loss was not due to enemy defences. A 98 Squadron Mitchell returned from an operation on 8 September 1944 with two 500lb (227kg) bombs hung-up in its bomb bay, which exploded on landing. The entire crew was killed and the runway severely damaged. The Squadron lost two more aircraft in support of Operation 'Market Garden' when the Wing was intercepted by Fw 190s. Incredibly these were the first 2TAF medium bombers to be shot down by fighters since its formation in November 1943.

Dunsfold's 139 Wing led the general move of Mitchell squadrons to the continent when it transferred to B58 Melsbroek on 9 October. The airfield became a satellite of Odiham on 15 January 1945, but continued as a reserve airfield in the Tangmere Sector. No 83 Group Support Unit transferred from Westhampnett on 22 February, holding a reserve of three aircraft for each No 83 Group squadron. At least two of the Spitfires then on charge survive to this day. Mk IX PV202 was later issued to 412 (RCAF) Squadron and is credited with three victories; post-war it served the Irish Air Corps as a two-seat trainer. After a long restoration it made its first flight in February 1990, fittingly at Dunsfold. The other survivor, Mk XIV RM689, was purchased by Rolls-Royce shortly after the war. At the time of writing, it is being rebuilt to fly after an accident.

At the end of the war in Europe, fleets of Dakotas arrived with ex-POWs liberated from German prison camps. An amazing 160 aircraft arrived on 9 May; the daily total was regularly more than 100, and by the end of the month nearly 44,500 former prisoners had passed through the station, before the task finished on 25 June. In early August No 83 GSU became the Group's Disbandment Centre; No 16 Squadron formally disbanded in late October, but the Air Ministry advised both 487 and 268 Squadrons in September that they were renumbered No 16! Eventually 268 won that privilege.

Dunsfold was reduced to Care and Maintenance on 2 February 1946 and was transferred to Training Technical Command on 2 September; it was leased to Skyways shortly after as its primary base. Skyways' occupation of Dunsfold started badly. On the evening of 8 December 1946 one of its newly delivered Lancastrians was burned out in one of the hangars, although the hangar was saved. The airline also used a Lancaster Mk 1 G-AKAB as a crew trainer with the appropriate name of *Sky Trainer* until it was broken up at Dunsfold during November 1948. The Berlin Airlift in 1948-9 produced rapid expansion until, at its height, Skyways at Dunsfold employed more than 1,200 personnel; but once the civil airlift was over, the staff were laid off and the company went into voluntary liquidation in March 1950.

Although Skyways was soon resurrected and continued to use Dunsfold for a while, the airfield's future lay with the renowned Hawker Aircraft Company, which was looking for a new flight test facility as its Langley airfield was being increasing compromised by the expansion of the new London Airport at Heathrow. Dunsfold, just 20 miles from the Kinston factory, was an ideal location, and in 1950 the tenancy was transferred to Hawker. Staff began to transfer from Langley from July 1951 and the two existing T2 hangars became the basis of a final assembly and flight test facility. The early production Sea Hawks were its first residents before the future development of the naval fighter was moved to Armstrong-Whitworth as Hawker concentrated on its beautiful and very successful Hunter.

The former Hawker/British Aerospace Final Assembly and Flight Test hangars at Dunsfold.
(DWL collection)

Although the prototype Hunter WB188 first flew from Boscombe Down in July 1951, it and the second aircraft did most of their development flying from Dunsfold. However, it was obvious that the T2s were insufficient for full production. Construction of a new three-bay final assembly facility started behind the wartime control tower in 1952, and a new tower was built across the airfield. The first production Hunter, WT555, made its maiden flight at Dunsfold on 16 May 1953.

With the first twenty production machines dedicated to development flying by Hawker, Rolls-Royce and the Air Ministry's experimental establishments, Dunsfold was a very busy airfield. The Avon-powered Mk 1 had trouble with the gun-firing/engine interface, but the Mk 2, with its Sapphire engine, was free of such problems. The test flying team was led by Hawker's then Chief Test Pilot, Neville Duke, who lived in the wartime squadron flight offices of the 17th-century Primemeads Farm on the former A281. The head of production test flying, Frank Murphy, had taken over Broadmeads/Rose Cottage; this building became known as Murphy's Cottage and, more recently, Canada House.

As the Hunter development continued, Hawker began work on its next project. Powered by the unique Bristol-Siddeley Pegasus engine, the Hawker P.1127, made its first tentative hovering flight at Dunsfold in the hands of Bill Bedford on 21 October 1960. The closure of Chilbolton in 1961 brought the production testing on the Folland Gnat to Dunsfold to join its Hunter and P.1127 stablemates. During 1964/65 the P.1127 entered limited production for tri-nation evaluation as the Kestrel, before evolving into the world-renowned Harrier. The initial production example first flew at Dunsfold on 31 August 1966 and, as the AV-8, the Harrier was sold to the US Marines and the Spanish. It developed from a marginally useful warplane but with a unique VTOL capability into a true multi-role machine when the BAe/McDonnell Douglas Harrier II first appeared in 1983. Throughout that time, Dunsfold was the HSA then British Aerospace Harrier production and development airfield.

The next Hawker-Siddeley product made its maiden flight from Dunsfold on 21 August 1974 when Duncan Simpson flew the first of 176 Hawks ordered for the RAF. On 20 November 1975 an HS 125 being flown by the renowned John Cunningham hit a flock of birds on take-off. The aircraft went through the boundary hedge and over the A281 and was damaged beyond repair, but its occupants escaped; tragically, it struck a car killing the wife of a fellow pilot and five schoolgirls. It was Cunningham's only crash in his long and distinguished flying career and, he said, the worst moment of that career.

Production of the Hawk T1 was completed by the late 1970s, but in 1983 BAe Dunsfold was given an order to convert eighty-eight Hawks to T1A standard capable of carrying a pair of Sidewinder missiles in a secondary defence role. Much development work was undertaken at Dunsfold on the armed single-seat Hawk 200, but without the overseas sales success that the two-seat trainer enjoyed. During 1988 DH Group Ltd acquired from a local landowner the last wartime Blister hangar just off the site to the south, replacing it with a modern new T2-type hangar with a new taxi-way to the perimeter track. Specialising in installing avionics in civil aircraft, the company started with an HS 748 and later the hangar was adapted with a cut-out above the doors to accommodate aircraft up to the size of the Boeing 737. In mid-1989 Surrey Police began to use Dunsfold as its base for operating the first of its helicopters.

In the early 1990s Hawk production was transferred to the BAe Brough factory, with final assembly and flight test at Warton, but work on the Harrier continued. The Canadians had placed a memorial in front of the wartime control tower commemorating the construction and hand-over of the aerodrome but, due to security, it was not readily viewable. In 1992, in conjunction with the publication of an excellent history of the airfield, the author Paul McCue organised the erection of a new memorial. The chosen location was the Alford Barn Inn on the A281 south of the airfield, which had been a popular venue in its wartime guise as 'The Gibbs Hatch Family Restaurant'. The memorial was dedicated on 20 June by the Rector of Alford in the presence of the former HSA Chief Test Pilot, Bill Bedford, local groups and veteran's organisations.

Harrier production finished in 1998, leaving Dunsfold restricted to maintenance and upgrading of the aircraft. The inevitable closure was announced in mid-1999 and urgent discussions ensued on its future. In April 2000 the Council recognised Dunsfold's importance by agreeing that there was no requirement for the land to be returned to agriculture and granted planning permission for the

Behind the memorial commemorating the airfield's construction by Royal Canadian Engineers is the extended wartime control tower. (DWL collection)

permanent use of the site by organisations other than BAE Systems for the assembly, repair and flight-testing of aircraft subject to a new set of conditions. When in 2002 the Rutland Group, an award-winning property company founded in 1984, took over the site, it was with temporary planning permission pending wide-ranging public consultation, which took place at the end of 2003.

The extensive range of buildings were soon being let out to new tenants for industry, offices and warehousing; one of the earliest new occupants was the BBC *Top Gear* programme, which took over the former paint shop as a studio and used the airfield as a test circuit. The main assembly hangars were leased to Cranleigh Freight and by the end of 2004 more than fifty separate organisations were tenants at Dunsfold. Surrey Police also has a driver-training facility on site. An unusual flying organisation trains birds of prey for Middle East customers. Another occupant, based

In 2004 the post-war control tower was unused, but has more recently been taken over by Aces High. (DWL collection)

in the control tower, is Aces High, a film and TV aviation specialist providing aircraft, helicopters and pilots; its most impressive recent acquisition is an ex-BA Boeing 747.

Flying is still a feature of Dunsfold, with a limited number of aircraft resident in one of the T2s, but its long-term future as an active airfield is not guaranteed, as Rutland's Chief Executive, Jim McAllister, told me: 'Airfields do not make money.' However, the company wants to recognise Dunsfold's history and hopes to create a museum, which would include examples of aircraft associated with the site, including the Mitchell. A possible location for the museum is the currently derelict Canada House. Subsequently a master plan for the future of the airfield was unveiled, which includes some 2,600 houses, about 350 acres of lakes and parkland, schools, shops and an enlarged business district. Consultation continues.

To the north of the airfield the accommodation areas are now in private occupation, one being a residential caravan park; the wartime Operations Block and the former battle headquarters both survive. For many years the regular Families Day gave an opportunity for a visit to this historic airfield, but these ceased as BAe left. However, August 2004 saw a successful evening concert and Spitfire display commemorating the 60th anniversary of D-Day. Among the crowd of 9,000 was Reg Day, one of the few remaining veterans of No 98 Squadron, who said, 'This is an evening that will live on in my memory for the rest of my life. To bring us back to the aerodrome where General Dwight D. Eisenhower addressed us before we left for the invasion, was a master stroke.' Since 2005 an annual 'Wings and Wheels' display organised jointly by the Brooklands Museum and Dunsfold Park has raised money for local charities and reinstated the opportunity to visit Dunsfold.

Main features:
Runways: 257° 6,000ft x 150ft, 210° 4,200ft x 150ft, 306° 4,200ft x 150ft, concrete with wood chippings. *Hangars:* two T2, eleven Blisters. *Hardstandings:* thirty-eight flying-pan type. *Accommodation:* RAF: 102 Officers, 103 SNCOs, 825 ORs; WAAF: 6 Officers, 10 SNCOs, 195 ORs.

In January 1917 the RFC's School of Aerial Gunnery, which operated RE.7 No 2400, became No 1 (Auxiliary) School of Aerial Gunnery. (JMB/GSL collection)

DYMCHURCH (Hythe/Palmarsh), Kent

51°03N/01°02E 1ft asl; TR127330. 2.5 miles SW of Hythe alongside A259(T)

The story of the creation of the Great War aerodrome that was variously known as Palmarsh, Hythe and Dymchurch reflects the apparent confusion over its name within the services themselves.

The unit that started this saga was the RFC's Machine Gun School, which moved from its Dover home to Hythe on 27 November 1915 to make better use of the facilities of the gunnery ranges to the west of the town. Although the HQ was established in the Imperial Hotel, its aircraft, which included RE.7s, BE.2cs and Vickers FB.5s, were based at Lympne, although occasionally operating from the range. Renamed the School of Aerial Gunnery on 3 September 1916, the increased activity led to a decision that the Kite Balloon Section should relocate away from the ranges.

A site near the ancient Napoleonic Dymchurch Redoubt was selected in November and an annual rent of £1 per acre offered to the farmer. Two balloon sheds and a winch were erected near TR125319 with the Redoubt itself being taken over for accommodation. By the time the War Office's financial branch got around to finalising the lease, the farmer demanded and got a 50% increase to 30 shillings (£1 10s) an acre.

Another change occurred during January 1917 when the SoAG became No 1 (Auxiliary) School of Aerial Gunnery, tasked with providing two-week courses for RFC observers. However, other demands on space at Lympne meant that the School needed to find another flying home as close as possible to the ranges. An area to the north-east of the Kite Balloon site on the very edge of the Romney Marshes was deemed suitable and in February 1917 the School moved into its new aerodrome. Twelve timber and canvas Bessonneau hangars were erected for the aircraft, which now included AW FK.3s and FK.8s, Scout Ds and DH.2s as well as the earlier RE.7s. There being no accommodation on site, personnel shared that available in the Redoubt.

The aerodrome, although called both Hythe and Palmarsh, became officially known as Dymchurch to differentiate it from the other establishments in Hythe. Although ideally located for the ranges, it was prone to severe winter flooding and liable to sudden sea mists, which limited its usefulness. Despite these limitations, it wasn't until 1 November 1918 that the No 1 (Observer) School of Aerial Gunnery moved to the better aerodrome at New Romney. The new title had come about on 9 March when Nos 1 and 3 (Aux) SoAG had merged.

Dymchurch became an emergency LG for aircraft using the Hythe ranges, but in early 1919 the School returned to be formally disbanded there on 14 February 1919. The site was closed shortly after, returning to farmland following clearance during 1920.

No evidence of the site's aeronautical use survives although a good view can be obtained from the famous Romney, Hythe & Dymchurch Railway as its track now bisects the field. Adjacent to the level crossing on the road to Botolph's Bridge is a works that might be a gas or sewage pumping station and there are extensive gravel workings to the east.

(Note: To continue the confusion over Dymchurch, a site in the area was chosen as a potential ALG during 1942. It was not built and, although its exact location is unknown, it was not on the Great War aerodrome at Dymchurch/Hythe/Palmarsh, nor apparently the Littlestone LG or its civil successor, which were both at St Mary's Bay.)

Main features in 1918:
Landing ground: grass. *Hangars:* twelve Bessonneau. *Accommodation:* requisitioned Dymchurch Redoubt.

EAST DEAN, East Sussex – see FRISTON

EAST GRINSTEAD, East Sussex – see HAMMERWOOD

EASTBOURNE, East Sussex

50°47N/00°18E 8ft amsl; TQ625015. 2 miles N of Eastbourne

It was the momentous cross-Channel flight by Louis Blériot that the founder of Eastbourne's aerodrome, Frederick Fowler, subsequently acknowledged as the event that aroused his interest in aviation. It is also likely that he viewed the historic aircraft nine days later on 3 August 1909, when it was exhibited in Eastbourne.

In late 1911, although he had yet to find a suitable aerodrome and to learn to fly, Fowler bought no fewer than five Blériot-type machines from the defunct New Hampshire Aviation School at East Boldre, Beaulieu. His airfield followed shortly after when he rented some 50 acres of marshy land between the gas works and St Anthony's Hill. The site was far from ideal, being crossed by many drainage ditches, some of which had to be covered by boards to give a maximum landing run of 1,640 feet (530 metres). The Eastbourne Flying School was created on 1 December 1911, and on 8 January 1912 Fowler attempted to deliver his first 50hp Blériot to Eastbourne. Having taught himself to fly at East Boldre (his formal RAeC Aviator's Certificate No 175 was not issued until 16 January), he lost control in fog and crashed into the Solent. Both he and the aircraft were recovered. The remaining machines were delivered by road on a purpose-designed trailer!

Among the buildings being erected was a £70 former corrugated-iron church, which included appropriate scriptural notices that were probably appreciated by the trainees about to embark on the hazardous business of learning to fly. Two hangars and a large workshop followed as the EAC also entered the aeroplane construction business, building Blériot-type machines. By the end of 1912 five of the first twelve pupils had already obtained their certificates on a range of aeroplanes including single- and two-seat Blériots, a Sommer biplane, a Bristol Boxkite and three Blériot types built by EAC. Frederick Minchin was one of the successful pupils, gaining his Certificate on 18 February 1913. After a distinguished RFC career in which he won a DSO MC and bar, he flew with Imperial Airways, but piloting a Fokker F VII with Princess Loewenstein-Wertheim as passenger in an attempt on the first east-west transatlantic flight by a woman, the aircraft and its crew disappeared without trace in August 1927. Another who learned to fly at Eastbourne was a Cyril Foggin, who qualified on 29 October 1912. He had ordered his own aeroplane, a Blackburn

Monoplane, which survives to this day as the oldest airworthy British aircraft, and is part of the Shuttleworth Collection.

Around this time Fowler had met Frank Hucks who, with his brother B. C. Hucks, later devised the Hucks Starter. On 24 February 1913 the Frank Hucks Waterplane Company changed its name to the Eastbourne Aviation Company as the two pioneers joined forces. Building on Hucks's experience, seaplanes were being added to the fleet. A site on the coast, adjacent to the Crumbles pond, was leased from Baron Willington from March 1913 for development as a seaplane base (TQ635007). A range of buildings were erected, including a large seaplane shed, workshops, offices and stores, plus a turntable and a launching railway that led down to the high-water mark. Thus, with both land and sea aerodrome facilities, Eastbourne was in the fore of UK aviation.

In 1913 EAC produced its first original design. The ELG monoplane was named after its Swiss designer, Emil Gassler, who had qualified for his Aviator's Certificate at Eastbourne towards the end of 1912. With no commercial sales, the sole example became a useful trainer with the Flying School. The second EAC design, a biplane to the order of Lieutenant R. Hunt for exhibition flying, was completed in February 1914, but again only one example was built. Fowler and Gassler's third design, the EAC Military Biplane, was exhibited at the March 1914 Olympia Aero Show. Sadly, no military orders were forthcoming, but the team pressed on to their final creation. A twin-float biplane with an enormous 54-foot (16.5-metre) wingspan powered by a 100hp Green aero engine driving a pair of tractor propellers, the aeroplane was to be entered into the Daily Mail Circuit of Britain. The outbreak of the First World War led to cancellation of the competition, and the EAC circuit Biplane was subsequently broken up, unflown.

Following the 4 August 1914 declaration of war, the EAC sites were taken over by the Admiralty. It already had an interest in the facilities having, in June 1913, leased an aeroplane shed on the airfield and contributed to the cost of a seaplane hangar on the Crumbles site. At Eastbourne all civilian flying was stopped as the aerodrome became an RNAS training station. Initial enlargement saw the original 50-acre site expanded to the west up to Lottridge Drove, while to the east the whole of St Anthony's Hill was included. The original sheds were supplemented by six Bessonneau hangars, and later a further nine were erected beside Lottridge Drove. The first RNAS Wardroom was Eversley Court on St Anne's Road, but later a large private house in Trinity Place was requisitioned.

By 1915 a wide variety of aeroplanes, including Avro 504s, Blériots, Caudrons, Maurice and Henri Farmans, White & Thompsons and Curtiss JN4As, were in service at Eastbourne, but by mid-1916 the fleet had been rationalised to just Jennies and Maurice Farmans. The flying field was further enlarged to the north-west with ever more drainage ditches being covered by boarding until, by November 1918, the site totalled 242 acres. Despite the constraints of the site, training continued throughout the war, and at its end 117 pilots had qualified, but eighteen airmen lost their lives in ground and flying accidents. On 5 September a formation of six aeroplanes, three of which were being flown by Brazilian officers, saw a collision between two Camels with both pilots, one a Brazilian, being killed. The last fatality was that of Private H. H. Hamil from Pueblo, Colorado, serving with the American Air Service as an engine fitter. He was struck by a propeller on 7 November and died three days later.

Short S.38 No 3144 was built by White & Thompson near Bognor Regis. Delivered to Eastbourne in November 1915, it was wrecked by wind four months later. (JMB/GSL collection)

Following the creation of the RAF in April 1918, No 54 Training Squadron was transferred from Castle Bromwich with a mix of machines including Pups, Camels, SE.5as and Avro 504s. On 15 July 1918 the unit was redesignated No 50 TDS in the 60th (Training) Wing. The Armistice saw a gradual run-down of activity, and in October 1919 the TDS moved to Manston, disbanding there on 24 October. In September 1919 the largest aircraft to visit Eastbourne ended up in a ditch during a precautionary landing. Carrying seven officers and other ranks, who were uninjured, the HP 0/400 was en route from Andover to Winchester when it suffered engine failure.

No 50 TDS operated a number of fighters, including this Pup D4016. (JMB/GSL collection)

Although the main activity at the Crumbles factory was repair work, twelve BE.2cs were built in the latter half of 1915. These were followed by forty Maurice Farman S.11s during 1916/17. Although 200 Avro 504s were ordered in late 1917, it appears that only just over fifty were delivered before the Armistice, the remainder of the order being subsequently cancelled.

Early in 1920 the two sites were handed back to Major Fowler, and Eastbourne briefly opened for civilian flying, but on 9 December 1920 it was formally announced that the aerodrome was no longer licensed for use. However, the seaplane base continued with EAC operating as a joy-riding concern using a fleet of red-painted Avro 504 and Short 184 seaplanes. The company also built six Avro 504L seaplanes, retaining two for its own use. In late 1921 EAC switched to building large charabancs based on an ex-Army chassis, which failed to sell, being found to be too wide for commercial use. On 16 December 1922 the company went into receivership, Eastbourne Corporation acquiring many of the seaplane base buildings for the storage and repair of deckchairs.

On the airfield one of the timber sheds was sold for use as a church in Five Ashes in East Sussex, being dedicated on 8 November 1921. It survives to this day as the Church of the Good Shepherd. During the Second World War the large hangar was used by the Canadian Army for storage, and post-war by Wenham's of Eastbourne Ltd as a furniture store. Its last use was to store vintage buses owned by the Eastbourne Omnibus Society, but following damage in the October 1987 gales the ancient shed was dismantled in late 1990, although its base survives to this day. The owner of Wenham's, Sidney Wenham, had purchased the former RNAS Guard House on Leeds Avenue for conversion into a bungalow, and it is now the last building of the EAC aerodrome to remain in situ.

There is, however, yet another relic of Eastbourne that survives, albeit in poor condition. One of the EAC-built Avro 504Ls, G-EASD, was sold to Sweden in 1921 but crashed in 1929. Its stored remains were returned to England in 1990. It has since changed ownership but hopefully it will be restored to fly once more from Eastbourne's beach; sadly, joy-rides are unlikely to be on offer.

The former Guard House, converted to a private bungalow, is a remarkable survivor of RNAS Eastbourne. (DWL collection)

Main features in 1918:
Landing ground: grass. *Hangars:* fifteen Bessonneau and three pre-war aeroplane sheds. *Accommodation:* requisitioned private houses and wooden hutting.

EASTLEIGH (Southampton), Hampshire

50°57N/00°12W 44ft amsl; SU0450168. 3.5 miles N of Southampton off A335

Of the million-plus passengers who now annually pass through Southampton Airport, the observant few may realise its historic connection with the immortal Spitfire; virtually none will be aware that aviation first came to these former water meadows of North Stoneham Farm between the River Itchen and the A335 as early as 1910.

Aviation pioneer Eric Rowland Moon's family ran the Moonbeam Engineering Company. In 1909 he decided to build his own aeroplane, a Demoiselle-like monoplane, which he called Moonbeam No 1. Test-hopped in June 1910, he developed it into the Moonbeam No 2, which was flown successfully at North Stoneham and elsewhere. Although it may be possible that the field was later used by Claude Graham-White, the next recorded use was following the farm's requisition in 1917 to be developed as an Aircraft Acceptance Park.

Construction of the GS hangars, workshops and storage sheds along Wide Lane (now the A335) began almost immediately. However, the needs of Britain's new ally intervened as the US Navy required a base to assemble the anticipated flood of American-built bombers in preparation for the planned attacks on the German U boat bases. Eastleigh's proximity to Southampton Docks made it an ideal location.

The first Americans arrived in the summer of 1918 and the handover of the incomplete airfield took place on 20 July, when the camp was designated Naval Air Station Eastleigh. Delivery of the American DH.4s was running behind schedule, so it was agreed that the UK would supply DH.9As in exchange for Liberty aero engines. Uncrated, assembled and flight-tested, the aircraft for the US 10th Bombing Group were quickly ferried to France.

The Armistice on 11 November 1918 changed all that, and within four days all assembly work stopped as the station began to accept equipment back from France for forward shipment to the USA. This continued until 10 April 1919, when Eastleigh was handed back to the RAF. The total area of the aerodrome was now 158 acres (64 hectares), of which buildings covered some 30 acres (12.2 hectares), and included Aeroplane Sheds of 170ft (52m) x 100ft (30m), twenty-one Storage Sheds with dimensions of 200ft (61m) x 60ft (18m), and five smaller Storage Sheds of 150ft (47m) x 60ft (18m).

The camp's accommodation was now used to house squadrons that had given up their aircraft prior to disbanding. During October 1919 Nos 45, 28 and 7 arrived, and by January 1920 all three squadrons had left or disbanded. With the last squadron gone, the station officially closed in May 1920. Renamed the Atlantic Park Hostel, the virtually new accommodation was taken over by shipping companies to house immigrants awaiting their voyage to a new life in the USA.

Although officially closed, the aerodrome was increasingly used as an unlicensed LG. By 1926 the Croydon-based Surrey Flying Services was regularly using Eastleigh for air taxi work, parachuting and joy-riding. When, in 1929, Southampton Corporation wanted its own municipal airport, it acquired 100 acres (40.5 hectares) of land, but the owners of the Atlantic Park Hostel were reluctant to sell. The negotiations were protracted, but flying continued when possible. In August 1931 Captain C. D. Barnard's Air Circus sponsored by the *Daily Mail* came to Atlantic Park with a Fokker F.VIIA, a Cierva Autogiro and a Spartan three-seater.

Finally, in January 1932 the Corporation was able to complete its purchase of the site. Renovations were put in hand, and on 11 August 1932 Sir Alan Cobham arrived with his National Aviation Day display. The potential of the aerodrome for experimental flight testing also appealed to Vickers-Armstrong, which obtained approval from the Air Ministry for Supermarine to use some of facilities on the aerodrome. Following the official reopening in November 1932, the Hampshire Aero Club transferred its operation here from nearby Hamble. Regular air services followed in August 1933 when International Airlines Ltd began 'The Western Express' Croydon-Portsmouth-Southampton-Plymouth service with two Monospar ST.4s.

Jersey Airways extended its Jersey-Portsmouth service to Southampton in mid-March and subsequently moved its HQ from Portsmouth to Eastleigh. At the end of July 1934 Railway Air Services began a Birmingham-Bristol-Southampton-Cowes summer service with a DH.84 Dragon. Before the end of the year, Spartan Air Lines also added Eastleigh to its routes. When a pundit beacon light flashing 'SN' was installed, the Hampshire Aero Club offered night-flying training and also formed a Civil Air Guard unit.

Supermarine used Eastleigh for the land trials of its Seagull V from June 1933 and subsequently leased two hangars to establish a flight-test centre; the first flight of the Type 224, progenitor of the Spitfire, took place on 19 February 1934. Other aeroplane manufacturers and sub-contractors arrived; Oddie, Bradbury and Cull built the second and third Kay Gyroplanes here for their Scottish designer, David Kay. G-ACVA first flew from Eastleigh on 18 February 1935, but insufficient funds meant that both machines were stored in Scotland. Now displayed at the Museum of Flight at East Fortune, G-ACVA is the oldest Eastleigh-built aeroplane to survive.

In 1935 the Air Ministry and the Corporation agreed that 10 acres (4 hectares) of land on the north-east perimeter of the airfield would be leased as an FAA base. For RAF Eastleigh (RAF Southampton from August 1936), ten Bessonneau hangars and a number of wooden huts were erected, and Nos 4 and 13 Squadrons brought their Audaxes for their summer camp. From August 1935 to August 1936, Nos 800, 801 and 802 Squadrons FAA all spent time at Eastleigh. The aerodrome had witnessed a very historic first flight when, on 5 March 1936, the prototype Spitfire, K5054, had flown in the hands of Vickers's CTP, 'Mutt' Summers. In early June the company received an order for 310 Spitfires, valued then at an incredible £1.25 million!

The Spithead Review of May 1937 attracted some forty Naval aircraft to Eastleigh, and in June Vickers (Supermarine) Aviation Ltd put on a private air display featuring all its products, including of course a Spitfire, but also Walrus, Wellesley, Stranraer, Scapa and Wellington aircraft. In August 1937 the Chairman of British-American Tobacco, Sir Hugo Cunliffe-Owen, founded a company at Eastleigh, renamed Cunliffe-Owen Aircraft in May 1938, to build the revolutionary American Brunelli 'Flying Wing' airliner.

Supermarine had completed a new flight shed for Walrus and Spitfire testing in April 1938, responding to a second order for a further 200 Spitfires. Despite the first production aircraft achieving its first flight from Eastleigh on 14 May 1938, Spitfire production was in deep trouble, mainly due to late deliveries of sub-contracted wings arising from lack of experience of stressed-skin construction. There was extensive adverse press coverage of the production delays – in 1938 the Spitfire was the Eurofighter of its day! In April 1938 the aerodrome came under the control of the Air Ministry, and a large municipal hangar costing £9,000 was erected, capable of housing five AW Ensign airliners. A terminal building was planned but overtaken by the forthcoming conflict.

No 814 Squadron FAA was formed at Eastleigh on 1 December 1938 with six Swordfish before embarking on HMS *Ark Royal* in January 1939. The Cunliffe-Owen COA-1 made its maiden flight on 12 January 1939, as the company moved into a new factory and a pair of Lamella roof hangars at Swaything on the southern edge of Eastleigh. The vacated Belfast Hangar 2 was taken over by Supermarine for Spitfire assembly, supplementing Hangar 1, which had been the company's since 1936. No 811 Squadron was formed from a flight of Swordfish in May 1939, and No 821 returned on 28 June (having been a regular visitor) just prior to the station becoming HMS *Raven* on 1 July 1939.

On 1 July No 758 Squadron had formed as a Telegraphist Air Gunner Training squadron with thirteen Sharks and six Ospreys. Skuas, Rocs and Proctors were added before the end of 1939. The outbreak of the Second World War meant the end of all civil flying as the buildings donned camouflage paint. On 2 October No 780 Squadron was formed; it used a wide range of aircraft types to convert volunteer civilian-trained pilots to Naval standards. No 759 Squadron formed as a Fighter School and Pool squadron with nine Skuas, five Rocs and four Sea Gladiators, and became the Fleet Fighter School after absorbing 769 Squadron on 1 December 1939.

The 'Phoney War' period saw the Southampton Corporation lease to the Admiralty another hangar on the western side of the airport together with a parcel of land to the east side. On 1 April 1940 No 760 Squadron was formed as No 1 Fleet Fighter Pool, initially with four Skuas, a pair of Rocs and a single Sea Gladiator. Defences were strengthened at the end of June by the arrival of No 924 Balloon Barrage Squadron, and aircraft planning to land at the aerodrome had first to call at Worthy Down to obtain authority to negotiate the gun and balloon defences. This did not help the luckless crew of a No 1 OTU Hudson who in August became the first of No 924's victims.

War came to Eastleigh on 11 September 1940 when the Cunliffe-Owen works at Swaything received nine direct hits, causing severe damage and much loss of life. The three FAA training squadrons departed within a few weeks – fortunately, as on 8 October a landing Hudson inadvertently led three He 111s of 6/KG55 through the balloon barrage. Thirty-eight 50kg (110lb) bombs were dropped on the aerodrome, and others landed on the town itself where the GEC works was damaged. One bomber was hit by Eastleigh's ground defences but was able to return to its Villacoublay base. Thorney Island's defences claimed two more 6/KG55 aircraft, one of which crashed near Rowland's Castle.

HMS *Raven* became an important ground training station with the Observers Part 1 Training School being joined by various artificer training courses. The Bessonneau hangars were reduced to a single example, the aircraft of a Salvage Depot and Major Inspections and Reserve Aircraft Storage being housed in the GS sheds on the civil side of the airport.

Cunliffe-Owen Aircraft Ltd was heavily committed to the modification, assembly and repair of a wide range of aircraft. An early contract was the conversion of the Hudson for ASR duties, carrying the Uffa Fox-designed airborne lifeboat. One Hudson was retained during June 1940 at Eastleigh in a 'special hangar' under conditions of total secrecy for use by 'VIPs' to escape to Canada if necessary. Nearly 120 early Spitfires were modified to Seafires, which led to a sub-contract from Westland for 350 new-build Seafire Mk IIIs. Setting up a production line took nearly twelve months but led to subsequent contracts for the Mk XV and finally the Seafire Mk XVII.

On 28 June 1944 No 716 Squadron formed at Eastleigh as the Safety Equipment School, operating a miscellany of aircraft including a Wellington together with Sea Otters and Barracudas. Other training units at HMS *Raven* included schools for Stokers and Wiremen and the Air Medicine School. With the final victory in the Far East, the units began to disband or disperse, and in April 1946 HMS *Raven* was 'paid off'. In May 1946 Eastleigh became a civil airport managed by the Ministry of Civil Aviation.

Although the airport was then still under FAA control, Channel Island Airways reopened its Jersey and Guernsey services from 10 September 1945 with six Rapide flights a day. At Cunliffe-Owen, modification work on Coastal Command Lancasters continued, but the company was planning its first post-war airliner. Cierva, who had moved to Eastleigh from Hanworth, sub-contracted COA to build much of its first helicopter, the Air Horse. On 18 October 1946

Southampton University Air Squadron arrived from Worthy Down with five Tigers and a single Oxford before moving on to Hamble a year later. In early 1947 Vickers-Supermarine decided to concentrate its flying operations at Chilbolton and South Marston, although retaining a manufacturing presence at Eastleigh until December 1957.

The medium-range ten-seat Cunliffe-Owen Concordia prototype made its maiden flight on 19 April 1947, followed in mid-October by the second example. Despite an extensive European sales tour, the airline market, flooded by war-surplus aircraft, was just not ready for a new aircraft. In November 1947 work on the initial production batch of six airframes was suspended. The substantial loss forced the company into liquidation. The factory was auctioned in 1948, and was taken over by Briggs Motor Bodies Ltd in 1949; acquired by the Ford-Iveco Motor Company in 1958, it was later used for production of the long-serving Transit commercial vehicle.

The unmarked Cunliffe-Owen Concordia prototype awaits its first flight in April 1947, with converted ASR Lancasters in the background. (ROC Museum via N. Cullingford)

The loss of its production facilities was a major setback for Cierva, whose giant Air Horse made its first flight at Eastleigh on 7 December 1948. Powered by a single Rolls-Royce Merlin engine driving three rotors via a gearbox, the machine was the world's largest helicopter. During the production hiatus, Cierva's design team conceived a small two-seat light helicopter, the W 14 Skeeter 1, which was shown statically at Farnborough with the Air Horse and first flew on 10 October 1948. Cierva was then leading the world in helicopter development; sadly, like many others, the company was to pay heavily for its innovation.

June 1950 was the month when it all went wrong. On the 13th the first Air Horse crashed at Eastleigh, killing Cierva's CTP, Alan Marsh, and his crew after the failure of a rotor hub. The Skeeter had been experiencing ground resonance problems, which reached a climax on 26 June when destructive vibrations broke up the machine. Cierva could not survive this double blow and closed as an independent company in January 1951. All was not lost, as Saunders-Roe, which had had a small presence at Eastleigh since 1937, took over the facilities, aircraft and most of the staff to continue the development of the Skeeter. The surviving Air Horse was put into storage and later broken up.

Although BOAC had resumed flying boat operations from the Solent, little commercial use was being made of Southampton's land airport, although Silver City Airways had started a Southampton-Cherbourg vehicle ferry service during 1952. To improve the facilities, the remains of the hutted camp and other buildings in the north-east corner were removed by 1954 and the main grass NNE/SSW runway extended to 5,050 feet (1,539 metres). The original GS hangars were retained and adjacent four-bay Belfast Truss workshops converted for passenger/freight handling. In 1953 Silver City introduced its long-nosed Bristol 170 Wayfarers onto a new Southampton-Bembridge service. BEA started a revolutionary new service between the London and Southampton airports in mid-June 1954 with Bristol 171 Mk 3 helicopters. The return fare was 50 shillings (£2 10s). The more effective Westland-Sikorsky S-55 was introduced onto the route in December.

A crowded Cierva works hangar in early 1950, with both Air Horses, a Cierva Autogiro and Skeeter production. (Fordyce via P. H. T. Green collection)

At Saunders-Roe, correction of the Skeeter's ground resonance problems was protracted and only solved when the Mk 5 was evaluated by the A&AEE during 1954. Full evaluation of the Mk 6 variant by the Army Air Corps as the AOP 10 and 11 finally led to production of the AOP 12, deliveries beginning in June 1958. The following month saw the first flight of the Skeeter's turbine-powered successor, the aerodynamic prototype Saro P 531 taking to the air on 20 July, followed by the second aircraft at the end of September. The improved P 531-2 flew in August 1959, in the same month that Westland Aircraft Ltd took over the Helicopter Division of Saunders-Roe. Named the Scout and Wasp for the Army and Royal Navy respectively, further development and the production line was transferred to Hayes during 1960. During its time at Eastleigh, Saro had also built major components for the Vampire, Venom and Swift, and Viscount wings for Vickers-Armstrong Ltd.

The sole Spitfire T8 two-seater, G-AIDN, carries race number 99 at Eastleigh in the 1950s. (L/Obs R. Shiels via N. Cullingford)

Eastleigh's Control Tower looks down on Grumman Super Goose G-ASXG. (N. Cullingford)

In 1961 Southampton Corporation took back its airport from the MCA and sold it to Southampton Airport Ltd on 15 May. The newly formed British United Airways proposed developing the airport with a totally new terminal across the River Itchen with a taxiway link to the existing site; this came to nothing, but it was obvious that Eastleigh needed to expand to retain its commercial services. The crucial concrete runway 03/21 was completed by Richard Costain Ltd in September 1965 and officially opened in January 1966, together with a large hardstanding adjacent to the terminal. The transformation of Eastleigh into Southampton Airport was complete when the Airport railway station opened in April 1966, giving a direct rail link to London.

British United and its successors made good use of Southampton with its London-Channel Islands rail/air link. British Airways withdrew its services in 1980 and a new airline, Air UK, took up some of the routes. A Channel Island link was also being flown by Aurigny Air Services, which had launched its service from Southampton in 1970 with BN Trislanders, the first operator of this aircraft. The resident flying club was the Hampshire School of Flying. The runway was lengthened to 5,653 feet (1,723 metres) in 1978 and redesignated 02/20. In 1988 a consortium led by Peter de Savary bought the airport, but in 1990 the ownership passed to BAA plc and the name changed to Southampton International Airport.

In 1993 construction of a new £23m terminal and car park began, being officially opened by HRH Prince Andrew, Duke of York, on 9 December 1994. The old terminal building was then demolished. Suckling Airways began to use Southampton in 1998, flying to Antwerp with Dornier 328s and carrying more than 41,000 passengers in its first year. Jersey European opened a Fokker F-27 service to Guernsey in May 1998 competing with KLM UK, which had acquired Air UK in 1997. In that year the airport handled more than 500,000 passengers, which had risen to over a million a year by August 2003. Most of that expansion was due to Flybe, which by 2004 was flying to sixteen destinations and carrying 50% of the airport's passengers.

In 2004 Jersey and Southampton celebrated the longest-established air link, which had been inaugurated on 29 March 1934 with a DH Dragon Rapide. In 2004 Flybe's service was four flights daily, and Eastern Airways, First Choice, Skybus and Scot Airways, the successors to Suckling Airways, were all operating from Southampton.

On the airport site, all the former Belfast hangars and the municipal hangar are now gone. The M27 motorway separates the airport from the former Cunliffe-Owen factory and its 'Lamella' hangars, which survive as part of the Ford factory. In 1999 BAA sponsored a commemorative window in the terminal, depicting the prototype Spitfire and recording the history of the Spitfire at Eastleigh. On 5 March 2003 Dr Gordon Mitchell, son of designer R. J. Mitchell, unveiled a two-thirds scale, 1-ton reproduction of the prototype Spitfire, sixty-eight years to the day since the original had made its maiden flight at Eastleigh. Mounted dramatically on the entrance roundabout on Mitchell Way, the sculpture by Southampton artist Alan Manning now greets all visitors to the airport.

Unveiled on 5 March 2003, this model of the prototype Spitfire welcomes visitors to Southampton Airport. (DWL collection)

Main features of HMS *Raven*:
Runways: NNE-SSW 3,810ft, WNW-ESE 2,040ft, 208° 3,600ft, grass. *Hangars:* one 65ft x 79ft Bessonneau. *Hardstandings:* none. *Accommodation:* RN: 48 Officers, 691 Chiefs/POs/Ratings; WRNS: 8 Officers, 183 Chiefs/POs/Ratings.

21st-century features:
Runway: 020° 1,723m x 37m, asphalt.

EGERTON, Kent, see HEADCORN

FARNBOROUGH, Hampshire

51°18N/00°45W 210ft amsl; SU856538. 2 miles NW of Aldershot on A325

Farnborough! An incredibly evocative name conjuring up, as it does, so many historical images and wonderful memories – from the most recent in mid-November 2008, as I watched the Vulcan taxi out to depart for Bruntingthorpe, a flight that I then feared was to be its last, to my first SBAC show in 1958, and what a show that was! 'Treble One' – the Black Arrows rolling and looping no fewer than twenty-two Hunters in close formation, a feat never to be repeated and never, ever forgotten. The Navy provided two formation teams: No 800 Squadron with Sea Hawks and No 803 with the mighty Scimitar. The RAF showed off a further forty-five Hunters in formation, nine Canberras and forty-five Javelins. The noise was awesome.

From the British Aircraft Industry there was the usual annual crop of new designs: the Fairey Rotodye, Saunders-Roe P.531 and a flock of Westland helicopters including the Westminster were part of the rotary element. Three Avro company Vulcans took part, including one demonstrating the LABS manoeuvre – a half loop and roll off the top! Rolls-Royce displayed its Conway-powered Vulcan Flight Test Bed, the prototype VX770. As a Nottingham resident, I regarded this as 'my' Vulcan, as it was flying virtually continuously from Hucknall on engine development. Tragically I also saw it and its crew perish at RAF Syerston a couple of weeks later. Prototypes of the English Electric P1B Lightning and Blackburn NA 39 Buccaneer demonstrated the future for the RAF and FAA – all this and much more on the airfield where British aviation began more than a century ago and where it was nurtured almost to the end of the 20th century.

From the early 1890s Aldershot had been the home of the Balloon Factory, constructing tethered observation balloons for the British Army. At the turn of the century the dirigible (steerable balloon) flights of Santos-Dumont in France and von Zeppelin in Germany eventually spurred a response from Britain. As the congested barracks were obviously unsuitable for such a machine, the northern end of Farnborough Common was chosen as a temporary location for a future airship and its shed.

The obvious attractions of the new location prompted the relocation of the Balloon Factory while the new airship shed was under construction. Accurately described as an 'Elongated Balloon Erecting House', the impressive new structure, 160ft (49m) long and 72ft

(22m) high, was completed by May 1905. Two gas holders, a number of smaller buildings and the iron-framed balloon house were dismantled at Aldershot, and before the end of 1905 were re-erected adjacent to the new airship shed with new-build workshops following in 1906. The transfer and consequent reorganisation somewhat delayed the appearance of the Army's first dirigible, which as the *Nulli Secundus* (*Second to None*) finally made its maiden flight on 10 September 1907. Under the command of Colonel J. E. Capper, the Superintendent of the Factory, on 5 October the airship circumnavigated St Paul's and Buckingham Palace before returning to Farnborough. Aboard that flight, as chief engineer, was Samuel Franklin Cody, the American-born entrepreneur and inventor.

Cody had originally arrived in Europe with a Wild West Show responding to the Victorian fascination with the American cowboy and his Red Indian foe. As the public's interest waned, Cody turned to experimenting with man-lifting kites, and patented his ideas in November 1901. Its potential as an alternative to the captive observation balloon led to demonstrations to both armed services. Initial military interest was limited to a sale of a Cody War Kite to the Royal Navy for wireless experiments. However, Cody was invited to use Aldershot's facilities for continuing experimentation at his own expense, which led to a contract in February 1905 as a civilian kite instructor. Thus Cody also moved to Farnborough to expand his interest, with Colonel Capper's support, into glider-kites while working on the propulsion and control systems of the *Nulli Secundus*.

As the Balloon Factory continued to develop its series of airships, Cody began construction of his first powered aeroplane. The influence of the Wright Flyer was obvious in the somewhat grandly titled British Army Aeroplane No 1. Although early taxiing trials, during which hops were made, took place on Laffan's Plain, it was from the Swan Inn plateau in the south-east corner of Farnborough Common that the aeroplane with its large wingspan of 52 feet (15.8 metres) first flew on 16 October 1908. After 27 seconds and some 1,390 feet (424 metres), including flying over a clump of birch trees, the left wing hit the ground, resulting in a crash from which Cody emerged unscathed. This historic event was acclaimed as the first sustained and controlled powered flight in Britain.

The damage to the British Army's first aeroplane was soon repaired and, with further improvements incorporated, trials resumed in early January 1909 despite the often difficult relationship between Cody and his Army masters. At the time airships appeared to have a much brighter future, which led to the Imperial Defence Committee concluding in January that funding of airships should continue, but that of aeroplanes should cease. This shattering news was given to Cody on 24 February. He was given the now unwanted aeroplane and the 'loan' of its Antoinette engine and, as he was still officially the Chief Kite Instructor, he was permitted to erect his shed on Laffan's Plain to continue his experiments on condition that he should keep the War Office informed as to progress!

Although Blériot's successful Channel crossing in July 1909 was universally hailed as a triumph, the Balloon Factory persevered with airship development. The 'improved' *Nulli Secundus II* (a somewhat ridiculous name!) had flown in July 1908, followed by the equally unsuccessful 'Baby'. From October 1909, under its first civilian superintendent, M. J. P. O'Gorman, the Baby was rebuilt as the *Beta*, which made its maiden flight on 26 May 1910. It was preceded by the non–rigid airship *Gamma*, which had flown on 12 February. Further investment at Farnborough was announced in the 1910/11 Army estimates. The outlay provided two more airship sheds, extended workshops and new gas plant and holders. But the progress of heavier-than-air flight could not be ignored for ever. Three aeroplanes were involved in the September 1910 Army manoeuvres on Salisbury Plain, and in October the Balloon Factory was tasked with repairing aeroplanes for the Balloon School. Repairing evolved into experimental rebuilding of mainly French designs with tractor monoplanes all receiving the 'B' designation after Blériot. Pusher designs were 'F' after Farman, and originally 'S' designs were based on the Santos-Dumont canard configuration.

Towards the end of 1910 a new employee joined the Balloon Factory, bringing with him an aeroplane of his own design. After successfully demonstrating it on a bitterly cold January day, the Farman-type 'pusher' biplane was purchased by the War Office for £400, to become the FE.1. Geoffrey de Havilland had begun his long and successful career in aviation. With effect from 1 April 1911, the Balloon School became the Air Battalion, Royal Engineers, and was allocated funds to construct two new sheds, having previously shared the facilities of the Balloon Factory. These two buildings became renowned as the famous 'Black Sheds', one of which survives to this day. Another original building from that period is the Air Battalion's first headquarters, now the home of the Farnborough Air Sciences Trust.

An aerial view of Farnborough circa 1912. What became the famous 'Black Sheds' are in the left foreground, and at the top is the historic portable airship shed, the frame of which is now the centrepiece within the Business Park. (MAP via P. H. T. Green collection)

The successful Army airship Gamma was part of No 1 Squadron RFC from 13 May 1912. (via P. H. T. Green collection)

Finally, on 26 April 1911 the Balloon Factory officially became His Majesty's Aircraft Factory, although generally called the Army Aircraft Factory, the Aircraft name being chosen to encompass both aeroplanes and airships. The two continued to be evaluated in parallel. One of the least successful airships was the Lebaudy *Morning Post*, purchased on behalf of the nation by readers of that newspaper. Although it arrived from France in late 1910, it only flew once in May 1911, after which it broke free, collapsing onto a nearby house. In his dual role of designer and chief test pilot, Geoffrey de Havilland flew the canard SE.1 at 05.30 on 7 June 1911, and the design was quickly followed by the FE.2 and the BE.1. The SE.1 only lasted until 18 August when it crashed, killing its inexperienced pilot, Lt T. J. Ridge. No further canard 'S' designs emerged, the designation becoming Scouting Experimental. During the summer the *Gamma* airship achieved a successful flight to Salisbury Plain for the Army manoeuvres.

Meanwhile, Cody independently persevered with his aeroplane, achieving a flight of more than 40 miles in 63 minutes on 8 September 1909. He began to regularly take passengers aloft, including his former employer, Colonel Capper, and the honour of Britain's first aviatrix fell to Cody's wife Lela. The immense size of the Cody machine in comparison with its contemporaries led to its nickname of the 'Flying Cathedral', a title that became the 'trademark' of a series of Cody Flyers that appeared at numerous meetings and races. He built up a huge public following, but had failed to sell a single Cody aeroplane until the announcement of a Military Trial to be held at Larkhill in August 1912 gave him fresh hope. The revised Mk III Cathedral was entered in competition with thirty-one other machines from British and European constructors. After weeks of tests only the Cathedral and three French aeroplanes completed the Trial, and it was the Cody that was formally adjudged the winner. Despite the antiquated appearance of his machine, the showman had finally triumphed over his critics! Sadly his triumph was only to last a year for, on 7 August 1913, his new 60-foot-wingspan hydroplane suffered structural failure over Laffan's Plain, and Cody and his passenger Lieutenant Keyser both died in the subsequent crash.

Ironically the real victor at Larkhill was the BE.2, which had made its first flight in the hands of Geoffrey de Havilland on 1 February 1912, but was debarred from competing as one of the judges was the Factory Superintendent. Subsequently an order for four BE.2s was placed with the British & Colonial Aircraft Company (Bristol). With the creation of the Royal Flying Corps on 13 April 1912, it absorbed the Royal Engineers Air Battalion a month later. On 13 May Farnborough saw the original No 1 (Airship) Company become No 1 Squadron RFC, with airships *Beta*, *Gamma*, *Delta* and *Zeta*. Also created on the same day was No 2 Squadron RFC from No 2 (Aeroplane) Company, flying a mix of early pioneer machines including various BEs.

In January the following year No 2 Squadron made an epic journey north to Montrose, and in June 1913 No 4 Squadron RFC, which had formed in September 1912, transferred its motley aeroplane assortment, including a Cody, a Breguet, a Longhorn and BEs, to Netheravon. Further squadrons were created at Farnborough, No 5 from a nucleus of 3 Squadron on 26 July 1913, and No 6 Squadron on 31 January 1914 with Longhorns, BE.2s and later a number of REs. On 1 May No 7 Squadron was formed with the Sopwith Tabloid, Longhorns and again various BEs. On the same day No 1 Squadron RFC became the RNAS Airship Detachment, although airships had formally become the responsibility of the Naval Wing on 1 January 1914. The unit remained at Farnborough until March 1915, when it moved to Kingsnorth. Prior to that, during August 1914, virtually the whole active strength of the RFC (Squadron Nos 2, 3, 4 and 5) had left for France via Swingate Down.

Farnborough now adopted a second-line training role as additional squadrons were prepared for service abroad. Although formed in January, No 6 Squadron had worked its way through an odd collection of machines including Longhorns, RE.1s and 5s and Farman F.20s before it left for Bruges on 7 October, the first echelon being under the command of Captain H. C. T. Dowding of future Battle of Britain fame. Two weeks later, 7 Squadron took its motley collection of aeroplanes to Netheravon before moving to France the following spring. To train pilots, the Reserve Aeroplane Squadron was formed in August with Blériot and early BE.2s, being renamed No 1 RAS in November as a second RAS was created at Brooklands. To manage the growing RFC, an Administrative Wing was set up to control the RAS, the Records Office and the Workshops, which had become the RFC Flying Depot, a repair facility and Aircraft Park. No 1 RAS provided the core of No 10 Squadron, which was formed on 1 January 1915 with Longhorns and Shorthorns, Blériot XIs, BE.2cs and Martinsydes before moving to Brooklands a week later.

During the rapid expansion, many of Farnborough's aeroplanes were housed in individual T-shaped canvas tents, but these were supplemented and later replaced by ten RFC sheds, some of which were transferred from Larkhill following their use during the 1912 Military Trials. Erected on Jersey Brow, these became No 1 (Southern) Aircraft Repair Depot in 1917. Construction of No 1 Officers' Mess and other quarters began in late 1914, together with the hutted Pinehurst Barracks for airmen adjacent to Farnborough Park. Also to the north of the Factory, rows of workmen's cottages appeared, and two wind tunnels were built during 1916/17.

The role of the Royal Aircraft Factory continued to be the design and prototype manufacture of new aircraft with associated research and development, particularly into armament and aerodynamics. Production was normally handed over to industry, although some small batches of FE.2B night-bombers, SE.5As and RE.8s were built as losses in France increased. The workforce, which had numbered some 1,250 in August 1914, had grown to more than 5,000 by 1917. The aerodrome now covered more than 286 acres (116 hectares), including Cove Common and Laffan's Plain.

The creation of the Royal Air Force on 1 April 1918 led to a change of name at Farnborough, which became the Royal Aircraft Establishment, a title it was to retain for many decades. Between 1914 and 1918 the Factory had constructed some thirty different types totalling more than 500 machines, many of them prototypes. Although production of aircraft at the RAE ceased with the signing of the Armistice, its future lay in aeronautical research.

By 1918 the No 1 (Southern) ARD had grown to cover some 80 acres (32.4 hectares), with a workforce of more than 3,000 men and women. The main types being worked on were DH.4s and 9s, SE.5As, Dolphins and Martinsyde F.3s, but the demand slowed dramatically with the ending of hostilities, and what was now the RAF Repair Depot turned to storage, rather than repair.

One of the few operational squadrons in the UK, No 4 Squadron was re-formed at Farnborough with Bristol Fighters on 30 April 1920 in an Army Co-operation role. A Flight moved to Ireland in November to combat the Irish republicans, returning in 1922 as the Squadron embarked in HMS *Ark Royal* for the Turkish Chanak Crisis. On its return in September 1923, it was housed in one of the black sheds to continue cooperating with Aldershot in artillery spotting, aerial photography and similar exercises.

One of the first aeroplanes to be tested by the RAE was the ill-fated Tarrant Tabor, a giant six-engined triplane that had been conceived to bomb Berlin. Although its raison d'être no longer existed, the machine was assembled and rolled out on 26 May 1919, but crashed on take-off, killing both pilots. Personnel numbers at the Establishment had been cut to 1,000 in early 1919, but had reached 1,316 by mid-1922 as trial work included catapults, pilotless aeroplanes and early oleo undercarriages. The first of the Cierva autogiros, the C.6A, made its first flight on 15 October 1925. Using an Avro 504K fuselage, it led to a successful line of rotorcraft at Cierva's Hamble factory.

On the military side, No 7 Group was renumbered No 22 Group in April 1926, its Farnborough HQ being responsible for the School of Photography, No 4 Squadron and other Army Co-operation units elsewhere. The stop-gap Atlas replaced the 'Brisfit' with No 4 Squadron in 1929 before being itself succeeded by the much improved Audax in February 1932.

Development work on catapulting culminated on 13 June 1930 with the launch of a Vickers Virginia IX by the RAE portable catapult capable of accelerating an aeroplane weighing up to 18,000lb to 60mph in 100 yards. From 1931 practical experiments with in-flight refuelling were undertaken, initially using a Virginia IX as a receiver and a pair of DH.9 tankers, later replaced by another Virginia. The procedure was somewhat hazardous. The tanker trailed a weighted wireless aerial connected to a hosepipe, which, when collected by the receiving aircraft, allowed fuel to be transferred. Sufficient confidence in the procedure permitted a public refuelling of a B&P Overstrand at the June 1931 RAF Hendon display.

The RAE began construction of a 660ft (201m) marine test tank in 1931 for hydrodynamic testing of model seaplane and flying boat hulls. The facility became operational in 1933 as the erection began of a huge 24-foot (7.3-metre) wind tunnel capable of testing complete aeroplanes and engines. This was officially opened on 5 April 1935 by the then Secretary of State for Air, the Marquess of Londonderry. The first aeroplane tested was the Gloster Gauntlet prototype J9125. Experimental work in high-altitude flight, which required pressurised flying suits, culminated in the design of the Bristol 138A, which, powered by a Pegasus IV engine, achieved a World Altitude Record of 49,976 feet (15,230 metres) on 28 September 1936.

The incredible 24-foot wind tunnel in which complete aeroplanes were tested is housed in the Grade 1-listed Building Q121 at Farnborough. (DWL collection)

The series of accidents to the incredibly popular home-built Mignet HM.14 'Pou du Ciel', or 'Flying Flea', led to an example being placed in the 24-foot wind tunnel in late March 1936, where an aerodynamic defect was found that, although correctable, caused the grounding of the type. A larger German-designed aircraft followed the 'Flea' into the wind tunnel. During August 1937 Rolls-Royce loaned its He 70 Kestrel-engined flight test bed for study into its aerodynamic efficiency. The design and its elliptical wing were acknowledged to have had an influence in the creation of the Spitfire.

February 1937 saw the long-time resident No 4 Squadron transfer to Odiham, with No 53 (AC) Squadron its replacement when it re-formed on 28 June with Hectors to specialise in night reconnaissance. After less than a year No 53 also moved to Odiham to make room for No 1 Anti-Aircraft Co-operation Unit on 11 April 1938, equipped with the Westland Wallace. Although the HQ and A Flight of the AACU remained at Farnborough, other Flights were deployed elsewhere on armament practice camps. The winter of 1938/39 saw the introduction of the Hawker Henley into service as a target tower.

At the declaration of war in September 1939 Farnborough housed the RAE, the School of Photography and the HQ of the AACU, which continued to spin off more Flights, one such of three aircraft being sent to Abbeville with the BEF, but returned by April 1940. As captured German aircraft became available, the RAE tested a Bf 109, a Bf 110, an He 111 and a Ju 88 during the summer of 1940. The importance of Farnborough, although not directly involved in the Battle of Britain, led to an intervention by the Luftwaffe. After two unsuccessful attacks, on 16 August eight Ju 88s of 1/KG54 dropped some twenty bombs, about half of which fell on the RAE, the rest on residential areas of the town. Fortunately adequate warning had allowed most people to reach shelters, although one bomb hit a shelter killing three Local Defence Volunteers. One hangar was destroyed and the work of the RAE disrupted for a few days as cleaning-up progressed.

An RAF ensign had been flown at the RAE since its inception, coming as it did under the Air Ministry, but in the autumn of 1940 it was the Ministry of Aircraft Production that took responsibility for the RAE. The rapid expansion, fuelled by the demands of war and larger aircraft, necessitated longer runways. Extensions were built on all four to give a maximum length of 6,150 feet (1,875 metres) to 07/25 runway by the summer of 1942. The range and complexity of the work undertaken at Farnborough during the war years far exceeds the available space in this book, but I can recommend *Farnborough: 100 Years of British Aviation* by Peter J. Cooper for readers who want to know more.

Visiting Farnborough circa 1938 is Hawker Hector K8112 of No 53 (AC) Squadron, RAF Odiham. Note one of the later famous 'Black Sheds' in the background. (via P. H. T. Green collection)

One of the highlights was designing and manufacturing in just twenty-five days the first catapult-launched fighter system to close the mid-Atlantic air cover gap, which the Luftwaffe's Condor bombers had been exploiting. By the spring of 1941 the first CAM (Catapult Aircraft Merchantman) ship was in service. Other research concentrated on bomb- and gun-sights, rocket projectiles and combating fire in the air.

By January 1942 the unwieldy No 1 AACU consisted of no fewer than twenty-five Flights, using every letter of the alphabet except 'I', based from Aberporth in Wales to Weybourne on the north Norfolk coast. The establishment totalled some 170 aeroplanes including Henleys, Queen Bees and Magisters. Something had to give, and in October 1942 No 1 AACU HQ was disbanded as each Flight gained an independent existence beginning with 'A' Flight, which became No 1600 Flight on 1 November. Farnborough also hosted a number of detachments from Army Co-operation Squadrons during 1943, including Nos 285, 290 and 667, to liaise with the Royal Artillery at Blackdown.

Some particularly hazardous experimental flying was carried out during 1943-44 by the RAE's test pilots into phenomena linked to high-speed flight. During one such test, Sqn Ldr J. R. Tobin dived a Spitfire Mk XI at full power from 40,000 feet (12,192 metres) and reached Mach 0.92, landing safely. In a subsequent test on 27 April 1944 by Sqn Ldr A. F. Martindale, the complete propeller and engine reduction gear failed and broke away, leaving the pilot to glide 20 miles back to Farnborough with the invaluable research data intact.

The RAF formally handed over Farnborough to the RAE during 1944. The RAE then controlled the complete site and the end of 1944 saw a new N-S concrete runway of 3,000 feet (1,874 metres) replace the former 04/22 runway, which became a catapult and dummy-deck landing strip. The RAE had received and tested a variety of captured Luftwaffe aircraft, but the last to arrive during wartime was the largest when an He 177 flew in on 10 September 1944.

As the war drew to its close, Power Jets (Research & Development) was established at Pyestock, which later became the National Gas Turbine Establishment. All rocket research was transferred to Westcott as the tempo of work slowed a little. This gave an opportunity to display an incredible range of captured German aeronautical technology. Invited guests from the armed forces, Government and the aircraft industry arrived at Farnborough between 29 October and 9 November 1945 to view an enticing selection of hardware. Over the weekend of 10/11 November the airfield was thrown open to the public with an extra display of the latest products of the British aviation industry ranging from the first Dove to the Martin-Baker MB 5. What I would not have given to be there!

The RAE came under the Ministry of Supply on 1 June 1948 as the long-time resident School of Photography moved with its Ansons to Wellesbourne Mountford. Taking over its accommodation was the ETPS from Cranfield, as that aerodrome became the College of Aeronautics. Other lodger units at Farnborough were the Institute of Aviation Medicine and the Meteorological Research Flight, which then operated a pair of Mosquito PR.34s and a couple of Halifax Mk VIs.

In September of that year a tradition started that continues to this day. After two post-war shows at Radlett, the home of Handley Page, the SBAC chose Farnborough as the location for its annual display of the products of the British aircraft industry. The show took place between 7 and 12 September, the last two days being open to the public. That first year saw 187 exhibitors housed in two of the RAE's hangars, and the flying encompassed everything from Geoffrey Tyson's inverted flight in the SR.A1 jet fighter flying boat and the AW.52 tailless flying wing to the prototype Viscount and much, much more.

The annual event grew in size, and from 1950 was allocated a permanent exhibition area on the south-east area of the airfield with the exhibitors' marquee very close to where Cody made his historic first flight. Later the exhibition halls were again moved to the present location, which gave an elevated view of the airfield and the RAE site. The 1952 show is sadly remembered for the tragic accident to the DH 110 prototype predecessor of the Sea Vixen, which broke up in mid-air with some of the wreckage landing in the crowd killing John Derry, Tony Richards and twenty-seven spectators.

The SBAC was not the only airshow held at Farnborough, for on 7 and 8 July 1950 a major RAF display was staged, attended by HM King George VI and the rest of the Royal party. During the show,

Right: *The Black Arrows at their best! Sixteen all-black Hunters of 111 Squadron dive out of a loop. (DWL collection)*

Below: *The morning parade of the products of the British aviation industry in the 1958 SBAC airshow. (DWL collection)*

thirty-seven Harvards spelled out 'RAF' and on a further pass the formation read 'GR VT'. A group of enemy tanks was destroyed by six rocket-firing Vampires – real rockets, not ground explosions! Mosquito B.35s of Nos 14 and 98 Squadrons escorted by Spitfire F.22s of 613 Squadron re-enacted the Amiens prison raid. The finale started with six Sunderlands, followed by Dakotas, Yorks and Hastings, then USAF B-29s and RAF Lincolns, and finally fighters of all shapes and sizes, including those from the French, Belgian and Netherlands Air Forces. Sadly, that was to be the last full-scale RAF Farnborough display.

The unspectacular but steady research work at Farnborough was brought into public prominence following the January 1954 loss of the BOAC Comet I G-ALYP in the Mediterranean Sea off Elba, followed on 8 April by a second disaster off Naples, which finally grounded the world's first jet airliner. In a major recovery exercise, much of G-ALYP was recovered and reconstructed on a purpose-made frame at Farnborough. The complete fuselage of another Comet I was placed in a large Braithwaite water tank for cabin pressure fatigue testing until finally the cabin ruptured.

The Meteorological Research Flight, originally formed in 1946, was by the mid-1950s operating a pair of much-modified Hastings, a Varsity and a Canberra, the latter involved in high-altitude air sampling following Soviet and USA atmospheric nuclear testing. The three types continued to be the mainstay of the Met Flight through into the 1970s until joined in January 1974 by the highly modified one-off Hercules W.2. Nicknamed 'Snoopy', the changes to the basic C.1 airframe had taken Marshall of Cambridge some three years to complete. The Varsity WF425 was retired to join the Imperial War Museum's collection at Duxford, where sadly, after twenty years of external storage, it was scrapped in 1995.

Catapult trials continued through the 1950s until, after some thirty years of research, the last launch of a Sea Venom FAW.21 was made on 20 September 1957. Earlier that year the first experimental runway arrester gear was tested, again by a Sea Venom. The forensic skills of the Farnborough scientists were again in demand in 1959 when an early Victor B.2 crashed into the Irish Sea on 20 August. About 70% of the airframe, totalling some 600,000 pieces of wreckage, was recovered from depths of 400 feet and pieced together to establish the cause.

During 1966 a new hangar was completed for the Army Air Corps detachment based at Farnborough, and Army flying returned to its historic roots on 20 July 1966 when the Scouts of No 21 Flight arrived. In May 1969 No 664 Squadron was re-formed from Nos 8 and 21 Flights, with Sioux and Scout helicopters, but was renumbered 656 Squadron in 1978, by then flying Scout and Gazelle machines.

When, in January 1968, the ETPS moved back to its birthplace at Boscombe Down with some two dozen aircraft, Farnborough's air traffic was significantly reduced. One aircraft it left behind, a redundant Devon XA879, donated its fuselage in September to fill a breach in the bank of the Basingstoke Canal caused by torrential rain. The resulting flooding of the Laffan's Plain end had caused the cancellation of the Monday's flying at the SBAC show, but with the fuselage entombed and the bank reinstated, the airfield drained sufficiently for flying to continue on Tuesday. An interesting task for a future *Time Team* episode?

As Farnborough moved into the 1970s, the RAE's work was in transition as it became much more concerned with electronics than aerodynamics. The fleet was divided into the Weapons Flight with a number of Buccaneers, a pair of Shackletons, a similar number of Canberras and a single Wessex, all developing weapons and their aiming and delivery systems. The Avionics Flight used a mixture of Wessex and Hunters whereas the Radio Flight, with Hastings, Comets and HS 748s, concentrated on landing and navigation systems. The small Structures & Mechanical Engineering Flight used a few Canberras, a Lightning and a Beverley. The last unit was the Transport Flight, which flew four Devons and later a Dakota.

The last annual SBAC was held in 1962, following a decision that it would in future be a biennial event, alternating with the Paris Air Salon. In 1972 the show was opened to European participation, and in 1974 Farnborough International was born with a major input from the USA that included the C-5 Galaxy and the Lockheed SR -71. The latter was displayed statically but had set a new transatlantic record on its delivery flight of just under 2 hours!

The last airworthy Blackburn Beverley was sold to Court Line in 1973. Following the airline's demise, it was displayed in the Army Transport Museum at Beverley, but can now be seen at the Fort Paull Museum near Hull. Another historic part of Farnborough was lost in 1978 when the northern part of the 'Black Sheds' was demolished, but the surviving section has Listed Building status, which will hopefully ensure its survival.

The aircraft the RAF never received! In 1964 the British Aircraft Corporation displayed a model of the TSR 2, which was cancelled in 1965. (DWL collection)

No 656 Squadron moved its eight Scouts and six Gazelles to Netheravon in March 1982, leaving just twenty-two aircraft based at Farnborough. The RAE experimental fleet was divided into three Flights based primarily where the aircraft were hangared, but all were expected to multi-task and might be used by any research department as an airborne laboratory. The types included Wessex and Sea Kings, Hunters, a Comet and a BAC 1-11, a pair each of Varsities and Andovers, and a number of Buccaneers and Canberras. The Transport Flight had acquired Dakota ZA947 in 1978, which served until 1993 when it became part of the Battle of Britain Memorial Flight.

The RAE's crash investigation department became the Accident Investigation Branch in 1946, when it was part of the Ministry of Civil Aviation and based in a T2 hangar on the southern boundary, moving into a new HQ building in June 1984. In November 1987 it adopted its present title of the Air Accidents Investigation Branch (AAIB). After 21 December 1988 the team undertook its most lengthy and complex investigation after a Pan American Boeing 747 was destroyed by a terrorist bomb over Lockerbie. The partly reconstructed fuselage still dominated the hangar during a visit I made to the AAIB in November 2008, but surrounded by the debris of other less-publicised tragedies. As all accidents and serious incidents have to be reported to the AAIB, it deals with more than 300 civil aviation incidents/accidents every year, together with a number of military accidents, usually fewer than ten.

The Transport Trust visited the AAIB in 1995, with the partially reconstructed fuselage of the Lockerbie Pan-Am Boeing 747 in the background. (DWL collection)

The creation in 1985 of the Farnborough Aerospace Development Corporation pointed the way forward, as its role was to promote some 23 acres (9.3 hectares) as an aerospace business park, which was officially opened in January 1989. Also in 1985 the now elderly Devons were replaced by three Navajo Chieftains. A subtle change to RAE's name was made in 1988 when it became the Royal Aerospace Establishment, but this was not enough to halt a process in which the Civil Service was being commercialised. Farnborough experienced this on 1 April 1991 when the RAE became DERA, the Defence Research Agency, and planned a move to a new £90 million centre on the other side of the airfield. This was achieved by 1997 and DERA became QinetiQ in July 2001.

The end of research flying at Farnborough came in 1994, as most of the fleet departed to Boscombe Down on 24 March. Just before this, in November 1993, the Farnborough Air Sciences Trust was created to protect the historic buildings and a vast collection of archives and artefacts. Although it gathered much influential support, the task facing it appeared insurmountable. Eventually, in December 1996 it was confirmed that a number of the historic buildings were to be listed, including G1, the original Balloon School and Trenchard's HQ. Sadly other historic structures, like the seaplane-testing tank, the balloon gondola shop and the earliest original workshop, were not included.

Slough Estates acquired the 125 acres (50.6 hectares) of the old 'Factory' site in March 1999, but was not convinced that the listed buildings could be saved and incorporated into their redevelopment plans. Finally, in early 2002, through English Heritage, the listings were upgraded to II* and the developers began to see the historic buildings as an asset rather than an encumbrance, although the majority of the RAE buildings were razed.

Out on the airfield proper, TAG Aviation took over from January 2001 with a plan to create a specialist business airport. Obtaining the requisite CAA licences took longer, as civilian requirements were much more onerous than those appertaining to military operations. In addition to significant earth-moving, it also involved more demolition, including the control tower, which closed to operations at the end of November 2002 and was rubble by the end of January 2003. A stunning new tower had been built and went into use on 26 November 2002. A futuristic three-bay hangar complex came into use during 2003, and in 2005 a stunning terminal building befitting the very expensive business jets and their wealthy passengers appeared adjacent to the hangars.

One of the buildings that was dismantled, the former RAE Foundry, had been constructed using the upper-section girders from an original portable airship shed, which had been dismantled in 1915. This historic frame, which dated back to the 1890s, was reassembled as the centrepiece within the business park complex and listed Grade II in early 2009.

On the approach to runway 24, the proximity of the Control Tower to the runway is apparent, which led to its demolition in January 2003. (TAG Aviation)

The stunning new TAG Aviation Control Tower complex, which opened in November 2002 to replace the RAE Tower. (TAG Aviation)

Farnborough is now a very dynamic site housing the HQs of both BAE Systems and QinetiQ, with much of its history preserved by FAST and home to the National Aerospace Library. TAG Aviation's massive investment will keep Farnborough alive with business aviation. The SBAC event continues as an important biennial aerospace business event, although the showcase flying bears no relationship to the spectacle of previous years. Although now very different from the highly secret centre of British aerospace technology it was in its RAE days, the varied attractions of 21st-century Farnborough are still enough to make a visit very worthwhile.

Main features:
Runways: 183° 3,000ft x 150ft, 223.5° 4,0800ft x 150ft, 251.5° 6,150ft x 150ft, 300° 3,000ft x 150ft, concrete. *Hangars:* four permanent, various Blisters. *Hardstandings:* ten diamond, seven circular. *Accommodation:* RAF: 185 Officers, 182 SNCOs, 867 ORs; WAAF: 16 Officers, 23 SNCOs, 534 ORs.

Main feature in the 21st century:
Runway: 06/24 8,000ft x 140ft.

FOLKESTONE, Kent, see CAPEL and HAWKINGE

FORD, West Sussex

50°49N/00°35W 20ft asl; SU995029. 2 miles W of Littlehampton on A2024

Every air show spectator over the past sixty-plus years will feel that they have experienced the awesome power and noise of a Rolls-Royce Merlin, whether fitted to a Spitfire, Lancaster, Mustang or Hurricane. Yet nobody has really had the best experience until they have stood beside an uncowled, trailer-mounted, 1,000hp V-12 Merlin Mark XX at or near full power! Amazingly, too, by an aero engine that crashed in 1941!

The story began at Ford when Bristol Beaufighter IIF R2355 was serving with the Fighter Interception Unit as an AI (Airborne Interception) radar equipment test bed. On the night of 3 September 1941 the aircraft crashed, fatally, 4 miles west of the aerodrome. In 1978 the crash site was excavated and the two much-damaged engines were recovered. After a restoration project lasting some 3,000 hours by a remarkably skilled engineer, Peter Grieve, engine number 26071 ran again in the year 2000 as a memorial to the three young airmen who lost their lives in that crash in 1941.

Ford has its origins in the rapid expansion of Britain's air arm, particularly the Royal Flying Corps, during the First World War. To achieve this expansion, many more training stations were required and Ford Junction, as it was officially known, was one such TDS. Work started on the 85-acre site between the villages of Yapton (by which it became known locally) and Ford in early 1918. The technical site, with its huts, three coupled General Service sheds and a single Aircraft Repair Shed (Belfast hangars), was to be located on the west side of the aerodrome.

Although initial planning had earmarked the field for US Air Service Corps use, the very incomplete station saw its first aeroplanes on 1 March 1918 when No 148 Squadron arrived from Andover with its FE.2b night-bombers. Two days later 149 Squadron was created from No 148, and both units had left for France by early June.

The Americans arrived on 15 August, formally taking over the station as Field No 1, Chichester Area Night Bombardment Section, American Expeditionary Force –not a designation that trips off the tongue easily! The plan was that the Americans would operate Handley Page 0/400s built in the USA with Liberty engines, and to that end a special Handley Page shed was to be added to the original Belfast hangars. As all the hangars were still incomplete, a row of eight Bessonneau canvas hangars was erected before the 92nd Aero Squadron arrived from the USA in late September. Two further Aero Squadrons were formed to operate a mix of BE.2c, Farman F.40 and US-built DH-4s.

A Night Bombardment Training School opened on 15 September and one, almost certainly UK-built, 0/400 was brought to Ford Junction in component form, but before it was assembled or any significant training undertaken the Armistice was signed. Just four days later the USASC aeroplanes were flown out to Tangmere and all American personnel left on 17 November.

The RAF returned to start demobilising its squadrons; the first was No 144, which arrived in December, followed in 1919 by Nos 10, 17, 115 and 215. No 97 escaped this fate, being re-equipped with DH.10 twin-engined bombers and departing to India in July 1919. With the last of the demobbed squadron personnel having left by December, the station was largely deserted and closed in January 1920.

For nearly ten years Ford slumbered, but in 1929 Dudley Watt and J. E. Doran-Webb, trading as DW Aviation, leased then renovated two hangars and formed the Sussex Aero Club, with its chief pilot being W. A. (Bill) Rollason. It was a mixed fleet consisting of two DW.1s (a modified SE.5a), three Le Rhone-powered Avros and a single DW.2. The intention was to build the DW.2 biplane, but this venture came to naught when Doran-Webb left to form the Wiltshire School of Flying at High Post. Rollason also moved to form his own organisation at Croydon.

The Ford Motor Company initially established a European base for its aviation activities at Hooton Park, but the synergy of the name attracted the company to Ford. A lease was agreed in 1931, and Ford TriMotors began to arrive in July. The hangars were emblazoned with the company name and the landing ground was similarly marked. As the aircraft failed to get a UK Certificate of Airworthiness, the few that were imported were all sold abroad with one exception, which survived to be impressed into the RAF in 1940. Although Ford left the airfield, the company retained the lease and sub-let the hangars.

The first arrival in April 1933 was Rollason Aviation Services, which was to stay for just over a year before being replaced by Sir Alan Cobham's National Aviation Day Ltd. In the same year Cobham formed Flight Refuelling Ltd, which in January 1936 commenced experiments in association with Imperial Airways from Ford using the AW 23, serial number K3585, on loan from the Air Ministry. Further aircraft, including a pair of HP Harrows, were acquired for trials in refuelling Short C class flying boats to achieve non-stop Atlantic services.

The aerodrome was used by RAF units for summer camps during the 1930s, including Nos 4 and 13 (AC) with their Audaxes in 1936. In 1937 the Oxford University Air Squadron, including Leonard Cheshire, camped at Ford and flew Hart trainers. The Air Ministry requisitioned Ford on 1 November 1937 and acquired more land up to the Ford to Climping road to erect nine Bellman hangars and a hutted camp along the eastern edge of the aerodrome at a cost of £109,000. RAF station Ford

A line-up of Ford TriMotors at Ford during 1931. (Ford Motor Co)

reopened on 1 December 1938 in No 17 (Training) Group of Coastal Command, and in early 1939 the School of Naval Co-operation began its move from Lee-on-Solent. Ford's brief reincarnation as an RAF station was to end on 24 May 1939 when it became HMS *Peregrine* under Admiralty control.

The RN Observers School consisted of three Squadrons, Nos 750, 751 and 752, which were joined by the Immediate Reserve Storage Unit and the School of Naval Photography. The vulnerability of Ford to enemy action was recognised, and Nos 750 and 752 Squadrons moved to a still incomplete Yeovilton in early 1940. However, they had been replaced by 753 and 779 Squadrons when the Luftwaffe targeted Ford on 18 August.

After a morning of raids on airfields further east, the all clear was sounded at Ford, just minutes before twenty-eight Ju 87s of II/StG77 descended upon a totally unprepared aerodrome. In moments hangars, the bulk fuel store, the MT, stores, both the ratings' and POs' canteens and many huts were smashed. Seventeen aircraft were destroyed, including the AW.23 and the two Harrows that Flight Refuelling had left in store when it moved to Malvern. Another twenty-six aircraft were damaged, but the human cost was even higher. Twenty-eight were killed and another seventy-five wounded. As the Stukas withdrew they were intercepted by Spitfires of 602 Squadron, which managed to shoot down three before being themselves attacked by Bf 109s. The Admiralty accelerated its move from Ford, but not before a memorial was dedicated in the churchyard of St Mary the Virgin at Climping in memory of those who died that day.

The memorial and the first two of the many gravestones in Climping Churchyard commemorating the dead of 18 August 1940. (DWL collection)

No 11 Group, Fighter Command, took over Ford on 1 October 1940 with the Blenheim 1Fs of No 23 Squadron in residence. Although another raid on 18 October caused further damage, it was relatively minor. The northern twin Belfast hangar and the single ARS had survived, as had at least five of the Bellman hangars. They were soon occupied by the Fighter Interception Unit, arriving from Shoreham with its Blenheims and Beaufighters. Both units worked on developing night-fighter skills. No 23 achieved its first intruder success on 2 January 1941 over Dreux in France when it shot down an He 111. The Squadron re-equipped with Havocs in March to pursue its targets over much of France and Holland.

During the rest of the year a significant redevelopment of Ford brought two tarmac runways of 6,000ft (1,828m) SW/NE, which necessitated the closure of the road to Yapton, and another aligned NW/SE of 4,800ft (1,463m). Extensive taxiways, blast pens and hardstandings were built, and twenty Blister hangars erected to supplement the original GS shed and Bellmans. A new Watch Office/Control Tower to pattern 12096/41 was constructed in front of the Bellman hangars on the eastern side of the field.

On 7 June 1942 No 605 Squadron re-formed with Bostons and Havocs, which it acquired from 23 Squadron. To aid the crews' conversion to the unfamiliar tricycle undercarriages of their new mounts, the one-off Owlet trainer was pressed into use. Although the Squadron undertook its first raid on Caen on 14 July, it was not fully operational and most of the personnel were temporarily transferred to Hunsdon as Ford began to fill up in preparation for Operation 'Jubilee', the combined operations raid on Dieppe.

The first to arrive was 88 Squadron, whose Bostons were joined by those of No 107 and a couple from 418 (RCAF) Squadron. Also present on the overcrowded field were the 'Hurribombers' of 174 Squadron. First off early on the morning of 19 August were four aircraft from 88 and 107 Squadrons, which linked with others from Thruxton squadrons to trail smoke to conceal the shipping. They were immediately followed by the rest of the Bostons bombing the massive gun batteries that defended the port. Although the Hurricanes were very busy trying to suppress the flak positions, a number of Bostons were hit. All the squadrons made two or even three sorties over the battleground during the day, closing with another smoke screen to cover the ships as they withdrew.

During the battle No 174 Squadron lost six Hurricanes, while 88 and 107 Squadrons lost a single Boston each, with many more damaged. In compensation, one claim for an Fw 190 was made by a Boston gunner. In retaliation, the Luftwaffe made a number of raids over southern England and Ford was attacked in the evening with a Boston being destroyed and others damaged. Later a solitary Fw 190 damaged three Beaufighters.

The Beaufighters of No 141 Squadron had arrived at Ford on 10 August, but played no part in Operation 'Jubilee', concentrating on trying to intercept the daytime fighter-bomber raids on coastal towns. Success was very limited, although on 16 December, without firing a shot, Flying Officer Cook brought down a Do 217 when it hit a gasholder. No 605 had by then developed an expertise in intruder work over the continent, but was scheduled to re-equip with Mosquitoes. This started in February 1943, but the Squadron moved to Castle Camps on 14 March to complete the conversion.

Familiar with Ford from its temporary secondment the previous year, No 418 (RCAF) arrived in March with its Mosquito IIs for intruder duties, achieving a total of seven victories over the next four months. A succession of squadrons including Nos 256, 29 and 456 followed in fairly rapid succession. The most successful night was on 24 February 1944, when 29 Squadron claimed an He 177, a Do 217, two Ju 88/188s and probably an Me 410. Sadly they lost their CO, Wg Cdr R. E. Mack DFC.

An interesting experiment was carried out at Ford on 8 October 1943. Ideas for temporary airfields were being evaluated as part of the planning for the future invasion of Europe. These included very oddball ideas like a floating iceberg, but 'Tentacle' was a floating landing strip, 1,800 by 75 feet, supported on steel pontoons. A full-sized replica was laid out at Ford and a number of types, including Spitfires, Mosquitoes, Beaufighters, Hurricanes, Mustangs, Typhoons and Fulmars operated from this strip. Since many aircraft overran the strip, it was concluded that at least 2,500 feet would be required. The logistics of towing such a construction, its vulnerability and the growing programme of ALG construction finally killed the idea. But this test heralded a change of role for Ford as the FIU transferred to Wittering in early April 1944, leaving the station free for tactical use, in the shape of the Allied Expeditionary Air Force.

The new occupant on 15 April was No 122 Airfield from Gravesend consisting of 19, 65 and 122 Squadrons with Mustangs. Commencing *Rangers* almost immediately, No 122 sent four aircraft to Dole/Travaux airfield on the Swiss border, shooting down six He 111s. Fitted with bomb racks, 65 and 122 Squadrons started fighter-bomber ops on 2 May when thirty-six 500lb bombs were dropped on railway marshalling yards. No 122 Airfield moved to Funtington on 14 May, being replaced by No 125 Airfield with the Spitfires of 132, 453 and 602 Squadrons.

On 15 May Airfields were redesignated Wings, and the Canadians of 144 Wing (441, 442 and 443 Squadrons) joined No 125 at Ford. Equipped with the Spitfire IX fighter-bombers, the Canadians plunged headlong into the preparations for the coming D-Day, then just three weeks away – not that anyone at Ford knew the date. The Squadron dive-bombed every conceivable target from airfields to railways, and especially radar stations.

D-Day, 6 June, saw Ford's fighters joining the all-encompassing umbrella over the Normandy beaches, but the Luftwaffe wisely failed to put in an appearance. In the following days the role changed to ground-attack in support of the advancing troops. Cover was on a 24-hour basis as a total of fifteen night-fighter squadrons were patrolling over Normandy, including No 456 from Ford, which had arrived in February with its Mosquito Mk XVIIs. The Aussies had a very good night on 7 June when they intercepted five He 177s, shooting down four. The following night was almost as successful with a further three being destroyed.

Once again the priorities changed, and from 24 June No 456's targets became the V-1 missiles as the Squadron started anti-*Diver* patrols. The arrival on 20 June of 96 Squadron from West Malling had heralded this change, as its Mosquito XIIIs had proved very successful in the task. This continued at Ford with the Mossie crews downing a further forty-nine flying bombs by the end of the month.

The Canadians had left Ford on 15 June, transferring to the ALG at B3 (St Croix-sur-Mer), followed ten days later by the last No 83 Group unit in the UK, No 125 Wing. A succession of Wings, including No 133 (Nos 129, 306 and 315 Squadrons), No 131 (Polish), with 302, 308 and 317 Squadrons, and No 132 Wing (66, 127, 331 and 332 Squadrons) passed through Ford on their way to the continent. No 96 Squadron also left, moving to Odiham in September, leaving the airfield with space for some previous residents to return.

The returnees in October were the FIU and 746 Squadron, which became part of the Night Fighter Development Wing operating a mix of Mosquitoes, Beaufighters, Seafires and Fireflies. The other parts of the Wing included the Ranger Flight and the Fighter Interception Development Squadron, which undertook some operational flights up to the end of the year. However, in early 1945 the Wing gradually transferred to Tangmere and 11 Group relinquished Ford on 31 July 1945.

The new owner once again was the Admiralty, as Ford was recommissioned as HMS *Peregrine*. No 746 Squadron remained in residence, being joined by 720 Squadron with four Ansons and some Barracudas operating as a photographic school. Two new front-line squadrons were formed in September, No 811 with Mosquitoes and No 813 with Firebrands. However, after many hectic years, the conditions at Ford had deteriorated to such an extent that what little hangarage was available was in very poor state. Despite this, an ATC unit, No 161 GS, arrived from Burgess Hill in early 1946, together with Flight Refuelling Ltd, which remained at Ford until the transfer to Tarrant Rushton in June 1948. Shortly afterwards, Ford closed for a major upgrading and refurbishing programme. A single B.1 was put up near Climping village south of the Bellmans and linked to the threshold of runway 33. Two additional B.1-type hangars were erected with hardstandings on the northern boundary.

HMS *Peregrine* was recommissioned on 1 February 1950 with 703 Squadron moving in from Lee-on-Solent as the Service Trials Unit with No 771, which were amalgamated together to form No 700 (Trials & FRU) Squadron. A steady stream of squadrons passed through Ford, working up prior to embarkation or returning from a commission. For many years it was the parent station for the four squadrons that constituted the HMS *Eagle* Air Group. June 1951 saw the newly formed No 1840 RNVR Squadron arrive from Culham with anti-submarine Fireflies.

An even more significant new squadron came into being on 22 August 1951, when the Royal Navy's first jet squadron was formed, No 800 with eight Supermarine Attackers, before embarking aboard HMS *Eagle* for sea trials. The second Attacker squadron, No 803 also formed at Ford and both came back many times until disbanding in June 1954. A number of Air Days were held, including one on 22 July 1955. Among the historic participants were the Swordfish, Fulmar and a Pup. Newer aircraft included the prototype Seamew, the Folland Midge and the DH.110. Martin Baker demonstrated its ejection seat using Meteor WA 634. The sight caused much concern in the crowd until it was realised that the falling figure was a dummy!

Firefly AS 6 WD851/206 taxies past the photographer at Ford. (M. J. F. Bowyer)

With a Sea Hawk in the background, Fairey Gannet AS 1 WN353 basks in the Ford sunshine. (M. J. F. Bowyer)

A further programme of rebuilding and upgrading was instigated, but a new Petty Officers' Mess, completed in 1956, was to be the only significant construction, for the days of HMS *Peregrine* were coming to an end. The creation of 700X Squadron on 27 August 1957 as the Intensive Trials Unit for the Scimitar was in effect Ford's swansong. This new powerful fighter, perhaps the most attractive and the last of the Supermarine jets, was a good type on which to end the military history of a famous airfield. Flying ceased in September 1958 and HMS *Peregrine* was paid off on 13 November.

Much of the main camp near Ford village was transferred to the Home Office, reopening in 1960 as an open prison. The Bellman hangars and the control tower (which had been enlarged in 1953 to a more typical Naval type) were all demolished around that time. It continues as a Category D training establishment for some 500 prisoners. Some of the original airfield buildings remain, although new construction and adaptations have changed their appearance. A total of eight barrack blocks, which were originally in Canadian Red Cedar, have been reclad in plastic. The Gym is now used as a dining hall with a stage. Even though the road from Climping to Ford bisects the site, photography is not permitted.

The two 'new' B.1s on the northern boundary were taken over for industrial use and are now used by Tarmac Topblock to manufacture concrete building blocks. An extensive, appropriately named Ford Airfield Industrial Estate has developed around this site, with mainly new buildings. A pair of Blister hangars are extant on the site of Northwood Farm to the east of the B2233, together with new buildings around the NE taxiway. Another Blister hangar survives on farmland on the south side of the airfield. The third B.1 remains in use on the Rudford Industrial Estate south of the prison. Many other original buildings have found alternative uses, and part of the main runway at the north-east end has been in use as the Ford Airfield Market for more than twenty years. The entrance to this Sunday market/car boot site is easily found, as Hunter GA.11 WW654 is dramatically mounted beside the Climping to Ford road.

In addition to the wartime memorial to those killed on 18 August 1940, a Ford Airfield Commemorative Garden was opened by Admiral Sir Raymond Lygo KCB in May 1989. An initiative by four local residents, the garden's role is:

'To commemorate all those service and civilian men and women who served at this airfield, the many who toiled and the few who died in the cause of British aviation and the defence of Freedom.'

A service is held at the Garden every Remembrance Sunday to remember those who gave their lives in the service of their country.

A more recent 'aeronautical' development is the Flying Fortress Family Fun Centre. Just what a B-17 has to do with Ford is unknown, but if you do need to find out, follow the brown tourist signs! Finally, a more potent threat to what is left of Ford arose in 2008 in the form of the Ford Airfield Vision Group. This consortium proposes to build an Ecotown of up to 5,000 houses, shops, etc, on the old airfield. If this development takes place, Ford will join so many of her sister airfields where only the memorials are left to tell their story.

Main features:
Runways: 249° 6,000ft x 150ft, 337° 4,800ft x 150ft, tarmac and wood chippings.
Hangars: five Bellman, one General Purpose, four Over Blister, sixteen EO Blisters.
Hardstandings: none. *Accommodation:* RAF: 227 Officers, 356 SNCOs, 1,59 ORs; WAAF: 4 SNCOs, 295 ORs.

FORELAND, Isle of Wight

50°41N/01°04W 32ft amsl; SZ6542877. Half a mile S of Bembridge off B3395

The Foreland landing ground came into existence to help counter the U-boat offensive of spring 1918. To supplement the floatplanes stationed in Bembridge Harbour, 51 acres were requisitioned at Lane End, Bembridge, and equipped with Bessonneau hangars. Linked with Foreland was a nearby field at Brading Haven, located to the west of Home Farm and south of the Bembridge to St Helens railway track. There were no permanent buildings and the personnel were billeted in the town.

The aircraft were DH.6s, an obsolete training machine that had gathered various uncomplimentary epithets during its inglorious RFC career, including 'The Clutching Hand', 'The Crab' and even 'The Flying Coffin'. It was not expected to sink any submarines, although it could carry up to 100lb (45kg) of bombs under its wings. The role for the DH.6s was acting as 'scarecrows', keeping the enemy submerged, thus minimising their threat.

With the formation of No 253 Squadron on 7 June 1918, the Brading/Foreland units became Nos 511 and 512 (Special Duties) Flights, but their monotonous flights along the patrol lines off the coast continued just as before with no action and very little to report. The Armistice came as a considerable relief, and both Flights were disbanded on 21 January 1919. The order for the disposal of the sites was promulgated in the autumn of 1919 and implemented in early 1920. The Foreland site was completely built over and no evidence of the Brading field now exists.

Main features in 1918:
Landing ground: grass. *Hangars:* unknown number of Bessonneau. *Accommodation:* requisitioned local housing/billeting.

FRISTON, East Sussex

50°46N/00°10W 355ft asl; TV534982. 4.5 miles W of Eastbourne off A259

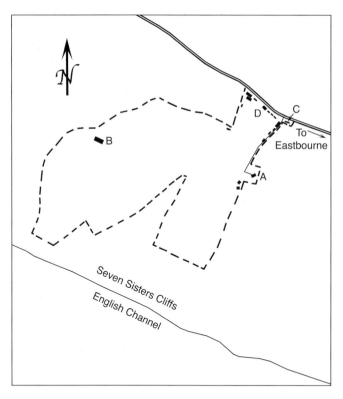

FRISTON, 1942-1945
A   Gayles SHQ
B   Blister hangar
C   Guardroom
D   Accommodation

The pre-war private landing ground changed little until the winter of 1941/42 when fuel, ammunition, accommodation and limited hangarage was provided. The flying field remained a good well-drained grass surface, roughly V-shaped, giving a maximum landing run in a NE/SW orientation of just over 5,000 feet (1,530 metres). The plan illustrates Friston in 1942.

The somewhat battered Spitfire port undercarriage door leads the eye towards the former grass aerodrome. (DWL collection)

'David, is this what I think it is?' I turned back to where my guide and local historian, Malcolm Finnis, was holding up a somewhat battered but easily identifiable Spitfire port undercarriage door, traces of the original 'Sky Type S' paint still adhering. In August 2004 we were making our way down a steep wooded hill, off the airfield, towards some possibly wartime structures, about which we had been told. These remained unidentified, but whereas I had been more concerned with staying upright, thanks to Malcolm's sharp eyes we had a unique wartime souvenir. On our return to the airfield we photographed our find with the original main grass runway leading off into the distance.

Located on top of the Seven Sisters cliffs, Friston was a pre-war private landing ground, known locally as Gayles or East Dean. An L-shaped area of level grassland, its longest landing run was orientated NE/SW with a maximum of 5,020 feet (1,532 metres). The aerodrome saw its first military use during Army Co-operation exercises in August and September 1938 when Hawker Audaxes of Nos 2 and 4 Squadrons flew from there. It became an ELG of Fighter Command in the summer of 1940, being upgraded to a satellite of Kenley in May 1941, but its use was limited to fighter emergency landings and ASR Lysanders detached from Shoreham.

Over the winter of 1941/42, the field closed for the construction of fuel and ammunition storage, together with much-needed hutting. With Kenley still as its parent station, Friston reopened on 15 May 1942, the first aircraft arriving by road at the end of the month. After assembly, the Spitfires were dispersed around the aerodrome, protected by Bofors AA guns. However, these were dummies intended to attract the attentions of the Luftwaffe, a ploy that totally failed. Real fighter aeroplanes arrived on 13 June in the shape of Hurricanes of 253 Squadron from Hibaldstow. Their equipment had arrived earlier and the groundcrews had been delivered the day before by 'Sparrow' – the nickname for the transport version of the Handley Page Harrow. Another Hurricane Squadron, No 32 was deployed from West Malling on 14 June amid much head-scratching as to why they were there. The rumours really began to fly when the aeroplanes gained zebra-like identification markings in early July. It was all in support of Operation 'Rutter', an abortive plan to destroy the heavy guns defending Dieppe.

Following the cancellation of the operation, both squadrons returned home on 7 July, but one unserviceable Hurricane remained behind. Two Bf 109s proved that the Luftwaffe could tell the difference between real and dummy Hurricanes when, on 9 July, they strafed the aeroplane, also hitting a new Blister hangar. Two 500lb (227kg) bombs cratered the N/S runway and damaged the SHQ. Even though the damage was still being repaired, a firepower demonstration was staged for around 5,000 official spectators by Spitfires of 602 Squadron, a pair of Mustangs, three Battles and a solitary Henley. From 20 July the Kenley Wing provided detachments from dawn to dusk to counter the tip-and-run fighter-bomber attacks that were causing consternation along the South Coast. This led to the death of two airmen whose tractor was hit by one of a pair of Hurricanes taking off just before first light.

Nos 32 and 253 Squadrons returned in mid-August as the Dieppe raid was reinstated as Operation 'Jubilee'. Both squadrons were called to readiness at 03.00 on 19 August and Sqn Ldr E. R. Thorn DFM led No 32 off at 04.45 with 253 following. Again their targets were the gun positions around Dieppe, heavy guns at first followed by machine-gun emplacements. Flak was intense and Flt Lt Ellacombe DFC was forced to bail out, but was picked up by one of the withdrawing ships. As one the closest aerodromes to Dieppe, a number of flak-damaged aircraft headed for Friston. The first arrival was a 614 Squadron Blenheim flown by Flt Lt J. E. Scott. In its crash-landing and subsequent fire, the gunner was killed, but a badly burned Scott pulled his unconscious Observer clear. The next forced-landings were by a pair of Hurricanes, followed by a Spitfire of 71 Squadron, which almost collided with the still-burning Blenheim. The last arrival was a 239 Squadron Mustang with a leaking oil tank. It had been a busy day for Friston.

Although more emergency arrivals were recorded in Friston's logs during the autumn of 1942, the only regular users were Spitfires of No 412 (RCAF) Squadron on detachment from Kenley, which lasted until January 1943 when the grass surface became too soft for use. There were no resident aeroplanes at Friston when, on 14 March, the aerodrome was warned of approaching raiders. After flares were dropped, two bombs exploded near the requisitioned Officers' Mess and incendiaries started two large gorse fires.

The low-level fighter-bomber raids on South Coast towns escalated during the spring of 1943, so the Griffon-powered Spitfire XIIs of 41 Squadron were deployed to Friston to counter the threat. A routine of cockpit readiness was instigated, which bore fruit on 4 June when eighteen Fw 190s were detected headed towards Eastbourne, to be met by eight Spitfires. The attack was foiled and two Focke-Wulfs were shot down, one by 41 Squadron, the other by AA fire. Although another attack occurred on 6 June, thereafter things were much quieter. This situation allowed for a greater offensive stance as No 412 (RCAF) Squadron with Spitfire VBs replaced No 41 on 21 June to undertake *Ramrod* and *Rodeo* operations over the continent, but only stayed until 13 July before moving to Redhill.

The aerodrome's first winter resident squadron arrived on 22 October 1943 in the shape of No 349 (Belgium) Squadron with its Spitfire Vs and began flying sweeps over France on 24 October. Apart from a brief detachment to Southend at the end of October, No 349 remained at Friston until 11 March 1944. Although there was no loss of life, the Adjutant, orderly room staff and a couple of dozen WAAFs billeted in the SHQ in the requisitioned Gayles lost all their belongings when it caught fire on 13 December; Tree Tops in East Dean was requisitioned to replace the SHQ.

The winter weather of 1943/44 was particularly harsh; no fewer than sixty-eight emergency landings were recorded in January 1944, and on the 21st of the month the Luftwaffe delivered one delayed-action bomb. The increased tempo at Friston saw a consequent improvement in facilities and the station became self-accounting. Accommodation in many forms, the most common being tents, had been found or created for 1,248 RAF personnel and 152 WAAFs. Hangarage consisted of two Over Blisters, which were used for servicing. The absence of any hardstandings was an operational constraint, although there was a perimeter taxiway that linked onto the approach road to the Gayles.

The next unit to arrive at Friston was familiar with the difficulties of its cliff-top location. No 41 returned on 11 March as 349 Squadron left for Hornchurch. Over the next six weeks the Squadron had a taxiing aircraft blown over by high winds and another crashed on landing before the unit departed for Bolt Head at the end of April. Although totally unsuitable for heavy bombers, Friston continued to be a magnet for B-17s and B-24s in distress. Most managed to get down successfully, but tragically, on 16 March, a Liberator of the 44th BG crashed and burned out while the fire crews could do little to control the conflagration.

In late April, Friston, now under Tangmere's control, became home to an 11 Group Wing led by Wing Commander D. Kingaby DSO DFM and two bars. The two Squadrons, Nos 350 (Belgian) and 501, both flying Spitfire Vs, began working up on Army exercises and attacks on a wide variety of targets on France. They didn't have it all their own way, as on 20 May the Luftwaffe deposited a single bomb adjacent to the primary runway, which shut down the aerodrome for several hours.

D-Day, 6 June, saw the Wing over the Normandy beaches at first light, but few Luftwaffe aircraft were to be seen and it was two days later that the first victory, a Bf 109, was achieved by 501 Squadron. The Allies' almost total air superiority can be illustrated by the fact that No 350 flew 1,192 operational hours in June, but only had one contact with the enemy. As the threat changed, both 350 and 501 Squadrons moved to Westhampnett in early July to make way for No 41 (yet again) with its Spitfire XIIs, and No 610 (County of Chester), also with Griffon-powered Spitfires, the latter being the Mark XIV.

The new threat was the V-1 flying bomb. Both squadrons learned that attacking the missile from astern was hazardous in the extreme as the resulting explosion could severely damage the attacker. They developed several techniques to destroy the 'Buzz Bomb', including that of flying alongside to position the Spitfire's wingtip under the missile, which interfered with the airflow, causing the bomb's gyros to topple and making it dive harmlessly into the sea. Another ploy that 610 used involved trapping the V-1 in the Spitfire's prop wash, which again upset the missile's equilibrium. As 610's Sqn Ldr Laurie commented, 'We shoot 'em down, we tip 'em up and we blow 'em over.' Every means possible was used to increase the Spitfire's speed, including using 150 octane fuel in place of the normal 130, removing the rear-view mirrors and deleting the machine-guns to rely on the pair of 20mm cannon. The aircraft were also highly polished. Despite these efforts, the Mark XIV's speed advantage over the Mk XII meant that 41 Squadron was replaced on 11 July by No 316 (Polish) Squadron with its Mustang IIIs. 610 Squadron's pilots accounted for thirty-one flying bombs while at Friston before transferring to Lympne in September as the V-1 threat diminished.

The Poles moved to Coltishall at the end of August, their replacements being 131 Squadron, again with Spitfire VIIs. The work now was mainly bomber escorts, interspersed with coastal patrols and fighter sweeps. Friston continued to be an emergency airfield of choice, but this was usually weather-related rather than due to enemy action. The field's resources were totally over-stretched on 8 September when no fewer than twenty-two C-47s were diverted to Friston. In preparation for a planned move to India, No 131 was taken off operations at the end of October as Friston reverted to its previous ELG role.

No 7 Fighter Command Servicing Unit took up residence in early 1945 and the Austers of 666 (RCAF) Squadron stayed for just over a month from 18 April before moving to the continent. But the active days of Friston were drawing to a close, the aerodrome being reduced to Care and Maintenance on 25 May and derequisitioned on 18 April 1946.

The next aerial residents of Friston were very different from its wartime occupants. The Southdown Gliding Club had found its old pre-war site at Devil's Dyke too dangerous following its wartime battle-training role, and re-established itself at Friston. With its hangar also transferred over, the club had nine years of very satisfactory cliff-top gliding in its fleet of two SG38s, a number of Tutors and a T-21 Sedburgh. The tenancy agreement ended in March 1955 and the Club moved 10 miles to Bo Peep Hill.

The field reverted to farming, but flying had not totally given up on Friston, although many years were to pass before the sound of powerful aero engines were again heard at this peaceful spot in Sussex. In 1983 author Derek Robinson published a novel called *Piece of Cake*, which told the story of a fictitious RAF fighter squadron from the outbreak of war through the Battle of Britain. It was chosen to be filmed as a television drama and shooting started in early 1988. One of the chosen locations was Friston and, when first surveyed, the site sported a good crop of peas! A deal was

Filming Piece of Cake *at Friston in mid-June 1988. (M. Finnis)*

An authentic setting for a 1940 fighter aerodrome, forty-eight years later. (M. Finnis)

struck with the farmer and grass was the next crop, seed being sown in early October; by May 1988 wartime Friston had been recreated. Original RAF vehicles, wooden sheds, a Nissen hut and many tents set the scene for a very authentic location. Replica Spitfires were dispersed around the field (shades of May 1942!) and the real aircraft arrived, most of them from Duxford. Ray Hanna was chief pilot, sadly now departed, as are a number of the other real stars, his son Mark, Hoof Proudfoot, Nick Grace, Reg Hallam and John Watts. Happily Stephen Grey, Walter Eichorn, John Romain and others are still with us. The flying was superb, but the story came in for a lot of metaphorical flak and sadly, to my mind, has never had a second airing on terrestrial television. However, I recently bought a two-set DVD of all six episodes and look forward to reliving the exploits of Hornet Squadron, despite their faults.

Main features:
Runways: ENE-WSW 5,025ft, NNE-SSW 2,850ft, grass. *Hangars:* two Over Blister. *Hardstandings:* none. *Accommodation:* RAF: 96 Officers, 175 SNCOs, 977 ORs; WAAF: 3 Officers, 3 SNCOs, 146 ORs.

FROST HILL FARM, Hampshire

51°16N/01°15W 450ft amsl; SU517525. 1.5 miles N of Overton alongside B3051

From the ancient Harrow Way, the land opposite Frost Hill Farm rises to the east to an open downland plateau some 475 feet (145 metres) above sea level. At the outbreak of war the site was chosen as one of the potential scatter fields for Odiham in the event of air attack or invasion. However, during the summer of 1940 its very suitability as an airfield led to it being obstructed by a forest of poles to prevent enemy aircraft landing.

Although apparently not used during the Battle of Britain, in December 1940 the field was chosen as a practice forced-landing ground for the Franco-Belgian FTS at Odiham. Its use by Magisters and the occasional Lysander continued through 1941. During June 1942, like many other sites, it was surveyed as a potential ALG for fighter operations. Although only a low-priority airstrip, two Sommerfeld track runways were laid during 1943. The main wire-mesh runway, orientated NW-SE, had a length of 4,800ft (1,453m) with a secondary E-W runway of 3,000ft (914m). No other improvements were made and no buildings erected. There is no evidence that the ALG was ever used.

With the war over, the tracking was lifted and mostly buried in the Nutley Bottom old gravel pit, from where small sections were recovered by locals for fencing. Briefly the site was retained for use by Maintenance Command for bulk fuel storage alongside the road, but the land was soon returned to agriculture. For a time the field was used by Army Air Corps helicopters from Middle Wallop, the old ALG seeing more aerial activity than during the Second World War, but sadly even that flying appears to have ceased. Having achieved nothing of note as an airfield, Frost Hill Farm is now better known as a good source of mushrooms.

Main features:
Runways: NW-SE 4,800ft, E-W runway 3,000ft, steel matting (Sommerfeld track).
Hangars: none. *Hardstandings:* none. *Accommodation:* none.

FUNTINGTON, West Sussex

50°52N/00°53W 115ft asl; SU790085. 5 miles W of Chichester south of B2146

Searching for a long-disused ALG, the last sight I was expecting to see was razor wire and a fenced-off high-security site. The new owner of the southern part of the former airfield is QinetiQ in the form of its Wind Farm Radar Impact Assessment Team. Its radar signature and antenna measurement range provides developers with the answer to what their wind turbines might do to local radar signals!

Apart from this visual aberration, nestling under the South Downs with the Racton Monument visible on the skyline to the north-west, it is still very obvious why Funtington was chosen as an airfield. Originally selected in the summer of 1942, the final plans, issued on 7 February 1943, showed a main Sommerfeld track runway of 4,800 feet (1,464 metres) roughly parallel to but south of the to-be-closed minor road from Funtington to Aldsworth. The secondary runway, to run SSE from Racton Park Farm towards Jubilee Wood, was 3,600 feet (1,097 metres). Completed in the late summer of 1943, the first occupant was the newly formed No 130 Airfield.

Moving in from the relative luxury of Odiham, Nos 4 and 268 Squadrons with their Mustang 1s found the primitive conditions of an ALG a severe shock. All accommodation was under canvas, and servicing was done in the open in preparation for what could be expected in France. The early Mustang's forte was low-level armed reconnaissance, and *Ranger* ops soon got under way despite indifferent weather. The evaluation highlighted many deficiencies in the facilities at Funtington, so the Squadrons returned to Odiham in October for much-needed improvements to take place.

These included the erection of four Extra Over Blister hangars, taxiways and additional hardstandings, the work being completed by late winter of 1943/44. 1 April saw the aerodrome formally handed back to the RAF, being immediately occupied by No 143 Airfield HQ. The three Canadian Squadrons, Nos 438, 439 and 440, flew their Typhoons in the following day. Although dive-bombing attacks on *Noball* V-1 sites were undertaken, the Typhoons left for Hurn on 19/20 April. Their replacements were the Spitfires of Nos 441, 442 and 443 (RCAF), which made up No 144 Airfield; its leader was the renowned Wing Commander J. E. 'Johnnie' Johnson DSO DFC and bar. They were immediately in the fight! A sweep by two dozen Funtington Spitfires in support of American B-24s and B-17s were met by Fw 190s, six of which were shot down. It wasn't all one way as two Spitfires were lost; Fg Off Sparling was killed and No 441's CO, Sqn Ldr Hill, became a POW. Accidents were relatively few although three Spitfires were written off on 8 May when one from No 422 Squadron swung on landing and collided with two more.

The next swap-over took place on 15 May when 144 was replaced by No 122 Wing (the change of designation from Airfield having taken place that day), consisting of Nos 19, 65 and 122 Squadrons. Two days later a most audacious *Ranger* raid took place. Five 65 Squadron Mustangs and two from No 122 refuelled at Coltishall to fly 400 miles (732km) across the North Sea to Aalborg in Denmark. Not unexpectedly, they caught the Germans totally by surprise! The claim was five Ju 88s, one He 177, one Bf 109 and two Ju 34s – all destroyed – and two Arado floatplanes damaged at their moorings, and that was from the five aircraft that returned! Flt Lt Barrett was killed but was believed to have got another Bf 109, and when Flt Sgt R. T. Williams finally returned via Sweden, he claimed a further two Ju 34s and an He 177. Quite a turkey shoot!

D-Day saw 122 Wing covering Coastal Command Beaufighters on anti-U-boat patrols before escorting the second wave of troop carriers and tug/glider combinations to their designated DZs and LZs. It wasn't until 8 June that the Wing met up with the Luftwaffe. In a successful bounce, three Fw 190s were shot down with no losses. Two days later the bounce was a Luftwaffe success when two Mustangs were lost to Bf 109s, although Flt Lt Collyns got one 109 in return. Soon afterwards six 19 Squadron Mustangs tangled with a similar number of 109s, claiming three of them. In preparation for its move to France, 122 Wing transferred to Ford on 15 June.

A succession of Wings then used Funtington for a few days to acclimatise them to ALG conditions before moving to the continent. These included No 145 (French) Wing with 329, 340 and 341 Squadrons. Their Spitfires arrived from Merston on 22 June and left for Selsey on 1 July. The Wing's replacement, No 135 Wing, stayed a little longer. The three Squadrons, Nos 222, 349 (Belgian) and 485 (RNZAF), arrived with their Spitfires on 4 July from Coolham to escort day-bombers. A new Wing Leader, Wg Cdr Harries, arrived in mid-July together with No 33 Squadron to create an enlarged Funtington Wing. On 26 July the Wing was escorting Mitchells and Bostons to Alencon when more than thirty German fighters interceded. In the resulting dogfight, three Bf 109s and a single Fw 190 were claimed for no losses. The Wing moved to Selsey on 6 August, being replaced by the four Spitfire Squadrons (Nos 66, 127, 331 and 332) of No 132 Wing. After only six days they left for Tangmere on the familiar path to the continent, but nobody replaced them! Funtington was left silent and empty.

The Grace Spitfire ML407 flew with No 485 (RNZAF) Squadron at Funtington for a month from 4 July 1944. (DWL collection)

The airfield was formally derequisitioned on 13 December 1944 and work began to clear the site. On completion, the land returned to agriculture, although it is believed that one or more of the Blisters were retained for storage for a period. Today there is nothing to tell of the hectic months of 1943/44 when Funtington was one of the busiest ALGs in the region. However, at least two of Funtington's Spitfires are still active. MK959 flew with No 329 (French) Squadron, but was transferred to the Royal Netherlands Air Force in 1946. After restoration in the USA, she is now operated by the Dutch Spitfire Flight in Amsterdam. The famous Grace Spitfire ML407 was also at Funtington with No 485 (RNZAF) for a month from July 1944.

Main features:
Runways: 083° 4,800ft, 343° 3,600ft, steel matting (Sommerfeld track). *Hangars:* four EO Blisters. *Hardstandings:* temporary Sommerfeld track. *Accommodation:* tented camp.

GAYLES, East Sussex – see FRISTON

GODMERSHAM PARK, Kent

51°13N/00°56E 300ft asl; TR049504. 2.5 miles N of Wye

Airships are a vulnerable mode of transport, particularly when filled with highly flammable gas, and are also very susceptible to strong winds. When the highly successful SSZ or 'Zero' class of airships evolved in late 1916 at the nearby airship station at Capel-le-Ferne and entered production, it was necessary to find appropriate mooring-out stations that were not only a suitable distance away but also afforded a degree of protection from the prevailing winds.

Godmersham Park, some 15 miles to the north-west of Capel, provided an ideal, heavily wooded, broad valley in the lee of the high ground of Kings Wood to the west and Godmersham village to the east. It was normal for a single airship to be moored out and records confirm that SSZ.36 was in residence on 22 June 1918. The vulnerability of the airship was underlined when SSZ.5 was destroyed by fire at Godmersham on 17 September 1918.

Polegate-based Airship SSZ.43 used Godmersham Park as a mooring-out site. (FAA Museum via Ces Mowthorpe collection)

The site was abandoned after the Armistice but the walkers who are willing to divert from the North Downs Way, which skirts the eastern edge of Kings Wood and overlooks what is now known as Airship Valley (which is private land), will find an overgrown pit in which the gondola of the airship would be located to minimise wind effects.

Main features:
Runways: none. *Hangars:* none. Airship mooring facilities.

GOODWOOD, West Sussex – see WESTHAMPNETT

GOSPORT, Hampshire

50°48N/01°10W 24ft amsl; SU590010. 4 miles W of Portsmouth off A32

For decades following the First World War, Gosport's name was synonymous with what to modern eyes was a rather basic means by which the instructor and his pupil conversed in draughty open-cockpit biplanes, the Gosport Tube. It was Major R. R. Smith-Barry who, as the CO of No 1 Reserve Squadron, after experiments with hand signals and early telephones had proved useless, created a modified speaking tube and designed a training scheme that in essence was adopted throughout the world right through to the jet age.

During his earlier service as the CO of No 60 Squadron on the Western Front, he had been appalled at how unprepared and relatively unskilled the replacement pilots were on arriving at the front. The then training philosophy had tended to avoid potentially dangerous manoeuvres, but Smith-Barry believed in allowing pupils to experience these and to gain confidence by recovering the aircraft to controlled flight. His appointment to Gosport in 1917 allowed him to develop what were then very revolutionary ideas of pilot training.

On arrival, Major Robert Smith-Barry reorganised the Squadron into three Flights: 'A' with the excellent Avro 504, 'B' with the equally good BE.2c, and 'C' with single-seat Moranes and Bristol Scouts. His staff, who had been accommodated in the gloomy 19th-century forts, were transferred to a requisitioned country house. His training curriculum was based on a mix of academic classroom training and dual-flight instruction, followed by solo flying by the pupils. Having proved that this worked, in May 1917 he wrote a set of training notes and began agitating for proper instructors' courses. He was successful in convincing General Salmond, who authorised the creation of a School of Special Flying at Gosport on 2 August 1917 by assimilating Nos 1, 2, and 55 Training (Ex Reserve) Squadrons. Early in 1918 all TSs were ordered to change to the Gosport training system once their instructors had passed through the SoSF. Training would never be the same again.

Aeroplanes and hangars of No 1 Training Squadron at Gosport in 1916/17. (JMB/GSL collection)

Flying had first come to Gosport in 1909 when two Naval Lieutenants attempted, unsuccessfully, to launch a powered aircraft from a ramp-like structure erected on the grass area between the two massive red-brick Victorian Forts Rowner and Grange. It did lead to the creation, in 1910, of the Portsmouth Aero Club, later to become the Hampshire Aero Club, which gained permission from the War Office to use Grange Camp Field for experiments in 'heavier-than-air' flight, sadly equally unsuccessfully. With the expansion of the Military Wing of the RFC during 1912/13, the area was an automatic choice for an aerodrome.

After work to smooth out ridges and furrows in early 1914, No 5 Squadron RFC transferred from Netheravon on 6 July with a mix of Maurice and Henri Farmans, Avro 504s and the SE.2 s/n 609. After the outbreak of war, the Squadron moved to France on 18 August, leaving Gosport deserted until No 1 Squadron (Naval Wing, RFC) was re-formed at Fort Grange in October equipped with Bristol Scouts. Later 'A' and 'B' Flights were formed with Avro 504s and Sopwith Tabloids before being sent to Dover in January 1915.

Concerned at this apparent take-over of one of its aerodromes, the War Office sent the newly formed 8 Squadron from Brooklands on 6 January 1915, and formed No 13 on 10 January, followed on 1 February by 17 Squadron, all flying various models of the BE.2. Personnel were accommodated initially in Fort Grange, but the creation of separate training flights on all home-based squadrons necessitated the acquisition of Fort Rowner on 24 September. No 8 Squadron and its men had already moved to France on 15 April. The frantic formation of new units, including Nos 22, 23, 28 and 29, despite a severe shortage of both men and machines, continued for the rest of the year. The congestion was eased in October when No 13 Squadron went to France and Nos 14 and 17 were dispatched to Egypt as part of No 5 Wing. The process of forming and working-up new squadrons continued throughout 1916, but perhaps the most significant new unit of that year was No 1 RS, which came from Farnborough on 22 May. By the end of the year training was the primary role of Gosport and it was, of course, the appointment of Major Smith-Barry as CO of No 1 RS that, as we have seen, was to revolutionise pilot training.

Hangarage from the beginning had consisted of the wood and canvas Bessonneau type, but these began to be supplanted by a line of wooden sheds adjacent to the road that formed the eastern boundary between the two forts. Workshops and flight offices were also constructed.

Although training dominated, a detached Flight from No 78 Squadron flying BE.12s had become responsible for the defence of the Portsmouth area. A similar detachment from 39 Squadron with Bristol Fighters took over the role in January 1918 and became the School of Aerial Co-operation with Coast Defence Batteries. When the RAF was formed on 1 April 1918, Gosport was put into No 2 Area under the command of No 8 Group at Southampton. In July the SoSF was renamed the South West Area Flying Instructors School. Although Smith-Barry had already departed, his legacy was destined to survive. During August, a new research unit was created under the deliberately vague title of the Development Squadron, whose role was clarified by its aircraft, the torpedo-carrying Sopwith Cuckoo. This unit and its task were to play a significant role in Gosport's future.

The Armistice brought rapid changes at Gosport: the School of Aerial Co-operation left and the SW Area FIS was disbanded on 26 February 1919. The station's future lay with air-dropped torpedoes, as No 186 Squadron was re-formed with Sopwith Cuckoos and Bristol Fighters. The station then became known as RAF Base Gosport, and its resident units were No 210 Squadron (re-formed on 1 February 1920 from 186 Squadron), an Observer Training Flight, and the Development Flight, which had evolved from the Development Squadron. The early 1920s were a period of much change. No 3 Squadron replaced the Observer Training Flight in October 1922, only to be disbanded, together with No 210, on 1 April 1923.

No 186 Squadron flew the Sopwith Cuckoo from Gosport for a year from February 1919. (H. J. Dyer via P. Swan)

The delivery of the first Blackburn Dart to the Development Flight on 9 March 1922 was to have great significance. A further example arrived in May and, after competitive trials with three Handley Page HP.19 Hanley prototypes, the Dart was adopted as the Fleet Air Arm's standard single-seat torpedo bomber, becoming a common sight at Gosport. The type was also remembered as making the night carrier landing after training at Gosport. Other types passed through Gosport in the 1920s, including the incredibly ugly Blackburn R.1 Blackburn. A much more elegant design, the Fairey IIIF powered by a Napier Lion engine, the final evolution of the Fairey III line, arrived at Gosport in 1928 for No 440 Flight. A further ten Flights over the next few years were also equipped with this remarkable design.

In April 1933 pairs of Flights were re-formed as squadrons: No 821 Squadron was created from 442 and 449 Flights, and similarly Nos 461 and 462 Flights became 812 Squadron. The Training Flights were also reorganised, becoming 'A' Flight (Army & Navy Co-operation), 'B' Flight (Telegraphist Air Gunner Training), 'C' Flight (Deck Landing), 'D' Flight (Torpedo Training) and later 'E' Flight for specialist experiments for the Air Ministry. In October 1934 'A' and 'B' Flights moved to Lee-on-Solent, while 'D' and 'E' were renamed 'A' (Torpedo Training) and 'B' (Torpedo Experimental Flights. 'C' Flight continued as the Deck Landing Flight.

The new Blackburn Baffin with its air-cooled Bristol Pegasus radial engine had been evaluated at Gosport in September 1933, and 'A' Flight was re-equipped with the type in January 1935 as the Baffin became the standard FAA torpedo-bomber. On 22 June 1936 a Gosport Baffin achieved a national notoriety. After dropping a practice torpedo, the aircraft, flown by Fg Off Horsey, struck one of the derricks on the French liner *Normandie* before crashing on the ship's bows. It had to remain there until the ship berthed at Le Havre, where it was recovered by an RAF working party. *Flight* magazine recorded on 23 July that the Court Martial was told that the aircraft was worth £7,000 before but only £1,000 after the accident!

Another very significant naval torpedo carrier arrived at Gosport on 19 February 1936 when the first pre-production Fairey Swordfish came for evaluation. In December 1936 Gosport came under No 17 Group control, and on 17 January 1937 No 813 Squadron was commissioned with nine Swordfish before embarking in HMS *Eagle* in February. A succession of FAA squadrons followed for re-equipping on shore at Gosport before going to sea. During the Munich Crisis, No 10 Mobilisation Pool was created, and in November 'B' Flight became the Torpedo Development Unit.

In the late 1930s Gosport's aeroplanes included the Magister, Nimrod, Swordfish, Avro 504N, Tutor, Shark, Osprey and Vildebeest. (Flight via P. H. T. Green collection)

The HQ of No 17 (Training) Group was moved to Fort Grange, Gosport, on 24 February 1939 from Lee-on-Solent, followed in May by No 2 AACU. At the outbreak of the Second World War Gosport was host to the Group HQ and the Training Squadron, the TDU, which became the Air Torpedo Development Unit, No 2 AACU and No 1 Coast Artillery Co-operation Unit (CACU), although the latter moved to Thorney Island almost immediately.

Over the years hangarage had steadily improved from the 'A' type of the 1920s, four of which were built at Gosport and supplemented by a single 'C' hangar in the mid-1930s. Two Bellman hangars were erected near Fort Rowner and the flying field was also expanded. Two tarmac runways had been laid down pre-war, largely for carrier landing practice. That orientated SW/NE was 2,100ft (640m) in length and the N/S runway was just 1,650ft (504m) long. In contrast to probably every other airfield in the UK, the hard runways were abandoned in favour of four grass runways, the longest, of 4,650 feet (1,417 metres), was N/S but the more suitable SW/NE run was only 150 feet (46 metres) shorter. This increased length permitted the operation of the modern torpedo-bombers like the early Bothas and Beauforts.

The war had little immediate impact of Gosport, and training/torpedo development continued much as before, that is until Monday 12 August when fifteen Ju 88s of KG51 bombed the airfield. A more serious raid occurred on 16 August when twelve Ju 88s, escorted by Bf 110s, bombed and strafed the hangars and buildings. They left several hangars and other buildings destroyed, six airmen killed, nine aircraft wrecked and a further ten damaged. Fighter Command's only VC was won by Flt Lt James Nicolson of No 249 Squadron trying to intercept this raid, although bounced by Bf 109s.

Just two days later, on 18 August 1940, a mass formation of more than 100 Stukas escorted by at least 150 Bf 109s was detected heading towards Tangmere, but, unlike two days earlier, that battered station was not the target. The formation spilled into four separate groups with twenty-two Ju 87s of 1/Stg 3 heading towards Gosport. Despite heavy defensive anti-aircraft fire, the attackers destroyed two more hangars and many other buildings, plus nine aircraft wrecked to a greater or lesser extent. Happily, there were no casualties this time and, despite more damage, Gosport continued to function. Also the Luftwaffe's intelligence sources were at fault since, however important Gosport's work was, it had no relevance to the outcome of the Battle of Britain.

Gosport was the venue on 6 December for the formation of No 86 Squadron, which worked up with its new Blenheim IV before moving north to Leuchars in early February. The Luftwaffe returned over the nights of 11 and 12 March when incendiaries fell on the field during heavy raids on Portsmouth. Expansion of the ATDU continued apace with the HQ and design offices moving into Moat House. The Ashley Wallpaper Works in Gosport was requisitioned to provide more machine shop space. The ATDU's own Marine Craft Unit provided range safety in Stokes Bay during torpedo-dropping and recovered the exhausted weapons. The range of types operated also expanded to include the Wellington, Hampden, Manchester and a single Albemarle, although in practice most routine drops were made by Swordfish and Albacore aircraft.

The Wellington evaluated the carriage of a pair of torpedoes while mines and depth charges were tested using the Hampden and Manchester. The arrival of the first 'Torbeau' Beaufighter in May 1942 was an exciting addition to the fleet, but it soon brought about the tragic loss of the unit's CO. Flown by F. O. Davenport with Wg Cdr Shaw observing, the aircraft was to carry out a torpedo drop over the Stokes Bay range when, at about 200 feet, an engine suddenly cut out. The Beaufighter rolled uncontrollably and crashed fatally near Alverstoke.

A further change of control took place on 23 August 1942 when Gosport came under No 16 Group, and No 3502 Servicing Unit was created from the FAA MU. The first result of this change was the arrival on 27 August of 608 Squadron with Hudsons for the fitment of long-range tanks. This unit was succeeded by No 500 Squadron for the same task, both squadrons departing in mid-September to Gibraltar for Operation 'Torch'. No 254 was the next new squadron to arrive at Gosport, but only for six weeks' torpedo training before leaving for North Coates on 7 November as part of the first Beaufighter Strike Wing. 3502 SU now specialised in major servicing of Hudsons from 38, 233 and 608 Squadrons. Later the Gibraltar Squadrons, Nos 48, 233 and 520, also came to Gosport for overhaul.

Although No 2 AACU disbanded, A Flight remained at Gosport as No 1622 Flight with Defiants, Gladiators and a single Roc, but on 1 December No 1622 was merged with No 1631 Flight to form 667 Squadron. Its Defiants towed targets for the RN gunnery schools, and Hurricanes were used for gun-laying assisted by a handful of Barracudas from May 1944. The

ATDU was enlarged in February 1944 by the addition of 764 Squadron, primarily to assess the early Firebrand aircraft. Gosport was little touched by the frenetic activity all around it as D-Day approached, and the day itself was rather an anti-climax for the station.

American Vengeances began to replace the Defiants in 667 Squadron from October, Oxfords having also joined the unit in June. Another squadron strengthened the naval presence at Gosport in January 1944 when No 708 (Tactical Trials) arrived from Lee-on Solent, while runway resurfacing was in progress. Its three-month stay was spent on Firebrand trials. Gosport was also much busier with Harvards, Fireflies and Masters from Lee. This detachment highlighted the Navy's need for more airfield capacity in the area, resulting in a formal hand-over on 1 August 1945 as Gosport became HMS *Siskin*.

Remaining as lodgers administered by Thorney Island were the ATDU and No 667, but they were joined by 707 Squadron on 14 August with Ansons and Avengers, then by No 711, with Mosquitoes and Martinets, and finally by 778 Squadron, which moved all the way down from Arbroath. As might be expected, the immediate post-war period was one of considerable confusion and change. 667 Squadron left in early December, followed in the spring of 1946 by Nos 707 and 778 Squadrons, and No 771 in April 1947. Although No 727 re-formed in May 1946 to provide officer training courses, it was the formation of 705 Squadron on 7 May 1947 that heralded a new era for Gosport.

Helicopters! Like them or loath them, when the Royal Navy's small number of Sikorsky R-4s began to collect at Gosport even their most ardent supporters could not have foreseen how helicopters would come to dominate the future FAA. Commanded by Lt K. Reed RN, 705 Squadron boasted seven Hoverflies, the total FAA complement, a similar number of pilots and just thirty ratings. Officially, No 705 was the Naval Helicopter Training Unit, but the versatility of the aircraft meant that they also undertook radar checks and transporting VIPs. The unit's equipment improved in January 1950 when the Westland Dragonfly started to replace the Hoverflies.

The RN Operational Helicopter Flight evolved from 705 Squadron during June 1951, leaving for Singapore aboard HMS *Warrior* the following month. The trial was an outstanding success, leading to an order for twenty-seven Sikorsky-built S-55s, which Westland was later to build under licence as the Whirlwind. No 848 was formed in October 1952 to operate them as they arrived by ship in late November. By 12 December, such was the urgency that the Squadron, with ten Whirlwind HAR 21s, was aboard *Perseus* on its way to Malaya to confront the communist uprising in that country.

The Hiller HTE-2 was chosen to fill the critical need for a good ab initio training helicopter and joined 705 Squadron in May 1953. The autumn saw more American-built Whirlwinds arrive to equip 706 Squadron, in this case the anti-submarine HAS 22 variant. After spending the winter in Northern Ireland, No 706 returned to Gosport and was renumbered 845 Squadron to work up its Whirlwinds in the sonar-dunking anti-submarine role. But Gosport's days as an airfield were numbered. The first squadron to depart, in November 1955, was No 705, which transferred to Lee-on-Solent, leaving the ATDU as not only the last flying unit but also the longest-serving. When it finally moved to Culdrose early in 1956, a thirty-eight-year association with Gosport was severed. HMS *Siskin* was formally paid off in June 1956.

The end of flying did not mean the end of military interest in Gosport, for as *Siskin* disappeared so HMS *Sultan* was commissioned on 1 June 1956 as a Mechanical Training & Repair Establishment. The base is now the Royal Navy's School of Marine & Aeronautical Engineering, supplying the fleet with engineering officers and ratings. It is the largest RN training establishment, employing up to 3,000 military and civilian personnel. The site, which covers some 179 acres on both sides of Military Road, also accommodates a number of other Naval departments including Centurion, the Navy's pay and pensions division. Among the very specialist training undertaken at *Sultan* is that of future nuclear submarine crews. The site has three Manoeuvring Room Trainers – the critical area of the boat from which it is controlled. Maintained by Rolls-Royce, these MRTs are complete replicas of the Manoeuvring Rooms of all three classes of RN nuclear submarine.

The airfield is now a housing estate, but the road names reflect both the naval and aeronautical history of the site, with Closes named Samson, Anson and Rodney, together with Nimrod Drive and Howe Road. Viewing HMS *Sultan* from Military Road, the most obvious airfield features to be seen are the single 'C' hangar near Fort Rowner and, to the north, the two surviving 'A' hangars, all much modified. A better view can be found on Google Earth or on the Royal Navy's own HMS *Sultan* website, which links to Microsoft's Virtual Earth. On both sites instructional airframes, including a Harrier GR.3 and a number of Sea Kings/Wessex, can be seen adjacent to the northern 'A' hangar.

On 28 May 1958 Air Chief Marshal Sir Arthur Longmore, who had commanded RNAS squadrons at Gosport in 1914, unveiled a memorial in the form of a stone plinth carrying a plaque surmounted by a globe and bronze eagle – a suitable commemoration of one of the oldest RFC/RNAS aerodromes, which evolved almost by accident but grew into an invaluable training and trialling station. Although flying ceased more than fifty years ago, the site continues to provide essential aeronautical engineering training. However, the future plans for military aeronautical training will see this role being transferred to the new Tri-Service Defence Training Campus at St Athan in South Wales from 2011, bringing to a final close all aviation connections at Gosport.

The Gosport memorial was unveiled in 1958, with an 'A'-type hangar in the background. (DWL collection)

Main features:
Runways: 317° 6,000ft x 150ft, 019° 4,200ft x 150ft, 084° 4,200ft x 150ft, concrete and wood chippings. *Hangars:* two T2. *Hardstandings:* fifty spectacle type. *Accommodation:* RAF: 7 Officers, 21 SNCOs, 742 ORs.

GRAIN (PORT VICTORIA), Kent

51°07N/00°43W 7ft amsl; TQ885745. 1.5 miles S of Grain village

About as far off the beaten track as it is possible to achieve in overcrowded South East England lies a virtually forgotten First World War aerodrome. Drive on to the low-lying Isle of Grain as far as the road takes you to enter the small settlement of Grain. Turn south towards a massive Power Station in the distance and you arrive at a much degraded concrete road. The nameplate says Port Victoria Road, which alludes to an earlier history when Queen Victoria chose Grain, complete with a railway station and jetty, as a departure point for trips to Germany. Ironically, in view of the future use of the site, the last Royal use of Port Victoria was by the Kaiser to return to Germany after attending the coronation of King George V.

The Admiralty chose the isolated, marshy site to be one of its first seaplane or 'hydro-aeroplane' bases. Strategically placed to defend the major ports along the Thames estuary leading up to London, Grain was commissioned on 30 December 1912. A slipway was cut through the sea wall and a number of coastguard cottages requisitioned as accommodation – on condition that the look-out was maintained! Eastchurch, which lay across the River Medway's estuary on the Isle of Sheppey, lacked seaplane access and in August 1913 Grain replaced Eastchurch as the primary air station in the Sheerness Naval District. In June of that year Grain had been allocated £20,000, to be spent on new sheds and other improvements. By January 1914 thirty-seven aeroplanes, approximately one-quarter of the RN's strength, were based at Grain.

An early test of the seaplane's efficiency occurred on 21 January 1914. A submarine, HMS A7, had failed to surface near Plymouth on 16 January and she could not be found. Grain's CO, Lieutenant J. W. Seddon, left at 09.15 in a Maurice Farman floatplane on a marathon journey around the coast. Refuelling at Calshot, he arrived at Plymouth at 16.40, too late for the search to start as it was virtually dark. The wreck was located on 22 January but bad weather prevented salvage at the time.

At the outbreak of war Grain began long-range patrols out into the North Sea; the first, on 9 August, took Seddon to the Belgian coast. Regular 2-hourly patrols provided air cover for shipping carrying the BEF to France. The unreliability of early aero engines almost led to the loss of Lt Seddon on 17 December 1914. With Leading Mechanic R. L. Hartley as observer, his Short Type 830 was forced, by engine failure, to land on the sea. To balance the loss of the port float, Hartley climbed onto the starboard wing. Finally, 8 hours after ditching the exhausted crew were rescued by the Norwegian SS *Orn*.

With the build-up of bases at Westgate and Clacton, 1915 saw Grain's role change to research and repair. An aerodrome was created by linking inland areas of rough pasture, boarding over the many dykes. A line of Bessonneau hangars was erected to supplement the seaplane sheds and a former Salvation Army Congress Hall sited to the west of the aerodrome requisitioned to act as the HQ for the new Royal Aeroplane Repair Depot, which was titled Port Victoria.

The Experimental Armament Section was formed in late 1915, followed in early 1916 by the Seaplane Test Flight. Grain became the Navy's equivalent of Farnborough when these units combined as the Marine Experimental Aircraft Depot. Sopwith Pups and 1½ Strutters operated from a dummy deck on early arrester wire trials. A redesign of an existing aeroplane led to the creation of the PV.1 (for Port Victoria), which was a much modified Sopwith Schneider. Grain's first original design, conceived as an anti-Zeppelin fighter, the PV.2 tractor seaplane, flew in June 1916 but was found to have poor lateral control. The PV.3 is believed to have been a two-seat landplane fighter, which was never built, followed by the pusher seaplane PV.4.

Nothing daunted, the PV.5 was a single-seat reconnaissance seaplane. The first flew on 27 July 1917 but was scrapped in September. The improved PV.5A survived at Grain until January 1919. The next Port Victoria designs were an attempt to build an anti-submarine scout capable of being flown from small naval craft. The resulting designs were tiny! The first, the PV.7 'Grain Kitten' had a wingspan of just 18 feet (5.5 metres) with power coming from a 35hp ABC Gnat. Very underpowered, it first flew on 22 June 1917, surviving until May 1918. The PV.8 'Eastchurch Kitten' was a little more successful, flying in September 1917 and, after evaluation, was sent to the USA for further tests in March 1918. The final PV design was No 9, which was another attempt at a seaplane fighter. It flew in December 1917 and later went to Felixstowe, where it was last recorded in October 1919.

Although none of the PV series were a great success and none went into production, this was only part of the work at Grain as the station evaluated a series of experimental designs from other sources. Tested during 1917 were the prototypes of the Fairey III series, final variants of which were only declared obsolete in 1940! Beardmore, Short, Felixstowe, Handley Page and Sopwith were among the many manufacturers who submitted prototype designs to Port Victoria for testing.

The last of the Grain designs, but one that did not carry a PV designation, was the most successful. Based on a Sopwith B.1 single-seat bomber, which was tested at Grain in December 1917, the two-seat 'Grain Griffon' featured folding wings and a hydrovane undercarriage. Seven were built, the first flying in March 1918, and three served aboard HMS *Vindictive* into early 1919, operating against Bolshevik forces. In addition to developing the hydrovanes as fitted to the Griffon, Grain also experimented with flotation systems and tested many experimental weapons including the Davis recoilless gun. By the autumn of 1918 a total of fifteen sheds had been erected, the majority just behind the sea wall, which had been pierced in three places by slipways. Staff numbers had increased to nearly 1,500 and a large camp had been constructed south of the village to house them.

In early 1918 Lt W. A. Yeulett arrived at Grain, although formally based at RNAS East Fortune, Scotland. He flew and photographed a number of aircraft there, especially the Sopwith Pup. On 19

Numbered N54 in the RNAS experimental series, the PV.5A survived at Grain into 1919. (W. A. Yeulett via W. Casey)

W. A. Yeulett gives scale to the diminutive 'Grain Kitten' N539. (W. A. Yeulett via W. Casey)

July 1918 Yeulett flew one of seven Sopwith Camels that were launched from HMS *Furious* to undertake the first ever raid conducted from an aircraft carrier. The attack on the Zeppelin sheds at Tondern was a great success, but sadly Lt Yeulett failed to return. He received a posthumous DFC.

Work at Grain slowed after the Armistice, but the closure of Orfordness in 1921 brought the Armament Experimental Squadron to Grain. Testing of new aeroplanes continued and included the Short Cromarty and the Fairey Atlanta, although the latter was probably the last new type to be evaluated. On 17 March 1924 the Marine Aircraft Experimental Unit moved to Felixstowe and, after a unique twelve-year history, Grain/Port Victoria was closed.

Much of the airfield is now under two power stations. The E.ON oil-fired Grain Power Station is most prominent and at least one original Admiralty stores building remains in use. Most of the flying field is covered by the Scottish Power Liquefied Natural Gas terminal and power

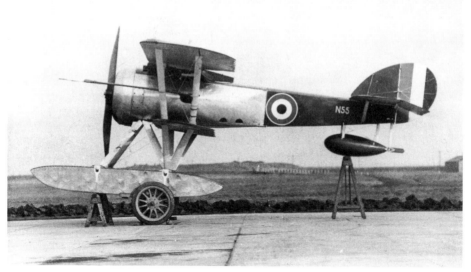

Another of the experimental Port Victoria designs, the PV.9 first flew at Grain in December 1917. (MAEE via P. H. T. Green collection)

N6176 scored four victories with No 4 Squadron before arriving at Grain in December 1917 for trials with a skid undercarriage. (W. A. Yeulett via W. Casey)

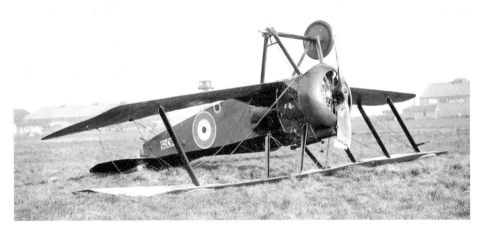

Also a combat veteran, Camel N6375 lost a wheel on take-off. Despite wheel-waving by groundcrew, Flt Lt N. E. Williams inverted at Grain on 8 March 1918. (W. A. Yeulett via W. Casey)

station. There is evidence of what may be old hangar bases to be seen from the path that is a continuation of Port Victoria Road. One jetty that was in use in 1918 is extant, but apart from two small buildings that may have a more modern drainage purpose, there is nothing to indicate that nearly a century ago this was ever a busy naval air station, testing aeroplanes that were then at the forefront of aeronautical technology.

Main features:
Runways: grass landing and take-off area, slipways to sea alighting and take-off area. *Hangars:* large number of aeroplane and seaplane sheds. *Accommodation:* wooden huts.

Port Victoria Road with the Grain Power Station in the background. (DWL collection)

GREAT CHART, Kent – see ASHFORD

GREAT SHEFFORD, Berkshire

SU364736. 3.5 miles NE of Hungerford beside A338

For an apparently anonymous new grass airstrip, Great Shefford achieved some early and unwanted publicity as recalled by Peter Marshall who, as a young lad, lived in nearby Shefford Woodlands where his parents ran the village Post Office. He recalls hearing 'Lord Haw-Haw' stating on the radio that they (the Germans) would add a few finishing touches. Sure enough, a few weeks later a German aeroplane dropped eight bombs on the landing strip! Another local resident, Mr Bill Weeks, who lived just opposite the landing strip's entrance, recalled:

> 'The night the bombs dropped, the blast broke every pane of glass in the house. I was woken by the noise of people running about and shouting. The bomb run was roughly south-east to north-west. There were eight craters about 6 feet across and 3 feet deep. The day after the incident, an RAF officer flying a Tiger Moth landed at the strip and taxied into one of the craters!'

This was not what was expected as the airfield had been created as a scatter field for the aircraft from Woodley near Reading. Woodley was not only the manufacturing site of Phillips & Powis Aircraft Ltd (later Miles Aircraft) but also the home of No 8 EFTS with its Tiger Moths and Magisters. With the Luftwaffe just across the Channel, the airfield was a likely target and, in the event of invasion, certain to be obstructed to prevent enemy aircraft landing. An emergency bolt-hole was required. The large, gently sloping grass field was apparently ideal for the purpose. From research undertaken by Roger Day (author of *Ramsbury at War*), there appears to have been an additional use for Great Shefford – communications. A number of Naval officers from Portsmouth had been evacuated to local large houses including The Goodings, Oakhanger House and Wooley Park, none of which was more than a couple of miles from the landing strip. A hostel for the WRNS who worked at the offices was established in Shefford Woodlands village. Vehicular entry to the airfield was through a gate near some farm buildings on the western edge of Shefford Woodlands village. A few RAF airmen lived in a tent in the field by the entrance. After a while they moved into the village hall (called the Reading Room by locals and now demolished). The only airfield accessory was a pole and wind sock!

Paratroop and invasion scares were rife during the early summer of 1940, but it appears likely that Great Shefford was first used officially in August. During that month there were a number of occasions that Woodley's resident aircraft abruptly departed to the west just before the air raid warnings sounded. The records do not confirm that Shefford Woodlands (the name the locals used) was their destination as Sheffield Farm (Theale) was then also being developed as Woodley's RLG. With a diminishing likelihood of invasion and bombing, Great Shefford became an ELG for all flying training units in its vicinity. Although it was originally thought that the strip continued in that role until the war's end, local information now suggests that the field was back in agricultural use by 1942.

Today the site to the north of Ermine Street (B4000) behind the Pheasant public house remains open farmland although the A338 has been re-routed over part of the airfield to link to Junction 14 of the M4. Sadly, because no buildings were ever erected there are no obvious signs of its wartime role, although it is reported that, in some conditions, evidence of the eight bomb craters may be discerned.

Main features:
Runways: grass landing and take-off area. *Hangars:* none. *Accommodation:* requisitioned private dwellings.

GREENHAM COMMON, Berkshire

51°22N/01°17W 390ft amsl; SU500645. 2 miles SE of Newbury off A339(T)

Greenham Common – for more than a decade from 1981 this airfield was never out of the news. The Cold War, Nuclear Armageddon, Cruise Missiles and the Women's Peace Camp! It is now a perfect example of the 'peace dividend' arising from the ending of the Cold War. It lies not just deserted, but Greenham Common Airfield is no more, it doesn't exist. The runways and taxiways have all gone and now it's just Greenham Common as nature re-establishes its dominance; gorse and grass have replaced concrete and tarmac.

Greenham Common lies on a ridge and came under the stewardship of Newbury Corporation in 1938 when it purchased the Lordship of the Manor. However, by early 1941 the town was being criticised for its lack of care. A local resident complained to the *Newbury Weekly News* that Greenham 'is now becoming a desolate waste and … a vast rubbish heap'. Thus when the area of heath and scrubland was requisitioned in May 1941, there was none of the usual farming resistance and local opposition was also muted.

Work to create a standard bomber OTU to act as a satellite of Aldermaston was quickly under way, with the closure of several minor roads that crossed the common. However, the main Newbury to Basingstoke road was retained but fitted with barriers and guard posts where it passed through the technical site. The accommodation sites were widely dispersed as usual, as far away as Symonton Common. The bomb dump and sewage works were located to the north-east of the airfield. A main 6,000ft (1,830m) runway orientated E-W was supplemented by secondary runways of 4,200ft (1280m) and 3,300ft (1,006m).

By the time the work was nearing completion in the summer of 1942 priorities had changed, and Greenham was earmarked for USAAF use. Passing through briefly were the HQ staff of the 51st TCW, who arrived in the September but moved on to North Africa in November 1942 for Operation 'Torch'. Pending the arrival of another American unit, the airfield was transferred to No 70 Group, the Oxfords of No 15 (P)AFU, moving from Andover in December, being joined on 29 April 1943 by those of 1511 (BAT) Flight. Pilot training continued until the end of September, with Greenham officially becoming USAAF Station 486 on 1 October 1943.

It was the 354th FG of the IXth AF that first arrived on 4 November to collect the new Merlin-powered P-51B aircraft to which it was converting, having trained in the USA on the Airacobra. As the first American Group to fly the type in combat, the 354th became known as 'The Pioneer Mustang Group', but with its aircraft it moved on to Boxted on 13 November. It was the first of a series of units that passed through Greenham briefly as the newly created IXth sought to settle down. The 71st FW HQ with one of its Fighter Groups, the 386th, arrived on 13 January to work up on its P-47 Thunderbolts. Declared operational, the unit made its initial fighter sweep on 14 March 1944, but was transferred to Chilbolton the very next day as it had been decided that Greenham Common's future did not lie with fighters.

The first C-47s of the 438th TCG arrived on 16 March as part of the 53rd TCW, but the TCG personnel were totally demoralised. Since disembarking in the UK, they had been pushed from pillar to post by new orders and counter-orders, residing in turn at Grantham, then Langar. Their aircraft had eventually reached them at Langar in mid-February, but all supplies were at Barkston Heath.

With 'Lilly Bell II' 2100766 in the foreground, the C-47s of the 89th TCS, 438th TCG, await their next mission in 1944. (DWL collection)

They were just beginning to settle down when told to move to Greenham! Despite their travails, they were declared operational in April 1944, being fully trained in both paratroop drops and glider towing.

To accommodate the C-47s a number of loop or 'spectacle' hardstandings were built to supplement the earlier 'frying-pan' type, raising the total to fifty. Large marshalling areas of steel mesh tracking were laid at both ends of the main runway to accommodate the gliders before they were linked to their tugs for a stream take-off. In addition to the pair of T2 hangars, special long buildings were constructed to store and service the tow cables.

Having so successfully overcome its earlier problems, the 438th was honoured to be chosen to spearhead the airborne forces assault on 5/6 June. Watched by the IXth Commander, General Lewis Bereton, the first aircraft, called 'Birmingham Belle', flown by the Group Commander, Col John M. Donaldson, was airborne at 22.48 on the night of 5 June. The first drop of nearly 1,500 men of the 101st Airborne Division and subsequent Hadrian and Horsa glider tows earned the 438th a Distinguished Unit Citation. In common with other TCGs, the mission changed to resupply drops then, as landing strips became available, cargo deliveries were made, returning with casualties.

A visiting Ramsbury crew, with the Volunteer public house and Waco CG-4 gliders in the background. (J. Antrim via R. Day)

A detachment was sent to Italy in July 1944, dropping paratroopers on 15 August as part of the invasion of Southern France, following up with reinforcement in Hadrians. The Group was returned to full strength before taking part in Operation 'Market', ninety aircraft dropping elements of the 101st around Eindhoven on 17 September. A further eighty aircraft towed gliders to the area the following day without loss, although two gliders aborted and eleven C-47s had flak damage. Subsequent lifts on 19 September were less successful, with two aircraft lost and many gliders released inaccurately. Further resupply missions were flown including two to Bastogne during the German surprise offensive later called the 'Battle of the Bulge' in the Ardennes in mid-December 1944.

With the move to France in February 1945 by the 438th, Greenham was devoid of flying units. This situation continued after the end of the war as the airfield came under the control of Technical Training Command. No 13 Recruit Centre gave new recruits an eight-week induction course, better known as 'square-bashing'. Declared surplus, Greenham closed on 1 June 1946, although was periodically used as an Army training camp. Over the years of neglect the site became ever more derelict and local feeling was very supportive of returning the land to its original state. The heating-up of the Cold War put paid to that hope, for in 1951 it was announced that Greenham Common would be rebuilt as a USAF nuclear bomber base! At a local public meeting on 22 March 1951 it was resolved to oppose the extension of the airfield. Thousands signed a petition opposing the development, but to no avail. Even as the petition was being circulated, work was beginning to construct the longest military runway in Europe.

On 21 April 1951 the 7501st Air Base Squadron was formally designated as the administrator of Greenham. The 804th and 817th Engineer Aviation Battalion started earth-moving, grading, levelling and drainage, with a British civilian contractor constructing the runway and hardstandings, the cost of reconstruction being shared between the British and US Governments. All the wartime buildings, including the two wartime T2 hangars, were demolished and a large technical site built to the south of the runway, the A339 being diverted along the edge of the ridge and through to Packmoor Copse. A new control tower was built north of the new 11,000ft (3,048m) runway, laid over and beyond the existing one with parallel taxiways. The work and road diversion meant the demolition of two pubs and many houses, with forty-four families being rehoused.

In September 1953, with the disbanding of the 7501st ABS and the creation of the 3909th Air Base Group, Greenham Common was formally available for USAF B-47 Stratojets, although the runway had been put to good use earlier by a 614 Squadron Vampire, which landed short of fuel. The first operational use was in March 1954 when the 303rd Bombardment Wing deployed from Davis Monthan AFB. After the first aircraft had landed, an area of the runway was found to have deteriorated such that all the rest of the Wing was diverted to Fairford. The cause was found to be a re-routed stream that had reverted to its original course and undermined part of the runway. The trapped B-47 was eventually flown out off the shortened runway with the aid of JATO bottles and minimum fuel.

Substantial runway reconstruction, additional parking for up to fifty-seven aircraft and resurfacing to raise the levels followed, together with extra culverts and water outfall tanks located adjacent to the runway and taxiways to collect the surface water. Thus it was not until October 1956 that forty-five Stratojets of the 310th BW began SAC's first full ninety-day deployment to Greenham Common. The local residents were appalled at the noise. Even on landing, the B-47s operated at high power settings against the drag of a brake chute. When added to ground running, noise was almost unbearable. Opposition to Greenham grew, reaching a crescendo after a very nasty incident on 28 February 1958. A B-47E on take-off developed an emergency that led to the dropping of the wing fuel tanks, which struck a hangar and a parked B-47. The resulting fire burned for 16 hours, totally destroying the aircraft and hangar. Two USAF personnel died and eight more were injured.

The ninety-day deployments were changed to a three-week Reflex Alert rotation of the bomb wings, significantly reducing the noise and number of flights. However, concern was again heightened when the runway and dispersals were strengthened to cater for the eight-engined B-52 Stratofortress. Although they were to make occasional training visits, none were ever based at Greenham. Another visitor on 16 October 1958 occasioned much excitement. The four-jet supersonic B-58 Hustler was a rare sight in UK skies, but this aircraft, appropriately named 'Greased Lightning', had flown non-stop from Tokyo, 8,028 miles (12,929km) in just 8hr 35min 20sec with five in-flight refuellings. That aircraft is now preserved at the Strategic Air & Space Museum near Offutt AFB, Nebraska.

Convair B-58 Hustler, appropriately named 'Greased Lightning', visited Greenham Common on 16 March 1958. (DWL collection)

A change of SAC policy saw the end of Reflex operations on 1 April 1964 and the return of Greenham Common to RAF control on 1 July. It was the withdrawal of France from NATO and the subsequent loss of US bases that renewed American military interest in Greenham. It became a storage annex for Welford during January 1967 before being upgraded to a NATO standby base. A number of Reforger (ie reinforcement) exercises passed through before the F-111Es of the 20th TFW were resident for three months from March 1976 as the Upper Heyford runways were resurfaced.

In 1973 a major air show called the Embassy Air Tattoo was held at Greenham in aid of the RAFA, with the sponsorship of W. D. & H. O. Wills. This was repeated in 1974, but from 1976 it became the International Air Tattoo in cooperation with the RAF Benevolent Fund; in 1977 it went biennial until 1983, when developments on the airfield caused its transfer to RAF Fairford.

A request from the USAF that Greenham Common become a KC-135 air-refuelling base was revealed in March 1978 to the unsurprising concern of the locals. Work to resurface the runway and repair buildings went ahead, but the public outcry had an effect for the decision was overturned. However, the next military decision would not be reversed. Following the NATO decision in December 1979 to base Ground Launched Cruise Missiles (GLCM) in Europe, it was announced that Greenham Common would be one of the two British airfields to house the nuclear-armed missiles. A planned total of ninety-six missiles would be stored in six protected shelters together with their launchers and control centres, to be deployed out into the countryside prior to the outbreak of a Third World War.

Although nobody could complain about noise, this plan brought an immediate and sustained protest from the Campaign for Nuclear Disarmament (CND), particularly in the form of a Women's Peace Camp, which was set up at the main entrance to the base in October 1981. Although work to build the six nuclear bunkers and supporting infrastructure continued, the protests became more and more vociferous, culminating in an estimated 30,000 women arriving at Greenham on 12 December 1982 to 'Embrace the Base'. Linking arms, they entirely surrounded the 9 miles of perimeter fence. Later, on New Year's Day, the security fencing was cut and a photograph of women dancing on the weapon silos at dawn went round the world.

Despite this publicity, in May 1983 C-5 Galaxies began to deliver the equipment to form the 501st Tactical Missile Wing, whose missiles arrived from November 1983. On the site, which was known as GAMA (GLCM Alert & Maintenance Area), each of the six shelters contained two LCC (Launch Control Centres) and four TEL (Transporter Erector Launchers), which would leave the base in convoys to secret preset dispersal sites via local roads and the surrounding villages. The protests grew even stronger as the 501st began its practice operational deployments. At its peak, when there were some forty women's peace camps spread around the base perimeter, it is rumoured that the base commander had an annual budget for fence repairs of £750,000!

Greenham Common in May 1983, with construction of the GAMA site in progress to the lower right. (DWL collection)

The United States and the Soviet Union signed the Intermediate-range Nuclear Forces treaty in 1987, which eventually led to the removal of the last cruise missile from RAF Greenham Common in March 1991, the 501st TMW being inactivated on 4 June. Just over a year later the USAF returned Greenham to the MOD and in February 1993 the airfield was put up for sale, although the peace camps remained at the site until September 2000. In March 1997 the land was purchased by the Greenham Common Trust for £7 million and returned to a variety of civilian uses, including a business park, the New Greenham Park, utilising the many buildings in the former technical site.

Where once nuclear bombers taxied, the northern taxiway now takes dog-walkers. (DWL collection)

With a fire hydrant in the foreground, the boarded-up control tower awaits an uncertain future. (DWL collection)

Most of the buildings on what is now Greenham Park are in use, but the former Commissary awaits a tenant. (DWL collection)

Large areas of the Common have been returned to something approaching its former natural state. A major part of this has been the removal of the runway (except for one central section) and hardstandings, which were used as foundations in the construction of the Newbury by-pass. The control tower was retained but plans to turn it into a visitor centre have come to nothing, and it remains derelict and boarded-up.

The GAMA site was put on the market by the MOD in May 2003 with a guide price of £100,000. However, as English Heritage had designated the site as a Cold War Monument, it was not expected to sell. Surprisingly, Flying A Services, which had evolved from the former Warbirds of Great Britain following the death of its founder, Doug Arnold, paid £317,500 for the 74-acre (30-hectare) freehold site. Since then the owners have had a number of planning battles with the local authority over their plans for the former bunkers, which include a Cold War museum.

In October 2002 the Women's Peace Movement dedicated a commemorative site just outside the Main Street entrance to New Greenham Park. The site features a stone and steel spiral water feature and a 6-foot-high steel sculpture of a campfire, within a circle of seven Welsh standing stones enclosed within a garden setting – perhaps a fitting tribute to an airfield that performed its allotted tasks over its fifty years of existence and contributed much to the ending of both the Second World War and the Cold War.

Main features:
Runways: 110° 6,000ft x 150ft, 140° 4,200ft x 150ft, 030° 3,300ft x 150ft, concrete and tarmac. *Hangars:* two T2. *Hardstandings:* fifty multi-engined type. *Accommodation:* USAAF: 470 Officers, 1,898 enlisted men.

GUSTON ROAD, Kent – see DOVER (Guston Road)

HAMBLE, Hampshire

50°52N/01°19W 70ft asl; SU477077. 4 miles SE of Southampton on B3397

The problem when writing a history of Hamble is to first define 'which?' and 'when?', for there have been six distinct aviation sites on the small peninsula between Southampton Water and the River Hamble.

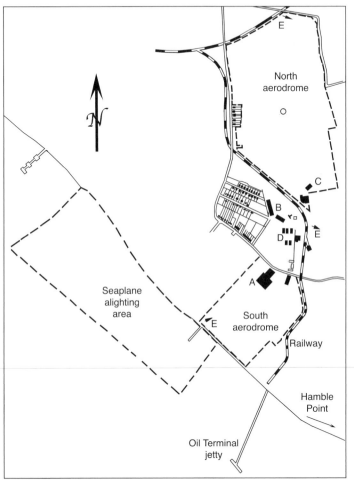

HAMBLE NORTH AND SOUTH AERODROMES: SEAPLANE ALIGHTING AREA, 1935

A Seaplane hangar
B Hangars
C Control Office
D Flying School Buildings
E Wind Indicator

This plan is an amalgamation of a number of drawings and includes information derived from the 3rd Edition of the Air Ministry's The Air Pilot, published towards the end of 1934. It illustrates three of the many flying locations that were called Hamble. What is labelled the Seaplane Hangar is the former A. V. Roe factory building. The Flying School buildings are those of AST, which from 1932 was the sole operator at Hamble. The School became No 3 E&RFTS in 1933.

The first Hamble was a simple landing ground known as Brown's Field, which aerial visitors to the Admiralty and Calshot used during 1913. Harry Hawker won the £500 Mortimer Singer prize for amphibians on 8 July 1913, flying the Sopwith Bat Boat No 1 from there, but the most notable visitor to fly from Brown's was Mr Winston Churchill, then First Lord of the Admiralty. According to *Flight* of 13 September 1913, he was flown for 15 minutes by Lt Spencer Grey in a Navy 90hp Austro-Daimler Sopwith tractor. The redoubtable Clementine also flew for about 10 minutes, despite her husband's concern.

In 1914 an incomplete HL-1 seaplane built by Luke & Co in partnership with the Hamble River Engineering Co at Hamble Point was exhibited at Olympia. The project came to nothing but the pair of sheds in which it was constructed were requisitioned by the Admiralty in December 1914, possibly for storage. They were offered to Fairey Aviation in 1915 to erect and test floatplanes that had been constructed at Hayes, Middlesex. The new occupant embarked on a major expansion, the slip was extended and new erecting shops built on substantial piers as the marshy land was prone to flooding. The first aircraft assembled and flown from Southampton Water were a number of Short 827s built as a sub-contract.

The attractions of the Hamble area had also reached the ears of A. V. Roe, as he was looking for a green-field site for a new factory to complement the ad hoc development in Manchester. A 100-acre (40.5-hectare) site was acquired on the edge of Southampton Water. The grand plan of a large open-plan factory and a 'Garden City' of 350 dwellings to house the staff was started in 1916. However, the plan fell foul of the Government's restrictions on building materials and work was stopped with only part of the factory and just twenty-four houses completed. The expected orders for the Avro 529 bomber and Avro 530 fighter failed to materialise and the factory spent most of the time in experimental work, although some 504s were built at the end of the war.

Virtually all of Fairey's wartime seaplanes were assembled and flown from Hamble, including the Campania, Baby and early Fairey IIIs. Because of the substantial increase in flying boat and seaplane production, in late 1917 the Admiralty authorised the construction of No 1 (Southern) Marine Acceptance Depot on a site between Hamble Point and the Avro factory. By September 1918 the twelve sheds (SU478061) and two slipways were partially complete, together with a railway spur, but work stopped after the Armistice. The sheds were demolished in 1919, the site becoming an oil tank farm served by the railway line – which were both extant in 2004.

Short 166 No 9751 is poised on the slipway at Hamble Point during 1916/17. (JMB/GSL collection)

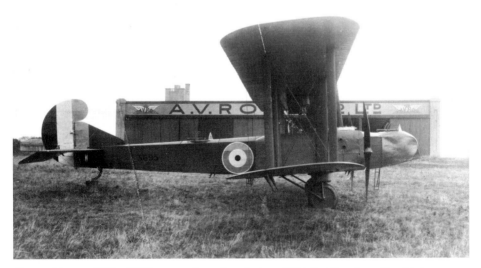

Powered by two 230hp BHP aero engines, the sole Avro 529A first flew from Hamble in October 1917. (JMB/GSL collection)

The end of hostilities brought a severe cutback in military orders for all aeroplane manufacturers and, unlike many companies, both Fairey and Avro just survived. Avro continued to develop variants of the 504 and new designs ranging from the tiny Baby up to the gargantuan Aldershot heavy bomber. One version had a 1,000hp Napier Cub installed – production models had to make do with just 650hp from a Rolls-Royce Condor. Test-flying started at Hamble in 1922 in the hands of 'Bert' Hinkler, but it was obvious that the aerodrome was too small for testing such large machines. In 1926 the company bought 200 acres (81 hectares) between Satchel Lane (now the B3397) and the railway to create a new aerodrome (SU 477077).

Avro at Hamble built the first two Cierva Autogiros based on the 504k fuselage, although a serious accident occurred in February 1927 when a rotor blade broke. The pilot, Frank Courtney, escaped serious injury. The original aerodrome was now restricted to autogiro testing and slipway access when all other landplane flying was moved to the new aerodrome now known as Hamble (North). When A. V. Roe sold his interests in the company to J. D. Siddeley of Sir W. G. Armstrong-Whitworth Aircraft in 1928, the design and development staff moved to Manchester and Cierva took over the Hamble design office, although the factory continued to build a few Avians, the autogiros and the Antelope.

Air Service Training Ltd was formed in 1931, taking over all the former Avro facilities at Hamble. The new company incorporated an Armstrong-Whitworth-operated flying school, which was transferred from Whitley at Coventry. Training recommenced in April as new hangars and buildings were still being erected on the southern boundary of Hamble (North). The fleet included Avians, Tutors, Atlases, two-seat Siskins and even a DH.9J. Instruction was given to civilian and military pilots from Britain and overseas.

When first Cierva, then the Hampshire Aero Club, moved to Eastleigh in 1932, it left AST in sole control of Hamble, its Reserve School becoming No 3 E&RFTS in 1933 as part of the Air Ministry's rationalisation plans. The School continued to operate with twelve Tutors and seventeen Cadets – all civilian-registered. November saw a rather different type join the fleet as a Calcutta was accepted to train Imperial Airways personnel. Two Cutty Sark amphibians and other redundant civil air transports were also acquired to facilitate navigation training. As AST continued to expand its remit to include advanced training, Harts, Hinds and even a few Battles were added to the E&RFTS fleet.

British Marine Aircraft Ltd was formed in February 1936 to build Sikorsky S-42 four-engined flying boats under licence. A new large factory was constructed on a 120-acre (48.6-hectare) site on

Looking north in 1934, Hamble South is in the foreground and Hamble North behind.
(A. M. Wood via P. H. T. Green collection)

An advertisement for AST appeared in Cobham's 1934 National Aviation Day Display souvenir
programme. (DWL collection)

THE LEADING AERONAUTICAL TRAINING CENTRE
OF THE WORLD

From the moment of its foundation in 1931 Air Service Training Ltd.
has set the standard in flying and ground training of all kinds. Its
personnel, premises and equipment are unequalled by any other
school in the country. Its courses extend from several years to
a matter of a few days and include the most expert tuition in Flying,
Engineering, Navigation and Wireless.

AIR SERVICE TRAINING LIMITED, HAMBLE, SOUTHAMPTON

AST79

The 1936 Christmas card from AST featured its aircraft and personnel. (via P. H. T. Green collection)

the shores of Southampton Water (SU469072) to the west of Hamble (North) aerodrome. The venture came to nothing and construction of the first incomplete aircraft was abandoned. However, H. P. Folland, the former chief designer at Gloster, was appointed as Managing Director as Imperial Airways began to use the main erecting shop for maintenance on its Short Empire flying boats. With sub-contract work coming from other companies, mainly Supermarine, the company was renamed Folland Aircraft Ltd.

Fairey had retained an interest on Hamble Point but the original Admiralty sheds were destroyed by fire in 1932 and replaced shortly afterwards. The Fairey Seafox, an attractive floatplane, conceived to operate from light cruisers, was designed and built at Hamble. Ordered in 1934, the first prototype flew on 27 May 1936 and a total of sixty-four were manufactured. On 13 December 1939 a Seafox from HMS *Ajax* participated in the Battle of the River Plate, which eventually resulted in the sinking of the German battleship *Admiral Graf Spee*.

The virtually unused former Avro factory was taken over by Armstrong-Whitworth to build the new Ensign airliners as its premises at Coventry were preoccupied with Whitley production. The transfer of jigs and tooling delayed production and it wasn't until 23 January 1938 that the first aircraft flew from Hamble (North) for test-flying to be undertaken at Baginton. A total of eleven machines had been built by the outbreak of the Second World War.

At AST, the unit became No 3 EFTS as Volunteer Reserve training ceased. Work was concentrated on camouflaging the buildings and airfield, siting gun positions and providing blackout curtains to the buildings. The fleet of thirty-two Avro Cadets were also camouflaged but kept their civil registrations. Before ab initio training resumed in November, the school trained new flying instructors, bringing the total to twenty-nine QFIs.

As the final Ensign left Hamble, a production line of Albemarle bombers was established using components from other factories in the Group. The first was completed in early 1940 and transferred to the aerodrome for engine and taxi trials. The first flight on 20 March 1940 was nearly a disaster when a fast taxi run had to be converted to a take-off as insufficient runway was left to stop safely. A further 10 feet (3 metres) was added to the wingspan before a second flight was attempted. Like the Ensign, test flying was carried out at Coventry.

On 1 June 1940 a section of No 3 Ferry Pilots Pool was set up at Hamble to cater for the increasing number of Spitfires being built in the region. Training was becoming more difficult with ever-increasing numbers of barrage balloons. A raid by a single He 111 on 12 July was the final impetus to move the EFTS to Watchfield on 20 July. In addition to its Spitfire sub-contracting, Folland was now manufacturing Blenheim and Beaufort parts, and these were followed by components for Beaufighters, Mosquitoes, Wellingtons and Sunderlands. At AST a similar path was being followed as it converted

Spitfires to Seafires and Hurricanes to Sea Hurricane 'Catafighters' to combat the Fw 200 Condor in the crucial Battle of the Atlantic. The company also became the country's largest fighter repair organisation, some 3,400 Spitfires having been repaired by the war's end.

The ATA set-up at Hamble became No 15 Ferry Pilots Pool in July 1941. Women pilots were a novelty at first, but the appointment of Miss Margaret Gore cemented their acceptance and gradually the Pool became virtually an all-women unit. By the summer of 1942 the unit had thirty pilots, two adjutants, maps officer, typists, drivers and canteen staff, plus twenty engineers to maintain the fleet of five Ansons and six Argus taxis that ferried pilots between aerodromes.

With so many manufacturing facilities together with RAF and Fleet Air Arm stations in the area, the variety of types they flew was amazing: Walrus, Albacore, Roc, Gladiator and Tomahawk, in addition to twins like the Blenheim, Oxford, Anson, Whitley, Hampden and Wellington. When Miss Gore was cleared to fly the Hudson, there was virtually nothing twin-engined that the Hamble 'girls' could not tackle. This critical work constituted the main flying activity at Hamble for the remainder of the war, until peace brought the disbanding of No 15 FPP.

Folland modified a Spitfire VB to a floatplane configuration, and it was flown in April 1945 before being shipped to Egypt for trials. However, immediate post-war aviation sub-contracts were now very limited, and in 1946 the factory began to produce a range of other products including the Folland Pony electric truck and the Power Master domestic refrigerator. 1946 also saw the return to their place of birth of the surviving Ensigns, but after a year they were all broken up. Hamble's recovery was slow, but the arrival of the Southampton UAS in early 1947 gave AST a contract for the servicing of its Tiger Moths. Flying training by AST for both British and overseas students began in the summer and No 14 RFS was formed on 15 August 1947 with a dozen Tiger Moths.

Down on the Point, Fairey Aviation had also been committed to repair and sub-contract work during the war; in 1945 the facilities were transferred to Fairey Marine, although aviation repair work continued. In 1948 production of ten Fairey Primer light trainers commenced, although only two were completed, both being dismantled by 1951. One of the last aviation tasks undertaken by Fairey at Hamble was refurbishing Fairey Swordfish G-AJVH, which continues to fly with the Royal Navy Historic Flight as LS326.

Hamble's specialisation in sub-contract work continued into the 1950s. At AST a number of Lancasters, Lancastrians and Lincolns were converted to jet engine test beds, the final example, a Lancaster, was delivered to Sweden in 1951. The company also maintained and refurbished the flying boat fleet of Aquila Airways; initially these were ex-BOAC Sunderlands, but gradually they were replaced by Solents. In addition to the serviceable aircraft, many others were stored on the slipway or moored in Southampton Water as reserves or to provide spares. Although Aquila was operating four Solents in 1957, they were becoming completely uneconomic and the airline shut down in the UK in September 1958.

It was Folland that attracted the most sub-contracts, building control surfaces for the Brabazon and wings for the Dove, Chipmunk and Vampire, but the retirement in 1951 of Henry Folland due to ill-health brought a most innovative designer to the company as Managing Director. Edward 'Teddy' Petter had been responsible for a series of fighters at Westland before moving to English Electric, where the Canberra and the Lightning's predecessor, the P.1, were his designs. However, his mounting concern at the ever-increasing size and complexity of fighters found an outlet at Folland. Construction of a private-venture prototype fighter called the Midge started in 1953, although its first flight on 11 August 1954 was made at Boscombe Down.

Although very successful, the performance of the Midge was limited by its Viper engine, but a new Bristol Siddeley engine, the Orpheus, promised much more power. With Government support, the Gnat was born and, like its predecessor, made its initial flight at Boscombe in July 1955. Although fighters were sold to India and Finland, the largest user of the Gnat was the Royal Air Force, which bought 105 two-seat versions as its standard advanced trainer. All were built at Hamble, although assembled and tested at Folland's Chilbolton airfield. The Gnat equipped the famous Red Arrows from it inception until 1978.

When in 1949 AST gained the contract to operate an Air Signals School for the Navy, Ansons from the former 783 Squadron transferred from Lee-on-Solent before the School's closure in November 1953. The number of Ansons had further increased when No 1 Basic Air Navigation School was created in January 1951 to teach navigation to National Servicemen, but this also closed in June 1953. Finally No 14 RFS was disbanded in August 1953, which made that a very difficult year for AST. Its civilian training contracts were slightly increased by the addition of Chipmunks to its fleet, joined in August 1955 by Hiller 12Bs and by Piper Apaches two years later. Southampton UAS also converted to Chipmunks, and in 1958 No 2 Air Experience Flight was created to cater for local Air Cadet Squadrons.

A rationalisation of the Hawker Siddeley group led in 1960 to the transfer of the AST school facilities to a new College of Air Training to provide aircrew for BOAC and BEA. The Chipmunks were supplemented by Piper Cherokees from November 1966 and Beech Barons replaced the Apaches two years later. However, in 1970 the Barons moved to Hurn, leaving Hamble to concentrate on primary training. The fluctuating requirements of the State airlines were difficult to forecast, so a 1975 contract from the RAF was most welcome. The service had a need for seventy-five pilots annually who were trained in asymmetric and airways flying. To cater for this the Barons returned from Hurn to be flown by RAF pilots.

The RAF contract was completed by 1977 and AST was again relying on British Airways contracts, which were becoming rarer. By the end of the decade it was obvious that the courses were becoming uneconomic and in 1982 BA cancelled its contracts. The college and airfield were sold to a consortium, Hampshire Airfield Properties Ltd. A new subsidiary, Specialist Flying Training Ltd, carried on with two Chipmunks and six Barons, the rest of the fleet being put into store. Southampton UAS had converted to the Bulldog in 1974 but, together with No 2 AEF and its Chipmunks, transferred to Hurn in 1979, severing the last military link at Hamble.

At Folland, the company had become part of the Hawker-Siddeley group, so work on the Gnat was supplemented by more sub-contracts from other parts of the consortium, including Avro 748 wings, Trident tailplanes and wings, and the Harrier T2 rear fuselage. Before the project's cancellation in 1965, Hamble had commenced manufacture of the wings for the Hawker P.1154 supersonic Harrier. The creation of British Aerospace in April 1977 further increased the flexible Folland factory's range of work.

Over on Hamble airfield, the situation became desperate after Specialist Flying Training transferred all its activities to Carlisle during 1983. The College of Air Training ceased trading on 14 February 1984, and thirty-two aircraft were sold by tender. Other assets were auctioned in mid-May and the land went to a property developer. Houses were built on much of the southern part of the airfield, but the history of the area was acknowledged in the naming of roads, including Aquila Way leading to Tudor Close and Spitfire Way to Cirrus Close. It is still possible to imagine Hamble buzzing with Tiger Moths as much of the former aerodrome is still open land – long may it continue to be so.

The former Folland Factory has gone through a number of metamorphoses. Aerostructures Hamble Ltd, a wholly-owned BAe subsidiary, was created in January 1989 when the primary workload involved Airbus wing sub-assemblies and Hawk fuselages. More recently an order was won for wing components for the C-17 Globemaster III airlifter. In 2000 the factory became part of Smiths Aerospace, which itself was acquired in January 2007 by the US Aerospace giant General Electric. Through all these changes, a Folland Gnat painted in Red Arrows livery proudly guards the gate.

The former Fairey sheds are still in nautical use at Hamble Point, but building boats not seaplanes. (DWL collection)

Ensign Way Business Park now occupies the area where the Avro and later the Armstrong-Whitworth factories stood. In 2003 a large former hangar workshop stood at SU475068, but apart from its name there was little to indicate that Ensigns and Albemarles had been built there. Moving south-east, School Lane leads to the Hamble Point Marina, a boating heaven, but for the discerning visitor a line of four sheds being used for marine activities are obviously former pre-Second World War Fairey hangars.

If all this aviation archaeology has created a thirst or hunger, return to Hamble Lane where, opposite the entrance to the General Electric (Folland) site, can be found the Harrier public house. You cannot miss the pub sign, which illustrates three Sea Harriers, fuselages of which were built just over the road.

Main features of Hamble (North aerodrome) c1934:
Landing area dimensions: N-S 3,600ft, NE-SW 2,100ft, E-W 1,860ft, SE-NW 2,700ft, grass. *Hangars:* two steel and corrugated iron, 300ft x 75ft and 175ft x 70ft. *Hardstandings:* not applicable.

HAMMERWOOD, East Sussex

51°08N/00°03E 340ft asl; TQ440391. 3 miles E of East Grinstead off A264

Very well camouflaged, being totally surrounded by woodland, the Hammerwood or East Grinstead airstrip was built on land belonging to Bowers Farm. A pair of landing strips was laid out and the first occupier was No 660 Squadron, 84 Group, which transferred from Andover on 20 November 1943. The HQ was established in Hammerwood House and the Auster III dispersed around the airfield. As an AOP squadron, No 660 operated detached flights to Hoyte and Ashington and practised liaison with local Army units for the future Second Front.

The Gipsy-engined Mk IIIs were replaced by Lycoming-powered Auster AOP IVs in February 1944 in preparation for the move to Westenhangar the following month. The replacement squadron on 23 April was No 659, which was already equipped with the AOP IV. Liaison work intensified through spring and early summer as D-Day came and went. Three days later 659 Squadron left for Old Sarum and then on to Normandy.

Like all the temporary airstrips set up in preparation for the invasion of Europe, Hammerwood was returned to its former owner and now it is impossible to find any evidence of its wartime role.

Main features:
Runways: grass. *Hangars:* none. *Accommodation:* none

Lycoming-powered Auster AOP IVs were flown by No 659 Squadron from Hammerwood in early 1944. (MAP via DWL collection)

HARTFORD BRIDGE, Hampshire – see BLACKBUSHE

HAWKINGE (Folkestone), Kent

51°06N/01°09E 540ft asl; TR213395. 2 miles N of Folkestone on A260

As I stand on the western boundary of Hawkinge beside one of the Pickett-Hamilton Forts placed to defend the beautiful grass airfield stretching out in front of me, I think that I can hear the pop-popping of a throttled-back Merlin as one of Hawkinge's fighters returns early from its sortie. Sadly, the illusion is broken as I realise that the engine is that of a tractor behind me in the next field and, looking to the left, the absence of the First World War Belfast hangars makes me remember that it is September 1987, not July 1940.

In the summer of 1940 Hawkinge could not have been more in the front line, sitting on top of Kent's North Downs with the coast just 4 miles away and visible from France on a clear day. The station's obvious vulnerability was underlined on Monday 12 August when a Tannoy announcement roused the station to life at 05.00hrs. Not long after 07.30 the personnel of the Dover Observer Corps post reported large formations of enemy aircraft coming from France. For the first time in the Battle their targets were fighter airfields and the vital RDF (radar) stations. Lympne was severely damaged in the early attacks, and the RDF stations of Dover, Rye and Pevensey were hit. By noon, when No 32 Squadron's Hurricanes were sent from their Biggin Hill base to Hawkinge, five radar stations were out of action and Fighter Command was forced to resort to standing patrols.

This was the Battle's busiest day so far, but Hawkinge appeared to have escaped the attentions of the Luftwaffe. This all changed around 16.45 when, eluding the patrolling 32 Squadron, a formation of fifteen Ju 88s from II/KG76 split into two groups; half headed for Lympne, but the remainder caught Hawkinge completely by surprise. Although the first formation created bomb craters over the airfield, the second wave of three attackers dropped their bombs among the station's buildings on the west side of the airfield with devastating effect. Hangar No 3 had received a number of direct hits causing it to partially collapse, and the main equipment store had been virtually obliterated, as had two former married-quarters houses. Casualties totalled twelve, with five dead.

No 32 Squadron had been mixing it with a formation of Messerschmitts over Dover, and was now desperately short of fuel. The station's telephones were out, but fortunately the Watch Office and its wireless network still worked. The Squadron was warned of the state of the airfield and some were able to return to Biggin Hill, but for six Hurricanes it was Hawkinge or nothing. Pilot Officer Barton's combat-damaged aircraft failed to make the airfield and was destroyed in the crash-landing; fortunately Barton survived, unhurt. Amid the smoke, craters and possibly unexploded bombs, Squadron Leader Mike Crossley brought his surviving fighters in for a nerve-wracking landing, but incredibly all made it safely. Suddenly, from the north-east, yet another formation of Junkers Ju 88s shattered the already overstrained nerves of the pilots and station personnel. As the station Tannoy wailed out its warning, bullets from the front gunners forced the airmen to dive for cover, and simultaneously No 5 (Handley Page) hangar disappeared under a direct hit, with debris being thrown all over the village. It was all over in a few minutes; incredibly, all five Hurricanes had escaped untouched, but it took some time for anyone to emerge from whatever cover they had found. Hawkinge had had its baptism of fire; by Herculean overnight efforts, the airfield was operational the following morning for a three-Hurricane dawn patrol.

The ordeal continued, for on Thursday 15 August the Luftwaffe again targeted the RAF's airfields and RDF stations. No 501 (County of Gloucester) Auxiliary Air Force Squadron deployed from its Gravesend base to the battered forward airfield of Hawkinge, and at 11.00hrs a formation of more than 100 enemy machines consisting of sixty Ju 87 Stukas with a strong fighter escort of Messerschmitt Bf 109s was detected by radar. No 501's Hurricanes were scrambled to meet this armada, which split, aiming for the Dover RDF station, Lympne and Hawkinge. No 501 Squadron, together with the Spitfires of No 54 from Hornchurch, caught up with the retreating Luftwaffe and shot down at least five Stukas with the loss of two fighters from each squadron to the escorting Bf 109s.

The afternoon continued this hectic pattern; formations of Heinkel He 111 and Dornier Do 17 bombers attacked from 10,000 feet. Fortunately the station's buildings survived this attack, but the already much scarred grass airfield was further pock-marked with bomb craters. This time a Home Defence detachment and local unemployed assisted the weary defenders as they filled in yet more holes in the once pristine Kent airfield.

All this was some thirty years in the future when 'flying' first came to the peaceful Kent village of Hawkinge in the form of a secretive Dutchman called W. B. Megone. Over a four-year period from around 1910, Megone lived in Bijou Cottage on Barnhouse Lane, to the west of the village, and rented a field from Lord Radnor. He erected a substantial corrugated steel shed in which he designed, built and constantly modified a pusher biplane, nicknamed 'Mayfly' by the sceptical villagers. Despite the best efforts of his assistant Victor Hunt, who arrived during 1912 in response to an advertisement in *Flight* magazine, the outlandish machine failed to achieve more than a few hops. In September 1914, a month after the outbreak of the First World War, Megone vanished as mysteriously as he had arrived, amid much speculation as to his motives for spending four years in rural Kent. The popular local conclusion was that he was a German spy, reinforced when Gotha bombers attacked Folkestone in 1917!

The demand for Royal Flying Corps aircraft in France grew from 1914, and the original jumping-off point of Swingate Down above Dover was quickly inadequate. Other suitable sites were sought, and 166 acres (67 hectares) of Lord Radnor's estate (including the field used by Megone) were requisitioned by the War Office. The records of No 1 Squadron RFC quote Folkestone (as the site was then called) as the departure point when the Squadron flew to France in early March 1915, and Nos 7 and 8 Squadrons used Folkestone during April. It is possible that the airfield they all used was Capel, which was also known as Folkestone and was brought into use by the Royal Naval Air Service as an anti-submarine airship station around this time. This is unlikely, as the RNAS rarely mixed aeroplanes and airships on the same station, especially one in such an early stage of construction. It would also be unlikely to welcome RFC squadrons as lodgers, even for a short time. However, a very reputable source suggests that it was not until September 1915 that the RFC first occupied Folkestone (Hawkinge), when the accommodation consisted of tents for the men and three canvas Bessonneau hangars for the aircraft.

During 1916 the flying area was expanded to offer a landing area with maximum dimensions of 2,400ft (732m) east-west and 2,000ft (610m) in a north-south direction. To aid safe arrival in France, two large-diameter compass bearing circles were cut in the grass and filled with chalk. As the aircraft on delivery overflew and aligned these two circles, the compass bearing led directly to the Acceptance Park at St Omer. Incredibly, one of these circles could still be detected from the air as late as the mid-1980s.

In January 1917 the airfield was officially renamed, becoming the Aeroplane Despatch Section, Hawkinge, under Headquarters 21st Wing RFC. The construction of permanent buildings also began in 1917 with the standard brick-built General Service (GS) sheds (now known as Belfast hangars) replacing the wooden-framed Bessonneaus. The original unsurfaced Barnhouse Lane could no longer cope with the construction traffic and became a virtually impassable morass; it was metalled and became the new Aerodrome Road.

The construction programme continued on both sides of Backhouse Lane, the buildings to the south virtually swallowing the whole of Megone's flying ground with a total of no fewer than nine GS sheds. From west to east, they were one double-bay (Hangar No 1), two triple-bays (Hangars Nos 2 and 3) and a single-bay (Hangar No 4). In addition, in late 1918 two large Handley Page-type sheds (Hangars Nos 5 and 6) were erected at the eastern end of the site nearer to Hawkinge village. These were designed to hold up to twelve Handley Page 0/400 twin-engined bombers with their wings folded. The continued expansion led to Hawkinge becoming No 12 Aircraft Acceptance Park (SE Area), and the airfield became the point from which all RFC aircraft would depart to France, with the consequent run-down of the Lympne AAP.

The expansion work was virtually complete when the 11 November Armistice finally silenced the guns on the Western Front. For a time the work continued, but by February 1919 the flow of aircraft was reversed as squadrons began to return home with their aircraft. In a matter of a few months the wartime RAF, created in April 1918 by the merger of the RFC and the RNAS, had contracted to a mere shadow of its former self. Some duties, however, remained for the peacetime RAF to fulfil, and Hawkinge, unlike so many airfields, still had a future in Britain's youngest service.

The closeness of the station to the continent enabled Hawkinge to be part of the earliest commercial use of the aeroplane. In response to a desperate request from the Belgian Government, Air Transport & Travel, a pioneer British airline, organised an airlift between Hawkinge and Ghent. Flown by RAF pilots in converted RAF DH.9s, the service, which began on 1 February 1919, carried urgently needed food, clothing and other essentials. A month later the first formal airmail link between England and the continent was inaugurated, carrying mail destined for British servicemen in occupied Germany. No 120 Squadron arrived at Hawkinge on 20 February to undertake this role, linking with an existing continental military mail service. On 1 March 1919 four of its aircraft, with the rear cockpits converted to enclosed mail compartments, carried more than twenty mailbags to France. Mail totalling more than 90 tons had been delivered without loss and with no casualties by the end of August, when the run-down of the Army in Germany led to closure of the service. With the move of 120 Squadron to Lympne, the AAP also closed in July 1919 and the station became inactive. However, a belated recognition of the potentially strategically important location of Hawkinge in the future air defence of Great Britain ushered in the role for which it would became internationally renowned.

No 25 Squadron, formed in 1915, had ended the war flying DH.4 day-bombers before officially disbanding on 31 January 1920. The following day, elements of the Squadron arrived at Hawkinge and officially took on charge all the aircraft then in store. With a potential strength of 127 Sopwith Snipe fighters, thirty-five Handley Page heavy bombers, including twenty-one giant 126ft (38.4m)-wingspan four-engined V/1500s, a single Bristol F2B Fighter and a pair of Avro 504K trainers, the Squadron only had sufficient cadre to operate the two Avros. As personnel numbers steadily increased and the best of the Snipes were selected, No 25(F) officially reformed on 26 April 1920 and was, for a time, the sole fighter squadron in the RAF. Thus began an association with Hawkinge that was to last eighteen years, albeit with a twelve-month deployment to Turkey from September 1922. On the return of No 25 in October 1923, the Squadron began to apply its unit markings (parallel black bands) to the fuselage and upper wings of the aircraft.

The standard two-squadron fighter wing was established at Hawkinge on 1 April 1924 when No 17(F) Squadron was re-formed, also flying the reliable Sopwith 7F.1 Snipe with its powerful 230hp Bentley BR2 rotary engine. The Snipe was, by the mid-1920s, becoming obsolete and in 1924 No 25 became the first RAF squadron to become fully equipped with the Gloster Grebe, which it showed off during the 1925 Hendon Pageant. Hawkinge finally bade farewell to the Snipe in March 1926 when No 17 became the second RAF squadron to receive the Hawker Woodcock.

With No 17 Squadron being officially a night-fighter unit and 25 its day-fighter partner, Hawkinge was now a fully fledged fighter station of the new Air Defence of Great Britain Command, much later to be better known as Fighter Command. However, the two-squadron status was only to last until October 1926 when No 17 was transferred to Upavon. With Hawkinge again a single-squadron station, No 25's Squadron Leader became the Station Commander. His duties included responsibility for the Wessex Area Storage Unit, formed in early 1926 and initially located in the twin Handley Page hangars. Very similar to Hawkinge's wartime role as an Aircraft Acceptance Park, the Storage Unit was charged with accepting new aircraft from the manufacturers, storing them and sometimes incorporating modifications before issue to the squadrons.

The lifestyle for many peacetime fighter pilots was distinctly leisurely, consisting primarily of flying practice, including aerobatics, formation flying, air-to-air and air-to-ground firing. Although much of the latter was practised over the nearby Lydd and Hythe ranges, occasionally Hawkinge itself was used. The potentially hazardous occupation of a fighter pilot was emphasised on 9 December 1926 when, during an exercise firing at a ground target, Flying Officer Purvis crashed fatally near Terlingham Manor Farm, his Grebe bursting into flames on impact.

From February 1929 the Grebes began to be supplanted by the Armstrong-Whitworth Siskin IIIa; the process was complete by July 1929 when, led by Squadron Leader Payne, No 25 took its new fighters to RAF Sutton Bridge near The Wash for its annual training exercise.

The spare hangarage at Hawkinge meant that it was a popular venue for summer camps by Auxiliary and Reserve squadrons from 1930 onwards. One of the first such visitors was No 602 (City of Glasgow) Squadron, which amassed no fewer than 451 hours on its Westland Wapitis during its camp.

The temporary buildings erected during the Great War were becoming inadequate and, as part of the expansion of the RAF, a two-year reconstruction programme began in 1931. The new buildings included a NAAFI, messes for both Officers and Sergeants, an Airmen's Dining Hall, two barrack blocks facing the original parade ground, and a number of married quarters.

In February 1932 Hawkinge became the second station, after nearby Tangmere, to receive the elegant and effective Hawker Fury I. With its 525hp Rolls-Royce Kestrel engine, the Fury was the first RAF fighter in squadron service to exceed 200mph. No 25 soon applied its black squadron markings together with, for the first time, the squadron's 'Hawk on a Gauntlet' symbol, marking its long association with Hawkinge, which was painted on the aircraft's fin. In December 1936 No 25 Squadron became the first unit to re-equip with the improved Fury II, which, with a 640hp Kestrel VI, could attain 223mph at 16,000 feet and climb to nearly 30,000 feet.

Like all RAF airfields of the 1930s, Hawkinge was available for use by private pilots with permission of the Officer Commanding. The 1934 edition of *The Air Pilot* recorded that the grass landing field gently sloped down towards the centre with maximum dimensions between 2,100ft (640m) and 2,400ft (732m). Caution was urged to avoid three radio masts, 70 feet high, on the north-west side of the airfield, and high-tension cables to the south-west, owing to the 'prevalence of sea mists and low-hanging clouds'. The RAF obviously did not fly on Wednesday and Saturday afternoons or on Sundays, since the private aviator was warned to expect sheep grazing on the landing area during those periods.

On 7 August 1933 No 504 (County of Nottingham) was at Hawkinge on summer camp. Flight Lieutenant Hartridge and his navigator were approaching over the village to land when the engine of their Hawker Horsley bomber failed, and Hartridge skilfully dropped the aircraft on the roof of the nearest single-bay hangar. As the crew scrambled down via a hastily provided ladder, petrol leaking into the hangar ignited; No 4 hangar, used by Wessex Area Storage Unit, was totally gutted and the six Blackburn Darts stored inside were destroyed. The station had also lost No 6, the more southerly of the two Handley Page hangars, probably before this time, but sources are very unclear as to what happened and when.

Despite this reduction, the station still had more hangarage than most airfields of the period, and with the expansion of the RAF it was inevitable that Hawkinge would get back its second squadron. When it arrived on 3 November 1935, it wasn't fighters – it was No 2 (AC) Squadron and its Audaxes, which were to be accommodated in No 3 hangar.

A flight of Audaxes depart from Hawkinge in about 1936. (NA3T)

During 1937 Hawkinge became solely a flying station as, after eleven years, the Wessex Area Storage Unit finally closed. In October No 25 received the unwelcome news that it was becoming a two-seat fighter squadron; the Fury IIs were flown to Catterick and exchanged for the Hawker Demons of No 41 Squadron. The second-hand Demons were old and showed distinct signs of decay; following detailed inspection, three aircraft were grounded due to structural corrosion. In November 1937 No 2 (AC) Squadron was re-equipped with the 800hp twenty-four-cylinder Napier Dagger-engined Hawker Hector.

The RAF was now preparing for the conflict that appeared more and more inevitable. 25 Squadron bade farewell to its unloved Demons in June 1938, albeit for yet another squadron's cast-offs. But at least they were single-seat fighters – the Gloster Gladiators of No 56 Squadron. No 2 Squadron began to receive the Westland Lysander in September 1938; the task was complicated by the Munich Crisis, when all leave was cancelled and camouflage applied to both aircraft and buildings. During the crisis No 25 had been operating from its war station of Northolt, but returned on 10 October 1938 to face a new role and yet another change of aircraft. The Demon had been bad enough for this proud fighter squadron, but now it was to be a night-fighter squadron equipped with the Blenheim 1F, a stop-gap fighter conversion of the Bristol Blenheim bomber! Shortly after the station had hosted what was to be the last Empire Air Day, it was decided that Hawkinge was too small for the safe operation of the relatively large twin-engined Blenheim. On 22 August, after an association of more than nineteen years, 25 Squadron left for Hornchurch.

At the declaration of war on 3 September 1939, No 2 (AC) Squadron was posted to France and for a time the sounds of aero engines over Hawkinge were replaced by the tramp of marching boots of No 3 Recruit Training Pool, Training Command. Fortunately, it was recognised that this was an indignity too far for a proud fighter station and, just in time for Christmas, a detachment of No 3 Squadron brought its Hawker Hurricanes to Hawkinge. The latter half of January brought heavy snowfalls and Hawkinge's airmen struggled to keep the airfield open. The recruits finally left in February 1940 and the station reverted to Fighter Command. The Hurricanes soon left and were briefly replaced by the Lysanders of No 16 Squadron before they joined the other Lysander units in France on 14 April 1940. Also in February one of Hawkinge's hangars became home to the Queen Bees of the Pilotless Aircraft Section.

One of Hawkinge's more interesting non-flying units also arrived in early 1940 when a listening post was set up in a disused airfield hut to monitor German radio transmissions. As the team grew, it moved into Maypole Cottage in the village, but after the fall of France moved again to a less vulnerable location. This was the start of the famous 'Y' service, which provided the raw material without which the Enigma code breakers of Station 'X' (Bletchley Park) could never have carried out the counterintelligence work that did so much to shorten the war.

Hawkinge now entered a spell as a forward satellite station: detachments from No 17 Squadron (Hurricanes) and No 25 (Blenheim fighters) both used the airfield to refuel and rearm after flying standing patrols over the rapidly changing front line. As communications broke down in France, a rear HQ was established at Hawkinge by AVM C. H. B. Blount, which began to collate reports from returning aircrew and the inputs from the Y service. This work became a vital part of the success of Operation 'Dynamo', which began on 27 May as Allied troops were evacuated from Dunkirk.

Prior to the miracle of Dunkirk, Hawkinge, like all South Coast airfields, became clogged with a mass of escaping RAF aircraft, most of which were hurriedly refuelled, repaired as necessary and flown to airfields further inland. Incredibly, offensive sorties by Hawker biplanes were still being flown from Hawkinge when No 613 (City of Manchester) Squadron sent six Hectors to attack German guns surrounding besieged Calais. Not only did they all return unscathed but a second attack on 26 May was also without loss. A third operation on 27 May saw 613 Squadron Lysanders escorted by Hectors drop supplies from just 200 feet to the beleaguered defenders of Calais. Yet again the German flak failed to gain a victim, although one Hector crash-landed near Dover. In early June the station became a forward airfield in the Biggin Hill Sector.

With the might of the Luftwaffe soon to be turned on the British Isles, the defences of Hawkinge needed urgent strengthening. To protect the fighters, six dispersal fighter pens were built; three in Killing Wood behind the White Horse Inn in the south-east corner, the others on the opposite side of the aerodrome across Gibraltar Lane. The more immediate defences had consisted of eight 0.303-inch Lewis guns manned by troops of 'E' Company of the 6th Buffs Regiment; these were supplemented by five 20mm guns, four Hispano and one Oerlikon, which had been salvaged from a sunken ship. A few Army Bofors were located off the aerodrome and towards the end of June the Parachute & Cable (PAC) device was installed. Derived from naval equipment, the PAC fired rockets to some 600 feet, each trailing a wire that then parachuted to earth; it was, however, largely ineffective. The anti-invasion defences were also improved by the digging of more slit trenches, the building of pillboxes and three Pickett-Hamilton hydraulic retractable forts were installed. Off the airfield, nearby fields were obstructed by a forest of wooden poles and road blocks were set up, together with demolition charges on strategic installations.

Initial attacks by the Luftwaffe began in early July and were concentrated on the Channel convoys in order to bring Fighter Command into combat. A relay of squadrons used Hawkinge on a daily basis as the intensity of fighting increased. No 79 Squadron was on standby on 7 July, and took off at 14.30 to intercept some forty Dornier Do 17s that were bombing a large convoy. They lost their CO, Squadron Leader Joslin, and two more pilots within two days, and on 10 July the remains of the Squadron were withdrawn from the fighting. A succession of Hurricane and Spitfire fighter squadrons, including Nos 501, 32, 72, 64 and 610, operated from Hawkinge over the next few weeks, and casualties mounted as the squadrons were frequently attacked while climbing to intercept. One of the worst days for a Hawkinge squadron took place on 19 July. The unfortunate unit was No 141 Squadron, which flew the Boulton-Paul Defiant, one of only two such squadrons in the RAF operating the gun-turret fighter. Unlike its sister squadron, No 264, which had claimed no fewer than thirty-seven victories over Dunkirk, 141 Squadron had yet to see combat. The Squadron was scrambled at 12.30, and was surprised by some twenty Bf 109s of the Richthofen Geschwader. As the pilots desperately tried to manoeuvre to allow their gunners to bring their guns to bear, four Defiants were quickly shot down for the loss of one Messerschmitt and all the rest had been hit, some critically. Of the nine Defiants that left Hawkinge, only four got back, two of which were written off on landing. With seven aircraft destroyed, four pilots and six gunners dead, No 141 Squadron had virtually ceased to exist after just one combat.

The Luftwaffe changed its tactics in August to target the Chain Home RDF stations and the airfields of the South East, and the devastating results of the first significant raid on Hawkinge have already been described. Six days later, on 18 August, a low-level formation of six Do 17s escorted by Bf 109s attacked again; no bombs were dropped, but the airfield and its surroundings were thoroughly strafed. On 24 August No 32 Squadron, operating from Hawkinge, lost five Hurricanes including that of the CO, Squadron Leader Mike Crossley; fortunately all the pilots survived. The airfield was the primary target again on Sunday 1 September, when a small formation dropped eight 125kg bombs, hitting the already damaged No 3 hangar and another small building.

No 72 Squadron arrived from Croydon on 2 September and was soon scrambled to intercept a formation over Dover. After a hectic day, it claimed eighteen victims out of the thirty-five aircraft known to have been destroyed for the loss of three of its Spitfires, with all the pilots surviving. Somewhat belatedly, with the threat of invasion imminent, it was decided to disperse some of the sections away from the station and work started to prepare a decoy dummy airfield, known as a Q-site, at Wooton. A surprise visitor on 6 September was a solitary Bf 109 with a dead engine, which made a perfect dead-stick landing. As the pilot, Feldwebel Werner Gottschalk, climbed out of the cockpit, the defences spotted the black Luftwaffe crosses and the Nazi swastika markings and opened up with every machine-gun on the airfield. Incredibly Gottschalk managed to reach the safety of No1 hangar without injury.

The Blitz on London started on Sunday 7 September, but the Luftwaffe continued its low-level attacks on airfields. At 11.20 the Folkestone Observer Corps post spotted a wave-hopping formation and telephoned a warning that got through just as the first wave of Bf 109s opened fire. The Bf 110s dropped their bombs on the Station Headquarters, the Officers' Mess and No 1 hangar; one soldier was killed and twelve other personnel wounded. Sadly a direct hit on a shelter in the village by a stray bomb caused six civilian fatalities. The attacks continued into October and, to provide more information on the make-up of enemy formations, trials at Hawkinge with a spotter Spitfire led to the formation of No 421 (Reconnaissance) Flight, which arrived on 15 November. After a series of attacks by one or two aircraft from the Downs direction rather than the sea, the Luftwaffe mounted a more determined raid on 27 October when two formations of Bf 109s destroyed the camp Post Office, and hit the old Officers' Mess. One raider crashed into the sea off Folkestone. The arrival of No 421 Squadron curtailed these activities and its Spitfires were also useful in countering aircraft that were spotting for German long-range guns on Cap Gris Nez. Their targets had included Dover Castle as well as Hawkinge itself.

The alert anti-aircraft gunners around Hawkinge had experienced so many surprise attacks that when, on 2 November 1940, a twin-engined, twin-fin bomber appeared out of the gloom at 200 feet with its undercarriage down, they immediately opened fire and scored a number of hits before the intruder sheared off. The unknown bomber was not a Dornier, but a Handley Page Hampden flown by Flight Lieutenant R. A. B. Learoyd VC, who had won his decoration on the night of 12/13 August 1940. With a wounded man aboard and more than thirty holes in the aircraft, Learoyd eventually landed at West Malling. As he later said, 'Being stationed in Lincolnshire, I had not realised how understandably trigger-happy they were down south.'

The resident Spitfires, although there primarily for reconnaissance, took every opportunity to attack whenever enemy aircraft presented themselves. Since the Flight had been formed it had carried out 199 patrols, claiming ten victories plus another thirteen damaged or 'probables'. The fighter/reconnaissance operations flown by the unit became known as *Jim Crows*, and its prowess was recognised on 11 January 1941 when the Flight was re-numbered 91 (Nigerian) Squadron. On 2 February Flight Lieutenant Billy Drake made the newspapers when, flying over northern France at 30,000 feet, his engine failed; although 70 miles from Hawkinge, he managed to stretch his glide back to land safely.

Hawkinge continued to be the target for 'hit-and-run' attacks with nine raids between February and April 1941. Four separate strafing attacks were launched on Friday 16 May in which one airman was killed and five injured. The first three caused some damage, but the Luftwaffe lost five Bf 109s to the gunners and patrolling Spitfires. However, the last raid caused significant damage to two shelters and to the temporary roof of No 2 hangar, which collapsed onto two Spitfires and the CO's Miles Magister 'hack'. This was the final straw for No 2 hangar, which was demolished shortly afterwards. The station's airmen worked through the night to clear up bomb damage and fill in craters on the airfield. Of the original hangars, only one was now usable, but three Extra Over Blister hangars were erected around the perimeter track.

During the Battle of Britain, the RAF's Air-Sea Rescue service had been a rather ad hoc affair, but a dedicated ASR Flight with two Lysanders was formed at Hawkinge in June, with two Walrus amphibians joining the unit during August. Other Flights at Martlesham Heath, Shoreham and Tangmere were brought together on 22 December 1941 when No 277 Squadron was formed at Stapleford Tawney. The expansion was a response to the growing offensive role of Fighter Command, and Hawkinge would frequently receive damaged aircraft returning from sweeps over France.

Hawkinge played a significant role in the so-called 'Channel Dash' by the German warships *Scharnhorst*, *Gneisenau* and *Prinz Eugen*, which left Brest harbour just after 22.00hrs on 11 February 1942. It was not until 10.20 the following morning that they were spotted by Squadron Leader Bobby Oxspring and his wingman from No 91 Squadron. Despite all the efforts of the RAF, and especially the gallantry of Fleet Air Arm Swordfish crews, the ships ran the gauntlet successfully. In April Bobby Oxspring made the first night sortie over France, an achievement that was soon copied by others on suitable moonlit nights. By the autumn No 91's *Jim Crow* flights were stretching the range of the Spitfire to its absolute limits, being called to fly as far east as Zuider Zee and to Le Havre in the west. The Spitfires of Nos 65 and 41 Squadrons arrived for a few weeks in June before they moved overseas. The airfield struggled to accommodate the additional men and machines, but that was nothing compared to the build-up for Operation 'Jubilee', the joint services raid on Dieppe.

From 18 August the airfield was sealed off from the outside, and that evening two more Spitfire squadrons arrived, Nos 416 and 616, the latter flying the high-altitude Mk VI. Both squadrons were there to fly top cover for 91 Squadron, which began its operations at 06.00 on 19 August; all three squadrons flew many sorties during the day. Few German aircraft were seen in the early stages but many Fw 190s intruded into the area as the day's operations drew to a close. It had been a very hectic period, with the groundcrews in particular involved in virtually continuous refuelling and rearming.

The next highlight in the story of No 91 Squadron and Hawkinge came late on Saturday 30 September when it intercepted a large formation of Fw 190s; the Squadron was credited with five kills and four damaged for the loss of one Spitfire and pilot.

For much of 1941 and 1942 No 91 dispersed one Flight to Lympne, but from November 1942 to January 1943 the position was reversed, with just one Flight remaining at Hawkinge. In April and May 1943 the Squadron was withdrawn from the front line for a month as the pilots converted to the Griffon-engined Spitfire Mk XII. It returned to Hawkinge on 21 May 1943, and four days later destroyed five Fw 190s in a chase across the Channel. While at Hawkinge 91 Squadron had destroyed seventy-seven enemy aircraft, with a further twenty-seven probable and seventy-eight damaged; the pilots had been awarded a DSO, eleven DFCs plus four bars, and five DFMs. The success of the Griffon Spitfire led to the formation of a Spitfire XII Wing in 85 Group, 2TAF, at Westhampnett; and this is where 91 Squadron was posted on 28 June.

The *Jim Crow* work was taken up by No 501 (County of Gloucester) Squadron on 21 June 1943, initially with the Spitfire V, but these were gradually replaced by the improved Mk IX from November until fully equipped by July 1944. During that time the unit spent some six months at Hawkinge, but also used Southend, Friston and Westhampnett. During the time No 501 was resident, it shared the airfield with a succession of Allied Spitfire VB squadrons that used the forward base for intruder operations into France.

To accommodate the increased activity, three more Blister hangars and nine extra hardstandings were installed during 1943, and the north-south grass runway was extended across the road to the village, which would be closed as required. This improvement was due to the increasing number of battle-damaged heavy bombers arriving at Hawkinge, often with wounded crew members; their pilots were desperate to put them down on the first English airfield they saw, however small! One of the first arrivals on 9 July 1943 was a 460 Squadron Lancaster returning, on two engines, from a raid on Cologne. After a number of attempts, the pilot got the aircraft down on the north-south strip, but hit a Nissen hut before reaching the runway extension; the crew survived with various injuries. The number of unscheduled arrivals accelerated as the strategic bombing offensive increased its momentum together with the build-up to the invasion of Europe.

The increased air activity also meant more work for Hawkinge's other resident unit, the air-sea rescue detachment from No 277 Squadron. In November 1943 the Sea Otter Mk II was added to its fleet of Spitfire IIs and Walrus amphibians, and one of these was involved in a rescue that typified the dedication of the unit. A Mitchell of No 320 (Dutch) Squadron had ditched just off the French coast on 18 March 1944 and the crew of five had all made it safely into their dinghy, so a Sea Otter was sent to their rescue. After embarking the whole crew, the pilot found his aircraft was too overloaded to take off, so he set off to taxi home! After 4 hours he was met by a high-speed launch, which accepted the Dutch passengers, enabling the Sea Otter to return to Hawkinge.

As part of the build-up to Operation 'Overlord', the Hawker Typhoons of No 137 Squadron were divided between Hawkinge and Lympne as they began their work of softening up the German defences with rockets and 500lb bombs. Even more unusual residents arrived on 23 May 1944 in the shape of Grumman Avengers of Nos 854 and 855 Squadrons, FAA. There as part of *Channel Stop* operations to prevent German U-boats and surface craft interfering in the coming invasion, the two Squadrons were to remain until early August. Sadly, on 5 June a fully loaded Avenger crashed on take-off, after which the total bomb load was reduced to 1,500lb (680kg).

The aerial activity around this time can be judged by the number of emergency landings: three Liberators on 1 April, another Liberator that crashed to the west of the field with four survivors on 20 April, and the following day no fewer than three Marauders and a Boston dropped in, one on its belly. At dusk on 27 April a Liberator landed successfully on three engines, unlike the B-17 that crashed on the aerodrome on 1 May without injury to the crew. Perhaps the most dramatic arrival took place seven months later on 5 January 1945. A Flying Fortress of the 388th Bomb Group had lost its port inner engine over Germany – the complete engine was shot away, both the pilots were killed and the navigator took over the controls. The first Hawkinge knew of this drama was when the crippled bomber appeared low over Killing Wood with its undercarriage down, but too fast to land. At the last minute the 'pilot' slammed the throttles open and the B-17 staggered away below the surrounding trees. It did not crash but appeared again, still too high and fast. Flying Control fired a red flare from its Very pistol and the machine limped around for another circuit. The crew were desperate to land and cut another engine, which windmilled as the bomber made a final approach just above its stalling speed. The pilot forced the machine onto the field and skidded across the grass with the tail high in the air before hitting a bank and ending across Gibraltar Lane; the 'pilot'/navigator and the tail gunner survived.

As the invasion force fought its way inland from the beaches of Normandy, a new threat emerged. From their camouflaged launch sites in France came a deluge of pilotless flying bombs – Hitler's Vergeltung (Retaliation) Weapon No 1, the V-1. Shortly after 04.00 on 13 June 1944 an initial four landed in various locations around London; the first mass attack began during the night of 15/16 June, when more than 240 bombs were launched from some fifty launch sites. By the end of June more than 2,000 had been fired. The fastest fighter aircraft were just able to intercept the V-1s, and the honour of destroying the first fell to one of Hawkinge's former long-term residents, No 91 Squadron, flying from West Malling in Kent. Under the V-1 code name *Diver*, many fighter squadrons were diverted to the task. Nos 350 (Belgian) and 402 (RCAF), with their Griffon-engined Spitfire XIVs, moved to Hawkinge in early August. No 350 Squadron shot down its first missile on 15 August, with three more being destroyed the next day by No 402; as the V-1 attacks lessened, both squadrons were withdrawn by the end of September.

Throughout the frenetic activity of D-Day and its aftermath, the detachment of No 277 (ASR) Squadron continued its life-saving duties. From 5 October 1944 Hawkinge became the primary base for the Squadron, although its detached Flights continued to cover the South Coast from Kent to Cornwall in the west. As the war in Europe moved towards its close, changing ASR requirements led to the disbandment of No 277 on 15 February; its duties at Hawkinge were taken over by a detachment from No 278 Squadron flying Walruses and Sea Otters.

Hawkinge's Station Commander in May 1945 was Wing Commander Mike Crossley, who had led No 32 from Hawkinge in the summer of 1940. It was with considerable satisfaction that he oversaw the ceremonial colour-hoisting parade on 9 May and the subsequent, rather wild, parties. Discipline was re-established as the station began to receive returning POWs, but the festivities resumed again on 14 August with the end of the war in the Far East.

The processing of returning POWs continued, and for a time it appeared that the peacetime role for Hawkinge would be as No 3 Armament Practice Station. However, that unit moved north at the end of October, and on 7 November Hawkinge was placed into Care and Maintenance.

During 1946 the airfield was used at weekends by No 166 Gliding School to teach ATC cadets gliding skills, but in the spring of 1947 Hawkinge was transferred to No 22 Group of Technical Training Command. This heralded the station's reopening on 1 June as the WAAF Technical Training Unit. Soon the neglect of nearly two years of so-called 'care and maintenance' was swept away and the station looked smart as an RAF station should. A Spitfire gate guardian also appeared near the Guardroom to mark the station's historic role in the past conflict. On 1 February 1949 the Women's Auxiliary Air Force became the Women's Royal Air Force, and Hawkinge became the depot for the new service.

No 166 GS was disbanded in early September 1955, and Hawkinge became the Home Command Gliding Centre in December 1955. In an echo of 1915, the gliders were housed in Bessonneau hangars along the eastern boundary.

In 1960 the station became the WRAF Officer Cadets Training Unit, as the airwomen's basic training role was transferred to Spitalgate. It was the beginning of the end; the OCTU then moved to Jurby, and Hawkinge closed on Friday 8 December 1961. In the closure ceremony, RAF and WRAF personnel paraded with the Central Band of the RAF in front of Hangar No 1, the sole example of Hawkinge's permanent hangars to escape the attentions of the Luftwaffe. As the Last Post sounded, the RAF ensign was slowly lowered for the last time in the presence of Marshal of the RAF, Sir William Dickson.

Although placed in the Care and Maintenance category, it was obvious that the station was unlikely to have a future RAF role. The Ministry of Defence finally relinquished the site when 50 acres (20 hectares) of land and buildings were auctioned off in July 1964, with the final 77 acres (31 hectares) going three years later. In June 1968 the airfield was restored to its pre-war appearance; hangars appeared on the bases of the old First World War hangars, together with dispersal crew huts, fuel and oil bowsers, trolley accs, and all the accoutrements of a wartime fighter airfield including Spitfires and Hurricanes. The miracle-workers were a company called Spitfire Productions, and Hawkinge was a film set for the movie *Battle of Britain*. One of the Spitfires restored to life for the film was Hawkinge's former gate guardian Mk IX, which had been removed in 1961, much to the displeasure of the citizens of Folkestone who had hoped to preserve it in the town. Sadly, when filming finished the Spitfire and all the rest of the paraphernalia of movie-making left, but MK356 survives to this day as part of the Battle of Britain Memorial Flight.

Watched by an alert AA gun crew, a 'vic' of Spitfires launches during the Battle of Britain movie. (Robert R. Rudhall collection)

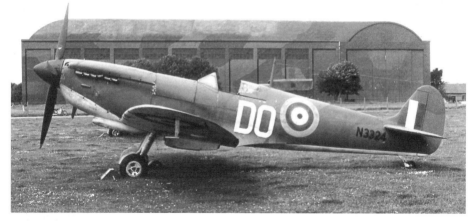

In 1968 a film-prop GS hangar provides a backdrop to Spitfire Mk IX MK397 painted as N332. (via P. R. Arnold)

The history that was made at Hawkinge is not forgotten, and today the thriving Kent Battle of Britain Museum occupies part of the site, with the historic Operations Block preserved and a number of full-scale replicas of the RAF and Luftwaffe fighters that fought over Hawkinge in one of the decisive battles of the 20th century. A memorial stone and commemorative plaque stands in front of the old gymnasium, and other original buildings have found alternative uses. The Officers' Mess was a totally vandalised wreck in 2008 and its demolition was imminent. That wonderful grass flying field, which I first saw in 1987, has succumbed to encroaching housing, leaving only a few road names like Grice Close as a reminder of the hallowed turf from which young men flew to defend these islands in that glorious summer of 1940.

In September 1987 a Pickett-Hamilton fort stands guard over Hawkinge aerodrome and the Battle of Britain Museum. (DWL collection)

The memorial stone and plaque stands in front of the former gymnasium. (DWL collection)

Main features:
Runways: NE-SW 3,300ft, N-S 2,700ft, E-W 3,300ft, grass. *Hangars:* four Extra Over Blisters, two Over Blisters, two double GS sheds. *Hardstandings:* nine, type unknown. *Accommodation:* RAF: 102 Officers, 157 SNCOs, 1,034 ORs; WAAF: 0 Officers, 3 SNCOs, 199 ORs.

HEADCORN, Kent

51°10N/00°41E 107ft asl; TQ878460. 3 miles NE of Headcorn on minor road

When originally chosen as a location for an ALG, the aerodrome was to be called Coldharbour after a farm to the north of the site. Early problems with a high water table led to a review of the runway orientation. When the revised plan was approved the name had changed to Headcorn, which was some 3 miles away. This has caused considerable confusion to airfield historians in recent years, as the former Lashenden ALG was constructed less than a mile south-east of Headcorn and adopted that name when reopened for private flying in the 1970s.

As built, Headcorn had two runways, the main E/W (09-27) of 4,140ft (1,262m) and N/S (00-18) at 3,600ft (1,097m), both surfaced with Sommerfeld tracking linked by a partial perimeter track. The construction had necessitated the burying of many telegraph wires as well as the demolition of a barn and oast house to the south of the site.

Ready for occupation in the early summer of 1943, the first flying residents were the Spitfires of Nos 403 and 421 Squadrons, which arrived on 20 August 1943. All accommodation was under canvas and maintenance undertaken in the open as the two squadrons tested their ability to operate under rudimentary conditions. Together with 416 Squadron, which resided at Merston, the three squadrons formed 127 Airfield. Operations included many *Ramrods* and, in early September, Operation 'Starkey', the spoof invasion of Boulogne that never was! Pre-invasion aerial activity in the areas was very high and on 6 September Headcorn was itself invaded by twelve B-17s, plus a Mitchell and a Marauder, to the consternation of the 127 Airfield HQ personnel.

Ramrods continued with probably the most successful occurring on 3 October. No 127 Airfield was operating as a diversion for a raid by Mitchells of No 320 (Dutch) Squadron. The subterfuge worked as the Squadrons tangled with the Luftwaffe in force with considerable success; 421 Squadron claimed seven victories for the loss of one Spitfire and No 403 claimed a further two.

As with all the early ALGs, operations had highlighted certain deficiencies. The Canadians returned to winter accommodation at Kenley on 14 October as the builders moved in. Nos 5003 and 5004 Airfield Construction Squadrons did most of the work. The main runway was extended to 4,800ft (1,463m) and the north/south to 3,900ft (1,360m). Headcorn had been earmarked for future USAAF use, so to cater for the expected heavyweight P-47 Thunderbolts the runways were reinforced by US steel planking. Taxiways were constructed parallel to the runways, and hardstandings, constructed from Sommerfeld track, were increased to seventy in number.

A steel-frame, canvas-clad Butler hangar was erected by an American Engineer Aviation Battalion and a few utility buildings plus sheet-metal protective structures for ammunition storage

George 'Buzz' Beurling autographs his victory record on his Spitfire IX in October 1943. (via A. Moor)

were also built. Some accommodation was to be in commandeered dwellings and farm buildings, but the majority of personnel were still expected to live in tents at Headcorn. 1 April 1944 was the formal completion date, but it was not until 13 April that the Americans arrived.

Three squadrons, the 377th, 378th and 379th of the 362nd Fighter Group, flew in from Wormingford with some seventy-five Thunderbolts. Initially operations were ground attacks aimed at destroying communication networks in Northern France and Belgium. However, on 6/7 June the Group escorted C-47s dropping paratroops over Normandy before reverting to a fighter-bomber role in support of the US Army as it fought its way inland from the beaches – a very dangerous role, but the P-47 was a rugged aeroplane and well able to soak up a lot of punishment. As airstrips were constructed in France, the tactical air units moved over the Channel, the 362nd transferring to A-12 (Lignerolles) on 2 July 1944, leaving Headcorn deserted.

By mid-July it was confirmed that Headcorn was no longer required and the American

The striking artwork on Lt Col 'Uncle Joe' Laughlin's personal P-47 at Headcorn. (via A. Moor)

engineers moved in to lift the metal mesh and Butler hangar for reuse in Normandy. The land was derequisitioned in September and the removal of telephones, buildings, stores and the rest of the tracking took several months before farming could resume.

A line of Canadian maple trees was planted to the north of the airfield in the early 1980s, and in September 1983 a memorial to the units and men who served at Headcorn was dedicated. The tablets indicate the layout of the airfield and name the Canadians and Americans who gave their lives operating from a tiny part of rural England. Another reminder of Headcorn may be found in the George Inn at Egerton (by which the locals know the airfield). A plaque and photographs of the two Canadian squadrons grace a corner of the bar – and they serve a good pint.

The roadside Headcorn memorial. (DWL collection)

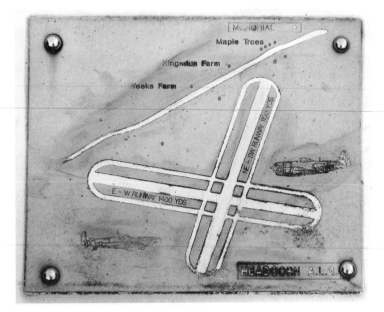

The aerodrome layout is depicted on the memorial plaque. (DWL collection)

Main features:
Runways: 090° 4,800ft, 180° 3,900ft, steel matting (US steel planking). *Hangars:* none.
Hardstandings: seventy temporary, Sommerfeld track. *Accommodation:* tented camp.

HEADCORN, Kent – see LASHENDEN

HIGH HALDEN, Kent

51°07N/00°42E 115ft asl; TQ890397. 7.5 miles WSW of Ashford on minor road

One of the many ALGs that were created near Ashford during 1943, High Halden was originally identified in 1942 despite local warnings that the land was liable to waterlogging. The final site plans were approved in December 1942 and involved the requisition of substantial portions of six farms, significant tree-felling and the burying of telegraph wires. Because the land on the 400-acre (162-hectare) site fell away to both the east and the west, an atypical landing strip layout was agreed. The main runway of 4,400ft (1,340m) was unusually aligned 04-22 with the secondary strip of 3,800ft (1,160m) in a more conventional 11-29 orientation.

An RAF Construction Squadron had built High Halden by the summer of 1943, complete with two Blister hangars, but on completion, lacking prospective customers, the land was released for grazing until the autumn of 1943. In common with the other local ALGs, significant improvements were authorised to cater for the heavy P-47s of the American IXth Air Force. The work was undertaken by a US Engineer Aviation Battalion, which virtually rebuilt the airfield.

The main runway was extended to 5,400ft (1,646m) using steel matting (US steel plank). Sommerfeld track was used to create linking taxiways, for holding platforms at the end of each runway and the seventy hardstandings. A portable Butler hangar supplemented the two Blisters. The airfield had been finished a few weeks on 13 April when the 358th Fighter Group moved from Raydon to adjust to its more spartan tent accommodation. Three requisitioned houses afforded shelter for a lucky few, and the house at Gate's Farm served as the Group Headquarters.

At High Halden, Gate's farmhouse was the 358th FG HQ. (G. J. Hukins via T. Matthews)

The three Squadrons, Nos 365th, 366th and 367th, quickly started fighter-bomber operations concentrating on rail marshalling yards and airfields. It was hazardous work, but work to which the powerful and rugged Thunderbolt was well suited. A few days after the Group arrived at the airfield, there was an unexpected visitor in the form of a battle-damaged 303rd Bomb Group B-17 from RAF Molesworth, which 'bellied in' on 24 April.

On D-Day the Group was on escort duty, protecting the fleets of C-47s as they ferried their paratroops to the DZ in Normandy. In the days that followed, the Group harried the defending German troops, their supplies and infrastructure until, on 3 July, they were able to move to A-14 (Cretteville), leaving High Halden deserted. For most ALGs this was the end of wartime excitement, but the war still had a need for High Halden.

Pulling through prior to an engine start of 'Chunky', a P-47 of the 358th FG at High Halden in 1944. (IWM via A. Moor)

The Allies' only jet fighter squadron, No 616, with Meteor Mk 1s, was based at Manston, but in August 1944, at the height of the anti-*Diver* campaign, there was a need for a forward operating base, so a small detachment was sent to High Halden. The Meteors normally operated in pairs against bombs that had penetrated the initial fighter screen. The Squadron lost one aircraft and its pilot on 14 August when Sergeant D. A. Gregg, short of fuel, crashed while trying to land at Ashford ALG.

By mid-September approval had been given for the Americans to recover the steel matting Sommerfeld tracking, the hangars and other equipment for use in France. During January 1945 a Flight of No 5027 Airfield Construction Squadron arrived to reinstate the land and return it to its former owners. Probably the last military aircraft to make use of High Halden was a battle-damaged B-17 that made an emergency landing on 19 March 1945. By this time much of High Halden airfield had been removed by construction engineers and only the main runway remained intact. The aircraft was repaired and flown out at a later date.

With most ALGs there is little or nothing to remind a visitor of its wartime role, but High Halden has a few mementoes. The Gate's farmhouse, which was the airfield HQ, is in excellent condition, unlike a solitary small brick building to the south-west of Gate's Farm, which may have been a pump house connected with the bulk fuel store. At what was the northern end of runway 04-22 lies the Spitfire Oast, with an excellent depiction of that iconic aeroplane as its wind vane. The original oasthouse was taken down during the war as a hazard to flying and only rebuilt some fifty years later.

Main features:
Runways: 040° 5,400ft, 110° 4,200ft, steel matting (US steel planking). *Hangars:* none. *Hardstandings:* seventy temporary, Sommerfeld track. *Accommodation:* tented camp.

HYTHE, Kent

51°04N/01° 04E 15ft asl; TR157341. Half a mile W of Hythe

During the early part of the 20th century a number of military establishments all carried the Hythe name, which causes considerable confusion for future historians. The School of Aerial Gunnery had its HQ in the town and its aerodrome was often called Hythe, but it is recorded as Dymchurch in this book. The unit whose history is noted here was No 14 Kite Balloon Base.

The No 14 Kite Balloon Base at Hythe on 27 November 1918. (JMB/GSL collection)

Its origins lay in the need, in March 1918, to combat the submarine threat around Britain's coast. A 9-acre (3.6-hectare) site was acquired between the Parkfield district of Hythe and the extensive Shorncliffe rifle range to establish a Kite Balloon Base. Four canvas balloon sheds together with offices were erected, but no living accommodation for the 148 officers and men who were billeted in the town.

Although an RAF unit, the four balloons were used to provide convoy protection under the control of the Vice Admiral, Dover. Closed shortly after the Armistice, the site is now under housing, as Hythe has expanded out to the edge of the rifle ranges.

Main features in 1918:
Runways: none. *Hangars:* four balloon sheds. *Accommodation:* none.

IVYCHURCH, Kent – see BRENZETT

KINGSNORTH, Kent (Airship)

51°25N/00°36E 6ft asl; TQ810725. 5 miles NE of Rochester on minor road

In the 21st century airships are an interesting aeronautical anomaly whose adherents now come across as somewhat oddball, but a century ago airships appeared to have a better future than the flimsy, unreliable short-ranged heavier-than-air aeroplane. By the end of 1912 both the War Office and the Admiralty were experimenting with airships at Farnborough. A naval airship base was started on the Hundred of Hoo peninsula, between the Thames and the Medway, close to Chatham Dockyard, and the new air station at Grain. When in January 1914 the Admiralty took over responsibility for all powered lighter-than-air machines, development work was transferred from Farnborough to the incomplete station that was commissioned in April 1914 into the Naval Airship Branch as Kingsnorth.

Sited about 2 miles east of Hoo village on very low-lying land, it was to become the most important and biggest airship station in the country. A railway spur had been built into the camp to bring in men and materials to speed its construction and the erection of two giant airship sheds, the first being 555ft by 109ft by 100ft (170m by 33m by 30.5m) and the larger 700ft by 150ft by 98ft (213m by 46m by 30m). Accommodation huts were built and a hydrogen production plant completed.

Renamed RNAS Kingsnorth from 1 July 1914, just over a month later it and the nation were at war. Airship No 3 *Astra Torres* was joined by *Parseval* (Airship No 4) and regular patrols were started between Dover and Calais to cover the transport of the British Expeditionary Force to

France. The CO at Kingsnorth, Wing Commander Neville F. Usborne, together with Commander E. A. D. Masterman at Farnborough, were tasked by Admiral Fisher on 15 February 1915 to urgently design some small fast airships for anti-submarine duties.

The first 'Sea Scout' or SS Class appeared in just three weeks! The team had taken a spare envelope from Naval Airship No 2 and suspended below it a BE.2 fuselage minus its wings and tail. The new airship flew for the first time on 18 March and the initial trials proved so successful that the admiralty placed an order for fifty. Kingsnorth had become a factory. The few remaining design staff and their equipment at Farnborough were transferred to Kingsnorth during March 1915 and a school was opened to train personnel in the operation and maintenance of the new airships.

The obvious limitations of the SS led in May 1915 to an improved variant appearing. The Coastal or C-type was larger and had twin engines for greater reliability. The design was based on the *Astra Torres* envelope with the fuselage and 150hp Sunbeam engine of an Avro 510, but in place of its rear fuselage a new section was grafted on, complete with a second pusher Sunbeam engine, giving room for a crew of four. The first flight was made on 26 May. After modifications, which brought the characteristic fore and aft single skids, the Admiralty approved production of thirty. Although Kingsnorth continued to build the SS class well into mid-1916, many were also built at Barrow, Folkestone (Capel) and at Wormwood Scrubs.

In addition to the many airships under construction and test at Kingsnorth, an unusual series of experiments took place in 1915/16. To combat the Zeppelin menace, an airship/aeroplane combination was conceived. Attempts to intercept enemy airships had been frustrated by the time taken by an aeroplane to climb to altitude and the very short endurance. By attaching a BE.2c to an SS-type envelope, it was hoped that the combination, called the AO.1 (Airshiplane) would climb to height quickly and detach the aeroplane to attack the Zeppelin, simultaneously actuating a rip valve on the SS envelope, which would float down to be recovered. First tested in August 1915, the combination was not fully controllable. Sources disagree on which date in February 1916 another trial was made and exactly what was the cause of the tragedy that enfolded.

Most likely it was on 21 February that Commander Usborne, accompanied by Squadron Commander W. P. de Courcy Ireland, took off in the combination and climbed to about 4,000 feet (1,219 metres) before an attempt was made to release the BE.2c. Apparently only forward pair of

Coastal airship C-8 landing at Kingsnorth in April 1916. (Ces Mowthorpe collection)

Sea Scout 'Zero' SSZ.59 was built at Kingsnorth in April 1918 but operated mainly from East Fortune. (W. A. Yeulett via W. Casey)

the four suspension cables released but the envelope 'ripped' as planned and the contraption began to descend. Ireland fell out. It is likely that he had climbed back to try to release the rear cables but was thrown off. His body was later recovered from the Medway near Strood. The aeroplane and envelope tumbled uncontrollably down to crash, fatally, in the goods yard of Strood railway station. The tragic loss of Kingsnorth's brilliant CO ended further combination trials, although the idea was resurrected with rigid airships.

The number of fully trained airship captains trained at Kingsnorth reached thirty-six by the end of 1915, plus many maintenance and handling ratings qualified via the Airship Station's training courses. Production of the original SS-type non-rigid airships reached sixteen as yet another new design was nearing completion. The NS or North Sea type received an order for six in January 1916, plus a further six of the SSP or Sea Scout Pusher. The latter arose from the success of the SS with a pusher Farman car rather than the original BE.2c. Only SSP-1 was built at Kingsnorth, the remaining five emerging from Wormwood Scrubs during 1917. With production being such a major role at the station, it was with some relief that training was handed over to Cranwell at the end of 1916 as Kingsnorth became known as the Airship Constructional Station (Non-Rigid), able to concentrate on assembly, repair and design work. Much of the workforce were civilians, with many female personnel employed in the fabric shops.

Production of the Coastal continued and Kingsnorth was to build twenty-seven C class for the Royal Navy, four for the Russian Government and one for France. Many of the later production had a 220hp Renault as the pusher engine. Initially problems were experienced with the NS class resulting in a halt in production in 1917 after the first five. While the faults were being eradicated, the Coastal Star class evolved as a temporary measure, all ten being Kingsnorth-built during 1918. The defects of the NS being overcome, a further eleven were completed during 1918 before the Armistice cancelled the final three under construction.

The last type of airship assembled at Kingsnorth was not one of its own designs; the SSZ or 'Zero' class originated at Capel and was an improved SS with a superb Rolls-Royce 75hp Hawk pusher engine. Of the seventy-seven SSZs built, twenty-four were from North Kent, the last starting its trials on 23 January 1919. The era of non-rigid airships in the Royal Navy was over, and during 1919 all such airship stations were closed down, although the rigid continued for a little longer. The giant sheds and the rest of the station were dismantled during the 1920s and the site is now occupied by an E-On UK Ltd coal-fired power station.

The history of Britain's most important airship station is remembered in the power station, which bears the same name, for in February 2009 the elderly daughter of one of the men who built the airships unveiled a commemorative plaque and presented a photograph of her father and many of the other men and women who were the Kingsnorth Airship Construction Station.

Main features in 1918:
Landing ground: grass. *Hangars:* two airship sheds, the larger one 700ft long, 150ft wide and 98ft high. *Accommodation:* wooden hutting.

KINGSNORTH, Kent (ALG)

51°06N/00°53E 125ft asl; TR025381. 3 miles SE of Ashford on minor road

Identified as a possible ALG in the spring of 1942, Kingsnorth was named after a small hamlet to the north-west. In a heavily wooded area with the western boundary being the Ashford to Rye railway line, the surveyors recognised that the creation of such an airfield would necessitate significant road closure, tree-felling and some demolition.

After approval of the plans by Fighter Command in October 1942, Kingsnorth was earmarked as a training ALG for mobile squadrons from June 1943. Work began, as a priority, in January 1943 with the closure of the roads, the felling of a large proportion of Buresland Wood, the absorption of the whole of Bliby and demolition of two buildings at Cheeseman's Green. Two farms, Brockman's and Chequertree, were requisitioned for use as HQ, stores and living accommodation. The runway arrangement was of cruciform layout with the longest NW/SE (13-31) at 4,700ft (1,430m). Although the site was flat, requiring little grading, it was subject to waterlogging during the winter months. Two Sommerfeld track strips and a partial taxiway were completed by June, together with PSP hardstandings and a Blister hangar.

No 122 Airfield, with its constituent squadrons (Nos 65, 122 and 602), all equipped with the Spitfire VB, arrived from Selsey and Bognor on 1 July 1943 to work up as a tactical unit. The HQ of 602 Squadron found itself in a nearby cottage, but its orderly room was a tent in the garden of the house serving as the Airfield Headquarters, which was not an ideal arrangement.

Although the Squadrons continued their *Rodeos* over France, the Spitfire V was less competitive and this was highlighted in a scrap with Bf 109s and Fw 190s, when No 602 lost four of its aircraft and only claimed two of its opponents. In mid-August No 19 Squadron exchanged with No 602, which moved to Newchurch as the Kingsnorth squadrons upgraded to the much-improved Spitfire IX.

As the summer moved into autumn, the state of the ALG deteriorated, resulting in a temporary closure for two days in September while the runways were relaid. Despite the poor conditions, there were very few accidents or incidents, although two Spitfires collided over the airfield on 22 September during a formation break prior to landing. Kingsnorth was handed back to the Airfield Construction units in October 1943 as No 122 Airfield left for its winter quarters at Gravesend.

As with most of the ALGs around Ashford, Kingsnorth was to be an American IXth Air Force P-47 base. The improvements, largely undertaken by an US Engineer Aviation Battalion, included re-laying the runways with PSP matting, extending the taxiways, building more hardstandings and erecting additional hangarage including a transportable metal-framed Butler combat hangar. On schedule, the ALG was ready for occupation on 1 April 1944, and four days later Thunderbolts of the 22nd, 23rd and 53rd Fighter Squadrons comprising 36th FG arrived.

Under the command of Lt Colonel Van H. Slayden, the Group struggled to adjust to its new location, UK weather and unannounced visitors like the crippled 44th BG Liberator, which gratefully crash-landed on 18 April, blocking the airstrip for some time. On 8 May the 36th was able to start missions in preparation for the coming invasion. Its D-Day role was to patrol the landing areas and beachheads, followed by days of close support and strafing missions in support of the advancing troops. As new airstrips in France were built, 17 July saw the Group transfer to A-16 (Brucheville), leaving Kingsnorth to the battered remains of yet another B-24, this time a 93rd BG aircraft, which had belly-landed on 27 June. In comparison with other Groups involved in hazardous ground-attack duties, the 36th only lost eleven aircraft while at Kingsnorth, although three were shot down on 22 May.

As soon as it was confirmed that the Allies had no further use for the ALG, the PSP was lifted and the hangars dismantled for use on the expanding number of continental airstrips. No 5027 Airfield Works Squadron sent a Flight to complete the dismantling of Kingsnorth, returning the land to a close approximation of its former condition. By early 1945 farming had restarted and the roads were reinstated, but no trees were replanted. There is no memorial at Kingsnorth, and apart from gaps in hedges, no evidence that the open arable fields ever held Thunderbolts and Liberators.

Main features:
Runways: 130° 4,500ft, 040° 4,725ft, steel matting (pierced steel planking and Sommerfeld track). *Hangars:* none. *Hardstandings:* seventy temporary, Sommerfeld track. *Accommodation:* tented camp.

LARKS BARROW, Hampshire

51°15N/01°21W, 380ft asl; SU455505. 1.5 miles NW of Whitchurch alongside A34(T)

The 500-acre largely grass site that took its name from a tumulus half a mile to the east was not an obvious choice for an airfield. However, with railway lines as the southern and eastern boundaries, sloping land, significant tree cover and Down Farm in the centre, in June 1942 it was selected as a possible secondary ALG. The subsequent detailed survey indicated that the proposed two 4,500ft (1,372m) strips would require extensive re-grading. As Down Farm would have been adjacent to the intersection of these runways, it would have been at least partially demolished and the telegraph wires along both railway lines would have had to be buried.

Although the site was requisitioned and formally accepted on 10 December 1942, it appears that little of the proposed work was done. Early in 1943 Larks Barrow was declared Surplus to Requirements; this may have been premature, as the field has been reported in use subsequently as a relief landing ground. It is possible that it was employed as an unmanned practice-forced-landing field by flying training units at Worthy Down or Andover. There is no record of any use by 2TAF or Fighter Command.

The present A34 trunk road follows much of the route of the old Newbury to Winchester line while cutting across the south-east corner of the former airfield as it bypasses Whitchurch. Down Farm survives in the centre of the site, but there is no evidence of any military activity having ever disturbed the tranquillity of this patch of rural Hampshire.

Main features:
Runways: grass. *Hangars:* none. *Accommodation:* none.

LASHAM, Hampshire

51°11N/01°02W, 585ft asl; SU677435. 4 miles NW of Alton off A339

In the overcrowded land-hungry South East, Lasham is a unique survivor. Of all the wartime airfields built in this congested part of England, there is more to be seen at Lasham than any other. Visitors at ground level might argue with that contention; they might ask, 'Where is the control tower, the four T2s, the many buildings on the technical site to the south-east?' To see the truth, go to Google Earth, put in 'Lasham, Hampshire' and a seemingly complete typical 'hostilities-only' three-runway airfield appears. In addition to the runways and many 'frying-pan' dispersals, close inspection reveals that two T2s do survive, one buried within the ATC Ltd aircraft maintenance complex, the other on the south-east side adjacent to the numerous bases of the technical support buildings. Some dispersals also remain, even off the present airfield boundaries, and evidence of the communal sites can be perceived. The bomb store area is recognisable, buried in a densely wooded area. Without doubt, it is an airfield that would reward a detailed on-foot survey, should one ever be granted.

It all began in September 1941 when farmland in the wooded rolling hills between Basingstoke and Alton was requisitioned for a planned satellite to the bomber OTU then being constructed at Aldermaston. McAlpine was the chosen contractor, whose first task was the diversion of the A339, which passed through Lasham village, onto the disused track of the former Basingstoke to Alton light railway. The runway layout was the classic wartime configuration with the primary orientated E/W (095-275) and 5,700ft (1,740m) in length. Three of the T2s were on the airfield proper, with the fourth to the north of an extensive group of dispersals, of which fifty-two were built in total. Accommodation on the dispersed communal sites was for 1,854 officers, NCOs and airmen, with room for a further 420 WAAFs. As the OTU plan had been overtaken by events, it was No 38 Wing, Army Co-operation Command, that accepted the new airfield on 9 November 1942.

The somewhat slower than expected build-up in airborne forces meant that the first aircraft did not arrive until March 1943, although a contingent of Canadian troops was in occupation when, on 2 January, a single Luftwaffe bomber strafed the airfield. The lack of defences was remedied just eight days later by the arrival of No 4165 AA Flight! It was No 175 Squadron with its Hurricanes that, together with the Spitfires of 412 (RCAF) Squadron, first used Lasham, for just a few days as part of mobility training during the *Spartan* exercise. No 175 moved on, but No 412 became part of No 124 Airfield for a month, being joined at times by No 181 with Typhoons and Spitfires of 602 Squadron before being caught up in the confused movements of squadrons as the new Airfield (later Wing structure) settled down. No 124 Airfield finally moved to Appledram on 2 June with its constituent squadrons.

Responsibility for Lasham then passed successively through Nos 10 and 70 Groups of Fighter Command before No 2 Group, Tactical Air Force, took over on 28 August 1943. Mitchells of No 320 (Dutch) Squadron arrived two days later from Attlebridge. Their first operational sortie with eleven aircraft was on 9 September when they bombed the heavy guns at Boulogne during Operation 'Starkey'. No 613 Squadron arrived with Mustangs on 12 October and, as a foretaste of things to come, immediately began to convert to Mosquito Mk VIs. The Squadrons became part of No 138 Airfield when, on 19 November, they were joined by No 305 (Polish) Squadron, also in the process of accepting Mosquitoes. The Mosquito wing was completed on 3 February by the arrival of 107 Squadron from Hartford Bridge, the Dutchmen of No 320 joining the other Mitchell units at Dunsfold.

No 138 Airfield was finally operational by 15 March 1944 when 107 Squadron attacked a *Noball* site. Although these were the high-priority targets at the time, No 613 was also tasked with night-bomber support missions and a few *Rangers*. This was a prelude to a low-level precision attack for which the Mosquito was famed. No 613's target was the Dutch Central Population Registry in the centre of The Hague, where the Gestapo kept many of its records. Six Mosquitoes flew to Swanton Morley for briefing and refuelling before setting off over the North Sea at 50 feet (15.2 metres). Attacking in pairs and led by Wg Cdr R. N. Bateson, they achieved complete surprise, with the leader's bombs 'going in by the front door'. Incendiaries followed and all six aircraft returned safely with just minor damage to one Mosquito. Later reconnaissance showed a perfect precision attack with the target destroyed and adjacent houses untouched.

Night interdictor sorties became the specialist role of the Mosquito squadrons in the lead-up to and during the invasion of Europe, with communications as the primary objective. On the night of 5 June ninety-eight Mosquitoes were dispatched by Nos 138 (Lasham) and 140 (Gravesend) Wings, bombing rail and road junctions, to cause as much chaos as possible. The task was repeated on 6 June and every night thereafter when the weather permitted. A second pin-point precision raid was mounted on 30 July, with the target being a chateau used as a rest centre for U-boat crews. Five Mosquitoes led by Grp Capt L. W. C. Bower, with his No 2 being Air Vice-Marshal Basil Embry (the AOC) but flying under the pseudonym 'Wg Cdr Smith', attacked the seemingly deserted building. Later intelligence revealed that more than 400 Germans had been killed.

The tempo of operations continued at a high rate and on 17 September a special effort was called for in support of Operation 'Market Garden'. Nos 107 and 613 were briefed on low-level attacks with 500lb (227kg) bombs on specific houses in Arnhem. Direct hits were achieved for the loss of two 107 Squadron aircraft. At the end of October No 138 Wing transferred to Hartford Bridge, and No 84 Group Support Unit, which arranged for replacement aircraft and crews for operational squadrons, moved into Lasham from Thruxton. The airfield, under No 11 Group Fighter Command, became a satellite of Blackbushe (renamed from Hartford Bridge in December 1944) on 15 January 1945. Fighter squadrons had started to bring their Spitfires and Typhoons for disposal from mid-December 1944, No 84 GSU becoming the Group Disbandment Unit. The Unit became a Centre on 1 August 1945, absorbing No 83 GDC in October before disbandment at the end of the year.

The next resident was General Aircraft, which occupied two T2 hangars to perform Mosquito overhauls and conversions. The development of the series of General Aircraft tailless gliders, which had started at Aldermaston, was transferred to Lasham during 1946. The third aircraft, TS513, made its first flight there on 30 May 1947 and the first example, TS507, crashed near the airfield on 12 February 1948, killing the pilot, gliding pioneer Robert Kronfeld. The programme was finally terminated during 1949. General Aircraft produced the ultimate version of the versatile Mosquito under the GAL Type No 59. Converted from B-XVI bombers, the incredibly ugly TT Mk 39 target tugs served with the Fleet Air Arm . Lasham was closed on 26 October 1948, and that might have been the end of a temporary wartime airfield.

Ironically it was gliders that were the salvation of Lasham. Permission for the airfield to be used by the Army Gliding Club was given in early 1951. It was joined by the Surrey Gliding Club and Imperial College Gliding Club in August. During July-August 1955 the airfield was the venue for the National Gliding Club championships, and around the same time the airline Dan-Air established its engineering base at Lasham in one of the T2s. The Lasham Gliding Society, incorporating the other clubs, was created in 1958 and acquired a long lease on the site.

General Aircraft GAL 57 TS513/B was the third of the tailless gliders and flew from Lasham on 30 May 1947. (RTP via P. Butler)

The prototype GAL 59 Mosquito TT39 PF489, converted from a B- XVI in 1947 for the FAA. (via DWL collection)

During the mid-1960s Staravia leased the dispersals and T2 hangar to the north of the airfield to operate a major aircraft scrapping business, especially of military machines. For some years it attracted much attention from enthusiasts, but the site was cleared by the early 1970s. Dan-Air Engineering Ltd prospered, maintaining its own fleet and that of other airlines. As the airline expanded and acquired new equipment, an active preservation group was established to care for a Dakota, York, Ambassador and eventually a Comet 4. Another museum was set up in January 1979 based in a former dispersal hut in the north-west corner of the airfield with the title of the Second World War Aircraft Preservation Society (SWWAPS). Sadly, its ambitions did not match reality and the collection that evolved was wholly of post-war aircraft.

Dan-Air's first Boeing 707, G-AYSL, in 1971, still carrying the numbers of its former identity, N721PA. (DWL collection)

Avro York G-ANTK at Lasham in November 1981, now preserved by the Duxford Aviation Society. (DWL collection)

The Lasham Gliding Society grew into one of the world's largest gliding clubs and included some famous names among its number. Derek Piggott was Chief Flying Instructor at Lasham during much of the period from 1953 to 1989, and Ann Welch and Peter Twiss were also members. The strength of the Society was such that in 2001 it completed the purchase of the freehold of the site, totalling some 500 acres (202.5 hectares). The airfield, in constant use throughout the year, regularly hosts national and regional gliding championships.

For some years the Royal Aircraft Establishment operated a research station at Lasham, centred around the wartime control tower on the south of the airfield. When it left the tower deteriorated, until in early 2003 – despite a proposal by the founder of SWWAPS, the late Bob Coles, to operate it as museum and visitor centre – it was demolished by the Gliding Society as a hazard to flying.

In 2001, just prior to the demise of Dan-Air, the engineering division was sold to FLS Aerospace, although two of the preserved aircraft, the York and Ambassador, had earlier been transferred to the Duxford Aviation Society at Duxford. Since 1995 the complex of hangars on the west side of the airfield has been let to ATC Lasham Ltd, which continues the business of civil aircraft engineering started by Dan-Air in 1955. In addition, 2008 saw a major rise in the cost of fuel and a world recession, which brought many repossessed leased aircraft to Lasham for storage. Other companies operating from Lasham include Southdown Aero Services, which has specialised in glider and light aircraft repairs for nearly sixty years.

A memorial to the men and women who served at Lasham during the Second World War was dedicated at the north entrance to the airfield on 14 September 2007. More than 200 people were in attendance while a Spitfire and Dakota of the Battle of Britain Memorial Flight made a flypast in salute.

Main features:
Runways: 095° 5,700ft x 150ft, 175° 3,600ft x 150ft, 063° 4,200ft x 150ft, concrete with wood chippings. *Hangars:* four T2. *Hardstandings:* fifty-two 125ft-diameter 'frying-pan' type. *Accommodation:* RAF: 142 Officers, 407 SNCOs, 1,305 ORs; WAAF: 10 Officers, 20 SNCOs, 390 ORs.

LASHENDEN, Kent

51°09'N/00°39'E 72ft asl; TQ855429. 1 mile SE of Headcorn off A274

Another of the many ALGs that were created in the relatively flat land to the west of Ashford, Lashenden was named after a small hamlet to the south-west of the chosen site. Like many of the other locations, the land was low-lying and rather prone to waterlogging, especially as, in this case, the River Beult formed the northern boundary. Despite this drawback, approval to create a second-line ALG was granted in July 1942.

Work started soon after the plans were approved in December 1942, which involved the closure of two minor roads to accommodate the approximately N-S (01-19) Sommerfeld track runway of 4,800 feet (1,460 metres). The secondary 11-29 runway was aligned parallel to the closed road from Smarden to Waterman Quarter. Shenley Farm, which was to be in the centre of the site, was requisitioned as an MT yard, Ebenezer and White Horse farms became stores and workshops, while Headcorn Hall was taken over for accommodation.

The first arrivals, on 6 August 1943, were the ground personnel of the newly formed No 127 (RCAF) Airfield, the 45-mile road journey from Kenley having taken 4½ hours. The Spitfires of Nos 403 and 421 Squadrons arrived somewhat faster the following day. From the luxury of Kenley, the rigours of tent living were a shock, but the adjustments had been made by the time they moved on to Headcorn on 20 August. Sadly the short period saw the loss of No 403's CO, Sqn Ldr Conrad DFC, on 17 August. To offset that loss, on the last sortie before the move 403 Squadron claimed one Bf 109 destroyed, while No 421 claimed another damaged.

The departure of 127 Airfield brought the Airfield Construction unit back for an upgrading programme, which included more hardstandings, and an extended taxiway linking the runways. No hangars were provided, which was unusual, as Lashenden had been earmarked for USAAF use. The first American aircraft to arrive was unscheduled: on 29 January a battle-damaged 4th FG P-47 crash-landed on the strip. The planned occupants moved in on 15 April 1944 in the shape of the 100th Fighter Wing HQ, which took over Headcorn Hall. It was the 354th FG of the four groups that made up the Wing that arrived from Boxted on 17 April. Operating the superb Merlin-engined P-51B, the first to do so, the three squadrons settled into their tents dispersed around the ALG and soon resumed their bomber escort duties.

'Home from home':
groundcrew of the 355th FS,
354th FG, make themselves
comfortable.
(LAWM via T. Matthews)

The Crew Chief undertakes an engine run on Lt Bob Stephens's P-51C 42-102997 'Killer' in
May 1944. (USAF via A. Moor)

Utilising the long-range capabilities of the Mustang to the full, the Group had much success, especially on 28 May when the bombers' target was Magdeburg, only 80 miles short of Berlin. The 354th claimed 19½ defending fighters for the loss of just two of its own. By the end of May, and after ninety-three missions, the Group had claimed an amazing 324 aircraft destroyed, thirty-nine probables and 212 damaged! Without a doubt, the claims were exaggerated in the heat of battle, but the Distinguished Unit Citation that was won at Lashenden was very well deserved. From mid-May the Group also undertook fighter-bomber operations as the Allied air forces did all they could to disrupt German communications prior to D-Day; however, on the day the Group was held in reserve until late afternoon, when it escorted the next wave of gliders and their tugs to their LZ in Normandy.

Lashenden's location placed it under the flight path of the V-1 missiles on their way to London, so the next task for the Mustangs was anti-*Diver* operations. On 23 June 1944, after a most successful couple of months, the 354th was one of the first to move to the continent, to A-2 (Criqueville). With no other aeronautical residents in the offing, the War Agricultural Executive Committee was pressing for the release of the land. The demand for the metal mesh for the new continental airstrips led to the lifting of all of it at Lashenden, and the land was returned to agriculture in January 1945. However, that was not the end of aviation at Lashenden.

The family that owned Shenley Farm – which was at the heart of the wartime airfield – had originally purchased the farm in 1927. It is believed that the son flew from a field on the farm, apparently in a BE.2. Aviation was therefore in the family tradition, and it was resurrected in 1963 when a surplus wartime Blister hangar was erected on the farm. A second was acquired two years later, half of which doubled up as a pigsty. Many famous pilots enjoyed the family's hospitality, including Sheila Scott, Neil Williams and Neville Browning. Parachuting began, and in 1970 the Lashenden Air Warfare Museum was founded by Trevor Matthews. Flying training started and the Tiger Club moved in during 1990. All was not plain sailing, however, as two public enquiries had to be fought and won.

The airfield now covers some 164 acres (66 hectares) and has a grass runway of 2,600 feet (796 metres) on the same orientation as the wartime 11-29. The grass cross runway is much shorter at only 2,130 feet (549 metres), but the River Beult is still its northern overshoot. The residents include the Headcorn Parachute Club, Thurston Helicopters, the Tiger Club, the Kent Police Flying Club, some forty privately owned aircraft and the excellent Lashenden Air Warfare Museum. Although formally still called Lashenden, the airfield is much more commonly known as Headcorn, causing much confusion within historic aviation circles.

Main features:
Runways: 010° 4,800ft, 110° 3,200ft, steel matting (Sommerfeld track). *Hangars:* none.
Hardstandings: seventy temporary, Sommerfeld track. *Accommodation:* tented camp.

Headcorn House, the HQ of the 100th FW, in 2004. (DWL collection)

LEE-ON-SOLENT, Hampshire

50°49N/01°12W 30ft asl; SU560020. 2.5 miles NW of Gosport off B3385

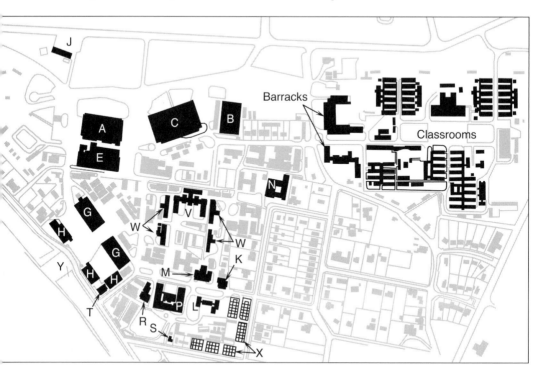

LEE-ON-SOLENT, 1965, WITH DETAILED PLAN OF THE MAIN SITE

A   'Swann' hangar, 'A' type
B   Bellman hangar, Nos 1, 4 and 5 ('Overlord' hangar)
C   'Dunning' hangar, 'C' type
D   Mainhill-type hangar
E   'Esmonde' hangar
F   Fromson hangar
G   Two Admiralty 'G'-type seaplane sheds
H   Three Admiralty 'J'-type seaplane sheds, Grade 2 Listed
J   Flying Control
K   Guardhouse
L   Eagle Block
M   Eagle Club and NAAFI
N   Wykeham Hall
P   Wardroom (Officers' Mess), Grade 2 Listed
R   Westcliffe House, Grade 2 Listed
S   Westcliffe Lodge
T   The Brambles, original CO's house
U   Ross House, Captain's (CO's) house
V   Triumph Galley (Dining room and Cookhouse), Grade 2 Listed
W   Type E Barrack Blocks named Anson, Blake, Cunningham and Duncan
Y   Slipway
Z   Explosive Stores

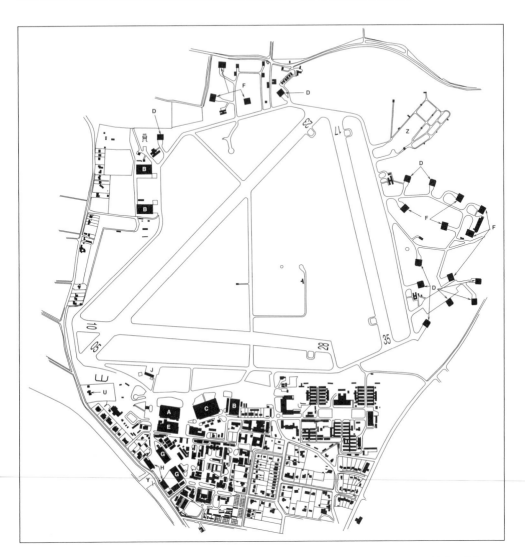

In 1965 Lee-on-Solent was at the peak of its expansion and importance. When HMS Daedalus was finally paid off in March 1996, nearly eighty years of Naval aviation had left a unique collection of historic buildings. Most of these have survived into the 21st century, but the major casualty is Ross House – the current structure of that name is not the original house. The detailed plan indicates the most important buildings, some of them now Grade 2 Listed, but the choice to list the three Admiralty 'J' sheds and not the slightly older 'G'-type is very puzzling. The core of the site is now a designated Conservation Zone, but the bulk of Lee-on-Solent has no protection at all.

On the airfield, what appear to be Blister hangars are the naval 'Fromson' type, which are much less common than their RAF equivalent; the same applies to the Mainhill type, which were only erected on RNAS stations. The pair of Bellman hangars are widely spaced because the inner pair were destroyed in the raid on 16 August 1940. The truncated 10/28 runway is unusual: there must have been a good reason why the easterly end was not continued to link with the taxiway/southern end of runway 17/35, but it is not apparent from the plan.

L ee-on-Solent had its origins in the upsurge of attacks by German U-boats on Britain's coastal shipping in the spring of 1917. The urgent need for more trained aircrew led to the CO of the seaplane training unit at Calshot to search for a temporary sub-station in the Solent area pending construction of a new school on Holy Island, Northumberland. The shallow cliff on the western edge of Lee-on-Solent town leading down to a gently shelving gravel beach appeared to be a near ideal location. The erection of Bessonneau canvas sheds in Westcliffe Paddock started in July 1917, with MT and stores sheds placed on the playing fields of Wykeham Hall, where a tent camp was also positioned. Nearby houses were requisitioned while the officers were billeted in the town.

The arrival on 30 July of the new CO, Squadron Commander D. C. S. Evill RN, two other officers and thirty men marked the official opening of the Naval Seaplane Training School, and the first ground instruction courses began at the end of August. Six Short 827 floatplanes arrived in late September and flying training started. The procedure needed to get the aeroplanes into the water was laborious in the extreme. From the Bessonneau hangars, they were carried on a rail-mounted trolley to the cliff edge where a crane transferred them to a similar trolley, running on rails that led into the sea. This could only be a temporary arrangement, and by November 1917 the cancellation of the Holy Island school confirmed the permanence of Lee-on-Solent. By early 1918 a single slipway had been cut through the cliffs by the sheds, while 30 acres (12.2 hectares) were acquired on the landward side of Marine Parade for new aeroplane sheds. A second double slip was started from this location.

In this aerial view circa 1918, the single slipway is on the right, Westcliffe House is centre and in front of the first 'G'-type seaplane shed is the CO's house, The Brambles. (JMB/GSL collection)

The creation of the Royal Air Force on 1 April 1918 saw Lee-on-Solent become No 209 TDS in No 10 Group RAF. By June the establishment had reached thirty-one staff officers, ninety-five pupils and 550 men. The two training squadrons operated twenty-four floatplanes and forty-eight small flying boats on a course of seven to eight weeks. With the second double slipway in use by September, the TDS was at full capacity at the time of the Armistice. Training continued with personnel reaching at peak of 827 in December 1918, with sixty-nine aeroplanes: twenty-four Short 184s, two Short 827s, twenty-seven FBAs and sixteen Norman Thompson NT2B flying boats. As demobilisation became the priority, it could not continue, and all training ceased on 1 January 1919.

Although a decision was taken that Lee-on-Solent would have a peacetime role as the RAF & Naval Co-operation School, later abbreviated to the RAF Seaplane School, this was only in existence from 19 June 1919 to early December, when the station was reduced to C&M status. Lee was reopened on 1 June 1920, as the post-war confusion began to clear, again in a seaplane training role. After various attempts at a suitable title, finally in May 1923 the unit became the School of

The waterline line-up in 1918 includes Short 184s, Short 827s and FBA flying boats.
(JMB/GSL collection)

Naval Co-operation. Equipped with the Fairey IIID, the courses included fleet observer and seaplane handling until the handling courses were suspended in January 1924. Some experimental work was also carried out using radio-controlled Fairey IIIDs.

The station began to specialise in the catapult-launching of seaplanes when No 444 Flight was formed with Fairey IIIDs strengthened for that role. It was joined by No 443 Flight, which converted to Fairey IIIFs and Flycatchers, before both units had spells aboard capital ships of the fleet. Lee was also the shore base for the Parnall Peto embarked aboard the ill-fated submarine M.2, which failed to surface after diving off Portland in January 1932.

In February 1930 the Fairey IIIF became the equipment of choice for the Naval Co-operation School and also, in June, for a re-formed Floatplane Training Flight. Two years later, Lee became the home for the HQ of Coastal Area, which transferred from London. This move prompted the acquisition of more territory inland of the hangars on which a new aerodrome was constructed. A new 'A'-type hangar together with barrack blocks, administration and technical buildings were built by the time the AMWD handed over the aerodrome on 25 October 1934. The School then absorbed units from Gosport, dividing into four Flights: 'A' with IIIFs for seaplane training, 'B' to instruct naval observers, 'C' Flight with a mix of IIIFs, Fairy Seals and Ripon-trained Telegraphist Air Gunners, and finally 'D' Flight trained Air Observer's Mates. A further reorganisation took place in September 1937, by which time all the Flights were operating the Blackburn Shark. Finally, on 1 January 1928 the School of Naval Co-operation transferred to Ford.

Lee-on-Solent was now the shore base for all Home Fleet catapult Flights and also a number of FAA front-line squadrons. To administer this diverse mixture, a new SHQ was created. Also during 1938 another building programme commenced, which was to increase both technical and domestic accommodation and add a ten-bay 'C' hangar. A new perimeter track was laid down and a row of four Bellman hangars erected adjacent to the maintenance area.

On 24 May 1939 Lee was transferred to the Admiralty and commissioned as HMS *Daedalus*. No 2 Observers School was formed using the Sharks of Nos 753 and 754 Squadrons for flying aspects of the training. No 765 Squadron was created from the former Floatplane Training Flight to operate a mix of Walrus, Swordfish and Seafox types, based in the original First World War sheds and using the double slipway, as had its predecessors in that conflict. A Service Trials Unit designated 778 Squadron and 710 Squadron with Walruses were both formed just before war broke out, although No 710 immediately moved to Mount Batten.

Camouflaging of buildings, digging slit trenches and shelters, together with locating gun and picket posts, became the absolute priority. With that completed, a deck landing squadron, No 770, was formed during November 1939 with a motley mix of Moths, Sea Gladiators and Skuas.

The public view of Lee-on-Solent in the late 1930s includes a Walrus amphibian. (via GSL collection)

Another Communications unit, No 781 Squadron, arrived operating the Walrus, but the 'Phoney War' period was generally just that as far as Lee-on-Solent was concerned. No 778 was flying a mixture of Swordfishes, Rocs and Skuas, and had to wait until 10 May 1940 before it received its first new trials aircraft, the Fairey Fulmar. On the same day, the war became very real as the German forces launched their Blitzkrieg through the Netherlands and Belgium.

After the evacuation from Dunkirk and the fall of France, the obvious vulnerability of *Daedalus* hastened the construction of more FAA airfields in the rear areas. No 764 Squadron was created from the Walrus Flight of the Seaplane Training Unit and moved to Pembroke Dock in July, as No 778 transferred to the still incomplete Arbroath – just in time, as Portsmouth and surrounding areas became Luftwaffe targets. Although some stray bombs had landed in the Lee area earlier, the airfield was not the intended target until 16 August 1940. A strong contingent of Ju 87 Stukas managed to evade the defending RAF squadrons, including No 213, whose Hurricanes had flown up from Exeter to reinforce the hard-pressed 11 Group. Lee was hard-hit: three hangars – including two of the new Bellmans – were destroyed and six aircraft lost. Fortunately the warning had been in time and there were no casualties.

By the end of 1940 the last of the training squadrons were forced out by a combination of enemy interference and the complications of the balloon barrage. No 763 transferred to Arbroath in October, followed by Nos 753 and 754 of No 2 Observer School. Their replacements were 780 Squadron from Eastleigh and the newly commissioned 702 Squadron, operating the Seafox to fly from armed merchantmen.

The duty that was to be Lee-on-Solent's main preoccupation for the rest of the war began early in 1941. This was the re-equipping of existing squadrons and the formation and working up of newly commissioned operational squadrons. Most were TBR units, in particular the Swordfish and Albacore, with which Lee became synonymous. A one-off was the Vought Chesapeake dive-bomber, which had been taken over from a French contract and was issued to No 811 in July 1941. The Squadron soon found that the underpowered machine required too long a take-off run for escort carrier operations. Foregoing the pleasures of an enclosed cockpit, the Squadron returned to the basic, but effective, Swordfish.

Training had returned in June 1942 with the creation of a Night Fighter School using Fulmars and AI-equipped Ansons. More Seafire and Sea Hurricane fighter units worked up during that summer, but they highlighted the limitations of the aerodrome. A new 3,000ft (914m) tarmac runway 24/06 was laid with a secondary 2,400ft (762m) strip orientated 13/31 and twelve blast revetments around the perimeter track. The end of 1942 saw the commissioning of 739 Squadron as a Blind Approach Development Unit. The initial Fulmar and Swordfish were supplemented by Oxfords and Ansons before the unit moved to Hinstock in February 1943.

The controversial Barracuda was the mount of No 810 Squadron when it re-equipped in the spring of 1943. More squadrons followed as the new torpedo and dive-bomber became the predominant HMS *Daedalus* type. Yet again a new aircraft type revealed shortcomings at Lee. Additional land was acquired up to the Lee to Fareham road to allow the E/W runway to be realigned and extended to 4,500 feet (1,372 metres). It is likely that this was when the current control tower was built to replace that originally adjacent to the 'A' hangar. A new N/S runway of 2.790 feet (905 metres) was also constructed. New dispersals were built on the land to the east and north with no fewer than twenty more hangars – twelve Mains and eight Fromson type. The latter could house several Naval aircraft with their wings folded within their 60ft (18.2m) by 70ft (21.3m) space.

Lee-on-Solent took on an additional role in the 1944 build-up leading to Operation 'Overlord'. The first evidence was the arrival in January of elements of No 3 Fighter Wing (Nos 808, 886 and 897 Squadrons) with their Seafire Mk IIs. They were joined in March by the newly formed 885 Squadron as all four re-equipped with the Seafire LF III, the first to have manually folding wings. They were the first elements of what was to become the unique No 34 Recce Wing of 2TAF. The other components, which arrived in April and May, were Nos 26 and 63 Squadrons RAF with Spitfire VBs, and VCS-7 of the US Navy, which also flew Spitfires. By 1 June the Wing, led by Commodore E. C. Thornton RN, could call on no fewer than 101 Spitfires and Seafires, plus a Flight, No 1320 with Typhoons. Just before D-Day, in case that was not enough, three Mustang squadrons, Nos 2, 268 and 414, arrived at the somewhat overcrowded Lee-on-Solent.

No 34 Recce Wing's role was as unique as its constituent squadrons – to provide air spotting for the fire support ships of the Western and Eastern Naval Task Forces. On the morning of D-Day, all aircraft were pooled. This meant that the pilots of VCS-7, for example, flew whatever Supermarine type was available, either Seafire or Spitfire. Typical spotting missions involved a pair of aircraft, the lead aircraft functioned as the spotter while his wingman protected the flight against enemy aerial attack. The first two Spitfires, resplendent in their newly applied invasion stripes, took off at 04.40. With the Mustangs, which had been withdrawn at noon for tactical reconnaissance duties, contributing ninety-six sorties, the Wing achieved a total of 435, far more than any other unit on the day.

Despite top cover by American P-47s and RAF Spitfires, their losses were three Spitfires, three Seafires and a Mustang. The CO of 885 Squadron, Lt Commander S. L. Devonald, ditched alongside an LST, and the Station's Commander Flying became a POW after an attack by six Bf 109s. One 109 was destroyed by Lt Mike Crossley for the expenditure of just forty cannon shells, justifying his post as the Wing Air Gunnery Instructor!

The Fairey Barracuda served at HMS Daedalus *from the spring of 1943. (MAP via DWL collection)*

The work continued over the following days, but from 15 June the demands for their assistance reduced significantly and, with the fall of Cherbourg, VCS-7 was withdrawn, followed by 63 Squadron. The targets for the Naval Wing and 26 Squadron became midget submarines, and Nos 808 and 885 managed to sink a number of these potentially dangerous craft. The Naval Wing was disbanded on 15 July, although 26 Squadron stayed until 6 October when it moved to North Weald, leaving Lee to its ever-present Barracudas and the communications aircraft of 781 Squadron. This unit included a number of Beech 17 Traveller (Staggerwing) light transports in its inventory via Lend-Lease, one of which, serial number FT507, was returned to the USA after the war and, as N18V, was flown in the UK from 1979.

As the war wound down in early 1945, Nos 1791 and 1792 Squadrons were formed with night-fighter Fireflies but soon moved to Inskip, leaving No 781 as Lee's main flying unit. By early 1947 No 781 (Southern Communications) was flying Expeditors and Rapides. No 799, which had arrived during 1946, was involved in refresher flying and No 771 flew the Martinet for target-towing duties. Over the next few months they were joined by No 807 Squadron from Germany and 783 from Arbroath, while 778 (the Service Trials Unit) returned with Seafires and Sea Furies.

HMS *Daedalus* hosted a display of the latest FAA aircraft and equipment in June 1947. The following year No 703 transferred from Thorney Island, absorbing the duties of No 778 Squadron. July 1948 saw the creation of the 51st Miscellaneous Air Group with Mosquitoes and Sea Hornets of No 771 Squadron and Ansons of 783 Squadron. With Ford closed for updating, 813 Squadron became a temporary lodger with its troublesome Firebrands. When Ford reopened in April 1950, both 771 and 703 Squadrons moved there, but the Firebrand remained. Problems limited their sea time, but that didn't prevent a spectacular demonstration of rocket-assisted take-off during the 1950 Air Day.

The *Daedalus* 'permanent' resident, 781 Squadron, continued to garner more tasks, growing in size to achieve them. By 1951, in addition to its VIP transport role, it had an Instrument Flying Examining Flight, a Training Flight and a Search & Rescue section, and operated a maintenance nightmare blend of Ansons, Oxfords, Harvards, Fireflies, Sea Furies, Sea Otters and a couple of Meteors. At least one Sea Otter, RD873, had joined No 781 in May 1948, staying until the end of October 1953, when it was sold for scrap. After a much-needed facelift during 1952, in which many temporary wartime structures were removed, HM the Queen visited Home Air Command on 21 November and watched a flypast of representative FAA aircraft.

That was just a foretaste of what was to come as Lee became responsible for planning a much bigger flypast and was to be the temporary base for many of the 327 Naval aircraft that participated in the Coronation Review of the Royal Navy. A new recruit to the Station Flight for the occasion was Fairey Swordfish NF389, which continues to be part of the RN Historic Flight to this day. Just prior to the great event, 813 Squadron finally returned to Ford in order to re-equip with the Wyvern. Two new types joined No 781 (JOAC) Flight during 1954: in April three Sea Balliols were the first, joined by a similar number of Sea Vampires in May.

What was to prove to be the Fleet Air Arm's last fixed-wing anti-submarine aircraft, the Fairey Gannet, joined its first squadron, No 826, on 17 January 1955. After working up, the unit embarked aboard HMS *Eagle* in May, but of greater significance for the future of the Royal Navy's air arm was the arrival in November of numerous helicopters from Gosport. No 705 Squadron brought over its mixture of Hilliers, Dragonflies and Whirlwinds, as No 845 was re-formed with the American-built Whirlwind HAS 22, the RN's first anti-submarine helicopter squadron. Although 845 soon moved on, 705 Squadron continued the *Daedalus* training tradition as the demand for helicopter aircrew expanded rapidly.

It was a shock when, in early 1956, the expansion of 781 Squadron was put into reverse, the unit losing all but its communications and air experience roles. A further sign that the future of anti-submarine warfare lay with the helicopter was the creation of a Flight within 700 Squadron to evaluate the new Westland Whirlwind HAS 7. The aircraft and crews moved on to 845 Squadron and embarked on HMS *Bulwark* in October 1957. January 1958 saw the departure of No 705 to Culdrose as 701 Squadron was formed to take over the responsibility for the SAR Dragonflies and Whirlwinds on board carriers. Before being disbanded in September, No 701 also carried out minesweeping trials and even tried glider-towing, but apparently this was not successful.

Despite its significant post-war improvements, Lee-on-Solent was very underutilised, which led to the decision to develop the station into a major technical training centre. When the Air Electrical School moved from Worthy Down, the station became HMS *Ariel* in 1959 to reflect its new role. By October 1960 the resident 781 Squadron had taken on a number of Whirlwind 22s for communication duties, being joined in October 1961 by the Sea Heron. At this time the servicing of the fixed-wing fleet was carried out by Airwork Ltd, which also ran the station on a daily basis under RN direction.

The abandoned slipway was brought back into use in 1962 following the formation of the Inter-Service Hovercraft Trials Unit, the craft being hangared in the First World War seaplane sheds. After six years of being *Ariel*, Lee reverted to HMS *Daedalus* in the autumn of 1965, with No 781 Squadron and the IHTU being the 'flying' residents. No 781 by then had four Sea Devons, three Sea Herons, two Whirlwinds and a Sea Hawk. Despite this aerial activity, it was in the ground activities sphere that Lee was expanding, that being reflected by the fact that in 1966, when the Freedom of Gosport was granted to the station, a total of 800 ratings and 'Wrens' were on parade. The January 1965 site plan listed more than fifty classrooms and laboratories, while the 'A' and 'C' hangars were named 'Swann' and 'Dunning' respectively.

The IHTU dropped the 'Trials' part of its title in 1968 as training on hovercraft began when the unit had one SRN 3, two SRN 5s, two SRN 6s and one large (50-ton) BH 7 on its strength. The Electrical School was absorbed by the Air Engineering School during its staged move from Arbroath, which was completed in 1970. In October the Naval Air Command HQ moved to Yeovilton. The arrival of three Whirlwind HAR 9 with 781 Squadron in February 1973 was the result of the RAF giving up its SAR commitment from Beachy Head to Start Point. The official role was assisting service airmen and mariners, but as usual the bulk of the calls were from civilians in distress.

When the IHU was recommissioned on 1 January 1975 as the Naval Hovercraft Trials Unit, specialising in mine countermeasures, it was because the Army and RAF had withdrawn from the unit. No 781 replaced its SAR helicopters with the Wessex 5 in 1977 and, if anything, the rescue task grew, such that in 1979 the Flight answered 161 call-outs and participated in rescuing ninety-five people. The communications part of 781's role had largely evolved into a weekly tour of FAA stations by the Sea Herons, since the Sea Devons were often committed to fishery protection, oil pollution detection and shipping checks. There were also three VIP Wessex 5s resplendent in the green and white livery of Naval Air Command, gaining the nickname of 'Green Parrots'.

After having been associated with Lee for more than forty years, 781 Squadron was finally disbanded on 31 March 1981, truly the end of an era. The Sea Herons and Sea Devons were parcelled out among the remaining RNAS stations, but the three SAR Wessex helicopters stayed at HMS *Daedalus*. The only other flying residents were the RN Gliding Club and helicopters on test after servicing at Fleetlands. Although flying had virtually ceased, Lee was still a very busy station. At least 650 men were under instruction at any one time with the Air Engineering School, and the hangars were filled with obsolete Naval aircraft. Many other resident units included the Naval Air Trials Installation Unit (NARIU) and the RN Accident Investigation Unit (AIU).

The ending of the Cold War accelerated the run-down of the FAA, which had been in progress for many years. In 1988 the Royal Navy handed over the Search & Rescue duties to the Bristow Helicopter organisation, although the station continued to be used by the Southampton University Air Squadron (SUAS) and the Hampshire Police helicopter. In April 1993 the SUAS moved to Boscombe Down. The previous year, two seaplane hangars near the double slipway were taken over for use by an embryonic Hovercraft Museum. But the transfer of the Air Engineering School to the nearby HMS *Sultan* at Gosport in December 1995 was the end for HMS *Daedalus*, which was paid off and formally closed as a Naval Establishment on 29 March 1996, ending seventy-nine years of continual Naval aviation presence.

A Planning Options Paper had been jointly published by the Gosport and Fareham Borough Councils and the Hampshire County Council in April 1994, but there followed a long period of uncertainty over the airfield's future. In August 1996 it was being rumoured that the whole site might be destined for gravel extraction, although the Coastguard SAR and Hampshire Police continued to use the airfield. In 1999 the MOD was offering the main site, totalling some 95 acres (38.8 hectares), for sale freehold. At the time the site contained more than 1 million square feet of buildings, although many had been severely damaged during police and security training.

However, in December 2001 it was being reported that Lee might not be sold after all, although plans for 500 new homes, a racecourse, a business park, a hovercraft museum and gravel extraction were still around. By 2002 a number of light aircraft were flying from the airfield, and the site's future was part of an MOD review, which could include 300 new married quarters for senior personnel. But it was a plan to use the domestic site to house male asylum-seekers that roused local opposition and the creation of the Daedalus Action Group in February 2003. Their protest was successful and the Home Office announced in February 2004 that 'for technical reasons' Lee was not suitable.

The Guardhouse and HMS Daedalus main gate in 2004. (DWL collection)

The slipway, 'G' and 'J' seaplane sheds and two SRN 4 hovercraft. (DWL collection)

The Wardroom and, on the left, Westcliffe House. (DWL collection)

Over the next few years private flying grew at Lee-on Solent, but then in 2007 it was announced that the airfield would close to general aviation. In November 2007 the following answer to a question in the House of Commons was published in Hansard:

'Part of the site of the former HMS *Daedalus* at Lee-on-Solent, including the runways, was acquired from Defence Estates in March 2006 in order to protect the Maritime and Coastguard Agency's (MCA) Search & Rescue helicopter facility. This land is currently managed and operated on a tenancy basis by the Hampshire Police Authority.

The remainder of the site, including the land on which the local general aviation community is based, was purchased by the South East of England Development Agency (SEEDA). Access to the runways at Lee-on-Solent from the SEEDA land has, I understand, been on a 'grace and favour' basis.

The recent decision to close the airfield to general aviation was taken, I am informed, by the Hampshire Police as the operator of the aerodrome due to safety concerns, and as such was not a matter for the Government.'

The ornate bar with the shutters only partially raised! (DWL collection)

With a 'minstrels gallery' at one end, FAA Officers could dine here in style. (DWL collection)

The formation of the Lee Flying Association to coordinate local and GA pressure resulted in a reprieve in 2008, but at the time of writing the future of private flying at Lee is still very much in doubt. The area of land acquired by SEEDA in order 'to provide a unique and exciting opportunity for a sustainable, high-quality mixed-use development' excludes the runways and the area that they enclose, but does include virtually all the technical and domestic site and the hangars to the east and west of the airfield totalling some 203 acres (82.4 hectares). Three of the original seaplane hangars are now listed buildings, as are Westcliffe House and the Wardroom (Officers' Mess), so hopefully some aspects of what was described as the most complete example of a Naval Air Station in the United Kingdom may survive for posterity.

The imposing Flying Control at Lee-on-Solent in 2004. (DWL collection)

Main features:
Runways: 178° 2,925ft x 150ft, 056° 4,260ft x 150ft, 107° 3,300ft x 150ft. *Hangars:* one 'A' type, one 'C' type, three Bellman, eleven Mainhill type, eight Fromson, five former seaplane hangars near slipway. *Hardstandings:* twelve. *Accommodation:* RN: 277 Officers, 4,502 Chiefs/POs/Ratings; WRNS: 50 Officers, 892 Chiefs/POs/Ratings.

LENHAM, Kent

51°14N/00°43E 442ft asl; TQ898528. Half a mile N of Lenham village off A20(T)

Lenham's origins date back to 1930, when the Kent Gliding Club kept its gliders in a Lenham village garage and used the fields to the north of the A20. The outbreak of the war closed down the club and in June 1940 a dummy airfield was constructed on or near the flying fields as a decoy for RAF Detling. The dummy Blenheims dispersed around the field were sufficiently realistic to attract bombs on 22 June. The site's close proximity to the village must have given the residents cause for concern, especially when Q-site lighting was added during the autumn to attract night-bombers. Sadly the lights were too successful, for on 17 October a Hampden of No 49 Squadron force-landed with the loss of one member of the crew and injuring three others.

The next aerial visitors were the Auster IIIs of B Flight 653 Squadron, which, although based at Penshurst, visited briefly in March 1943, followed in April by C Flight of No 655 as the Army Co-operation squadrons practised flying from unprepared strips under operational conditions. Although the decoy was again bombed in early 1944, the active role of Lenham ceased after VE-Day, the site was cleared and the present agricultural fields give no hint of any past military purpose.

Auster AOP III of 653 Squadron flew from Lenham in the spring of 1943. (DWL collection)

Main features:
Runways: grass. *Hangars:* none. *Accommodation:* none.

LEYSDOWN (Shellbeach), Kent

51°26N/00°56E 7ft asl; TR040698. Half a mile SE of Leysdown-on-Sea on minor road

Leysdown's long-standing and generally recognised claim to have been Britain's first aerodrome was challenged in 2009 by Fambridge in Essex. Whichever was actually used first, Leysdown was emphatically the first successful aerodrome in the UK, as Fambridge was abandoned very shortly after being brought into use.

It was the renowned balloonist and UK agent for Wright aeroplanes, Griffith Brewer, who suggested to the Short brothers, Oswald, Horace and Eustace, that the land between Leysdown village and Shell Ness point would make a suitable aerodrome and factory site for their planned production of Wright aeroplanes. As a member of the Aero Club, he also recommended that the site would make a suitable club aerodrome.

Frank McClean of the Aero Club bought a farmhouse, then called Mussel Manor, as a club building and obtained flying rights over the adjoining marshland as the Shorts purchased land on Shellbeach. Work started in February 1909, with the first Short factory building being erected in March. Adapted from a standard corrugated-iron-clad shed made by William Harbrow Ltd of St Mary Cray in Bromley, it was 120ft (36.5m) by 45ft (13.7m) with sliding doors giving a clear opening of 40ft (12.2m). Other club members were encouraged to build their own sheds and a number did so, with McClean also constructing a bungalow alongside his shed.

On 2 May 1909 J. T. C. Moore-Brabazon flew his Voisin biplane from Leysdown, which was subsequently recognised as the first flight in the UK made by a British national. Two days later the Wright brothers, Orville and Wilbur, were brought to Leysdown by the Hon Charles Rolls to inspect the aerodrome and the Shorts' aeroplane factory – again later recognised as a world first. A famous photograph was taken at the door of Mussel Manor of the Shorts, the Wrights and other leading Aero Club members; the group are now known as 'the Founding Fathers' of British aviation.

From June 1909 overnight accommodation was available in the Manor and some abandoned cottages near the coastguard station were also acquired and refurbished. By August the second Short factory building was nearing completion as the manpower reached eighty, many being accommodated in temporary huts erected nearby. The *Daily Mail* had offered a prize of £1,000 to the first Briton to fly an all-British aeroplane on a circuit of more than a mile. On 30 October Moore-Brabazon achieved the feat at Leysdown in a Short- built version of the Wright powered by a Green engine.

The flying ground at Leysdown was very rough in places and, despite the numerous drainage ditches, was very prone to flooding. This prompted a search for an alternative site, which was found at nearby Eastchurch. In May 1910, having completed their sixth Short-Wright aeroplane for Charles Rolls, Shorts also moved its factory to the new site, although flying and development work continued at Leysdown, especially into floatplanes.

During the early wartime expansion of the Naval Flying School at Eastchurch, Leysdown was used to practice forced landings, but when in 1917 bombing and gunnery ranges were set-up offshore, it was redeveloped into a 115-acre (46.6-hectare) aerodrome. The sheds from 1909 were swamped by standard WD wooden huts, a large aircraft shed and a pair of Bessonneau wood and canvas hangars. The Gunnery School from Eastchurch moved in, but on the creation of the RAF on 1 April 1918 the somewhat clumsy title of Pilots & Observers Aerial Gunnery & Aerial Fighting School (SE Area) was chosen. The fleet of a dozen Avro 504Ks and six DH.4/9s were utilised to give up to fifty pupils instruction in gunnery and bombing.

The end of First World War brought a rapid run-down of the School, which was closed in early 1919, but the aerodrome remained in use by Eastchurch aeroplanes operating over the ranges. This situation continued throughout the Second World War, the airfield being especially active while No 18 APC was based at Eastchurch.

Leysdown towards the end of the Great War. (via W. Croydon)

A camouflaged Curtiss R-2 at Leysdown on 23 June 1917. It was used for home defence and nicknamed 'Night Hawk'. (JMB/GSL collection)

Mussel Manor was released soon after the war, but the aerodrome remained MoD until disposal in 1981, although much of the site had been cleared earlier. Renamed Muswell Manor, the house became a country club with an adjoining caravan park. During 2009 a series of celebrations took place to mark the centenary of aviation at Leysdown.

Main features in 1918:
Landing ground: Two grass landing strips NW/SE 2,100ft, NE/SW 1,200ft.
Hangars: one large aeroplane shed, two Bessonneau, a number of Harbrow-type sheds. *Accommodation:* Mussel Manor, local housing and WD wooden hutting.

LITTLESTONE, Kent – see NEW ROMNEY

LYDD, Kent

50°58N/00°52E 7ft asl; TR015230. 2.5 miles NW of Lydd on minor road

It was as long ago as 1886 that aviators in the shape of the artillery observation balloons of the Royal Engineers first used a site in the marshlands of Kent and called it Lydd Camp. This was the first of number of other sites also named after the nearby town, to the future confusion of aviation historians. The balloon trials continued in the 1900s but had apparently finished by the time a four-aeroplane detachment of No 3 Squadron RFC arrived early in 1914 to pursue the gunnery experiments that had started at Shorncliffe Camp, Hythe.

From the outbreak of the First World War, Lydd Camp was dedicated to training courses but aviation returned to the Lydd area in April 1916 when an RFC Training Brigade was formed as No 2 Balloon School. It was located north of Lydd between the present B2076 and Derring Farm (TR037212), from where the students could observe the activities on the ranges to the south of the town. Shortly afterwards, 60 acres (24.3 hectares) of Derring Farm was requisitioned as an aeroplane LG. A square of roughly 1,800 feet (549 metres) to the south-west of the farm (TR322208) was developed for an Artillery Co-operation Flight by January 1917 to operate in conjunction with the range. By August the aerodrome was designated an SE Area Third Class LG as one of a network of such equipped for home defence emergency night landings. The nominated user was the newly formed No 112 (HD) Squadron.

A visiting BE.2E is photographed as it departs at 15.40 on 27 September 1917. (JMB/GSL collection)

The Armistice brought the disbandment of the Artillery Co-operation Flight, the Balloon School having closed in September 1918, and Lydd was returned to agriculture to await the next conflict. When it came in early 1940, the site chosen as a decoy airfield was at Midley, some 2 miles north-west of Lydd. Two years later the Aerodrome Board selected Midley as a very promising future ALG with excellent approaches to the proposed SE/NW and SW/NE strips. The disadvantages were a total absence of camouflaging tree cover, very poor road access over the Walland Marsh, the necessity for significant piping of ditches, and the objections of the Agricultural Emergency Committee. Despite these major defects, Midley, as it was known locally, was given priority status in January 1943 as a mobile fighter unit training ALG.

The requisitioned land was taken from the Newland, Upper Agney and Scotts Marsh farms, and apart from the extensive drainage and filling-in of ditches the work was very straightforward. Well before the arrival of No 121 Airfield in June 1943, the aerodrome was ready with two Sommerfeld track runways, the longer SE/NW of 4,800ft (1,463m). The three Typhoon squadrons gathered from separate aerodromes, No 174 from Merston, No 175 from Appledram and No 245 from Selsey, to spend the summer working up as a team. Nissen huts on either side of the road from Hawthorn Corner provided mess facilities and the Squadron HQs were set up in nearby houses. Aircraft maintenance was done in the open and all personnel were accommodated under canvas.

Nos 174 and 175 Squadrons concentrated on fighter-bomber operations. Initially No 245 commenced Army support training, but when operational from 27 July it escorted 'Bomphoon' squadrons in *Ramrods* and *Rhubarbs*. Operation 'Starkey' in September involved the whole Airfield providing cover to the mock invasion force. There were no casualties during an isolated attack by the Luftwaffe on 15 September and operations continued without interruption although there were, of course, losses during operations. The wear and tear on the steel mesh runways was exacerbated when a hung-up bomb fell off a 174 Squadron 'Tiffie' on landing. Finally, during the second week in October 1943 the Squadrons were relieved to move to their comfortable winter quarters of Westhampnett.

Like many other ALGs, the winter was spent upgrading with five Blister hangars erected and access and perimeter tracks laid, but all in vain for the squadrons never returned, Lydd being kept in reserve. Some ground and RAF Regiment units occupied the airfield in the spring and summer, but by September all was silent. Derequisition approval was received on 13 December and in early 1945 the hangars were dismantled and the metal tracking was lifted. The return to agriculture was virtually total, but even in the 21st century some remnants survive. A Nissen hut believed to have been the office/living quarters for the OC No 121 Airfield, and a loop of concrete is probably the location of the stores and technical site.

The typical wartime concrete road identifies the location of the ALG's stores and technical site. (DWL collection)

Main features:
Runways: SE-NW 4,800ft x 150ft, SW-NE 4,200ft x 150ft, steel matting (Sommerfeld track). *Hangars:* five Blister. *Hardstandings:* three hardcore. *Accommodation:* tented camp.

Places of interest nearby:
The present Lydd Airport is also known as London Ashford Airport, but has no wartime connections, having been opened as Ferryfield in April 1956 to operate car ferry services to France. Although not an 'Action Station', it is still worth a visit with two wartime-type T2 hangars and interesting murals in the terminal.

LYMPNE, Kent

51°04N/01°01E 345ft asl; TR115355. 2.5 miles W of Hythe on B2067

A field between the present B2067 and Folks Wood to the east of the village was the first Lympne flying field, chosen for the Machine Gun School at Hythe in October 1915, but it was soon discovered that the lower section became a quagmire after winter rain. The site was abandoned and by March 1916 a new location north-west of Lympne between the lane to Otterpool Manor and what is now Harringe Brooks Wood had been selected as a night ELG for home defence.

By October 1916 Bessonneau canvas hangars and technical buildings had been constructed, while Lympne Castle was requisitioned as the Officers' Mess. Wooden huts for airmen's accommodation were assembled to the south of the road on what had been allotments. The Machine Gun School had become the School of Aerial Gunnery, operating a varied fleet of FE.8, FE.2B, AW FK.8, Camel and RE.8 aircraft over the nearby ranges to the west of Hythe.

In January 1917 Hythe became No 1 (Auxiliary) School of Air Gunnery, a portion of which flew from Lympne as the Advanced Air Firing School. To accommodate the planned No 8 Aircraft Acceptance Park, six GS sheds, eleven corrugated-iron sheds, workshops and offices were built close to the road along the southern boundary. Construction was incomplete when, on 25 May 1917, the

Armstrong-Whitworth FK.8 B3326 at Lympne with the School of Aerial Gunnery during 1916. (D. S. Glover via P. H. T. Green collection)

Gotha crews of Kagohl 3, prevented by bad weather from reaching London, bombed Lympne aerodrome and Folkestone. Formed on 1 September 1917 to ferry aircraft to France, No 8 AAP also undertook aircraft modifications arising from experience of operational use in France.

When building work was completed in early 1918, the aerodrome was designated a First Class LG with landing runs approaching 3,000ft (914m) on a 175-acre (71-hectare) site. No 120 Squadron was formed as a DH.9 day-bomber unit on 1 January, being joined by 98 Squadron from Old Sarum on 1 March before leaving for St Omer a month later. The next resident was the descriptive Day & Night Bomber & Observation School, which flew a full set of de Havilland bombers, the DH.4, 9 and 9A.

The Armistice brought a degree of uncertainty to Lympne although the presence of the AAP prevented any immediate closure plans. The FE.2Ds of No 108 Squadron returned from France in February 1919 and much of 120 Squadron's effort were directed towards the cross-Channel mail link. With No 108 being disbanded on 3 July, and the amount of mail rapidly reducing, 120 Squadron also disbanded in October.

With two first-rate aerodromes, Hawkinge and Lympne, in close proximity, it was inevitable that the Air Ministry would not need both for the much-reduced post-war RAF. The solution was a sensible one; instead of closure and demolition, Lympne would become a civil aerodrome. In the optimistic glow of novel civil aviation, North Sea Aerial & General Transport began a Leeds-Lympne-Amsterdam cargo service on 6 March 1929 using Blackburn Kangaroos. Regrettably the market was not there and the service closed as Lympne entered yet another period of uncertainty.

What roused Lympne from its doldrums were the Light Aviation trials of 1923, 1924 and 1926. Prizes totalling £1,500 were offered by the *Daily Mail* and the Duke of Sutherland for a single-seat aeroplane that could travel the furthest on just one gallon of petrol; this was amended to a flight of more than 50 miles over a 15-mile triangular course. The competitors gathered at Lympne in early October 1923 to first demonstrate the transportation test. After removing or folding the wings, the machine had to be manhandled a mile along the road before passing through a gate. This latter test initially proved too difficult for the DH.53 Hummingbird. The wings passed through, but the tailplane span was too great. The solution – judicious use of a saw!

Soon fifteen entries had passed the test and the flying could begin. The usual fickle British weather limited flying opportunities, but eventually the prizes were divided between the English Electric Wren and the ANEC, which both achieved almost 90mpg. The rules for the 1924 contest were laid down by the Air Ministry, which was to provide the main prize of £3,000. This time the entry had to have two seats. Again there were fifteen entries, but technical problems, mainly with engines, restricted the number flying to just eight. Practical designs that were to be successful later were eliminated and the prize was awarded to the Beardmore Wee Bee, of which little more was ever heard. The subsequent competition in 1926 introduced much more practical designs such as the Hawker Cygnet and the Avro Avian and pointed the way towards the famous de Havilland Moth series.

G-EBHS was the RAE Hurricane entrant for the 1923 Light Aeroplane trials – unsuccessfully. More successful was the de Havilland DH.53 G-EBHX, which still flies with the Shuttleworth Collection. (JMB/GSL collection)

The RAF now expressed an interest in using Lympne for its summer camps by Auxiliary Squadrons. The first in 1927 brought six DH.9A and four Avro 504Ns of Nos 600 and 601 Squadrons, followed by another camp in 1928, but then interest waned for many years. Short Brothers used Lympne for a few years from the mid-1920s and flew its Gurnard landplane version from there in May 1929. The East Kent Flying Club, later renamed the Cinque Ports Flying Club, was formed at Lympne in 1928, but the aerodrome was once again experiencing a quiet period.

It was a flight in July 1928 by Lt Pat Murdoch SAAF, who flew from the aerodrome in a successful attempt to beat Alan Cobham's UK to the Cape record, that made Lympne the aerodrome of choice for many long-range record flights, by such personalities as the Duchess of Bedford, Jim Mollison and Amy Johnson. One of the last of these was in February 1936 when Flt Lt 'Tommy' Rose left for the Cape, arriving in 3 days, 17 hours and 38 minutes, easily beating Amy Johnson's record.

Expansion of the RAF was now in vogue and Lympne was needed again as a No 1 (Bomber) Group aerodrome, reopening on 28 October 1936. The Hawker Hind day bombers of Nos 21 and 34 Squadrons arrived on 3 November and took up residence in the GS sheds (Belfast Truss hangars). Lack of accommodation was a problem and the Hinds left in the summer of 1938, as Lympne was transferred to No 24 Training Command as the School of Clerks & Accounting – a most odd decision for an obvious Fighter Command station in a forward defensive position! The School soon departed, but it was the Admiralty that moved into what became HMS *Buzzard* on 1 July 1939. Although six Skuas and three Rocs from HMS *Ark Royal* were in residence until September before joining the *Ark* again, Lympne was recommissioned as HMS *Daedalus II*, an out-station of Lee-on-Solent, to house a naval Air Mechanics School.

Lympne's strange not-really-wanted existence continued as the war gathered strength all around it. The retreat of the AASF across the Channel temporarily brought the Blenheims of Nos 18, 53 and 59 Squadrons and the Lysanders of No 2 to Lympne, but they all soon moved to less vulnerable stations. However, the Lysanders of Nos 16 and 26 Squadrons stayed on to fly Tac/R sorties over Dunkirk and also dropped water and ammunition to the besieged garrison of Calais. The confusion even led to unique visitors dropping in on 31 May. Bloch 152 fighters of GCII/8 refuelled prior to an unsuccessful operation to escort Aeronavale Vought 156Fs (Chesapeakes) to bomb Gravelines. In all this activity the Naval Air Mechanics School departed to Newcastle-under-Lyme as Lympne returned to the Air Ministry.

An aerial view of the north hangar looking south-west, possibly during the 1935 International Rally on 25 August. (via DWL collection)

At last, Lympne became a forward satellite aerodrome in the Biggin Hill Sector of 11 Group, squadrons being held at readiness during daylight hours with a small cadre of airmen to look after them. The first Luftwaffe interest on 3 July caused little damage, but just over a month later Lympne was hit hard. On the beautifully clear summer morning of Monday 12 August a concerted attack by Bf 110s on the South Coast RDF stations succeeded in temporarily putting Dover, Pevensey and Rye stations out of action. Thus fifteen Do 17s of 1/KG2 were able to approach low over Romney Marsh, climb over the old sea cliffs and catch Lympne totally by surprise!

The three 1918 GS hangars were all hit, as was the SHQ, the Cinque Ports clubhouse and many accommodation huts. As the CO, Sqn Ldr D. Montgomery, and his small team were starting to tackle the fires, a further wave dropped some 240 more bombs; fortunately nearly one-third fell outside the perimeter, but the field was badly cratered. Amazingly, two wounded 54 Squadron pilots force-landed their Spitfires amidst the chaos of unexploded and delayed-action bombs and survived. Remarkably, casualties were very light, only one killed and two badly injured. Thirteen civil aircraft stored in No 2 hangar were destroyed by fire and Lympne was definitely out of action. However, the temporary loss of Lympne had virtually no effect on the operations of the Biggin Hill Sector.

Luftwaffe intelligence was obviously unaware of the limited importance of Lympne, for just three days later about forty Ju 87s of II/StG 1 launched an unopposed attack in ideal conditions. What had been untouched after 12 August was now in ruins, with all electricity and water supplies cut and the site littered with delayed-action bombs. This time Lympne was totally unusable for forty-eight hours and was then only available for emergency use by battle-damaged fighters. Personnel were evacuated to accommodation in the area, the Officers to Port Lympne, the

Sergeants' Mess to French House, and airmen were housed in Lympne Palace. The village hall became the NAAFI and WAAFs were billeted in local houses in the village and at Bellevue, but the station took no further part in the Battle of Britain.

Little use was made of Lympne until the spring of 1941 when it was decided to bring the aerodrome up to full satellite standard. Three Blister hangars and dispersed hardstandings were provided together with temporary accommodation alongside the Bellevue estate as the station housed squadrons from Biggin on a daylight-only basis for fighter sweeps. Although No 72 spent a week at Lympne in June 1942, it was Operation 'Jubilee', the flawed combined services assault on Dieppe, that proved that the aerodrome had a worthwhile part to play.

Two Squadrons, No 133 (Eagle) and No 401 (RCAF), moved in from Biggin Hill in August 1942. The American volunteer Eagle Squadron led by Acting CO Flt Lt Don Blakeslee DFC had yet to prove itself, but four missions on 19 August confirmed its worth. In the first sortie, starting at 07.20, the Squadron tangled with Fw 190s over Dieppe, the CO and Pilot Officer W. H. Baker each scoring one victory. The Canadians escorted B-17s of the 97th BG to the Abbeville area, during which they claimed one Fw 190 destroyed and another damaged for the loss of one Spitfire and another written off on landing back at Lympne – honours even.

On No 133's second sortie at 10.15 it again claimed two Fw 190s plus a Ju 88. The third mission began at 12.25, during which the Squadron intercepted six Do 217s as they were about to bomb Allied shipping, destroying one. Sadly 401 Squadron was bounced by Fw 190s over Dieppe, losing two Spitfires without scoring. Both Squadrons provided cover for the returning ships and No 133 finally landed back at Lympne at 20.55, after a very long but satisfying day. As the Squadrons departed, Lympne returned to its pre-'Jubilee' somnolence, although it was occasionally used for a week of fighter sweeps during late 1942/early 1943.

However, the success of 'Jubilee' from the Lympne point of view brought further upgrading to enable the station to operate with two squadrons for a longer period. Additional dispersals and a further Blister hangar were provided by the time No 1 Squadron brought its Typhoons in on 15 March 1943 to initiate a most unusual period of sustained activity. The initial task for No 1 was to counter the low-level fighter-bomber tip-and-run attacks by Fw 190s, which achieved a measure of success although generally considered boring. The airfield was a tight fit for a 'Tiffie' and the first of several accidents occurred on 19 March when one aircraft overshot on landing and overturned. However, it was a popular move as both Officers and NCOs enjoyed very comfortable accommodation. A detachment of 245 Squadron also arrived in March to assist No 1, staying for about six weeks when No 1 Squadron changed to escorting the bomber-Typhoons using Lympne as a forward operating base.

Like many South Coast airfields, Lympne became a magnet to bombers in distress, however unsuitable the airfield was for a heavy bomber. The need to land as soon as possible was understandable, but a four-engined bomber on its belly would close a grass airfield for many hours. The second Typhoon squadron to be based at Lympne, No 609, arrived in mid-August and soon both units were working up for the unsuccessful Operation 'Starkey', after which No 609 concentrated on low-level intruder operations while No 1 began fighter-bomber duties. Taking a fully loaded Typhoon off Lympne's short grass runways, the longest being only 4,200ft (1,280m), was a distinctly hazardous occupation. On the first *Ramrod* on 10 November, 609 Squadron escorted eighteen 'Bomphoons' at 50 feet (15.2 metres) over the Channel, climbing to 11,000 feet (3,353 metres) to dive-bomb what were later revealed as V-1 launch sites.

No 609 departed in December 1943, being replaced by rocket-firing Hurricanes of No 137 Squadron, whose hazardous task was anti-shipping strikes. To re-equip with Typhoons, No 137 transferred briefly to Colerne, returning on 4 February just before No 1 reluctantly moved to Martlesham Heath, having enjoyed its stay at Lympne. No 137 Squadron started Typhoon operations on 8 February but moved to Manston on 1 April, overlapping with the tired Spitfires VBs of 186 Squadron, which arrived on 1 March; the Squadron was renumbered 130 before leaving on 30 April 1944. The new arrival was a complete Spitfire IX Wing from North Weald, and Nos 33, 74 and 127 Squadrons started pre-invasion sweeps and bomber escorts over France.

On D-Day the Wing escorted glider and tug combinations to their LZs in Normandy, then undertook standing patrols over the beachheads. When the V-1 campaign started, 74 Squadron was put on to anti-*Diver* interceptions as the rest of the Wing dive-bombed *Noball* sites. In early July the Wing was transferred to 2TAF, being briefly replaced by a Czech Wing of Nos 310, 312 and 313 Squadrons. As anti-*Diver* patrols became the priority, a new Wing with Spitfire IXs of Nos 1, 41 and

165 Squadrons arrived on 11 July 1944. Although the Mark IX's speed advantage over the V-1 was marginal, the Wing's score mounted, helped by Flying Officer Davy, who shot down four in one day.

As the *Noball* sites in France were overrun, Nos 1 and 165 Squadrons transferred to Detling and No 41 returned to fighter sweeps when its conversion to the powerful Spitfire XIV was completed. The unit's particular target was the jet-powered Me 262, which was proving a problem for the American VIIIth Air Force. The Wing was re-formed by the arrival of 130 and 610 Squadrons, and all three Spitfire XIV units participated in supporting sweeps during Operation 'Market', the landings in Arnhem. At the end of September 130 Squadron were replaced by No 350 (Belgian) Squadron in preparation for a move to the continent as part of 2TAF, which finally occurred on 4 December 1944.

Lympne's hectic period was over and the station reverted to an emergency LG role, although in April 1945 the Spitfire XVIs of Nos 451 and 453 (RAAF) Squadrons briefly operated from there. The end came swiftly as the Lympne ATC was withdrawn on 22 May and the airfield closed shortly afterwards.

Lympne returned to civil control on 1 January 1946 and the Cinque Ports FC restarted in April. Air Kruise was set up during the summer to provide pleasure flying, but the most important event took place on 13 July. On its inaugural flight from Lympne, a Silver City Airways Bristol freighter carried an Armstrong-Siddeley Lancaster car to Le Tourqet. Although the service closed during the winter, demand was very high the rest of the year, leading to the erection of a Super Robin-type hangar on the base of one of the old GS sheds. During 1953 Dakotas were introduced on an expanded network of routes, but heavy rain made the airfield unsafe, leading to a transfer of the service to Southend Airport. When this problem was repeated in the autumn, Silver City decided to create a new airport near Dungeness – the present Lydd Airport. When its last service departed on 3 October 1954, it had carried more than 54,500 cars and nearly 208,500 passengers in just over six years.

In yet another slump period, Lympne closed to commercial traffic and parts were sold back to the original landowners. Just in time, Eric Rylands of Skyways Ltd obtained a long lease to operate a coach/air service to the continent and relicensed the airfield in 1955. A London-Lympne- Beauvais-Paris service began on 30 September, later extending to include Lyon, Brussels and Antwerp as Skyways Coach Air. The HS (Avro) 748 was chosen in 1960 as a replacement for the aging Dakotas, the first arriving in November 1961 with scheduled flights commencing in the following April. A severe setback occurred on 11 July when a landing 748 cart-wheeled and ended up inverted but with, amazingly, no serious injuries to the passengers and crew, although the aircraft was written off.

To improve the all-weather capabilities, a 4,400ft (1,341m) concrete runway was laid down over the winter of 1967 orientated SE/NW, and Lympne was renamed Ashford Airport in April 1968. A new terminal building was in use by April 1969 but the economics of the operation began to unravel and on 20 January Skyways Coach Air ceased trading. A management buy-out secured the 748s and the new company, called Skyways International, began services on 8 February 1971, being in turn bought out by Dan-Air a year later, which operated the Ashford-Beauvais service until October 1974, when it moved to Lydd (Ferryfield). When the Cinque Ports FC, Business Air Travel and Skyfotos also transferred their allegiance to Lydd, the future of Lympne was once again in the balance.

This time it was the final curtain for Lympne as an airfield. Industry started to take over the hangars and in 1982 an Industrial Park was formally created on the airfield. Aviation did briefly return during 1982/3 when the Valiant two-seat microlight was manufactured in one of the new industrial units. Also a company called the East Kent Memorial Flight began the restoration of a Sea Fury, but both ventures succumbed to financial pressures. By 1985 the control tower and runway had gone and as an airfield Lympne had ceased to exist. For an aerodrome that was in existence for almost seventy years, Lympne had great potential and had short periods of fulfilment, but overall promised more than it was to achieve.

However, the knowledgeable visitor can still find plenty of evidence of the site's aeronautical past. Within the industrial estate, what at first glance appears to be a modern building is the post-war twin hangar built on the base of the most northerly GS hangar. At what was the original entrance from Aldington Road can be found what looks very much like a timber-clad gatehouse. Travelling up Otterpool Lane, passing some air raid shelters, a large group of wartime brick huts survive, and on the date of my visit the elevating section of a Pickett-Hamilton airfield fort was nearby. Across the fields to the north, the underground Battle HQ remains in good condition and at least two pillboxes are in situ elsewhere. Some of the domestic site is now part of the Port Lympne

Skyways Air Cargo DC-3 at Lympne on 10 April 1971. (DWL collection)

Surviving wartime huts with a Pickett-Hamilton fort in the foreground. (DWL collection)

Zoo Park, which also has Port Lympne House, the former Officers' Mess. Much of the actual flying field is still open space and the line of the 1967/68 runway can be easily seen on Google Earth.

Main features:
Runways: NW-SE 4,200ft, NNE-SSW 2,700ft, NNW-SSE 3,000ft, grass. *Hangars:* four Blisters. *Hardstandings:* one, type unknown. *Accommodation:* RAF: 70 Officers, 123 SNCOs, 847 ORs; WAAF: 3 Officers, 2 SNCOs, 88 ORs.

A timber-clad former gatehouse at the original entrance off Aldington road. (DWL collection)

MANSTON, Kent

51°20N/01°21E 168ft asl; TR333662. 2 miles W of Ramsgate off A253

In the summer of 1940 Manston was in the front line. Germany's blitzkrieg through the Low Countries and the fall of France had placed the historic aerodrome as the nearest RAF Fighter Command station to the enemy. It was destined to be bombed repeatedly and was probably the most attacked and damaged RAF airfield during the Battle of Britain; in many respects the ordeal of Manston was greater than any other.

The first attack was on 3 July when a number of light bombs were scattered over the aerodrome, destroying a grass mower. This bore no relationship to what was to come just six weeks later. On Monday 12 August the Luftwaffe concentrated its attacks on Manston, Lympne and Hawkinge. After a quiet morning during which No 65 had been scrambled to give protection to two small Channel convoys, they had landed, refuelled and rearmed and at 12.50 were about to take off when Manston was strafed by Bf 110s from the Erprobungsgruppe 210 as eighteen Do 17s from KG2 bombed from higher level. All but one of the Spitfires was able to get airborne as the aerodrome disappeared under a cloud of smoke, debris and chalk dust. A total of 150 high-explosive and fragmentation bombs had been dropped, destroying the maintenance workshops, where a civilian clerk was killed, damaging two hangars and leaving the flying field pitted with more than 100 bomb craters. One Blenheim was destroyed and several Spitfires damaged.

After a day of filling in craters and cordoning off unexploded bomb sites, the battered aerodrome reopened on what to the Luftwaffe was Adler Tag (Eagle Day) – the air offensive aimed at the final destruction of the RAF – but Manston was spared for a further 24 hours. At 13.00 on 14 August, the Erpr Bf 110s returned in force, dive-bombing to destroy three Blenheim IF fighters of No 600 Squadron and badly damaging four hangars on East Camp. The airfield was again severely cratered, but honours were almost even as the attackers lost two aircraft to the AA defences.

On Thursday 15 August No 266 Squadron moved in from Eastchurch, which had been heavily bombed the previous day, only to be strafed by Bf 109s, losing two Spitfires in the attack. Manston's location and lack of any natural cover meant it was an obvious target of opportunity for any Luftwaffe aircraft returning home with unexpended ammunition or bombs. This almost continuous atmosphere of danger and the virtual absence of any advanced warning led, not unexpectedly, to a reduction in morale in some instances.

No 266 found itself severely outnumbered in a dog-fight with Bf 109s on 16 August, losing their CO, Sqn Ldr R. Wilkinson, and three other pilots; only one of the three aircraft that returned was undamaged. A group of strafing Bf 109s swept over the aerodrome at 17.45, destroying a Blenheim and a Spitfire and damaging another two aircraft. Further low-level fighter-bomber attacks occurred on 18, 20 and 24 August with losses of aircraft, personnel and buildings. No 600 Squadron's Blenheims were withdrawn to Hornchurch on 22 August and thus missed the cataclysmic events of Saturday 24 August.

The Defiants of 264 Squadron had deployed from Hornchurch to act as airfield defence despite the by then known weaknesses of the type against the enemy fighters. The first combat occurred at 11.35 over Manston as bombs caused a cloud of dust and chalk to totally obscure the target for the second wave of bombers, which instead attacked Ramsgate town and airport, with devastating consequences in loss of lives and houses. No 264 was being refuelled at midday when the third wave of bombers arrived. A quick scramble being impossible in Defiants, the Squadron was only just airborne when the bombs started dropping. but was able to claim four Ju 88s of KG76 before its fighter escorts dispatched three Defiants with the loss of all six aircrew.

The survivors returned to a scene of utter chaos on the ground. With seven dead and many more injured, craters and unexploded bombs were everywhere, fires blazed in the wrecked buildings and the water main was severed, leaving the fire crews desperately short of water. All external telephone contact was lost for several hours. As the weary ground personnel started on the hopeless task of clearing up, yet another raid took place. It could not go on! Manston was abandoned for the rest of the battle except as an ELG. A small aircraft servicing team camped in nearby woods – virtually everyone else moved to Westgate.

That was all twenty-four years in the future when Manston came into existence in early 1916. The limitations of the nearby aerodromes at Westgate and Detling in providing Zeppelin air defence for London led the RNAS to seek a larger site suitable for night-flying and chose a field near Ramsgate. The first wooden huts and a demountable hangar from Westgate were erected in

February 1916 as the site became Manston LG. Initially aeroplanes were positioned in from the other aerodromes but, after a formal inspection on 27 April, No 3 (Aeroplane) Wing with two BE.2Cs, one Short biplane, four Sopwith 1½ Strutters and a single Curtis biplane moved in on 29 May from Detling, which was put into C&M. They were joined in June by the Westgate War Flight with six aeroplanes and about fifty men, who were accommodated under canvas.

The intention was that No 3 Wing would transfer to France when fully trained but the opening of the Somme offensive had increased the RFC's need for reconnaissance aircraft and No 3 Wing lost most of its Sopwiths to its sister air arm. The arrival of the second prototype Handley Page 0/100 'bloody paralyser' increased the training needs as this new large aeroplane was evaluated. Further 0/100s arrived and eventually, by the end of July 1916, some aircraft and crews including a few 0/100s had moved to Luxeuil. A pair of HPs was retained as the Handley Page Training Flight, which necessitated a major increase in hangarage, personnel and accommodation.

In spring 1917 the War School was set up at Manston from the nucleus of the Eastchurch pilot training school. Flying Avro 504s and a mix of operational types, the School gave advanced training before the pilots transferred to the front-line units, in effect the equivalent of a modern OCU. The War Flight was responsible for patrolling a line between Ramsgate and Whitstable. Equipped with a mix of machines including the Bristol Scout, an attempt to intercept an LVG reconnaissance aeroplane on 28 November was unsuccessful, as was another interception at dawn on 16 February 1917. But as the night-time threat to London from the Zeppelin receded, so that from the Gotha twin-engined day-bomber increased. More unsuccessful interceptions were made in June, but on the morning of 7 July twenty-one out of twenty-two Gothas dispatched bombed London but were intercepted on their return by the Manston War Flight and other units. One Gotha was definitely destroyed and three more were claimed.

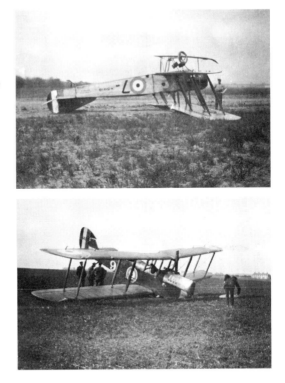

Avro 504G N5818 was delivered to the Manston War School in September 1917. (H. J. Dyer via P. Swan)

Powered by a 200hp RAF 3A engine, this DH.4, coded 9, possibly from the War School, has come to grief at Manston. (H. J. Dyer via P. Swan)

The daylight Gotha raids had started on 25 May 1917, but changed to night operations after 22 August and the Manston War Flight played a prominent role in that decision. From the end of June Manston had included three Sopwith Camels in its fleet, the first time that this potent fighter had been used for home defence. On the morning of 22 August fifteen Gothas of Kagohl 3 left their base in

Belgium to attack the targets in the Thames estuary and Dover. Five had to turn back with technical problems and the remainder were detected in time to alert the defences and the Manston War Flight was scrambled. Flt Lt Arthur Brandon, flying Camel B3834, named 'Wonga Bonga' for reasons that are lost in time, intercepted the formation over Margate. After setting one engine on fire, the doomed Gotha broke up, the main wreckage falling on Vincent Farm adjacent to the airfield. Two more of the bombers were destroyed, one by the RNAS unit at Dover, and virtually all those that returned had been damaged and their crews injured. There were no further daylight raids on the UK during the First World War and thus ended what future historians were to call the 'First Battle of Britain'.

More 0/400s arrived from Redcar on 2 October 1917 to form 'A' Squadron RNAS, which departed for Ochey two weeks later, but night-flying by the Handley Page Training School was causing false alarms with the Home Defence forces. Reluctantly, the RNAS transferred the School to Stonehenge in January 1918. A critical shortage of Air Mechanics led the aerodrome to become a primary instructional station called the Southern Training Base, and a decision made in 1917 that Manston would become a permanent station led to a major expansion, especially of hutted accommodation and hangars. At least two of what were known as Bessonneau underground hangars were constructed, one at Alland Grange (TR322664) and the other along the Manston road (TR340674). Neither were actually underground but were below ground level and the spoil thrown up on three sides, a ramp being provided on the fourth side.

The formation of the RAF on 1 April 1918 brought a three-squadron day-bomber training unit, No 203 TDS, and the War School became a Pilot's Pool to supply aircrew to counter the German offensive of that time. In July the War Flight became part of No 219 Squadron based at Westgate with three Flights at Manston, No 470 with Camels and Nos 555 and 556 with DH.9s. The TDS was renumbered 55 TDS and moved to Narborough on 12 September, as No 2 School of Observers was formed to provide an output of 500 trained aircrew per month. Manston then had an establishment of 2,539 personnel, of which 750 were under training, and 125 aircraft.

It is believed that the 'underground' hangars were never finished, but by the Armistice Manston had eight large and one small aeroplane sheds, two MT sheds, three large workshops and innumerable wooden huts covering about 100 of the 680 acres (275 hectares) of the aerodrome. The Pilot's Pool had moved to Joyce Green in October, but 219 Squadron and the Observers School continued, albeit with reduced activity until the School closed in September 1919, followed by 219 Squadron on 7 February 1920.

The decision that Manston would continue as a peacetime aerodrome led to one tricky problem. Among the requisitioned properties was Pounce's Farm, which was slated to become the OC's dwelling. Its former owner, an elderly German lady, Miss Luhn, was not willing to accept its loss and entered into a long battle to return home. Eventually, at the end of 1919, she had to accept the situation and submitted her claim for compensation with ill grace.

When the School of Aerial Gunnery closed at the end of 1919, it was replaced by the first elements of the School of Technical Training (Men) with courses commencing in May 1920. In the summer of 1921 No 6 FTS arrived from Spitalgate to provide refresher courses on Avro 504s, Snipes, F2Bs and Vimys for pilots posted overseas. A major, albeit temporary, increase in the station's establishment occurred during the 1921 Railway Strike, when eighty officers and 589 airmen were mobilised from the Reserve. A year later the establishment moved in an opposite direction as the 'Geddes Axe' led to the closure of No 6 FTS in April 1922 and the down-sizing of the SoTT courses.

A modest expansion began in 1924, with money for married quarters allocated, and on 31 March the Bristol Fighters of No 2 (AC) Squadron flew in from Andover. 1 April saw Britain's meagre fighter defences enhanced by No 3 Squadron, which re-formed at single Flight strength with five Sopwith Snipes. Before it had chance to find its way around Manston, the Squadron was sent to Upavon to exchange with No 9 (B) Squadron because apparently No 9's Vickers Vimys would not fit in the Upavon hangars!

1926 saw Manston involved in another industrial dispute – the General Strike. No 9 Squadron, now equipped with the Virginia, helped distribute the Government newspaper, the *British Gazette*. By July the situation having returned to normal, and the station hosted the DH.9As of No 600 Squadron AAF on its annual summer camp. No 2, still with the F2B, deployed to the Shanghai Racecourse, China, on 20 April 1927, returning to Manston on 27 October. After ten years (an unprecedented length of service at the time) 2 Squadron finally traded in its Bristol Fighters for the AW Atlas in January 1930. In November No 9 Squadron moved to Boscombe Down, but the

In the early 1930s Pounces Farm (the CO's house) can be seen between No 3 SoTT hangar in the foreground and the School's accommodation huts. (via DWL collection)

formation on 16 March 1931 of No 500 (County of Kent) Special Reserve Squadron brought Virginias back to Manston. The half-regular, half-reserve manpower policy worked well, helped by the naming of the Virginias – the first being christened *Isle of Thanet* on 4 June. After a year the Squadron was at full establishment and flew six Virginias and two Avro 504N trainers.

Two Fairey IIIF squadrons, Nos 821 and 822, spent a short time at Manston during 1933 while disembarked from HMS *Courageous* and HMS *Furious* respectively. The first Empire Air Day in May 1934 attracted an attendance of 6,000, from which the RAF Benevolent Fund received £146 4s 6d. No fewer than three Squadrons, Nos 500, 501 and 503, gathered at Manston in July for the annual air exercise. Working with regular bomber squadrons from the Salisbury Plain area, they constituted 'Southland', being opposed by the 'Northland' fighters from Biggin Hill and North Weald.

With the expansion of the RAF demanding more technicians, the School of Technical Training was enlarged into No 3 SoTT (Men). Training became the primary role at Manston as No 2 Squadron moved to Hawkinge to make space for the School of Air Navigation. Created on 6 January 1936 by merging the Air Pilotage School from Andover with the Navigation School from Calshot, it operated an exotic collection including the Saro Cloud amphibian and Avro 626 Prefect. No 48 Squadron was posted to Manston at the end of 1935 to provide the flying element for the SoAN. Manston was by now bursting at the seams as more and more trainees were found beds in the most unlikely locations.

The resident 500 Squadron became a light bomber unit in January 1936 when it exchanged its vintage Virginias for Hawker Harts. On 25 May the unit was transferred from Special Reserve status to the Auxiliary Air Force and the Hind began to replace the Hart from February 1937. No 48 had found the Cloud unsuitable and, with relief, received its first Avro Anson in March 1936. As the RAF's first retractable undercarriage monoplane, the Anson was an advanced aircraft at that time. However, the wheels did require 172 turns on the handle to manually retract them! Officially No 48 was a coastal reconnaissance unit, but in practice it was fully committed to the deluge of navigation trainees and soon reached an establishment of no fewer than eighty Ansons! The rapid expansion of the RAF also meant that two more squadrons were spun off from them: No 206 in June 1936 and No 224 during February 1937. Finally the School took on responsibility for its flying and 48 Squadron was able to retreat to Eastchurch on 1 September 1937 as a proper operational unit.

The Munich Crisis of autumn 1938 found Manston's personnel digging slit trenches, camouflaging aeroplanes and locating gun posts. On 26 September No 500 moved the short distance to Detling as the crisis eased on Chamberlain's return from Munich on 30 September with his 'peace in our time' speech. The lack of accommodation reached a critical point as at least 700 trainees were sleeping under canvas; more temporary wooden accommodation huts were erected to ease the pressure at the overcrowded station.

The declaration of General Mobilisation on 1 September 1939 brought chaos to Manston. On 2 September the SoAN left for St Athan and No 3 SoTT dispersed some courses before disbanding on 13 September. No 3 Squadron passed through on its way to Croydon, as the deserted station was officially in C&M for a short period. Finally, at the end of October Nos 235 and 253 Squadrons were formed, initially on Fairey Battles although both expected to become fighter units. For No 235, this occurred in February 1940 when it received Blenheim Ifs and moved to North Coates. 253 Squadron received Hurricanes on its transfer to Northolt in mid-February.

The transfer to Fighter Command took place on 15 November 1939 and Manston welcomed its first resident fighter units, No 79 with Hurricanes on 12 November and No 600 with its Blenheim night-fighters just after Christmas. It was hoped that the AI-equipped Blenheims would catch He 115 floatplanes, which were mining the Thames Estuary, but success eluded the Squadron. A new Flight, officially No 1 General Reconnaissance Unit (a cover name), was created at Manston on 19 December 1939 to operate the experimental DWI Wellington. These aircraft were fitted with an enormous degaussing ring, 48 feet (14.6 metres) in diameter, energised by a 500-amp petrol-electric set installed within the fuselage. In theory, by flying low over a mined area the magnetic mines would be exploded. The consequence to the aircraft and its crew was yet to be discovered. Escorted by fighters and with a rescue launch on standby (reassuring!), Squadron Leader H. A. Purvis exploded the first mine on 8 January 1940, returning safely to Manston. Further successes followed until May, when the unit flew to Egypt to operate over the Suez Canal

No 79 moved to Biggin in March but, with 32 Squadron, continued to send detachments to Manston on alternate weeks until No 79 was posted to France as part of the BEF. During the evacuation from Dunkirk, 600 Squadron temporarily exchanged with No 604 as the latter operated over the beaches. A number of evacuating squadrons passed through in dribs and drabs. Confusion was universal and some 615 Squadron pilots attached themselves to No 604 to fly Gladiators as local airfield defence. As order was re-established, a decoy airfield was established on the Ash Level marshes, 2 miles to the south-east. With No 600 as Manston's only permanent resident on night-fighter duties, Spitfires of 54 and 74 Squadrons detached daily from Hornchurch. The scene was set for the cataclysm that, as we have already seen, was to descend on Manston in August 1940.

The importance of Manston and the trials of its personnel were recognised on 28 August by a visit from the Prime Minister, Winston Churchill. Expressing concern that it was taking so long to get the station serviceable, as usual he had a solution: special mobile airfield repair teams with transport, equipment and materials to repair raid damage. Thus Works Flights were created. By the end of September Manston was able to accept a pair of Lysanders from No 4 Squadron to liaise with the ASR launches from Ramsgate. The Luftwaffe did drop four bombs on 30 September without effect, but dropped in more permanently on 17 October. Oberleutnant Walter Rupp force-landed his Bf 109E after tangling with the Spitfires of No 603 Squadron. Amazingly, the situation was repeated on 27 November 1940 when a Bf 109 fighter-bomber being flown by Leutnant Wolfgang Teumer crash-landed virtually outside Manston's flight office. The aircraft was taken to the Rolls-Royce factory at Hucknall where it was restored to flight and became part of No 1426 Enemy Aircraft Flight at Duxford and elsewhere. It is now displayed in the Battle of Britain Exhibition at the RAF Museum, Hendon.

Despite its vulnerable location, Manston was too valuable to be left empty for long. No 92 was the first to arrive in January 1941 and almost immediately scored a success with its canon-armed Spitfire VBs, destroying an He 111 on 3 February. Blenheims also returned with No 59 Squadron on 1 February, but with bomber rather than fighter variants to reconnoitre and bomb the French ports. On 20 February No 74 Squadron replaced No 92 and was welcomed by a strafing attack by fifteen Bf 109s, which damaged barrack blocks and a Spitfire.

Manston's strategic position was again exploited in April 1941 when the Blenheim IVs of 101 Squadron arrived for daylight anti-shipping sorties for *Channel Stop* operations, a very hazardous occupation. Three aircraft were despatched on 28 April on the inaugural operation and two returned. Losses mounted with little success, and a pause was called on 9 May. When the operations resumed with No 110 Squadron, No 242 was posted to provide a dedicated Hurricane escort service. Operations were undertaken at wave-top height with the Hurricanes silencing the flak ships as the Blenheims bombed. Losses were reduced but it remained an extremely unhealthy occupation.

By the time the Blenheims were withdrawn in September 1941, Manston-based squadrons had sunk 44,600 tons of shipping and damaged a further 27,500, but at a terrible cost in the lives of aircrew.

On 11 September 615 Squadron swapped places with No 242 and spent just over two months roaming off the French and Belgian coast with its four-cannon Hurricane IICs. The new station CO, Wg Cdr R. (Tom) Gleave, arrived in October 1941 with a brief from the AOC 11 Group to return Manston to full operational status. The bombed-out debris was cleared away and the airmen's accommodation refurbished using salvaged materials. The grass airfield was extended, giving an E/W landing run of 4,800ft (1,463m) and the longer NE/SW strip achieved 5,700ft (1,737m), although the latter crossed the public road through the camp. However, the real need was for a permanent hard runway, but Manston would have to wait for that.

Since March 1941 the two German battlecruisers, *Scharnhorst* and *Gneisenau*, together with the cruiser *Prinz Eugen*, had been bottled up in Brest harbour, subject to many RAF Bomber Command attacks that, although causing damage, failed to sink them. In early 1942 intelligence assessed that the Kriegsmarine planned to move its valuable assets to somewhere safer and the likely scenario was a dash up the Channel at night. RAF and FAA assets began to gather at Manston and other suitable locations. The RAF Beaufort torpedo-bomber squadrons positioned detachments in the region and the newly formed No 825 Squadron, then working up at Lee-on-Solent, transferred six Swordfish to Manston on 4 February. The German ships left Brest in really foul weather at 22.45 on 11 February but they were not detected for 13 hours and then only by accident. The six Swordfish led by Lt Commander Eugene Esmonde DSO RN took off at 12.20 escorted by eleven Spitfires from No 72 Squadron.

The German capital ships were escorted by numerous destroyers and smaller craft together with a full fighter screen of Fw 190s and Bf 109s. The latter engaged 72 Squadron as the six puny Swordfish tried to force a way through the incredible defensive gunfire, which included 11-inch shells from the battlecruisers. Esmonde managed to launch his torpedo before being shot down, followed shortly afterwards by his two wingmen; five survivors were later rescued. The second wave failed to get anywhere near its targets, and none of the aircrew were ever seen again. None of the torpedoes hit a target. A posthumous VC was awarded to the leader and lesser awards to the other brave men who knew that such a daylight attack was virtual suicide. Even the Germans acknowledged the incredible bravery of that attack.

Although other attacks by surface and by air were attempted, the delayed detection prevented any successful operation and the ships reached their harbours in Germany, although the *Scharnhorst* struck a mine. Although it had been a tactical defeat for the British, the consensus was that it may have been a strategic victory. In Brest harbour, the ships were a threat in the Battle of the Atlantic, whereas that threat was much diminished for ships in the German Baltic ports. As Roosevelt commented to Churchill, 'The location of all the German ships in Germany makes our joint North Atlantic naval problem more simple.'

The 'Hurribombers' of No 174 Squadron were joined by regular detachments of 23 Squadron Havocs on their intruder sorties, and from the end of May 1942 four Typhoons from No 56 stood by at Manston to defend Canterbury from any German Baedeker raid. Tragically, in June the Typhoon's resemblance to the Fw 190 caused two of 56 Squadron's aircraft to be shot down by No 401 Spitfires with the death of one pilot. Manston regularly hosted Spitfire VBs from the North Weald Wing on *Rhubarbs* and No 23 Squadron transferred from Ford in early August to send its Mosquito IIs on long-range intruding over the continent.

Operation 'Jubilee' against Dieppe brought the complete North Weald Wing, Nos 242, 331 and 332 Squadrons, to Manston, together with No 403 (Canadian) Squadron, all with Spitfires. On 19 August the first wave of thirty-six Spitfires arrived over Dieppe simultaneously with Luftwaffe fighters and a major dog-fight ensued. The Norwegians of Nos 331 and 332 claimed five Fw 190s destroyed and three damaged for the loss of two Spitfires. The Canadians also shot down two fighters but lost three Spitfires. On the second sortie, the Norwegians and Canadians attacked a heavily escorted unit of Do 217s, claiming three Dorniers and two Fw 190s without loss. As the ships withdrew Nos 242 and 403 covered their retreat and the OC of 403 Squadron, Sqn Ldr L. S. Ford DFC, claimed his second Fw 190 of the day. The Wing's total score for the day was forty enemy aircraft destroyed for the loss of nine Spitfires.

Inevitably aircraft in distress began to find Manston an irresistible target. The first of many USAAF bombers, a B-17E, landed on 24 August with three injured crew, but that was nothing compared with the night diversions of 28/29 August. At dusk, forty-five Spitfires of the Northolt

Polish Wing arrived, followed later by a 305 (Polish) Squadron Wellington, which crash-landed on the flare path. Three more Wellingtons and three Stirlings landed safely but another Stirling, when told to aim to the right of the still blocked flare path, chose too far to the right and collided with the line of Polish Spitfires. Yet another Stirling managed to avoid the burning Spitfires but went through a wooden hut before colliding with a hangar! Before the night was out, two more bombers landed safely. At first light the scene was reminiscent of August 1940. The report, supported by photographs, did much to further the case for a crash runway, which was destined to transform Manston.

The now totally outclassed Hurricanes of 174 Squadron were supplemented from September 1942 by No 137 Squadron flying the Whirlwind fighter-bomber, attractive but plagued by problems. Three Whirlwinds were lost to flak during the Squadron's first operation on 31 August. The AA defences of Manston also had its successes, bringing down an Fw 190 in early October. As the number of low-level attacks increased, the Typhoons of No 609 Squadron arrived on 2 November to counter this threat. Led by Sqn Ldr R. P. Beamont, later a renowned English Electric Test Pilot, the Squadron was not content to just provide standing patrols but started night offensive *Rhubarbs*. Such was its success that the week's temporary deployment ended up lasting nearly nine months.

With 'A' Flight of No 832 Squadron embarked in HMS *Victorious*, B Flight's Albacores arrived to lay mines off the French coast, joining the Albacores of No 841 Squadron, which had been at Manston since the autumn of 1942. No 841 was replaced in early 1943 by No 823 Squadron from Tangmere. The successful activities of 609 Squadron brought No 198, also with Typhoons, to Manston at the end of March, initially to escort the Whirlwinds of No 137 but later to carry out its own *Rhubarbs*. In April one of Manston's hangars became very closely guarded as it received a number of top-secret items followed by a group of boffins, one of whom was Barnes Wallis of Vickers-Armstrong. They were there to carry out trials of the Wallis-designed 'bouncing bombs', code-named 'Upkeep' and 'Highball'. Both weapons gave considerable problems, but at the end of April 'Upkeep' worked successfully, just three weeks before No 617's raid on the Moehne, Eder and Sorpe dams.

Manston was used to unexpected night visitors, but one arrival early on 20 May 1943 was definitely out of the ordinary. Having flown over the Thames Estuary, Unteroffizier Heinz Ehrhardt landed under the impression he was at St Omer, presenting a perfect example of the Fw 190A fighter-bomber to the RAF. The Focke-Wulf fighter-bomber was becoming a regular visitor over Kent, but a group of twelve on 1 June received a very hot reception. Intercepted by 609 Squadron, Flt Lt J. C. Wells shot down two and Fg Off L. J. Davies destroyed one over Kent, another low over the Channel and a third over Ostend. With the AA defences claiming a sixth, it was not a good day for the Luftwaffe. Evidence that lightning can strike twice came on 20 June when yet another Fw 190 landed in perfect conditions.

Finally the long-standing request for an emergency runway had been approved, but the contract, awarded to John Laing & Son Ltd, was much bigger than anyone at Manston had expected. Work started on 15 June 1943 on a monster runway, 9,000ft (2,743m) long and 750ft (229m) wide, a dispersal loop of 6,000ft (1,829m), and twelve crash bays. With work in progress to the south, flying continued on the original aerodrome as No 137 departed in favour of the Hurricanes of 184 Squadron. This was not a retrograde step as these were Mk IV variants armed with a mighty punch of eight rockets. No 137 returned in August with No 164 to create an all-Hurricane IV Wing. 137 Squadron's aircraft were armed with a pair of 40mm cannon, whereas the other squadrons carried rockets.

Typhoon operations continued with No 3 Squadron, and No 56 briefly replaced No 609 before 198 Squadron arrived in August to partner No 3. When the long-resident 841 Squadron disbanded in November, six Albacores were taken on by 'A' Flight of 415 (RCAF) Squadron to continue the anti-shipping task. The Hurricane Wing, having had little success, was withdrawn by the end of the year and No 3 Squadron moved to Swanton Morley as 609 returned, linking with 198 to smite the German forces wherever they could be found. A particularly successful day was 30 January 1944 when a total of fourteen aircraft were destroyed in the air and on the ground. Manston's score dominated No 11 Group in January with forty-three victories – three-quarters of the Group's total.

The return of No 3 in mid-February created a three-squadron Wing, but that was not the chosen title at the time, for No 123 Airfield, No 84 Group, 2TAF, took over command of the three Typhoon squadrons at the end of February. However, it was a time of considerable flux and, after various changes, the Airfield had departed by 1 April.

Working around the clock, progress on the massive runway had been rapid and at 14.25 on 5 April 1944 it was brought into use. The statistics of this project give an idea of its magnitude. A workforce of

600 men and 149 trucks had excavated more than 370,000 cubic yards (282,880 cubic metres) of soil, which was replaced by hardcore and covered by 379,000 square yards (316,840 square metres) of concrete 7 inches (178mm) thick on the main runway and a further 462,000 square yards (386,230 square metres) of tarmac over taxiways and dispersals. At each end of the runway was a 1,500ft (457m) overshoot and Mk II runway lighting, and a FIDO fog dispersal system had been installed.

The need for this very expensive facility was confirmed when, in the first three weeks of use, fifty-six emergency landings were made. The overstretched Servicing Wing was assisted by an American contingent, which dealt with the USAAF aircraft. They made use of the two surviving GS sheds and a single Callender portable hangar for maintenance, together with a further seven Extra Over Blister hangars dispersed around the airfield.

In April No 605 Squadron brought its Mosquito VIs to Manston for night-intruder work over Dutch and Belgian airfields, but the formation of No 155 (GR) Wing of 16 Group Coastal Command was a departure from the usual Manston units. The black-painted Swordfishes of No 819 Squadron were matched with the similarly bedecked Avengers of 848 Squadron. The Wing's role was to prevent the enemy moving fuel by coastal tankers, as the rail and road services were disrupted by 2TAF and USAAF intruders. Equipped with ASV Mk V radar, the Swordfishes sought out targets for the rocket-firing Typhoons of 137 Squadron, which had returned in early April. The Avengers dealt with any shipping in the Scheldt Estuary, which was the end of the convoy route.

As D-Day approached, the use of Manston's emergency runway in May soared to 535, reflecting the intensive air activity. Beaufighters of 143 Squadron arrived at Manston on 23 May to seek and destroy E-boats, sometimes in conjunction with flare-dropping 415 Squadron Albacores, but often on their own. 605 Squadron was concentrating on airfields and AA gun and searchlight positions. On D-Day it had a roving commission with eighteen Mosquitoes out looking for trouble. One Me 410 was found and dispatched while the Beaufighters made a succession of attacks on E-boats.

The big runway continued to receive its full share of bomber diversions, most fairly routine but some causing severe problems, like the B-24 that accidentally jettisoned eight bombs during its forced landing on 13 June. Later on that day, a 500lb (227kg) bomb on board a Mosquito at its dispersal exploded, causing many casualties. Two days later Manston and the RAF achieved their first V-1 victory when a 605 Squadron Mosquito met and destroyed a flying bomb. As the campaign grew, 137 and 605 Squadrons and many others were dedicated to anti-*Diver* patrols, Manston destroying thirty-six by the end of June. On 10 July the Albacore Flight of 415 Squadron was numbered 119 Squadron but its work continued unaffected.

Manston's attraction to Luftwaffe fighters was sustained on the night of 20 July when a pair of Bf 109G-6s orbited the airfield, flashed their downward identification lights and landed, one on its belly. Six and counting! If that was not sufficiently exciting, a totally new sight and sound appeared over Manston on 21 July as a pair of 616 Squadron Meteors landed. The rest of the Squadron, still flying Spitfire VIIs, arrived from Culmhead later; the Spitfires soon relinquished as more Meteors became available. Declared operational on 26 July, the Meteor opened its V-1 score a week later in an most unusual way. Fg Off 'Dixie' Dean attacked a missile but his guns jammed. Nothing daunted, he flew alongside and eased his wing under that of the bomb. The disturbed airflow tipped the V-1 over, and it crashed 5 miles south of Tonbridge. A few minutes later another bomb was destroyed by Fg Off Rodgers, but in a more conventional manner.

Tempests of No 501 Squadron were the next new type to serve at Manston. They concentrated on night anti-*Diver* operations, accounting for thirty-three during August. Two more Tempest squadrons, Nos 80 and 274, arrived before the end of August but, as the V-1 sites in France were overrun, scores diminished rapidly, the Tempest Wing returning to armed recce over the continent. In addition to the continuing flood of emergency landings, at the end of August Manston was host to no fewer than eight squadrons, three with Tempests and one each with Meteors, Mosquitoes, Spitfires, Beaufighters and Avengers. The station was certainly getting revenge for its suffering of 1940 with a unique combination of squadrons.

Albemarles of Nos 296 and 297 towed ninety-seven Horsas into Manston to make use of the broad runway during Operation 'Market'. During 17/18 September they carried troops to Arnhem in two lifts as the Tempest Wing supported in a flak-suppression role. Over the summer there was little use of the FIDO installation on Manston's runway, but it came into its own on 21 September. The afternoon had been rather hazy with visibility down to 1,500 feet (460 meters) and the burners were lit as a precaution. Over a 6-hour period, FIDO's glow, distinguishable up to 8,000 feet (2,438 metres), attracted nine Spitfires, two Mustangs, three Norsemen and a Stirling. By the end of the month Manston had received about 600 emergency landings with nineteen crews being saved by the use of FIDO, and there were to be many more as the winter deepened.

The squadrons at Manston grew by another three on 25 September when Nos 118, 124 and 229 arrived with Spitfires for bomber escort duties. The usual squadron changes saw No 91 replace No 229 in October and No 118 was succeeded by No 1 Squadron in mid-December. The resident night-fighter Mosquito unit changed during January 1945 when No 406 arrived with Mk XXXs, with which it interdicted Luftwaffe fighter airfields during bombing raids. Yet another Spitfire Wing took up residence on 27 February as the Czechs of Nos 310, 312 and 313 Squadrons flew in from Bradwell Bay for bomber escort and *Ramrod* duties. Their last major operation was on 25 April when they escorted 446 Lancasters and Halifaxes to Wangerooge.

The end of the war in Europe gave time to assess the important role that Manston had performed, particularly in the later stages. From 1942, some 100,000 landings had been made at Manston, an estimated 5,800 of them being in an emergency, of which approximately 140 had been assisted by FIDO. Air Traffic Control was always busy but perhaps the most hectic period was between 15.00 and 16.00 on 13 January 1945 when sixty-four B-17s and sixty-seven Mustangs were landed safely. As many as fourteen fighter squadrons had flown from the aerodrome in any one day, and Manston's squadrons had officially sunk 123 enemy ships, destroyed 234 aircraft and 161 V-1 flying bombs – an impressive score for an aerodrome that had been virtually counted out in September 1940.

The FIDO tanks at Manston photographed in 1987. (DWL collection)

Although the fighting was over, flying continued and squadrons still moved around. No 29 Squadron arrived in June to replace No 406. The Czechs departed to Prague in late August with a full complement of new Spitfire IXs as thanks for their invaluable service, leaving the night-fighter Mosquitoes as Manston's only operational fighters; however, they also left at the end of October.

As the RAF was everywhere being run down, a decision was made in December that Manston would have a future as a fighter station and as a transport staging post. No 91 Staging Post came into existence on 1 April 1946 and Manston was authorised as an RAF and Civil Customs Aerodrome. Some of the first civil users were Yorks of Skyways Ltd on contract to the Anglo-Iranian Oil Company, and RAF Dakotas were bringing large numbers of servicemen back from Europe. It was No 46 Group of RAF Transport Command that took control on 15 July 1946 to coordinate the processing of the personnel and freight that were the Staging Post's tasks. No 1 Overseas Ferry Unit based itself at Manston from May 1948, delivering aircraft to the Middle and Far East.

A tragedy occurred during Battle of Britain Day on 18 September 1948 when a display by a Mosquito went wrong. During practice, the pilot had made a single roll at about 50 feet (15.4 metres), but on the day he attempted a second, unsuccessfully. In addition to the loss of the pilot, twelve members of public died. The Staging Post disbanded at the end of July 1950 and No 1 OFU moved to Chivenor because Manston was to get the fighter units promised in December 1945.

However, the uniforms were not blue as Manston was transferred to the American 3rd Air Division for use by a SAC fighter escort wing. In preparation, the 7512th Air Base Group arrived on 11 July 1950 as officially the station was transferred from No 46 to No 11 Group to preserve the RAF interests with a small liaison team. The first arrivals were Republic F-84E Thunderjets of the 20th FB Wing on detachment from Langley Field. They stayed until replaced by the 31st FEW in January 1951, which was succeeded by the 12th FEW six months later. April 1951 saw the arrival of a detachment of the 9th ARS with SA-16 Albatrosses and SB-29 Superfortresses carrying an underslung lifeboat.

When the USAFE took over in November 1951, new hardstandings were constructed to accommodate the Thunderjets of the 123rd FBW, Kentucky Air Guard. The very wide runway was divided into three sections; the centre strip, 200 feet (61 metres) wide, was the runway, and the outer sections were for taxiing. On 10 July the 123rd was deactivated, its aircraft and personnel being re-formed as the 406th FBW with 512, 513 and 514 Fighter Bomber Squadrons changing to a Fighter Interceptor Wing when their Sabres arrived in November 1953. The air rescue detachment had become the 66th ARS during 1952. Further unit exchanges took place during 1954, but the station hit national headlines in August 1955 for all the wrong reasons. An American airman went on a 2-hour rampage with an automatic weapon, killing two including an RAF police corporal and wounding many others before killing himself.

Manston became a Master Diversion airfield in April 1956, open 24 hours a day, 365 days a year to accept aircraft in emergency or with weather problems. The deactivation of the 406th FW in May 1958 led to the station being returned to RAF Fighter Command and reduced to C&M on 1 August. Despite its magnificent runway, Manston remained closed until it reopened as a Master Diversion airfield, parented by West Malling, on 28 March 1959, but still with no resident RAF flying units.

The closure of Blackbushe led to Silver City making Manston its main base, moving aircraft and personnel in during April 1959 and utilising the SHQ as its offices before moving to the eastern end of the airfield, which became the civil area. When customs facilities became available, it promoted more traffic, including some BEA training flights. In January 1960 the Air Ministry Fire Establishment formed its Central Training Establishment at Manston to become a long-term resident.

The arrival of 'D' Flight No 22 Squadron in March 1961 with a pair of Whirlwind helicopters for SAR duties at least meant that a small RAF flying contingent was present. Since the role of a Master Diversion airfield was to receive Bomber Command's V-Bombers in the event of an emergency, it was logical that the station was parented by No 3 Group, which took place on 1 October 1962. Around the same time, the Central Training Establishment came under RAF control as it gathered a significant collection of obsolete military aircraft for fire training duties. More flying returned in early 1963 when No 618 Gliding School was formed, and No 1 Air Experience Flight arrived from White Waltham. Also during 1963 Manston became one of three UK airfields capable of laying a foam carpet on the runway to reduce the risk of fire during a wheels-up landing. The first of many users of the 'foam runway' was a Valiant in May 1964.

Air Ferry commenced services at Manston from 30 March 1963 with a pair of Vikings and a single DC-4, and was joined in 1965 by Invicta Airways. The consequent increase in civil traffic caused the Gliding School to transfer to West Malling. Although remaining a Master Diversion airfield, No 19 Group, Coastal Command, took over control from Bomber Command during August 1967.

In early June 1968 Manston again received the attentions of the Luftwaffe! Twenty-eight years earlier the aircraft with black crosses and swastikas had arrived without warning; this time the publicity was such that crowds turned out to welcome a pair of Heinkel 111 and fifteen Messerschmitt 109s as they landed at Manston. In fact, they were Spanish-built CASA 2 111s and Hispano HA 1112s, all powered by Rolls-Royce Merlin engines, clearing customs before proceeding to Duxford for the forthcoming filming of the *Battle of Britain* movie.

The closure of Air Ferry on 31 October 1968, Invicta's reduction in services in early 1969 and the announcement that the ASR helicopters were to be withdrawn made the future of Manston look very bleak. Even the rumour that the airfield would become London's third airport had a very mixed reception. On the positive side fire training continued and foam carpets were still in demand;

Vickers Merchantman G-AXNT operated by Invicta Air Cargo at Manston on 11 April 1971.
(DWL collection)

during 1969 a Canberra, Comet and Vulcan all landed safely with minimal damage. As the station moved into the 1970s, the foam saved two Bassets, two Argosys and single examples of Victor, Britannia, Canberra and a Vulcan aircraft. In 1971 a Rotary Hydraulic Arrestor Gear was installed for hook-equipped aircraft, the first grateful user being a Buccaneer in January 1972.

After two years with no ASR, the Bristow International Helicopter Company was awarded a contract to provide the service from June 1971. However, after three successful years 'D' Flight of 72 Squadron returned with Wessex HAR 2s until handing over to 'E' Flight of No 22 (SAR) Squadron in June 1976. Sea Devons of 781 Squadron from Lee-on-Solent were regular visitors, operating in support of HM Coastguard's Channel radar surveillance unit at Dover, but the foam carpet equipment was removed in September 1980 on economic and technical grounds. A total of sixty-two aircraft; forty-four military and eighteen civil, had safely used the service in its seventeen years of existence.

The new decade brought little new RAF activity to Manston. The resident No 1 AEF continued to give flights to Cadets with its four Chipmunks and the ASR service received its regular calls from members of the public in distress with an occasional military job to justify its existence. Manston kept up its 'open arms' role for aircraft in distress. During January 1982 the station welcomed forty civil airliners, all weather diversions; the busiest day was 17 January when Manston was the only southern airfield that was snow-free, and 1,698 passengers arrived on twenty-five aircraft. An unusual visitor arrived from France on 7 July 1982. *Solar Challenger* was the first aircraft to cross the English Channel powered solely by the sun. July 1982 also gave Manston a reminder of 1940 when a series of pipe mines were discovered under the old grass runway. Installed in 1940 as an anti-invasion precaution, they were safely dealt with by the Army Bomb Disposal team.

Invicta International Airways finally ceased trading in April 1982 and a freight company, Seabourne Aviation, took over the lease on the hangar and other Invicta assets. April 1984 saw the main runway closed until September for resurfacing, part of the northern taxiway being used while work was in progress. During 1985 Manston handled nearly 44,000 civil and military aircraft movements, of which twenty were diversions. After almost twenty years as part of Coastal Command, the station returned to 11 Group (Strike Command) on 6 January 1986. At the end of August 1988 'E' Flight of 22 Squadron with Wessexes moved to Coltishall, exchanging with 'C' Flight of 202 Squadron operating the more capable Sea King.

In 1989 Kent International Airport opened as a 38-acre (15.4-hectare) civilian area within RAF Manston, including a new terminal opened by the Duchess of York. Under a contract the RAF agreed to maintain the runway and air traffic control and to provide ongoing emergency services. A 1993 report by the Government's Department of Trade & Industry looking at future airport requirements in South East England concluded that Manston was unsuitable for development as a major airport.

Although the disbandment of 'C' Flight of 22 Squadron in July 1994 was accepted with resignation by the local population, who expressed thanks for the years of ARS support, it left No 1 AEF and 618 VGS as the only RAF flying units. In April 1995 the Gliding School went to Odiham and the AEF transferred to St Athan. In 1996 Manston's satellite radar station, RAF Ash, shut down, and on 31 March 1999 RAF Manston also closed, although the MOD decided to retain the fire training facility, and almost all of the 'domestic' side of the base became FSCTE Manston (Fire Service Central Training Establishment).

The operation of Manston International Airport has not been without problems. An attempt to make it into a budget airline hub using an Irish airline EUjet failed in July 2005 when the airline suspended services. Then London Manston Airport plc went into liquidation and all operations, including air traffic and radar services, were temporarily suspended until a sale to the owner of Glasgow Prestwick Airport was completed on 26 August 2005. Early in 2009 the Chief Executive of Kent International Airport launched an ambitious master plan for the future of the troubled airport. It is hoped that, still with one of the best runways in the area and a history of defeating its enemies, Manston will survive and develop to make full use of its potential.

Main features:
Runway: 010° 9,000ft x 750ft, concrete and tarmac with 1,500ft grass extensions at each end. *Hangars:* one Callender portable, two GS sheds (Belfast Truss), seven EO Blister. *Hardstandings:* twenty-six single-engined type. *Accommodation:* RAF: 150 Officers, 283 SNCOs, 3,126 ORs; WAAF: 7 Officers, 6 SNCOs, 414 ORs.

21st-century features:
Runway: 010° 9,000ft x 200ft

Places of interest nearby:
There are three museums at Manston. The oldest is the Spitfire and Hurricane Memorial Building, which grew from the need to put the original RAF Manston gate guardian Spitfire XVI TB752 under cover. What was initially called the Spitfire Memorial Building opened in June 1981, joined by the Hurricane seven years later. It is much more than two historic aircraft – and, what is more, it is free!

The second collection is the RAF Manston History Museum, housed in what was the old MT building and telling the full story with many artefacts from the long and glorious military history of Manston.

The Manston Fire Museum is the final collection, and is housed in the old RAF Fire School building within the MOD FSCTE and opened in June 1995. So, if you are flying from Manston on your holidays, arrive early and learn something of its remarkable history.

The 'For Johnny' statue and the Spitfire Memorial at Manston in 2004. (DWL collection)

MARINE PARADE, Kent – see DOVER (Marine Parade)

MARLBOROUGH (High Trees), Wiltshire

51°24N/01°43W, 623ft asl; SU193678. 1 mile S of Marlborough off A346

Perched near the top of Salisbury Hill on the western edge of the beautiful Savernake Forest, the Earl of Cardigan chose a delightful spot for his unlicensed aerodrome when it opened in 1935. Although the land fell away steeply both to the north and the south, the E-W airstrip gave a run of some 1,800ft (549m) and a shorter but still useable 1,500ft (457m) orientated N-S, more than sufficient for the Avro 504N that the Duke operated from the airstrip, which he called High Trees.

In January 1936 the Central Flying School at Upavon began using the LG for weekday practice force-landings, mainly with Tutors. Among the other private aircraft hangared at High Trees were four exquisite Chilton DW.1 aeroplanes that had been designed and built in the grounds of Chilton Lodge at Chilton Foliate, Berkshire. Although first test-flown by Ranald Porteous in April

1937 from Witney Aerodrome, virtually all subsequent testing was done at High Trees. Being too small for impressments at the outbreak of the Second World War, the four Chiltons were stored at the airstrip and, on instructions from the police, immobilised by severing all the plug leads.

The Marlborough LG, as it was known to the military, continued in use until early 1942 when the nearby Overton Heath took over. When visited on a misty early November in 2003, what was believed to be the Duke's original hangar had been incorporated into farm buildings and was unrecognisable as such, although a small Nissen hut remained in situ. Although a concrete farm track crossed the aerodrome, much of the area was still open grassland ready to receive the pair of Chilton DW 1As, which are still airworthy.

A wartime Nissen hut recorded on a misty November morning. (DWL collection)

Main features:
Runways: grass landing and take-off area with maximum E-W run of 1,800ft and N-S of 1,500ft. *Hangar:* unknown type. *Accommodation:* none.

MARWELL HALL, Hampshire

51°59N/01°16W, 140ft asl; SU508212. 3.5 miles NE of Eastleigh off B2177 (former A333)

The small, attractively named Robin Type B hangar with its sloping side walls was never as common as its larger wartime cousins. Used as a dispersal hangar on aircraft storage units and satellite landing grounds, the Robin was designed to merge into the countryside, often being camouflaged as an agricultural building. Today a number still survive, most now having a genuine agricultural use. One of the largest concentrations of original Robins can be found on the former Cunliffe Owen Aircraft flight test airfield at Marwell Hall.

The Managing Director of Cunliffe Owen lived at the Hall during the early 1940s at a time when his factory at Swaything, Southampton, was busy with modification and repair war work on both British and American designs. Southampton was of course a major Luftwaffe target, although well protected by both barrage balloon and artillery defences. Flying within this area was potentially hazardous and getting the necessary special permissions and clearances very time-consuming. For pilots, delivering or testing aircraft, anything that could make their work easier was to be welcomed.

It was therefore recommended that part of the large estate to the south of Marwell Hall be developed as a flight test airfield, being outside the balloon barrage. The work was relatively straightforward, involving the joining of two large fields, cutting gaps in hedges and a stand of trees, and the closing of a minor road from the then A333 and Hurst Farm to give a suitable grass runway on approximately an E-W orientation. The heavily wooded estate also provided excellent camouflage for a large number of Robin hangars, each capable of holding up to four single-seat fighters. Others in more vulnerable locations were disguised as farm buildings, while Hurst Farm and the Hall were pressed into use as accommodation. The cellars of the Hall became crew rest rooms for the ATA pilots who ferried the aircraft into and out of the airfield, the planning of these flights being handled by administrative staff housed in the old cheese room.

Marwell opened in September 1941 and the first aircraft to arrive were Spitfires and Blenheims. Although the ATA provided the outside link, it was company test pilots who flew the aircraft to and from the factory, but as much work as possible was actually undertaken at Marwell. In addition to British aircraft, larger American designs such as the Boston and Hudson successfully used the airfield. It was a smaller, single-seat, design that caused the most problems unless the wind was blowing strongly down the airstrip. The revolutionary Bell Airacobra with its tricycle nose wheel undercarriage and engine mounted behind the pilot proved most reluctant to take off unless conditions were near perfect. Although the type had entered service with 601 Squadron at Duxford in September 1941, the Squadron quickly reverted to the trusty Hurricanes and the Airacobras, after modifications, were passed to Britain's Soviet allies.

Modification work, especially on American types, continued to grow, reaching a peak in 1943. The aircraft involved included Venturas and the mighty Liberator. This wasn't the only heavy bomber to fly into Marwell, as Cunliffe Owen had obtained a contract to modify the Handley Page Halifax for Coastal Command. With the grass airstrip being just 600 feet (61 metres) wide at its narrowest point, strong crosswinds could make it very tricky, if not unusable, the problem being accentuated by the numerous tall trees that generated significant turbulence in adverse conditions. The ATA pilots who delivered their charges to Marwell had to be very experienced, but even the most blasé airman could not fail to be impressed when the pilot who climbed out of the massive Halifax proved to be a young woman. For everything except the four-engined bombers, when the pilot would have the help of a flight engineer, an ATA pilot of either sex flew alone, doing all his or her own navigation. Unlike many of the airfields the ATA used, Marwell was exceptionally difficult to find. It never appeared on wartime RAF maps and its wooded surroundings provided excellent camouflage. The only landmark that helped the pilot find this semi-secret airfield was the long narrow fish pond of the unimaginatively named Fisher's Pond a mile to the west.

As the war moved into its penultimate year, the risk of air attack being much reduced, Cunliffe Owen moved back to Eastleigh and Air Service Training took over the site for design work on modifications to Mustangs and Mitchells. There was very little flying, and with the end of the war the designers returned to Hamble. The last aeronautical use of Marwell Hall was by the little-known company of Willmot & Mauser Experimental Aircraft, which soon moved on to Beaulieu.

One of the many Robin hangars still in use at Marwell. (DWL collection)

Today the Hall is a well patronised zoological park with brown tourist signs helping airfield hunters find their alternative target. To the south of the road, the alignment of the former runway can still be followed by gaps in the hedges. More obvious evidence of the wartime use of the area is the still numerous Robin hangars. From a plan held by the owner of Hangar Nurseries, there were originally up to thirty; in 2003 at least five could be found relatively easily. The Robin, which gave the nursery its name, is now used by Neptune Outdoor Furniture, another forms part of a complex of modern farm buildings at Marwell Grain Store, and a pair, one semi-derelict, form part of a mushroom farm. The best survivor is used by Marwell Industries. It can be found right beside the road, in excellent condition, having been reclad after storm damage following the infamous 1987 Michael Fish 'What storm?' weather report.

Main features:
Runways: E-W grass landing and take-off area. *Hangars:* large number of Robin Type B. *Accommodation:* local housing.

MEMBURY, Berkshire

51°28N/01°33W 676ft asl; SU308754. 3 miles SW of Lambourn alongside M4

Few of the millions of travellers along the M4 motorway realise that, as they pass the Membury Services, they are travelling over a wartime aerodrome from which American paratroops flew into France on D-Day and later to Holland during the ill-fated operation to capture the bridge over the Rhine at Arnhem. A few more who choose to stop at the westbound services might notice an aeroplane propeller blade mounted on a concrete base on the north side of the car park and be curious enough to wander over to read the plaque and learn that it is a memorial:

'Dedicated to the personnel of the RAF and USAAF 8th and 9th Commands who served at Station 466 Membury during 1941 to 1947. Remember them all.'

Although there is nothing more within the confines of the Services to remind them of the airfield's past, they would only have to travel a short distance away from the car park to find much surviving from those times of nearly seventy years ago.

Construction of Membury as a bomber OTU started in 1941 with the typical three-runway layout, the longest, at 4,544ft (1,388m), aligned SW/NE, four T2 hangars and the normal technical area and dispersed domestic sites. The largest of the dispersed sites required for instructional purposes was located to the north-east of the airfield along Ermine Street, the old Roman road. The entry of the USA into the war after Pearl Harbor and the decision to establish the VIIIth Air Force in the UK altered Membury's future, although it was No 91 Group, Bomber Command, that accepted the still incomplete airfield from the contractors in August 1942.

The first of the assigned units to USAAF Station 466 arrived in early September 1942, consisting of the 3rd Photographic Group, the 67th Observation Group and the 153rd Liaison Squadron. Still very much understrength, the new arrivals were a few hundred partly trained men, six Boeing F-9s (photo-reconnaissance B-17s) and a handful of Piper Cubs. Although nine F-4s (photo-recce P-38s) subsequently arrived with the 5th Photo Squadron, they departed with the 3rd PG in October. The build-up for Operation 'Torch' prevented the Membury units from getting anywhere near full strength. By the end of the year the 67th OG could muster a total of thirty-six second-hand Spitfire VBs divided among the 12th, 107th, 109th and 153rd Squadrons.

In effect the 67th was being used as a training unit, as its Spitfire pilots were posted away as soon as they were qualified on type. However, by March 1943 training was being given in observation, photography and artillery spotting during joint manoeuvres with the Army. During the *Spartan* exercises the Americans were joined by the Spitfires of No 19 Squadron for a three-day under-canvas camp.

Renamed the 67th Reconnaissance Group in June, although still primarily a training unit, some pilots were detached to RAF squadrons for sorties over France. A small number of target-towing A-20 Bostons that had arrived earlier in the year also flew on operations with similar RAF squadrons. Two crews from the 153rd RS joined No 107 Squadron in an attack on Schipol airfield on 30 July 1943, losing one when it spun into the sea; another operation on 18 August was completed without loss. On 13 November the 67th RG was transferred to the IXth AF, leaving for Middle Wallop in December.

The decision that Membury's next resident would be the 53rd TCG meant that a longer runway was needed. Because of the topography, it was only possible to extend the 17/35 runway to the north, although the prevailing south-westerly winds would create a crosswind on this alignment. The extension took the 6,000-foot (1,829-metre) runway almost up to Ermine Street and was ready for the hand-over to the IXth AF on 22 February 1944. However, interlopers had descended on Membury six weeks earlier in the form of the 366th FG, whose three squadrons (the 389th, 390th and 391st) were awaiting the arrival of their P-47 Thunderbolts. They then spent two months getting used to their mounts and the British weather before moving to Thruxton.

Membury was empty for just two days before the 436th TCG arrived from Bottesford on 3 March 1944. The four Troop Carrier Squadrons, the 79th, 80th, 81st and 82nd, flying C-47 Skytrain troop/cargo aircraft and CG-4 Hadrian gliders, immediately embarked on intensive glider towing and paratroop exercises at night in preparation for D-Day.

'California Honey' of the 82nd TCS, 436th TCG, at Membury during 1944. (S. Risher via R. Day)

The Group's first Normandy operation, code-named 'Albany', involved ninety aircraft taking paratroops of the 101st Airborne Division just after midnight on 6 June to a DZ south-east of Ste Mere Eglise without loss. A second drop was not so well positioned and bad weather delayed the return to Membury. The 436th participated in the second glider lift of the 82nd Airborne using mainly British Horsa gliders. D-Day+1 saw Membury resupplying the 101st Airborne, but it was the 442nd that had deployed forward from Fulbeck. In poor weather fifty-six C-47s dropped on the wrong DZ, the supplies being partially retrieved by the 82nd Airborne. Further relatively small-scale glider and parachute drops concluded the work of the 436th during Operation 'Overlord', for which the Group received a well-deserved Distinguished Unit Citation.

The 436th sent a detachment of C-47s to Italy in July for Operation 'Anvil'/'Dragoon' taking paratroops and glider troops to LZs inland of the assault beaches on 15 August to cut communications. After a number of resupply missions, the various elements of the 51st TCW

The flight simulator of the 1940s: Membury's invaluable Link Trainer. (Col R. A. Stone via R. Day)

returned to the UK in late August to prepare for the next airborne operation, 'Market Garden'. Back under 53rd TCW control, on 17 September the 436th carried the 506th PIR to a DZ near Zon to capture the critical Wilhelmina Canal. After a resupply mission to the 82nd Airborne, the last 'Market Garden' mission on D+6 took more gliders to the Nijmegen area.

Pending more airborne work, the 436th concentrated on freight transport duties supplying the Army in France, but kept up training in both glider-towing and para-dropping. On 25 February 1945 the Group was transferred to Melun in France, leaving the rear party behind to tidy up the airfield before handing over to No 47 Group Transport Command in mid-June.

It was on 15 July 1945 that the Dakotas of 525 Squadron arrived from Lyneham, joined in September by No 187 Squadron. Its task – to carry out long-range trooping flights to and from India – started on 1 October. Restrictions on the all-up weight of the Dakota initially limited the number of troops to seventeen, then to just fourteen on part of the route. Fortunately the availability of four-engined transports curtailed this duty in March 1946. The more appropriate task of continental mail and newspaper schedules followed, involving more than nine aircraft per day.

The transfer of Membury and its squadrons to No 46 Group took place on 1 April 1946 before both squadrons left in October, No 187 to Netheravon and 525 to Abingdon. Parented by Welford, Membury was put into C&M; it was considered as a possible SAC base, but rejected because of its runway orientation.

Membury was used by the Hungerford-based Campbell Aircraft Ltd to flight-test its gyrocopters during the mid-1960s before transferring their workshops there in 1967. The Campbell Cricket was built and tested at Membury, production reaching two per week before the company closed in 1976.

Despite the M4 motorway crossing the airfield and the two Service Areas, much of wartime Membury can still be seen. Although the control tower has gone, the engineering factory on the site is called the Tower Works. Many original buildings on the technical site are still extant, including both

T2s. To the south of the main runway, Walker Freight Services has reclad the pair of T2s and also uses former technical buildings as offices. Much of the instructional and domestic sites around Ermine Street are still in use as Industrial Estates. The largest of these to the north of Ermine Street was the Officers' and Sergeants' Club areas, still with the gymnasium/chapel, cookhouse and a power house, which on the day of my visit provided shelter to Fairey Gannet XA459! Just to the south of the Roman road an instructional site housed a pallet company, and in an adjacent field was a double bombing teacher building, which cannot have had much use during the 436th occupation of Membury.

Cut from the cinema wall, the 'Flying Horse' symbol of the 436th TCG is preserved in the Ridgeway Group's museum at Welford. (DWL collection)

The former Officers' Club, north of Ermine Street, is now an industrial estate. (DWL collection)

Flying has not deserted Membury as it boasts two grass strips parallel to the original runways, 16/34 of nearly 3,000ft (900m) and 04/22 a little shorter at nearly 2,000ft (600m). Southern Sailplanes, based near the strips, will maintain or repair your light aircraft up to Dragon Rapide size. Elsewhere on the Industrial Estate, Aviation Enterprises is into very high-tech designs including the Magnum VLA light aircraft and QR5 Quiet Revolution wind turbine. The future of Membury looks very bright.

Main features:
Runways: 220° 4,550ft x 150ft, 170° 6,000ft x 150ft, 270° 3,300ft x 150ft, concrete with wood chippings. *Hangars:* four T2. *Hardstandings:* fifty-nine dispersed concrete. *Accommodation:* USAAF: 470 Officers, 1,898 enlisted men.

MERSTON, West Sussex

50°49N/00°44W 50ft asl; SU885030. 1.5 miles SE of Chichester off A259

At first sight Merston would appear to be another of the many local temporary ALGs built for the invasion of Europe, but in fact its history dates back to before the outbreak of war. The land was requisitioned in July 1939 for development as a decoy site for Tangmere, just over 2 miles away, but the decision was made to convert to a full satellite. A small domestic site was built near Marsh Farm and the technical area on the western side of the airfield. A 30-foot (9.1-metre) perimeter track encircled the roughly square grass landing area. Although nominally ready for occupation by the autumn of 1940, heavy rains left the land waterlogged. Over the winter the opportunity was taken to add six Over Blister hangars and a number of single-engined fighter blast pens. The station was officially opened in the spring of 1941.

The first occupant was No 145 Squadron, which moved its cannon-armed Spitfire IIBs over from Tangmere on 28 May but continued to operate as part of the Tangmere Wing. After a couple of months it moved north to Catterick, changing places with No 41 Squadron, which was soon re-equipped with the Spitfire VB, spending the rest of the year on *Rhubarb* sweeps over enemy-occupied France. The Squadron moved to Tangmere's other satellite of Westhampnett in December as the winter rain had made Merston totally unserviceable. As the airfield dried out, No 41 returned on 1 April 1942, being joined by No 131 on 14 May.

In mid-June No 412 (RCAF) replaced No 41, preparing for Operation 'Jubilee', scheduled for 19 August 1942. During the Anglo-Canadian raid on Dieppe, No 131 was exceptionally busy. Its first incoming raid proved to be a returning Boston under attack from Luftwaffe fighters. The bomber having ditched off Shoreham, the Squadron then escorted a Walrus to rescue the crew from their dinghy. Before 09.00 it was providing low cover over the shipping and claimed one of the defending Fw 190s without loss. A few hours later it escorted the Bostons of Nos 88 and 197 Squadrons without incident. A subsequent top-cover mission was more eventful. A small force of three Do 217s was intercepted, two being destroyed and the other damaged. The final scramble was prompted by another incoming raid, which proved to be a mixed formation of Ju 88s and Do 217s. No 131 dispatched a Ju 88 and damaged a pair of Dorniers for the cost of one Spitfire, which crash-landed near Selsey. It had been a long but most satisfactory day for No 131.

Within a few days of Operation 'Jubilee' both squadrons moved over to Tangmere to make way for the 307th FS of the 31st Fighter Group. Merston had formally become Station 351 back on 4 June 1942, but the American Spitfires did not arrive until 24 August. With the other two squadrons based at Westhampnett, the 31st had the distinction of being the first FG to begin operations with the VIIIth Air Force on bomber escort duties. The Group was assigned to the XII Air Force in mid-September and departed for the Mediterranean in October, leaving Merston to the birds.

The grass of the airfield, despite the frequent waterlogging, had stood up well to Spitfire operations, but with much heavier fighters in prospect and thought being given to the Second Front, the opportunity was taken to 'all-weather' the airfield surface. An Airfield Construction Unit moved on to the site over the winter of 1942/43 to lay two Sommerfeld track runways, which extended significantly beyond the original perimeter taxiway, the SW-NE strip closing the road to the west. The domestic site was also enlarged.

Merston reopened in May 1943 and received its first squadron, No 485 (RNZAF) with Spitfire VBs, on 21 May. It was joined at the end of May by Hurricane IVs of No 184 Squadron, which practised with its rocket-armed fighter-bombers until replaced on 12 June by the mighty Typhoons of 174 Squadron. However, their sojourn only lasted until the end of the month, and when 485 also departed to Biggin Hill on 1 July, silence fell over Merston for just over a month.

In early August the Spitfires of the Canadian Wing (Nos 402 and 416 Squadrons) from RAF Digby were attached to 11 Group for *Roadstead* operations, being joined from Coltishall by No 118 to escort Coastal Beaufighters on hazardous anti-shipping strikes. One of No 118's Spitfires at this time was the famous 'Darlington Spitfire', W3320. Over $3\frac{1}{2}$ years of service, it served with six operational squadrons, recording three enemy aircraft destroyed, another three and a half probables and one damaged.

On the fourth anniversary of the outbreak of war, Merston was honoured by a visit by the 'Father of the RAF', Marshal of the RAF Lord Trenchard, who gave 'an interesting and inspiring address', according to 118 Squadron's ORB. Shortly after, while No 118 was temporarily detached back to Coltishall, its Canadian partners escorted Marauders to the marshalling yards of St Lô, destroying six enemy aircraft with two more damaged for the loss of a single Spitfire, with the pilot saved. The pilots of 118 Squadron were somewhat miffed to have missed the party. By mid-September the Wing had been broken up as Merston was prepared for a Tactical Air Force role.

It was a Typhoon Wing (Nos 181, 182 and 247 Squadrons) that moved in from New Romney during mid-October, a move that was greatly appreciated by the Squadron's personnel as living conditions were much superior. Although all the squadrons suffered losses, No 181 was especially hit. On 25 October three Typhoons were hit by flak near Caen, one crashing and killing the pilot, while the others were able to force-land with the pilots becoming POWs. Worse was to come, for on 12 and 13 November No 181 lost four aircraft and their pilots over France, almost certainly all to flak. The Wing became No 124 Airfield on 15 November and subsequently specialised in fighter-bomber attacks on the V-1 launching sites, often called 'ski' sites.

After Canadians and Americans it was Merston's turn to play host to the aircraft of yet another ally when No 145 Airfield replaced 124. The Free French Wing of Nos 329, 340 and 341 Squadrons arrived from Perranporth on 17 April 1944 with the superb Spitfire IXB. As the impending invasion of Europe drew closer, the Wing's offensive sweeps over France had brought a sad loss when the Wing Leader collided with a 329 aircraft, both pilots being killed. With wing bomb racks fitted, dive-bombing practice began in May, leading up to D-Day when the Wing provided low-level shipping cover. No contact was made with the Luftwaffe on 6 June, but the following day saw a Ju 88 destroyed north of Caen.

The Frenchmen moved to Funtington on 22 June, being replaced by another Spitfire IX Wing for a few days before the arrival of Nos 130, 303 and 402 Squadrons at the end of June. Although only resident at Merston until the end of the first week in August, the Wing provided escorts for No 2 Group aircraft. When it left, the flying history of Merston came to an end. The station was reduced to C&M status and on 16 March 1945 the domestic site was used to accommodate 700 men attached to the Air Disarmament Unit until May, when the Admiralty used the hangars for storage until the end of 1945.

The Sommerfeld tracking was lifted and the Blister hangars removed as the airfield reverted to agriculture. Today some of the perimeter track survives, although that to the south was being relaid and widened in late 2003 as part of a new industrial estate on the old Marsh Farm site. A large area of glasshouses covers the western part of the airfield, and to the north the Chichester Food Park is served by a new road that crosses the old taxiway. A solitary, very overgrown original building is barely visible on the northern boundary of the old airfield, which is rapidly disappearing with no acknowledgment of its important role in the world conflict of the mid-20th century.

Main features:
Runways: 045° 4,775ft, 135° 4,200ft, steel matting (Sommerfeld track). *Hangars:* six Over Blister. *Hardstandings:* twenty single-engine type. *Accommodation:* RAF: 78 Officers, 106 SNCOs, 955 ORs; WAAF: 1 Officer, 60 ORs.

MIDHURST, West Sussex – see COWDRAY PARK

NEW BEMBRIDGE, Isle of Wight – see FORELAND

NEW ROMNEY (Honeychild), Kent

51°00N/00°56E, 3ft asl; TR063269. 1.5 miles N of New Romney off minor road

With so many landing grounds in the Romney Marsh area that were used in either or both of the 20th-century conflicts, differentiating between them is a problem for an airfield historian. The surveyors in 1942, having rejected the Great War sites of Dymchurch and Littlestone, chose 400 acres (162 hectares) of farmland between St Mary-in-the-Marsh and the New Sewer (a Romney Marsh drainage channel). Although lacking woodland to provide natural cover, the site needed little grading, the primary tasks being the piping or infill of numerous channels, ditches and streams and the burying of telegraph wires.

With approval granted on 19 December 1942, work commenced shortly after with March 1943 as a target completion date. Since it was impossible to hide what was being prepared, a decoy site was also created at Romney Salts. Two Sommerfeld track runways were laid down, the longest, at 4,800ft (1460m), being aligned NE/SW with the shorter cross runway running SE/NW.

Honeychild Manor farmhouse and farm on the north-west boundary, together with four local cottages, were requisitioned as accommodation. Huts on a nearby Army searchlight battery were also taken over.

It was not until 2 July 1943 that No 124 Airfield moved in from Appledram with the fighter-bomber Typhoons of Nos 181 and 182 Squadrons, which were quickly dispersed around the aerodrome. With the Honeychild Manor farm buildings becoming the MT yard, the many support vehicles were hidden in and around the buildings. The third squadron, No 247, arrived on 13 August with fighter Typhoons, but the welcome was far from warm as the accommodation camp sites were still a quagmire from recent heavy rain.

Anti-shipping strikes started in mid-August with No 247 tasked with suppressing the flak guns while the 'Bomphoons' (as the press liked to call them) of Nos 181 and 182 dive-bombed with their 500lb (227kg) bombs. 247 Squadron was then diverted into standing patrols to counter the Luftwaffe's hit-and-run fighter-bomber raids on South Coast towns, but the other two squadrons undertook *Rhubarbs* over France, targeting road and rail communications as well as airfields and army camps. No 182 Squadron also tried its hand at some night ops.

There were some losses and the usual accidents occurred, some humorous, others tragic. The most spectacular with a happy ending involved a 182 Squadron pilot who stalled his Typhoon on approach, cartwheeling over the airfield, shedding bits of the aeroplane on the way until just the cockpit remained intact, the occupant escaping with just bruises. The two pilots of 247 Squadron who collided over the landing ground on 15 August were not so fortunate.

One of No 247 Squadron's Typhoon Mk 1s at New Romney during 1943.
(KAHRS Archive via A. Moor)

With the onset of autumn, No 124 Airfield moved to Merston in early October as the Airfield construction team built more hardstandings, a partial perimeter track and four Blister hangars. But New Romney was not to play a major role in the invasion of Europe as it remained a Reserve ALG, only hosting a ground signals unit awaiting its move to Europe and a servicing party to deal with only emergencies. One of its customers was a B-24, believed to be called 'Queen of Hearts', of the 466th BG from Attlebridge in Norfolk, which crash-landed with battle damage on 17 July 1944.

Honeychild Manor farmhouse was damaged by fire on 1 November, but shortly afterwards New Romney was derequisitioned to allow a Works Flight to clear the metal mesh tracking, Blisters and other debris of wartime occupation. The land and buildings were handed back to their owners early in 1945 as farming re-established its historic role. Apart from some culverted streams, there is no evidence of wartime use, but if visitors wish to visit the many aerodromes of Romney Marsh perhaps they should base themselves in Honeychild Manor farmhouse, which provides comfortable bed & breakfast on a working arable farm with its own dairy herd.

Honeychild Manor farmhouse and farm were requisitioned for accommodation in 1943. (DWL collection)

Main features:
Runways: NW-SE 4,125ft, NE-SW 4,800ft, steel matting (Sommerfeld track). *Hangars:* four Blister. *Hardstandings:* one MT, three refuelling. *Accommodation:* tented camp.

NEW ROMNEY (Littlestone), Kent

51°00N/00°58E 7ft asl; TR089275. 2 miles NE of New Romney on A259(T)

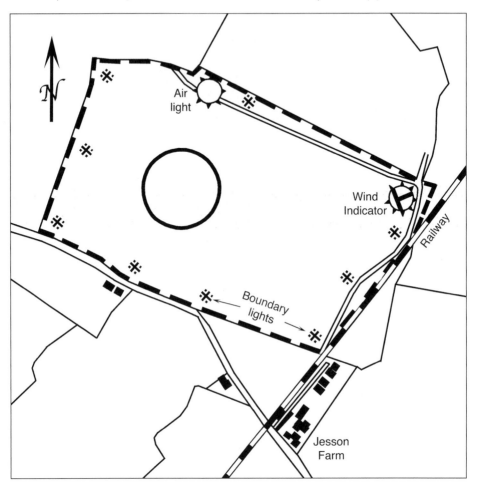

NEW ROMNEY (LITTLESTONE), 1934

*After New Romney closed in 1919, it was reopened in the 1920s as the Littlestone civil
Emergency Landing Ground for use as a diversion when Lympne was unavailable. The
maximum landing run of 1,800 feet (550 metres) was in the E-W direction. Equipped with
boundary lights and an Air Light beacon, it was under the control of Lympne and maintained
by the Directorate of Civil Aviation. It closed in the mid-1930s.*

No 3 (Auxiliary) School of Aerial Gunnery was formed on 1 August 1917 at the newly opened
New Romney/Littlestone training aerodrome. Created on two adjacent sites at St Mary's Bay,
the main part was to the north of the New Romney to Dymchurch road and the outfall of the New
Sewer. The other site was south of the road on a triangular portion of the Littlestone golf course,
known as the Warren (TR085264). A very odd arrangement!

*No 3 (Auxiliary) School of Aerial Gunnery operated RE.7 No 2353 during 1917.
(JMB/GSL collection)*

A pair of MT sheds, two workshops and three hangars were erected on the north-east side of the main site, together with numerous wooden hutted accommodation. As no buildings were placed on the Warren, it is assumed that most flying was done from there, which, despite the limited vehicular traffic of the period, must have caused problems at the crossing places.

After amalgamation with No 1 (Auxiliary) School of Aerial gunnery at Dymchurch/Palmarsh, the expanded unit became No 1 (Observers) School of Aerial Gunnery on 9 March 1918. Both aerodromes continued in use until 1 November 1918 when staff, students and aeroplanes, which included Bristol F2Bs, DH.4s and 9s and the ubiquitous Avro 504Ks, were concentrated at New Romney, which despite its traffic problems had proved to be a more suitable aerodrome.

*Polegate-based Airship SSZ.8 overflies Bristol F2B fighters and a Bessonneau hangar at
Littlestone. (JMB/GSL collection)*

Training slowed significantly after 11 November 1918, but it was not until September 1919 that the School moved to Manston, and by November 1919 the aerodrome was closed when it came under the control of the Government Surplus Property Disposals Board. That might have been the end of a temporary wartime LG, but the establishment of regular air services between Croydon and Paris led to a requirement for civil ELGs to be established along the route. Although Lympne was the local Customs aerodrome, a nearby diversion field was considered desirable.

As the track of the Romney, Hythe & Dymchurch miniature railway had been laid over part of the northern site, it was an area inland of the railway just north of the St Mary's Bay station that was selected as the ELG (TR088280). The maximum landing run of 1,800 feet (550 metres) was in the E-W direction. Equipped with boundary lights and an Air Light beacon, it was under the control of Lympne and maintained by the Directorate of Civil Aviation. By the mid-1930s, with larger and more reliable aeroplanes operating on the route, it was no longer required and reverted to farmland. Housing now covers the main aerodrome site and the Warren has returned to a golf course, leaving nothing to indicate its flying role of ninety years earlier.

Main features in 1918:
Landing ground: grass. *Hangars:* three Bessonneau. *Accommodation:* wooden hutting.

NEWCHURCH, Kent

51°02N/00°55E 3ft asl; TR045315. 7 miles SSE of Ashford on minor road

Romney Marsh hosted four wartime ALGs, of which Newchurch was the most northerly. Located immediately to the west of the village, its boundaries were minor roads to the east and south but it cut the road leading to Will's Farm on the west. After selection and approval in the early summer of 1942, the site plans were being studied by Fighter Command at the end of October with authority for work being granted with a start in mid-December for 1 March 1943 completion.

The site required little grading, a few trees were felled and telegraph wires buried. The Rectory and Brooker farmhouse and buildings were requisitioned for accommodation, with the MT park being also at the Rectory. Two Sommerfeld track runways were laid nearly at right angles to each other. The longer, at 4,800ft (1,463m), was orientated 08/26 and its N/S partner of 4,200ft (1,280m) ran parallel to the Newchurch to Bilsington road.

To appease the War Agricultural Executive Committee it was agreed that the land could be used for grazing when the airfield construction teams had finished their work, but the arrival of No 125

Pilots of No 132 (Bombay) Squadron pose around one of their clipped-wing Spitfires during 1943. (via A. Moor)

Airfield on 2 July 1943 curtailed that use. Initially comprising only two squadrons, Nos 19 and 132 with Spitfire VBs, it was immediately in business escorting USAAF light and medium bombers on raids over France. As with all early ALG exercises, most of the personnel were under canvas, testing the Airfield's ability to be independent of fixed permanent facilities. However, Orchard House in Bilsington was requisitioned for additional accommodation.

A decoy site was constructed at Burmarsh, some 3 miles to the east – a precaution not normally associated with ALGs. The Airfield grew to three squadrons as the Hurricanes of No 184 joined Nos 132 and 602, which had replaced 19 Squadron. An escort task on 15 August by 602 Squadron went very wrong through no fault of its own. Nineteen Marauders of the 323rd BG were scheduled to bomb the Abbeville marshalling yards, but flak so disrupted the formation that the bombs, with one exception, were scattered over the countryside. The exception wasn't on target as it had been dropped by mistake near Redhill on the way out! The Luftwaffe intercepted a raid by thirty-six Marauders of the 387th BG on the Courtrai marshalling yards on 4 September, without effect but losing an Fw 190 to 602 Squadron.

The rather tired Spitfire VBs were finally replaced by the much improved Mk IX by early October, but that was virtually the end of 125 Airfield's sojourn at Newchurch as it moved to winter quarters at Detling on 12 October. In common with other ALGs, improvements were made over the winter, including extending the taxiway and erecting four Blister hangars. Unusually no metal mesh hardstandings were provided as the grass was firm enough. It was No 150 Airfield that reopened Newchurch in April 1944. Although it was ready, No 150 was not. Intended to be a Tempest Wing, only No 3 Squadron was operational with the new type on arrival. No 486 (RNZAF) had a mixture of Typhoons and Tempests; No 56 had Typhoons but was receiving the Spitfire IX as its future mount.

The tailplane of a No 3 Squadron Tempest serves as a briefing table in 1944. (via A. Moor)

Led by the future legendary Wing Commander R. P. 'Bee' Beamont DSO DFC and bar, the Airfield started with pairs on shipping recces but soon extended its role to include targets in France. On D-Day, as No 150 Wing, the Tempests provided top cover over the beachhead while the Spitfires of No 56 escorted tug/glider combinations on both 6 and 7 June. D-Day+2 was a busy day for the Tempests, when two dozen aircraft undertook a sweep from Le Havre to Cherbourg. Warned by GCI radar of 'bogeys', the Wing achieved the perfect bounce on a group of Bf 109s. When the results were totted up, the Wing had shot down four and damaged two without loss, although Beamont returned with a large hole in his starboard wing.

The opening of the anti-*Diver* campaign against the V-1 missiles saw the Wing transferred to ADGB on 18 June, although it had opened its score on 16 June when a total of eleven had been destroyed. The V-1s were a dangerous target as the attacker could easily be damaged when the warhead exploded at some 600 feet (183 metres), the distance at which the Tempest's guns were harmonised. Beamont formally requested that the harmonisation be extended to 900 feet (274 metres) but permission was refused. Typically 'Bee' went ahead regardless, resulting in both improved scores and less collateral damage, but he had to take a reprimand from Command HQ.

No 56 did get one V-1 with its Spitfires, but completed its conversion to the Tempest during July. The Wing had been tasked to tackle the V-1 at night and was having problems. To assess the complexity of the task, two night-fighter pilots were seconded from the FIU at Ford. After converting to the Tempests they found that, under radar control and in good visibility, the missile's pulse-jet exhaust made them easy to spot, but assessing the range was the problem. When a special sight was developed, the FIU detachment commander showed how it was done by destroying seven over the night of 23/24 July. After a hectic summer, the Wing moved to Matlask in Norfolk on 19 September to recuperate, leaving Newchurch deserted.

With no further role, approval to derequisition the airfield was given on 13 December and the lifting of the runways and removal of all other signs of military occupation followed shortly after, being completed in early 1945 when the land was returned to its owners. The only physical sign that a most successful ALG ever existed on the land is the absence of hedges on both sides of the road south of Will's Farm where the main runway had crossed the road.

Main features:
Runways: 350° 4,200ft, 260° 4,800ft, steel matting (Sommerfeld track). *Hangars:* five EO Blisters. *Hardstandings:* seventy temporary, Sommerfeld track. *Accommodation:* tented camp.

Place of interest nearby:
Not far away is an evocative memorial to a casualty of 1940 (TQ062302). Pilot Officer Arthur William Clarke of 504 Squadron went missing in combat on 11 September. Although the crash site of his Hurricane was subsequently identified, the family wished that his remains be undisturbed. On 11 September 1986, forty-six years after his death, a headstone in the style of those of Commonwealth War Graves Commission was dedicated on the roadside nearby.

The roadside memorial stone to PO A. W. Clarke. (DWL collection)

NEWHAVEN, East Sussex

50°47N/00°04E 10ft asl; TQ456002. Half a mile SE of Newhaven town

The busy little port of Newhaven saw its first aeroplane in early 1912 when Lt Spenser Gray had to make an emergency landing in his Short S45 en route from Sheerness to the Naval Review at Portsmouth. His recommendations took some time to bear fruit, but it was the declaration of unrestricted submarine warfare by the German Navy that led to the strengthening of anti-submarine defences around the South Coast. To accommodate a new seaplane base, 5 acres (2 hectares) of shingle foreshore on the eastern side of Newhaven harbour was requisitioned.

A twin-bay wooden hangar was erected well above the high tide level with a concrete hardstanding and slipway. The men were accommodated in wooden Army huts while the Officers lived in nearby Bishopstone, with the Tidemill being taken over as the Wardroom. On the main site, three old railway carriages supplemented a number of wooden huts as workshops, stores and offices.

As an outstation of Calshot, RNAS Newhaven opened in May 1917 with four Short 184 floatplanes. Although operating from the open sea, the flying area was protected from all but south-easterly winds by the long breakwater, but a heavy swell was a problem at times. When weather permitted, flying began at dawn, only ending at dusk, with each patrol being 4-5 hours in length with no reward for the monotonous duty. Aircraft numbers increased to six and the formation of the RAF led to the erection of a new steel-framed aeroplane shed alongside the existing sheds. A second slip and permanent workshops followed.

Another 6 acres (2.43 hectares) were acquired beyond the coast railway line and became known as the drill ground, but may also have been used as an occasional LG for visiting aeroplanes. In May the unit became No 408 Flight and a second Flight, No 409, was formed with the Fairey Campania. Patrols continued between Dungeness and the Isle of Wight, usually without any result, but on 7 July a Short 184 crew spotted the track of a torpedo. It missed the convoy they were escorting but then, to their amazement, the U-boat surfaced, presumably unaware of the seaplane. Spotting the Short, the U-boat started to crash-dive as Lt E. M. Ackery and his observer Lt Dangerfield dropped a 112lb (51kg) bomb close to the diving boat. Although oil was seen, a sinking was not credited.

In August 1918 No 242 Squadron was formed from Flight Nos 408 and 409 at Newhaven and 514 on the nearby Telscombe Cliffs aerodrome. The Armistice led to the disbanding of 409 Flight, but it is believed that the remaining Flights continued until No 242 was disbanded in May 1919. Newhaven closed in the autumn of 1919 and the buildings were auctioned off. Although apparently little was achieved by the long hours flown by the flimsy floatplanes at Newhaven, the mere presence of an aeroplane over a convoy was sufficient to keep a U-boats submerged and restrict their ability to attack.

Carrying the RNAS experimental number N117, the Sage 4c crashed at Newhaven during flying instructional tests in early 1919 and was written off. (JMB/GSL collection)

The Short Cromarty, an F5 and an F3 from the Seaplane Development Flight visited Newhaven in August 1922 during a cruise along the South Coast evaluating possible future anchorages, but nothing came of the visit. Of the former RNAS Newhaven, the concrete hardstanding is extant and the truncated remains of the concrete slip are still visible to remind visitors of a virtually forgotten 'Action Station'.

Main features in 1918:
Take-off and alighting area: open sea protected by breakwater. *Hangars:* two Admiralty seaplane sheds. *Facilities:* slipways and hardstanding. *Accommodation:* wooden hutting and requisitioned housing.

ODIHAM, Hampshire

51°14N/00°56W 400ft asl; SU740491. 6.5 miles ESE of Basingstoke alongside B3349

In June 1924 fields forming part of Down Farm, a mile south-west of Odiham town, were selected by No 13 Squadron, based at nearby Andover, as a potential summer landing ground for its Bristol F2B Fighters. After the land had been bought by the Air Ministry, the first summer training camp took place in 1926, with all the equipment being trucked over from Andover.

Simulating field conditions, tents and Bessonneau hangars were erected alongside the track from Down Farm to Snatchangers Farm. The occupants were No 13 from Andover and No 4 from Farnborough, both initially flying the F2B in an Army Co-operation role. The camps were repeated each summer as both squadrons received new aeroplanes. The Armstrong-Whitworth Atlas was the first RAF aeroplane specifically designed for the Army Co-operation role, No 13 receiving its examples from 1927 and No 4 in 1929. The much-improved Hawker Audax joined both units during 1931/32.

The site at Odiham was an obvious early choice when the RAF Expansion Schemes started in the 1930s. A further 150 acres (61 hectares) were purchased and Lindsey Parkinson Ltd was appointed as contractor in 1934. The planned three-squadron Army Co-operation airfield had the standard technical and domestic site located alongside the Alton road to the north-west of the grass flying field. Three 'C'-type hangars, an SHQ, stores, boiler house and H-Block barracks were all completed by November 1936 at a cost of £315,000.

Handed over to No 22 Group on 3 December 1936, the first occupant on 11 January 1937 was the newly formed No 50 (Army Co-operation) Wing. The constituent Squadrons, 4 and 13, arrived in mid-February with their Audax aeroplanes, which were replaced by the Hector during May, the first Squadrons to operate the type. Although derived from the very successful Audax, the somewhat temperamental Napier Dagger engine initially gave problems during the regular round of artillery spotting, photography and recce with the Army.

The new station and its relative proximity to London led to a number of VIP visitors, but perhaps the first was the most unlikely. Chosen to officially open RAF Odiham on 18 October 1937 was the German Secretary of State for Air, General Erhard Milch! The all-grass flying surface, as at many other aerodromes of the period, was vulnerable to heavy rain during the winter. A most unusual experimental aircraft arrived from Farnborough in early 1938. The Whitley had been fitted with an enormous beam between the undercarriage legs and had oversized Dunlop wheels and tyres. The test was to establish if the new heavier bombers could safely operate from standard grass surfaces. Initially loaded to 24,000lb (10,886kg), the taxiing Whitley became bogged down, and although eventually it was able to taxi at weights of up to 40,000lb (18,144kg), the experiment did show that regular operations would be impractical during the winter. The test over, the aeroplane returned to Farnborough.

The third Squadron to complete the Wing, No 53, finally arrived from Farnborough on 8 April 1938. The following January Odiham embarked on a total re-equipment programme. No 53 received the Blenheim Mk IV while Nos 4 and 13 Squadrons became Lysander operators. Capable of flying from very short strips and a great improvement on the Hector, the Lysander did have some difficult characteristics that could and did catch out inexperienced pilots.

Whether it was the Whitley experiment or the frequent waterlogging after heavy rain, but Odiham was chosen to be one of the first aerodromes to receive concrete runways, which were completed by the spring of 1939. Both were 2,100 feet (640 metres) in length, orientated 10/28 and 05/23. A planned summer mobilisation exercise became for real on 23 August as the Odiham Squadrons were listed for service with the BEF in France. The first to leave was No 53 on 18 September, followed a few days later by Nos 4 and 13.

Replacement Squadrons, Nos 613 and 614, both Auxiliary Air Force, arrived on 2 October. No 614 had Hectors and was immediately divided, its 'B' Flight becoming 225 Squadron with Lysanders on 11 October. No 613 arrived with Hinds, but converted to the Hector during November. After spending the winter liaising with the Army, a few Lysanders arrived for No 613 in March 1940. After the German blitzkrieg through the Low Countries on 10 May, both squadrons ferried Lysanders to France to make up the number of available aircraft.

After the fall of France No 1 Fighter Training Squadron of the Free French was created at Odiham on 3 August with a diverse collection of French aeroplanes, mainly Bloch 151 and Dewoitine 520 fighters. General de Gaulle visited the unit a week later, but the intention to operate as a Free French fighter squadron in Britain failed when it went abroad.

Odiham was an intended target on 12 August by the Ju 88s of KG54, but the successful interception by 43 Squadron disrupted the attack, which failed to find the aerodrome. The only time that Odiham was bombed was on 15 August – by mistake, as the Ju 88s of LG1 thought that they were bombing Andover. Damage was minimal, but as a precaution a decoy was built at Froyle, some $3^1/2$ miles to the south.

The Franco-Belgian FTS was formed at Odiham on 2 November with a dozen Magisters for basic training and a motley collection of more advanced machines including Blenheims and Lysanders for service training. The transfer of Odiham from No 22 (AC) Group to No 70 Group in the newly formed Army Co-operation Command on 1 December was not really noticed by the station's polyglot residents.

The New Year changed the camp into a building site as the runways were resurfaced with a taxiway linking them to the hardstanding in front of the hangars. The work was briefly interrupted on 23 March when a dozen bombs were jettisoned by a Ju 88 under attack by a Hurricane and another was shot at by the station's defences as it flew low over the aerodrome. No bombs landed on Odiham, which continued to have a charmed existence.

No 110 (RCAF) Squadron, which arrived from Old Sarum with Lysanders during 1940, was renumbered 400 (RCAF) Squadron in March 1941 to avoid confusion with the RAF Squadron, and began to receive its Tomahawk recce-fighters in April. Although ineffective as a pure fighter, the Tomahawk, with a good low-level performance, proved to be a vast improvement on the Lysander. As the flow of recruits from the continent had slowed to a trickle, which the RAF Flying Training Schools could absorb, the Franco-Belgian FTS disbanded at the end of May 1941. No 13 Squadron returned to its familiar home on 14 July as it began to re-equip with the Blenheim IV, although it was September before the last Lysander departed.

Back in May 1941 a Douglas Havoc had carried out tests on the runways, which proved that they were too short for regular operations. Thus in September more land was acquired to permit the extension of both runways, which required the demolition of the Isnams farmhouse. When completed in 1942, the E/W 10/28 runway was 5,100ft (1,550m) and that aligned 05/23 reached 4,200ft (1,130m).

The first tactical recce by No 400 on 6 November was spoiled through lack of cloud cover, but it built up experience over the winter as No 13 Squadron concentrated on low-level bombing and smoke-laying operations. Planning for the 1,000-bomber raid even involved 13 Squadron as it joined Blenheims of No 2 Group on diversionary raids on the first two operations without loss. However, on the third raid No 13 sent five aircraft to Wattisham from where they bombed Bremen, one being shot down on the Dutch-German border.

No 400 received the excellent Mustang Mk 1 in July and detached to Gatwick in August for Operation 'Jubilee'. No 13's Blenheims were also allocated to 'Jubilee', operating from Thruxton, whose longer runways permitted higher all-up weights for their smoke-laying operations. With three other Army Co-op Mustang squadrons, No 400 operated in the rear areas behind Dieppe monitoring German troop movements. No 614 Squadron had arrived in August with Blenheim IV/Vs and, as No 13 converted to the Mk V, both units left for North Africa in mid-November for Operation 'Torch'.

For a short time it looked as though Odiham might have an Army Co-operation Mustang Wing when 400 was joined by Nos 168 and 239 Squadrons on 18 November, but No 400 was sent to Dunsfold and 239 Squadron to Hurn in early December, leaving No 168 to concentrate on monitoring Channel shipping and coastal activity. It was joined briefly by the Hurricanes of No 174 and 175 Squadrons, but neither stayed long as more Mustangs arrived in May and June 1943. The newcomers were Nos 170 and 268 Squadrons, as Odiham and its units became part of Fighter Command on 1 June 1943.

The HQ of No 123 Airfield took up residence on 21 June, camping in the old bomb dump, and on 10 July it formally took control of the Mustang squadrons, which continued on Tac/R operations over northern France looking for radar stations, enemy supply bases and HQs. They were joined by No 2 Squadron on 10 August as night-intruder and the occasional interception patrol added variety as the summer moved into autumn and early winter.

The creation of the 2nd TAF and ADGB in mid-November occasioned a wholesale shuffling of units, which resulted in the Mustangs departing in favour of No 511 Forward Repair Unit from Henlow; the latter received its first aeroplane, a Spitfire IX, for repair on 4 December. A pair of Typhoon squadrons, Nos 181 and 247, were resident for a couple of weeks in early 1944 on *Noball* duty, but February saw the return of 400 Squadron, converting to PR Mosquito XVIs and Spitfire XIs. They restarted operations in March and were joined by Nos 168, 414 and 430 Squadrons to form No 128 Airfield of No 83 Group.

All personnel were living under canvas at Broad Oak and Long Sutton when the Airfield became No 128 Wing on 15 May, and operational intensity increased in the build-up to D-Day. From a fairly quiet start, No 511 FRU had expanded until its personnel numbers reached nearly 3,000 by May – not all at Odiham. Detached parties were preparing Halifax, Stirling and Albemarle glider tugs off site in preparation for the invasion, but the pressure on aircraft hangarage at Odiham saw six Blisters being erected around the perimeter. With the aerodrome overflowing with aircraft and personnel, it was with eager anticipation that D-Day dawned on 6 June.

No 128 Wing was operating at full stretch throughout the day, particularly No 168 Squadron, which in 18 hours flew thirty-six Tac/Rs. Four Mustangs from No 430 were intercepted by six Fw 190s and lost one of their number, but generally the Luftwaffe was noticeable by its absence. As continental ALGs became available, Nos 430 and 168 Squadrons moved to B8 Sommervieu, near Bayeaux, on 29 June, being joined by the Spitfires of 400 Squadron on 1 July. The Mosquitoes and No 414 Squadron left to join up with what was then called No 39 (Recce) Wing in mid-August.

Odiham was not quiet for long as No 130 Wing with Nos 4 (Spitfire XI), 2 and 268 (Mustang) Squadrons arrived from Gatwick on 27 June. It was renamed No 35 (Recce) Wing in early July, reflecting the dual role of the unit. While the Spitfires continually updated the photo coverage of Normandy, the Mustangs, flying as many as sixty sorties a day, hunted out troop and transport movements. The Wing followed its predecessors to France in stages; the first to leave for B-10 Plumetot at the end of July was No 2 Squadron, followed by No 268 on 10 August, which had also been flying Typhoons alongside the Mustangs since late July. No 4 moved to B-4 Beny-sur-Mer on 16 August.

In common with all southern airfields at this time, Odiham had its fair share of unheralded visitors in the shape of battle-damaged 'heavies' from both Bomber Command and the USAAF, but at least it did have a good repair organisation on site. However, in July No 511 FRU was renamed Forward Repair Unit (Mobile Aircraft Repairs) within No 85 Group, and moved to Old Sarum on 1 September in preparation for a transfer to the continent.

With no operational units, it must have been an uncanny quiet that descended on Odiham, and the arrival of No 1516 (BAT) Flight with Oxfords in mid-September changed little. Somewhat better was the appearance of the Mosquitoes of No 96 Squadron from Ford on 24 September, but it was not to last, as lack of V-1 targets, in which No 96 had specialised, led to the unit being disbanded on 12 December 1944. No 147 Wing, with 264 and 604 Squadrons, operated its Mosquitoes from Odiham for a brief period in December before transferring to B-51 Lille/Vendreville.

Although Dunsfold became a satellite in January 1945, activity remained limited to the BAT Oxfords, until April when a flood of ex-POWs began to arrive by Dakota. It was inevitable that Fighter Command had no further use for Odiham and, on 7 June, the station transferred to Transport Command with the arrival of the SHQ personnel from Blakehill Farm, followed the next day by No 233 Squadron and its Dakotas. A regular scheduled service was flown to and from the continent, taking a wide range of materials including medical supplies, fuel and food, and returning with troops. Although No 233 was posted to the Far East in August, it was replaced by No 271 Squadron, which maintained the schedules until October when it departed to Broadwell.

The new occupant in early November was No 120 (RCAF) Wing, with No 437 (RCAF) Squadron being joined in April 1946 by No 436 (RCAF) Squadron from Down Ampney to provide a transport link between the UK and Canadian units on the continent. Their task completed, the two Squadrons were disbanded by mid-June as Odiham was returned to the RAF on 28 June 1946 as a No 11 Group fighter station.

The three squadrons that moved in during July operated a mix of types: No 54 had Tempest IIs, No 247 flew the Vampire F.1 and No 130 was still flying the Spitfire IX. Both 54 and 130 Squadrons exchanged their piston-powered fighters for Vampires in October 1946, but No 130 was renumbered 72 Squadron on 1 February 1947. The new jets' exhaust was found to be damaging the runway surface, necessitating emergency repairs and later concrete ends, which were provided on the main runway during 1948/49.

As the RAF's first Vampire Wing, the three squadrons received the improved F.3 variant during 1948 and No 54 was to achieve the first jet fighter crossing of the Atlantic when it went on a goodwill tour of the USA and Canada in July 1948. In exchange, the 56th FG arrived at Odiham with sixteen F-80A Shooting Stars in late July. By late November 1949 the Wing had converted to the Vampire FB.5, but in March 1950 No 72 moved to North Weald, being replaced in January 1951 by No 421 (RCAF) Squadron from Canada for ten months to gain experience with jet equipment before conversion to the Sabre.

Further airfield improvements were scheduled for the early 1950s. The main 10/28 runway, which had been resurfaced in 1948, was extended at the western end to 6,030ft (1,838m), a revised peritrack and ORPs being added. Large areas of concrete were provided in front of the 'C'-type hangars and a pair of T2s, which were erected on the south and east sides of the airfield. Most of the work had been completed when both 54 and 247 Squadrons converted to the Meteor F.8 during April 1952.

Two years later, both squadrons were temporarily transferred to Tangmere as Odiham was prepared for what to be the most important event in its history. In just ten weeks, on 15 July 1954, Odiham was to stage the Review of the RAF by Her Majesty the Queen. A tent city on the south side of the airfield housed the 3,000 officers and men who were to transform the station while a Bessonneau hangar on the parade square provided additional messing facilities. On the day, 318 aircraft and 1,200 personnel represented every RAF command in Europe and many Commonwealth units. Overhead flew forty-seven separate formations at 30-second intervals, beginning with a solitary Sycamore and concluding with a Supermarine Swift – nearly 1,000 aircraft in total, of which 641 were in the air, a spectacle that could never be repeated.

As Odiham's two Squadrons returned at the end of July, a third Meteor squadron, No 46, was formed in mid-August, with the long-nosed radar-equipped all-weather NF.12 and NF.14 variants. The long-awaited Hunter F.1 arrived for the two day-fighter squadrons in early 1955, but was soon replaced by the improved F.4 version, and in 1957 by the superb F.6. In March 1956 No 46 Squadron became Fighter Command's first Javelin unit, which meant more building work at Odiham with a new radar workshop and armoury to house the Firestreak missiles. Sadly, defence cuts brought the disbanding of No 247 in December 1957, leaving Odiham as a two-squadron station. That is until July 1959, when a decision to close Odiham as a fighter base led to the departure of No 46 to Waterbeach and No 54 to Stradishall as Odiham went into C&M.

When Odiham reopened on 15 February 1960 as No 38 Group RAF Transport Command it ushered in an era that has continued to the present day. Planned to be the primary UK station for RAF transport helicopters, these were in short supply at the time, but eventually No 225 Squadron came over from Andover in May with a mix of Sycamore HR.14 and Whirlwind HC.2 and HC.4 machines. As they were considered to be virtually helicopters, the STOL Pioneers and 'Twin Pins' of No 230 Squadron joined the station on 30 May 1960.

A quantum leap forward in size and technology arrived at Odiham on 4 July 1960 when the Belvedere Trials Unit was formed to guide the new twin-rotor helicopter into service. Its job done by September 1961, the Unit became the nucleus of the new No 66 Squadron. Two months later a second squadron, No 72, was formed on this revolutionary design, followed by a third, No 26, on 1 June 1962. No 66 Squadron had left for the FEAF in May 1962, where it gained a good reputation and a nickname of the 'Flying Longhouse' from the Borneo natives. Aden was the destination for No 26 in March 1963, leaving 72 Squadron as the No 38 Group medium-lift helicopter specialist. Probably the most famous exploit of the Belvedere was the attachment of the 80-foot (24.4-metre) spire of the new Coventry Cathedral. That required precise flying but the subsequent location of the 'flying cross' took a week to complete as the wind and weather had to be exactly right.

The turbine-powered Whirlwind Mk 10 was the next new helicopter at Odiham, the first recipient being No 225 in March 1962 followed by 230 Squadron in June, both departing in 1963,

No 230 to Germany in January and 225 Squadron to Malaysia to participate in the Indonesian Confrontation. No 230's cast-off Twin Pioneers joined the Odiham Station Flight with a training remit, but the creation of the Wessex Trials Unit on 1 July 1963 was a more significant event. After six months' evaluation, No 18 Squadron absorbed the Unit at the end of January 1964. No 72 Squadron also adopted the Wessex in exchange for its Belvederes in August 1964.

The Helicopter Operational Conversion Flight evolved from the oddly named Short Range Conversion Flight on 1 July 1967 when the last of the Twin Pioneers departed. The Wessexes were joined by the first Pumas in January 1971 as the unit was renamed the Air Training Squadron in May, and finally No 240 OCU on 1 January 1972. No 18 moved to Germany in 1965 as 230 Squadron returned to Odiham with its Whirlwinds until March 1969, when it went to Wittering. No 33 Squadron re-formed on 14 June 1971 with the Puma, joined by No 230 from October, although its Whirlwind detachment at Wittering continued until December 1971.

As Odiham entered an eight-year period of stability, 72 Squadron with its Wessex HC.2s had evolved to become the largest Army support unit in Britain, with two operational Flights and an HQ at Odiham. Both 33 and 230 Squadrons operated three Flights, which were fully mobile and air-transportable. Flights were quickly deployed to Cyprus after the Turkish invasion of the northern part of the island, supported troops in Belize for many years and went to Rhodesia/Zimbabwe during the transfer to majority rule. The Puma was a workhorse for both the military and civilian authorities.

The long-standing lack of a true heavy-lift helicopter was finally resolved when an order for thirty American Chinooks was placed in February 1978, and later forty-one Boeing Vertol Chinook HC.1s, with deliveries starting in December 1980 to No 240 OCU at Odiham. No 230, with its Pumas, was deployed to Germany, allowing No 18 Squadron to return to Odiham to become the first Chinook squadron on 4 August 1981. The rapid build-up of mighty Chinooks put pressure on accommodation with the result that No 72 decamped to Aldergrove with its Wessexes to concentrate on anti-terrorist role.

An Odiham Chinook is framed by the tail of a visiting Puma. (H. Watson)

The arrival of the Chinook was only just in time, for the Argentinean invasion of the Falkland Islands resulted in the dispatch in April 1982 of the Task Force, which included four of No 18 Squadron's Chinooks. One aircraft, coded BN – Bravo November – had been assembled and was on air test when an Exocet missile sunk the *Atlantic Conveyor* with major loss of life and the three other Chinooks. The achievements of the sole survivor became the stuff of legend as it frequently carried loads far in excess of what was officially possible. On one occasion, eighty-one troops were carried into battle when thirty seated troops was the official capacity.

The second Chinook Squadron, No 7, was formed on 1 September 1982 with No 18 moving to Gutersloh in Germany in May 1983. For the next ten years Nos 7 and 33 Squadrons, together with 240 OCU, continued to operate at Odiham. During 1993/94 the Chinook HC1 fleet was updated to HC2 standard, and 240 OCU became No 27 (R) Squadron. A rationalisation of the Support Helicopter Force (SHF) took place during 1997. No 33 Squadron and its Pumas departed to Benson as No 18 Squadron returned from Germany. In January 1998 No 27 (R) Squadron became a fully operational Chinook squadron, losing its Reserve (R) status.

A number of the resident Chinooks were on display during the Odiham Families Day in 2001. (H. Watson)

In 2000 the responsibility for operating the Conversion Flight transferred to No 18 Squadron, and No 657 Squadron Army Air Corps (AAC), operating the Lynx AH7, arrived from Dishforth. Also in July 2000, No 618 VGS re-formed with four Vigilant T Mk 1s to provide basic flying and gliding training for Air Cadets. The final flying unit at Odiham is the Kestrel Gliding Club, which became part of the Royal Air Force Gliding & Soaring Association in 2006. The Joint Helicopter Support Unit is also based at RAF Odiham to provide specialist underslung load support and landing site management.

Odiham's Mission Statement, taken from the Station Handbook circa 2000, is a perfect summation of what Odiham is about: 'To provide an effective, efficient, sustainable and field-deployable Chinook capability to support UK joint operations world-wide'. Since that handbook was published those worldwide conflicts and commitments have multiplied and the Chinook is in constant demand. I was greatly disappointed that the only operational RAF station in my 'patch' refused a visit, but with its aircraft spread so thinly from the Falklands through Iraq to Afghanistan, perhaps it was to be expected. Sadly it meant that it was not possible to see the memorial and to reflect on the sacrifice made by one Chinook crew whose aircraft so tragically crashed on the Mull of Kintyre on 2 June 1994 with the loss of many members of the Northern Ireland security team.

Odiham Main Gate and Guardroom. (H. Watson)

The pre-war 'Fort'-type Watch Office. (H. Watson)

The wartime control tower, built to Drawing No 343/43 with subsequent modifications. (H. Watson)

The modern Operations Block in 2001. (H. Watson)

Main features:
Runways: 102° 4,100ft x 150ft, 045° 4,200ft x 150ft, concrete with wood chippings. *Hangars:* three 'C' type, six Blister. *Hardstandings:* six twin-engine, twenty-nine spectacle, five 'frying-pan' type. *Accommodation:* RAF: 193 Officers, 167 SNCOs, 1,368 ORs; WAAF: 7 Officers, 3 SNCOs, 62 ORs.

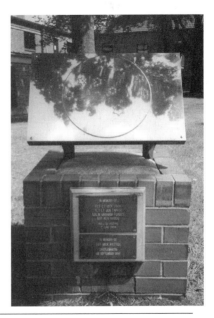

The memorial to the casualties of the conflict in Northern Ireland, including the aircrew lost on the Mull of Kintyre on 2 June 1994. (H. Watson)

OVERTON HEATH, Wiltshire

51°23N/01°44W 613ft asl; SU180658. 2 miles S of Marlborough alongside A345

In the rapid expansion of the RAF in the immediate post-war period, the Central Flying School at Upavon sought additional RLGs to ease congestion at home. One of the chosen sites was an area of heathland at Clench Common above the Vale of Pewsey. Work started almost immediately with the aim of having the site useable by October 1940 but, as might have been expected with heath, the field suffered repeated waterlogging.

The aerodrome was still closed when inspected by the AOC during a visit to the CFS in April 1941, but opened later and by October was being considered as a flying training research and development unit led by the 'father' of RAF flying training, R. Smith-Barry, back in harness as a Squadron Leader. Although Hullavington was later chosen, it was decided to improve Overton Heath by laying Sommerfeld track runways and providing some additional facilities.

No 5 Works Squadron began in February 1942 to upgrade the aerodrome, creating the longer runway at 5,250ft (1,600m), aligned 11/29, and the shorter, at 4,500ft (1,370m), orientated 06/24. Two standard and five Over Blister hangars were dispersed around the field, and a communal mess, barrack huts and stores were built to the south alongside the Clench Common to Wootton Rivers road.

When the CFS became No 7 Flying Instructors' School on 1 April 1942, Overton Heath reopened to operate Oxfords, some of which were based on the aerodrome. The closures of Marlborough/High Trees and, in November 1943, New Zealand Farm led to increased use of Overton Heath, more personnel and improved medical facilities. The establishment then totalled eighty-five, consisting of two officers, three SNCOs and eighty other ranks.

New Year's Day 1944 brought a very large surprise visitor when an 8th Air Force B-17 force-landed successfully on the metal mesh runway without injury to its crew. Oxfords of No 1537 BAT Flight from Upavon also used the aerodrome for a time, but after VE-Day and the acquisition by No 7 FIS in July 1945 of Lulsgate Bottom as a satellite led to Overton Heath being abandoned by August 1945. It was retained as an inactive site until June 1948, when it was handed over to the Ministry of Agriculture.

Most of the land is now farmed, but remnants of the wartime infrastructure survive. During a visit on a misty November morning in 2003 one Blister hangar was found to be in use by a local farmer and a brick hut with its water tower shrouded in ivy and a small Nissen hut remained in very poor condition. However, flying has returned to Overton Heath as the Clench Common Airfield, which is a thriving microlight field operated by GS Aviation adjacent to Cutley's Farm on the western side of the wartime aerodrome.

The Blister hangar at Overton Heath emerges from the mist in November 2003. (DWL collection)

Main features:
Runways: 110° 5,250ft, 060° 4,500ft, steel matting (Sommerfeld track). *Hangars:* two 45ft Blister, four 65ft Blister, one 69ft Blister. *Hardstandings:* none. *Accommodation:* RAF: 2 Officers, 3 SNCOs, 80 ORs.

PALMARSH, Kent – see DYMCHURCH

PARHAM PARK, West Sussex – see PULBOROUGH

POLEGATE, East Sussex

50°48N/00°14E 70ft asl; TQ581035. 3.5 miles NW of Eastbourne

Polegate was another of the airship stations created during 1915 along the South Coast to counter the increased threat from the German U-boat fleet to Britain's coastal shipping, particularly that passing through the English Channel. The location south of the village of Polegate appeared ideal – 142 acres (57.5 hectares) of sheltered meadowland with good road and rail access.

When work started in early 1915, the contractor, Arrol Ltd, found that it was a far from ideal site, low-lying and prone to waterlogging for most of the year. They manage to erect the large airship shed, but all efforts to drain it were unsuccessful. Despite being far from complete or ready for use, Polegate was officially opened on 6 July 1915, the officers taking over a pair of thatched cottages at Wannock while the ratings were billeted in Polegate, Wannock and Willington. By the end of 1915 the situation had improved to such an extent that three SS-type non-rigid 'blimps' were undertaking daily patrols along the Sussex coast.

A second wood and corrugated iron shed was completed in early 1916 and the establishment of fourteen officers and 137 ratings was accommodated in wooden huts clustered around the famous Polegate windmill. On the night of 30 May 1916 the SS.40 airship was demonstrated to War Office personnel. Specially modified at Kingsnorth for secret night flights over enemy territory, the airship had a silenced 100hp Green engine and the gas envelope had an overall black finish. After further tests, and nicknamed 'Black Ship', SS.40 left Polegate on 6 July 1916, arriving at Boubers-sur-Canche near Arras the following day. Some night-reconnaissance flights were made over enemy lines during August and September but the airship returned to the UK in October.

In 1917 Polegate was transferred from Dover to Portsmouth Command and began to assemble a series of the new SSZ airships. The first was SSZ.6, which started its trials on 5 July, followed in succession by SSZ.7, 8, 9 and 10, the last being on test by 4 August. In September the Commander-in-Chief, Portsmouth, Admiral Sir Stanley Colville, flew with a group of airships, but strengthening winds caused a general recall and soon three airships, including that carrying the Admiral, were struggling to return to Polegate. Eventually all returned safely.

A sixth blimp, SSZ 19, was also assembled in early October to join the earlier five as the Polegate Squadron, but SSZ.7 and SSZ.10 collided while landing in fog on 20 December 1917; both were destroyed by fire and Flt Sub Lt Swallow was killed. Replacements were SSZ.28 and SSZ. 30, both being delivered from Wormwood Scrubs during February 1918. The arrival of women on board a ship, even a land-locked naval establishment, caused consternation in March 1918. The WRNS took over clerical tasks, cooking, driving and fabric repairs and were soon accepted.

In April 1918, shortly after Polegate became an RAF airship station, SSZ.41, 42, 43 and 44 were delivered from Wormwood Scrubs, followed in June by SSZ.39, which had been delayed by damage to its controls. The latter airship created a record for endurance between 11 and 13 August when captained by Lt Bryan; she flew 1,000 miles in 50 hours 55 minutes.

When No 10 Group, Warash, took control in October 1918, Polegate had eleven SSZ blimps on charge, but following the Armistice flying was severely reduced and by early 1919 all of Polegate's airships had been deflated. The station closed later that year and its airships were struck off charge. Most of the wooden huts were auctioned, but the hangars were demolished. The concrete road that served the station now serves the large housing estate that covers the site, leaving no evidence of its former role in the Great War.

Polegate-built SSZ.19 commenced trials in October 1917 and was deflated in January 1919. (MAP via P. H. T. Green collection)

With its deflated envelope behind it, the car of SSZ.9 appears relatively undamaged after an accident on 13 November 1917. (RAeS via Ces Mowthorpe collection)

Main features in 1918:
Landing ground: grass. *Hangars:* two large airship sheds. *Accommodation:* wooden hutting.

PORT VICTORIA, Kent – see GRAIN

PORTSMOUTH, Hampshire

50°49'N/01°30'W 12ft amsl; SU670035. 2.5 miles NE of city centre off A2035

During times of high unemployment, governments tend to produce schemes to encourage greater use of labour. These proliferated in the 1980s, but a much earlier scheme was responsible for the creation of a municipal airport for Portsmouth. It was in 1928 that an Air Ministry letter was sent to all population centres of 20,000 or more, reminding the city fathers of the benefits of a civil aerodrome and that construction would qualify for financial assistance from the Unemployment Grants Committee. The information found a sympathetic ear in Portsmouth, as the city's councillors had encouraged aviation from as early as 1919.

It was in June 1919 that Mr E. J. Hucks reached an agreement with the city to operate a joy-riding concession with a third of the profits benefiting the War Memorial Fund. This and a further contract were not a success, but subsequently Surrey Flying Services operated Avro 504s and 536s from an area to the north of the city on the north shore of Langstone Harbour. A much more elaborate project was proposed by a city councillor in 1924, which would have seen a seaplane base in Langstone Harbour, an international airport on Portsea Island and a further municipal aerodrome on Farlington Marshes. Although far too ambitious for its time, it did mean that Portsmouth seized the more realistic opportunity that was presented to it in 1928.

The chosen 276-acre site was on Portsea Island to the north of the city and included the compulsory purchase of Highgrove Farm, the farmhouse of which was retained, converted to a clubhouse for the flying club. The construction was not straightforward, including as it did the demolition of part of the city's old Napoleonic fortifications with their substantial ramparts, much of which went to fill in the old moat. Finally, on 2 July 1932, the superb new aerodrome with its 204-acre grass landing field together with two hangars, refreshment cabin, customs office and a control tower were officially opened by Sir Philip Sassoon, the Under Secretary for Air. More than 50,000 spectators attended the opening ceremony and the flying display that followed. One of the many highlights was a brief flypast by the giant Graf Zeppelin airship.

Before the official opening, the first commercial resident, Portsmouth, Southsea & Isle of Wight Aviation (PSIOWA), had started passenger services to the island and local joy-rides. It was soon joined by a much more substantial organisation when, in March 1933, Airspeed Ltd was persuaded to transfer its business from York to a new corporation-financed factory. Airspeed had been founded two years earlier by four prominent aviation businessmen including Sir Alan Cobham and Nevil Shute Norway, later better known as the novelist Nevil Shute. They arrived with a partially completed prototype Airspeed Courier, on which the future of the fledgling company depended. The aircraft successfully flew for the first time on 11 April in the hands of the Schneider Trophy pilot, Flt Lt G. H. Stainforth.

Later in 1933 the airport achieved a first in Britain when it opened five passenger boarding gates: No 1's destination was Ryde Ferry, No 2's Shanklin Ferry, No 3's Shoreham Ferry, No 4's pleasure flights, with No 5 being a spare. On 18 December Jersey Airways started a daily Portsmouth-Jersey service with six-passenger-seat DH Dragon aircraft, the actual schedule being at the mercy of the tide as they landed on the beach on Jersey. They were joined in January 1934 by Provincial Airways, which started using Portsmouth as an intermediary stop on its Plymouth to Croydon service. Also in 1934 PSIOWA introduced a Shoreham-Portsmouth-Bournemouth service. The increased activity led to the establishment of a radio station, callsign 'Portsmouth'. The 1934 *Air Pilot* warned of two radio masts, 70 feet high, on the south side of the airfield. Other local hazards included a gas works with an obstruction 140 feet high within 350 yards of the airfield in the south-west corner. It also noted that the extreme western area of the landing field was also used as a sports ground with red and white boundary markers indicated the limit of the airfield when sporting activities were taking place.

The Courier was the third Airspeed design to be built; only the three-engined AS.4 Ferry intended for Sir Alan Cobham's National Aviation Displays had brought in any profits. The AS.5 Courier was a very advanced concept, being the first British design to have a retractable undercarriage, but sales were slow to appear. Airspeed was soon in financial difficulties with what today would be called 'a cash-flow problem'. The saviour proved to be the Tyneside shipbuilder Swan Hunter Wigham Richardson Ltd, which acquired the company; with the additional financing, it became Airspeed (1934) Ltd, a public limited company. The date was dropped ten years later. With this new injection of cash, the company was able to proceed with an enlarged twin-engined version of the Courier called the Envoy under the designation AS.6. First flown on 26 June 1934, it immediately attracted orders including one from

£ s. d.

DOES COUNT

It must in the long run. That is why Sir Alan Cobham uses

AIRSPEED FERRY

aeroplanes for all the really hard work. All they require is petrol and oil, and not much of that. For his personal use Sir Alan prefers to save time by using his 160 miles per hour

AIRSPEED COURIER

The first British machine to be fitted with a retractable undercarriage

BUILT BY THE FIRM WHO SET THE PACE

AIRSPEED LTD., THE AIRPORT
PORTSMOUTH   TEL. 2444

An advertisement for Airspeed appeared in Cobham's 1934 National Aviation Day Display souvenir programme. (DWL collection)

PSIOWA, which used the type to inaugurate Portsmouth's first international service to Paris on 22 July 1935. The Air Ministry also expressed an interest in the aircraft.

Sir Alan Cobham had been experimenting with aerial refuelling using Handley Page W.10 airliners, converted by Airspeed to tanker aircraft. In September 1934, a few weeks after the Envoy's first flight, he attempted a non-stop aerial-refuelled flight to India in the prototype Courier. Sadly, a minor engine fault led to an emergency landing in Malta. This was the origin of Flight Refuelling Ltd, which, seventy years on, still exists as a world leader in aerial refuelling, but now trades as Cobham plc in honour of its founder.

During 1936 the possibility of the use of Langstone Harbour as a flying boat terminal was again under discussion, but subsequently the City Council decided that the £400,000 grant on offer from the Government towards the forecast £1.2 million development cost was insufficient. Portsmouth received more unwelcome publicity on 20 August 1936 when two Airspeed employees stole a Courier, which they hoped to sell in Spain, then in the throes of a horrific civil war. Their plan was to cross the Channel and turn right – neither were qualified pilots and their navigation aid was a school atlas! The aircraft crashed on take-off; one 'pilot' was killed and the other was sentenced to three months in prison.

The success of the Envoy was confirmed by a very prestigious order for an Envoy III 'for the transport of Royalty and State personages'. The RAF unit flying this aircraft, which was delivered in June 1937, was to become the King's (later Queen's) Flight. Another significant order was from South Africa for seven convertible civil/military Envoys for use by South African Airways and the Air Force. The Air Ministry interest had crystallised into an initial order for fifty of a military trainer version under the designation of AS.10 and called the Oxford, the first flying on 19 June 1937. As more orders were expected, the factory was extended, with the first deliveries to the RAF beginning in November 1937 to the RAF Central Flying School.

Another Airspeed design ordered by the RAF was the Queen Wasp radio-controlled gunnery target aircraft, conceived to replace the earlier Tiger Moth-based Queen Bee. First flown on 11 June 1937, of the sixty-five ordered only five, including the land and floatplane prototypes, were built. More Queen Bees were ordered instead. An even more extraordinary design was the AS.39 Fleet Shadower, which as its name suggests was conceived as a carrier-based aircraft suitable for maintaining contact with an enemy fleet for up to 7 hours at very low speeds down to 40 knots. The concept lapsed after the start of the war, but with its four Pobjoy Niagara radial engines mounted on a wing capable of folding, the first and only example eventually took to the air in October 1940.

In 1938 the Government placed a contract with the Portsmouth Aero Club to train potential future RAF pilots under the subsidised Civil Air Guard scheme. The club was so successful that by early 1939 it had flown more CAG hours than any other British aero club. The outbreak of war in September 1939 saw the airport being requisitioned by the Air Ministry and led to many changes. The PSIOWA fleet was evacuated to Wales, the company receiving contracts for the overhaul and repair of RAF aircraft. During 1943 the company became Portsmouth Aviation, and by the end of hostilities it had repaired more than 5,000 aircraft.

In June 1940 the Swan Hunter shareholding in Airspeed was acquired by the de Havilland Aircraft Co. Ironically the changeover coincided with an attack by the Luftwaffe when, just after 17.00 hours on 11 July, a formation of what turned out to be twelve Heinkel 111s escorted by Messerschmitts approached Portsmouth. It was believed that the bombers' original target was the naval dockyards but, harassed by fighters from Tangmere and anti-aircraft gunfire, at least one bomber unloaded over the factory and airfield. Although damage was fairly limited, it was decided that the project design team should move out of the front line to Hatfield and later to Salisbury Hall. The production team did not have such an opportunity and sadly one man was killed on 9 April 1941 when a stray bomb hit the factory.

One of the Airspeed designs initiated at Salisbury Hall was the AS.51 Horsa assault glider, but production drawings were prepared at Portsmouth. Construction of complete Oxfords continued at Portsmouth throughout the war, but further production lines of major Horsa components were also established there and at other centres. Most Horsas were assembled at RAF MUs, although complete examples were built and flown at the Airspeed shadow factory at Christchurch. Portsmouth was, however, used for some Horsa experimental work, with the airfield seeing somewhat larger four-engined aircraft than the earlier abortive Fleet Shadower. For a time the mighty Halifax bomber was flown in trials as a Horsa tug. Much smaller Cadet and Grunau Baby gliders appeared at Portsmouth from October 1943 when No 163 Gliding School was formed to give instruction to ATC cadets, remaining until September 1946 when it moved to Gosport.

Most of this other activity was peripheral to the main task of the Portsmouth factory – building Oxfords. The works were the primary production centre for the type, with other manufacture at Christchurch and Hatfield, Standard Motors at Coventry and Percival at Luton. Of a total of 8,586 Oxfords built, more than half – 4, 411 – were built at Portsmouth. Of course they all had to be delivered to their destinations. One example was PH480, which was collected on 3 January 1945 by a No 6 Ferry Pool ATA pilot, Peter George. On that day he had already delivered a Typhoon from Litchfield to Westhampnett, flown the ferry Anson to Portsmouth and finally took the Oxford back to his home base at Ratcliffe, a typical busy day for the ATA. When the last Oxford was rolled out of the factory on 14 July 1945, the occasion was marked by an official party. On display at the time was the seventh production Oxford, L4542, which had been delivered to the RAF back in January 1938.

Post-war, the future of the airport was reviewed by Portsmouth Corporation, but the councillors were divided on the need for a civil airport. A proposal to enlarge the airfield and lay a tarmac runway came to naught. Despite this lack of civic interest, Portsmouth Aviation had begun design work on a revolutionary light commercial aircraft, and in April 1946 re-established commercial flights using a Rapide for charter work. Airspeed remained busy, but was now converting military Oxfords to the six-passenger-seat civil Consul. The first example, originally a de Havilland-built machine, was certified in March 1946 for the Bata Shoe Company. In parallel, a number of Oxfords were refurbished for export, notably to Burma and Turkey.

When, in May 1947, the ban on private flying was lifted, the Portsmouth Aero Club celebrated with a large public air display. Just a month later, on 18 June, the work of Portsmouth Aviation was revealed when the Aerocar Major flew for the first time. A twin-boom design powered by two Blackburn Cirrus engines, it carried a pilot and five passengers in a fuselage pod. The design was a development of the slightly smaller Aerocar Minor, the construction of which was abandoned in 1947. Although the Aerocar was exhibited at both the 1948 and 1949 SBAC Shows, no orders were received and the aircraft was scrapped in 1950. This left Airspeed as the only aircraft manufacturer at Portsmouth, but the independent existence of the company was to survive only until June 1951, when the formal merger with de Havilland was announced. In practice the independence of the company had ceased in 1948 when the holders of Airspeed shares had exchanged them for those of de Havilland. The factory survived by producing components for the Ambassador, Comet and Vampire for de Havilland until the deH name, like that of Airspeed earlier, disappeared when Hawker-Siddeley Aviation Ltd came into existence on 1 July 1963. The HSA logo flew in front of the factory for a few more years until it was finally closed in the mid-1960s.

Commercially the airport was used by a number of airlines, but predominately by Channel Airways, initially with the DC-3 Dakota. The short-sightedness of the city fathers in refusing to consider a hard runway was highlighted in June 1949 when an RAF Anson failed to stop on the wet grass and slid onto the electrified main Portsmouth to London railway line. Fortunately all the occupants escaped before the aircraft was destroyed by fire. Worse was to follow in 1967. Channel Airways had replaced the Dakotas with the much faster Dart turboprop-powered HS (Avro) 748 in 1966 on the Ipswich-Southend-Portsmouth-Jersey service. For a time it looked as if the good times had returned to Portsmouth, with even the City Council making a profit from the airport. Then after a torrential storm on 15 August 1967, a Channel Airways 748 arriving from Southend skidded on the sodden grass, the undercarriage collapsed and the aircraft stopped with its nose buried in a grass bank. Fortunately there were no serious casualties among the twenty-one passengers and crew. Incredibly, just 90 minutes later the service from Jersey suffered the same fate, breaking through the boundary fence and ending up on its belly across the Eastern Road. The only saving grace was again the absence of serious injuries.

The Avro 748 was a very successful 'DC-3 replacement', but two of the Channel Airways fleet overran the runway at Portsmouth on 15 August 1967. (via DWL collection)

The subsequent enquiry ruled that Portsmouth was too small for 748 class aircraft, so Channel Airways re-routed its service to Southampton Airport, Eastleigh. With no scheduled services, the end of Portsmouth as a viable airport came closer. One last attempt was made by John Fisher, the Chairman of the City's Docks & Airport Committee, to persuade the Council to run its own airline. Not unnaturally it was unwilling to agree and Fisher resigned to form, with two other businessmen, JF Airlines in January 1971. Operating the short-take-off-and-landing Twin Pioneers together with the Islander, the airline was moderately successful. However, the Council had formally agreed in 1970 that the airport would have to close, and this was finally implemented on 31 December 1973. Hundreds of spectators and scores of light aircraft spent the day at Portsmouth to witness the official final day of flying.

Some buildings were taken over for non-aviation uses, building bus bodies in the case of those of the former Portsmouth Aviation, while others, like those last used by Channel Airways, were demolished to make way for houses. Over the ensuing years more and more of the original aviation buildings have disappeared, some under new industrial estates, others being obliterated by new domestic housing.

A visitor seeking the former Portsmouth Airport has to look fairly hard to see any indication of the use of what is now an extensive industrial estate. The easiest evidence to spot travels west from Eastern Road: the Airport Service Road no longer serves an airport, but along its length can be found other aviation names such as Merlin and Kestrel Roads, Sywell Crescent, Mitchell Way and Airspeed Road. The former Rat Lane, which bordered the airport, was renamed Norway Lane after Neville Shute Norway, the author and aircraft engineer, who jointly founded Airspeed on the site. Also on the Airport Service Road can be seen the hangar and workshop buildings that were last used by Hawker-Siddeley Aviation, now in the care of Nicoll Food Packaging Ltd. Elsewhere, a red-painted former Blister hangar is now Boarhead Garage, agent for Renault cars. Through all these changes one company remained at Portsmouth, giving a degree of continuity. H&S Aviation, the former Hants & Sussex Aviation, founded in 1946, is now one of the world's leading aviation engine overhaul and repair organisations. Part of BBA Aviation since 1998, the company is still resident on the historic site that was Portsmouth Airport.

The Boarhead Garage is housed in a former Blister hangar. (DWL collection)

Main features in 1938:
Landing ground: grass, 204 acres. *Hangars:* three plus aeroplane factory (Airspeed).
Accommodation: Aero Clubhouse.

PULBOROUGH (Parham Park), West Sussex

50°55N/00°28W 112ft amsl; TQ072147. 1 mile NW of Storrington

Flying in this part of southern England dates back more than a century to 1909 when, on 27 June, a young Gordon England achieved the first soaring flight in Britain in a glider designed by José Weiss. The site of this 58-second flight was Amerley Mount on the South Downs just 2½ miles to the south-west.

Powered flight arrived in the 1930s when a private aerodrome was created on land to the east of the Park and north of the A283. In July 1940 the 100-acre (40.5-hectare) site was requisitioned as a dispersal ELG for Tangmere. There is no recorded use by the squadrons at Tangmere, but some evidence exists that an Auster AOP unit made some use of it prior to D-Day.

Post-war private flying returned to what is now called Parham Airfield in the form of the Southdown Gliding Club. Formed in 1930, it is one of the oldest in Britain and, with some fifty club and privately owned gliders and motor gliders at Parham, it is also one of the busiest. All residents make full use of the lee waves from the South Downs, which Gordon England accidentally discovered all those years ago.

Main features:
Runways: grass. *Hangars:* none. *Accommodation:* none.

RAMSBURY, Wiltshire

51°25N/01°36W 500ft asl; SU269703. 4.5 miles E of Marlborough on minor roads

I was standing on the intersection of the main and secondary runways on a dank, dismal November morning with the powerful scent from a local pig farm wafting on the easterly breeze. With a solitary crow the only aerial movement, it was hard to imagine the frenetic activity of nearly sixty years before when Ramsbury had been USAAF Station 469.

It all began in early 1941, when the land on which the airfield was to be built was requisitioned under the 1939 Emergency Powers Act. Located on a plateau above the River Kennet, it was an area of small fields and their hedgerow boundaries with occasional woodland and a few public roads, the closure of which was notified to Ramsbury Parish Council in May. As with the other airfields in the area, Ramsbury was conceived as a bomber OTU. The main contractor of the site, covering some 500 acres, was Percy Trentham Ltd of Dagenham, with numerous local sub-contractors. Its three runways – the main one, aligned 08/26, stretched to a usefully long 6,000ft (1,829m) – were linked by the perimeter track along which were provided thirty-three pan dispersals (later supplemented by more loop hardstandings). Two T2 hangars were erected in the technical areas, together with living accommodation for 2,368 officers and men. The whole airfield cost some £1m at 1940s prices.

During construction the planned future occupants had changed and when, on 18 August 1942, the still incomplete airfield was handed over to its new owner, it was the VIIIth Air Force rather than Bomber Command that took charge. While the contractors struggled to complete the domestic and technical sites, the first ground echelons of the 64th TCG arrived on 21 August followed shortly after by the personnel and C-47 aircraft of the 16th, 17th, 18th and 35th TCS. Despite wartime security, a couple of days after the Group's arrival it was unofficially welcomed in a broadcast by 'Lord Haw-Haw', who announced that it would shortly receive a Luftwaffe visit. Having lost one of its aircraft and its crew during the transit flight from the States, it was around a week later, when bombs were dropped on the airfield, that the Group realised its war had really begun. Fortunately the attack caused minimal damage and no casualties.

Initially the Group was tasked with freighting duties to acclimatise it to European conditions, but some parachute training then began with the 2nd Battalion of the 503rd PIR billeted at nearby Chilton Foliat. The purpose behind this was finally revealed on 14 September when the 64th was transferred to the newly created 12th Air Force prior to its deployment to North Africa for Operation 'Torch'. All fifty-one of the Group's aircraft were equipped with long-range tanks, and in late October they left for the Cornish ferry airfields where they collected their troops, finally leaving for Algeria on 9 November.

Ramsbury next became a satellite airfield, together with Greenham Common, for No 15 (P) AFU, then moving to Andover from Leconfield to provide multi-engined conversion training to Commonwealth Air Training Plan aircrew unused to the European climate. 'S' Flight with its

Oxfords arrived at Ramsbury in mid-December in atrociously wet weather, although the first intake of twenty-five pupils did not arrive until 5 January 1943. The intensive six-to-eight-week flying programme began immediately, and sadly with such training accidents were inevitable. During the nine months that 15 (P) AFU used Ramsbury no fewer than twelve local accidents were recorded, including three mid-air collisions. The first fatality occurred on 2 March when an RNZAF pilot on a solo night sortie misjudged his height, hitting trees on the downwind leg of his circuit to land. Later that month, during a low-flying exercise, the instructor and his pupil were both killed; the latter, an Australian, Sgt B. Francis, lies in Ramsbury churchyard. The instructor, WO J. R. T. Hazelton, had already completed one operational tour with Bomber Command!

A typical trainee, Ernest 'Bill' Berry, an Australian who trained in Canada, arrived at the end of April, having previously flown all single-engined types, Tiger Moths, Yales and Harvards. The airfield was, incredibly, still far from complete, with roads, paths and buildings still being built. 'Bill' recalled for Roger Day in *Ramsbury at War* that, 'It was easy to get an aircraft bogged down in the mud if you misjudged your position on the perimeter track, and I also remember how surprised I was to see women driving the big gravel trucks – something unheard-of in Australia.'

'Bill' lost a friend from his course on 7 June when the Oxford that Ken Deacon was piloting dived into the ground with no apparent explanation. Onlookers felt that he was probably trying to join the upwind leg of the circuit when the aircraft suddenly went into a wide steep diving turn to the right with the engines still running under power. Recent research has found evidence that the port outer flap linkage mechanism was a very poor fit. This, coupled with the pilot inadvertently lowering the flaps at too high an airspeed, may have caused loss of lateral control and the subsequent crash.

A sixty-strong contingent of WAAFs was stationed at Ramsbury from December 1942, working as parachute packers, drivers, cooks and in administration. They led the RAF parade through Hungerford for the town's fundraising 'Spitfire week' during 1943. But the RAF's temporary occupation of Ramsbury was drawing to a close. It left towards the end of October to make way for the Americans, who returned on 1 November.

C-47s of the 83rd TCS (coded T2), 437th TCG, which was resident at Ramsbury from 5 February 1944. (via DWL collection)

As Station 469, Ramsbury came under the IXth Air Force, but delays in the build-up of the troop carrier groups delayed its permanent occupation until 5 February 1943, although both the 434th and 435th TCGs temporarily used the field during December and January for exercises with the 101st Airborne. The new resident was the 437th TCG, which had left West Palm Beach in early January on the hazardous southern Atlantic ferry route, arriving eventually at Balderton on 21 January before moving on to Ramsbury. It was joined on 12 February by its ground echelon that had travelled by ship, train and truck. The Group was part of the 53rd TCW and was equipped with around seventy-two Douglas C-47 aircraft set up primarily for glider towing. Each of the Group's four squadrons was allocated an individual identity code: the 83rd carried 'T2', the 84th 'Z8', the 85th '9O', and finally '5K' was displayed by the 86th TCS.

Commanded by Colonel C. E. Hudgens, the 437th concentrated on glider towing of both the British Horsa and American Hadrian aircraft, working up to mass night formation flights of up to forty-eight combinations. As elsewhere, the main runway width was increased by the addition of metal planking on either side to accommodate the gliders for a rapid Group launch. This intensive flying inevitably brought accidents, particularly in bad weather. It was during a snowstorm on 4 March 1944 that the 437th suffered one of its worst accidents. The Group had taken off on a cold clear evening for a simulated parachute drop, but after running into thick cloud the exercise was aborted. Some C-47s were able to get into Ramsbury, others reached Membury or Welford, but an 84th Squadron aircraft with a crew of three plus two paratroopers became lost and crashed near Chisbury with the loss of all aboard. Just a week later an apparently minor incident would have serious consequences.

During a glider-towing exercise, a Horsa became detached from its tug, landing safely in a small ploughed field above the village of Axford. Major Donald Bradley decided that it was possible to retrieve the glider rather than wait for it to be dismantled for recovery. With Lt Gaylord Strong as co-pilot and the 83rd Flight surgeon, Captain Lee Gillette, as observer, he landed uphill beside the Horsa. With the glider attached the take-off began, but just as the C-47 got airborne it hit power cables, crashing into the River Kennet. Both pilots were fatally injured, but 'Doc' Gillette eventually returned to duty after weeks in hospital. The glider pilot was able to make another safe landing across the valley. Today a memorial stone commemorating this wartime sacrifice stands in the car park of the Red Lion in Axford.

437th TCG C-47s tow their CG-4A gliders past the Ramsbury control tower. (J. Antrim via R. Day)

As the unknown day for which the Group had been practising so assiduously came closer, an unusual formation visited Ramsbury. On 24 May 1944 the troops had the opportunity for a little aircraft recognition as a mixed group of RAF, USAAF and Luftwaffe aircraft of the 'Rafwaffe', or, more formally, No 1426 (Enemy Aircraft) Flight, arrived. In fact, the day – which was still unknown to the troops – had already been chosen by General Eisenhower on 23 May. He had selected 5 June as D-Day, although bad weather was to force a 24-hour postponement. Thus, a minute before 2.00am on 6 June the 437th went to war. The first of fifty-two combinations was a C-47 flown by Col Hudgens towing a CG-4A carrying 82nd Airborne HQ personnel. Within 30 minutes all fifty-two pairs had taken off destined for an LZ near St Mere-Eglise. Although one Horsa detached from its tow, it was able to return to Ramsbury and a spare C-47 delivered it to France only 30 minutes behind schedule. A second serial of twenty-six C-47s towing eight Hadrians and sixteen Horsas left for an evening reinforcement mission and for the first time the Group had a clear view of the vast armada that was Operation 'Overlord'. A further mission was scheduled before dawn on 7 June when fifty C-47s delivered thirty-two CG-4As and eighteen Horsas to Normandy. Thereafter the Group concentrated on resupply missions, initially by parachute, then, as landing grounds became available, the aircraft began to return with casualties.

A nucleus of four aircraft from each squadron continued with the resupply mission when the rest of the Group was deployed to Italy on 16 July for the invasion of southern France. The remnants of the 437th were temporarily transferred to Welford on 7 August. Their replacement at Ramsbury was the 98th TCS from Exeter, the 441st from Merryfield, the 93rd from Upottery and the 306th TCS from Weston Zoyland, all to ensure an uninterrupted supply of essential supplies to the battlefield in Normandy. The 437th detachment returned to Ramsbury on 24 August to prepare for its next task.

That job was to join the rest of the airborne forces in the joint land/air Operation 'Market Garden', whose objective was a corridor of strategic bridges through Holland to the German border, culminating at Arnhem. On 12 September the 101st Airborne Division moved onto the airfield and, with two days to go, the 437th was briefed on its mission. Sunday 17 September dawned a beautiful autumn day. As the congregation in Ramsbury church commemorated the fourth anniversary of the Battle of Britain, they could hear the C-47 aircraft making ready to leave, and many a quiet prayer was said for their safe return. An impressive seventy combinations left Ramsbury from 11.00 to link up with their comrades to form history's largest airborne armada. However, with glider pilots in short supply each glider flew with a single pilot.

It was to be the worst day in the history of the 437th, the Group losing seven C-47s, more on this single mission than were lost in all its other operations in total. Its objective was near Son en Breugel in the Eindhoven Sector, but strong anti-aircraft defences caused losses even before the German lines were reached. Further C-47s were brought down near Eindhoven and two Wacos collided over the LZ with heavy casualties. A resupply mission was flown the next day, but although some were damaged by ground fire, all aircraft returned safely. A further mission was completed safely on 19 September, which ended the 437th's involvement in Operation 'Market Garden'. It was not quite the last for Ramsbury, for on 20 September twelve aircraft from the 442nd TCG carried 75mm howitzers and troops of the 337th Parachute Field Artillery into Holland.

Ramsbury returned to the routine of resupply and casevac missions, enlivened at the end of the year by the efforts to drop supplies to the garrison at Bastogne encircled in the German Ardennes offensive. Sadly, on 23 December one 85 TCS aircraft was lost to flak. Persistent rumours of a move to France were finally confirmed on 25 February 1945 when the 437th deployed to A8 Coulommiers/Voisins, some 20 miles east of Paris. Like the other local IXth stations, the USAAF retained Ramsbury for rear echelon use until finally relinquishing control with effect from 8 June, when the airfield became part of No 4 Group, Transport Command.

The station became a satellite of Welford and some of the dispersed accommodation sites were taken over by Glider Pilot Regiment personnel. The first aerial activity was not until early September when Dakotas from Welford began to practise 'circuits and bumps'. The first gliders to arrive at the end of September were eight Horsas delivered from Cosford, followed by a further seven from Brize Norton. The purpose of these was revealed when the Glider Pick-up Training Flight arrived from Ibsley on 29 October. As the name suggests, the unit trained Dakota pilots to snatch a glider out of a field without landing. The system was remarkably successful. From the glider a special tow-rope led to a pick-up loop suspended between two poles. The Dakota, equipped with a hook and winch, collected the loop in a low pass and the glider inevitably followed! However,

The absence of turrets and guns reveals that this is a visiting C-109 flying tanker. Note the PSP surface. (W. Ladwig via R. Day)

Dedicated to honor the members of the
437th Troop Carrier Group
United States Army Ninth Air Force
World War II
who were stationed at Ramsbury Airfield
and participated in the campaigns of
Normandy, Ardennes, Northern France,
Rome-Arno, Southern France,
Rhineland and Central Europe.

Where the River Kennet flows over
the small weir below this spot,
Major Donald E. Bradley
and 1st Lt. Gaylord Strong
members of the 83rd Squadron,
437th Troop Carrier Group,
died in the crash of a
Douglas Dakota C47 aircraft on
March 11th 1944.
They were attempting to retrieve a
Horsa glider that had broken free
in a practice mission and landed in the
field above this spot.

Captain Lee Gillette, 83rd Squadron
Flight Surgeon, although seriously injured,
survived the accident and returned to duty
after 5 weeks in the US Army Hospital at
Burderop Park, Wroughton, Wilts.

The impressive 437th TCG memorial shortly after its dedication in 2000. (H. Watson)

the future of gliding was under review with no likelihood of immediate future conflict, and on 15 November the GPTF was disbanded, reducing Ramsbury to C&M status.

For a brief time from 22 January 1946 it looked as if Ramsbury might have a post-war role as a training station when 'F' Flight of No 7 FIS arrived with its Oxfords from Upavon. For a couple of months night-flying training continued, but the Flight returned to its parent station on 29 March and Ramsbury reverted to the dreaded C&M status. Apart from an emergency landing by a Spitfire Mk 22 on 4 January 1947, all flying at Ramsbury had ceased.

During 1947 some of the accommodation buildings were taken over by the Wiltshire Agricultural Committee as a hostel for the Women's Land Army, still an important source of labour on Britain's farms. Other buildings were taken over by displaced persons, mainly Polish and Ukrainian, who worked with the Land Army girls. Gradually the DPs found more permanent homes and by the time the WLA was disbanded in 1950 most of the hostel buildings were already derelict. The airfield was gradually returned to agriculture, although sales of war surplus materials during 1948 had already disposed of such equipment as generators, filing cabinets and other office paraphernalia.

During the celebrations for the fiftieth anniversary of D-Day and the dedication of the Axford memorial, an original 1944 aircraft returned to Ramsbury in the shape of Ken Wakefield's L-4 Grasshopper, which landed to refuel. In November 1997 veterans of the 437th TCG held their annual reunion in the area, all posing for a photograph on the end of runway 26.

Although very few of the wartime buildings survive, most of the southern perimeter track is still its original full width except where it is used by the public road from Ramsbury to Chisbury villages. The southern end of the NW/SE runway still joins the taxiway, which survives at full width, albeit with two modern houses built thereon. The western perimeter track leads to the site of the control tower, sadly now gone, although the roofless fire tender building just hangs on to existence. To the east on Bridge Farm, the largest group of original technical site buildings lives on. The buildings that remain were site numbers 42, 43 and 44. The northern brick-built structure was a gas clothing store and the other two Romney huts were main stores with an office block.

Main features:
Runways: 260° 6,000ft x 150ft, 200° 3,300ft x 150ft, 320° 3,300ft x 150ft, concrete and tarmac. *Hangars:* two T2. *Hardstandings:* fifty concrete, two steel planking. *Accommodation:* USAAF: 470 Officers, 1,898 enlisted men.

Places of interest nearby:
A permanent reminder of wartime Ramsbury is the memorial to be found in the village church. The original plaque is dedicated to the memory of the men of the 437th who lost their lives in the war and below it has been added a list of those names. This was formally dedicated on 7 May 2000 in the presence of a group of 437th veterans on a pilgrimage back to their wartime haunts. In the Memorial Hall, a bronze plaque presented to the village by the veterans of the 506 PIR was dedicated on 18 June 1999, and finally on the village square are two seats carrying the appropriate notice: 'Donated by the Yanks of the 437th Troop Carrier Group stationed on the Hill, 1944-1945.'

RAMSGATE, Kent

51°21N/01°21E 164ft amsl; TR375673. 1.5 miles N of Ramsgate town

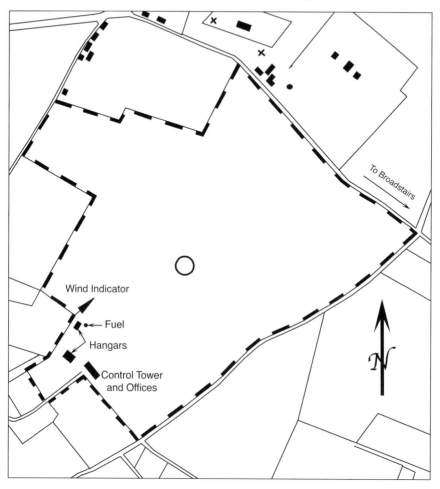

RAMSGATE, 1934

In 1934 Ramsgate had just opened as municipal aerodrome for Ramsgate and Broadstairs. The approximately square field gave a maximum run of 2,700ft (823m) in an E-W direction. Two hangars were available, one of wood and the second, slightly larger at 75ft (23m) by 60ft (25m), was steel, clad in asbestos. Alongside the hangars in the south-east corner of the field was a control tower with a clubhouse/restaurant. After minimal wartime use, Ramsgate was reopened in 1953, closing just fifteen years later.

Although the use of land near Ramsgate by Home Defence aeroplanes was formally agreed in December 1914, there is no record of any actual activity, and it took twenty years for aviation to reach the town. After a vociferous campaign by local councillors, a site 1 mile west of Broadstairs came into use during 1934.

Crilly Airways started a Norwich-Ipswich-Southend-Ramsgate 'Sunday only' service from 7 July to the end of September 1935. Over a similar period Hillman Airways flew daily Stapleford-Ramsgate-le Zoute services, but neither airline used Ramsgate in 1936. The Thanet Aero Club was formed in April 1937 and the aerodrome was officially opened on 3 July as Ramsgate Airport Ltd, operated on behalf of the Corporation of Ramsgate. During August three RAF squadrons occupied the aerodrome during their summer camps. The Thanet AC participated in the Civil Air Guard scheme in 1938 and the Straight Corporation (Southern Airways) operated a Ramsgate to Ilford service from the end of July until September.

All civil flying ceased at the outbreak of war, but in 1940 Ramsgate was reopened as a scatter field for Manston. During the heavy raids on Manston, Ramsgate airport was bombed, particularly on 24 August when the town also suffered badly. After the Battle of Britain, the landing ground was obstructed and handed over to agriculture for the rest of the war, continuing post-war.

The airport was officially reopened on 27 June 1953 by Minister of Civil aviation, Mr A. T. Lennox-Boyd, on behalf of Air Kruise Ltd. The high-profile event was marked by an excellent flying display, which included three Meteors from No 500 (County of Kent) RAuxAF, an F-86e of the RCAF, an S-55 from the USAF and civil displays by an Aerovan, Dart Kitten and Fairy Junior. Air Kruise started a scheduled service through Lympne to Le Touquet, but in the spring of 1958 Skyflights Ltd took over as operator using a Hornet Moth for pleasure flights for the rest of the season.

Activity remained at a low ebb until Chrisair restarted joy-riding in 1961, moving to Sywell in June 1963. A further attempt to revitalise Ramsgate was made by East Kent Air Services in 1967, but to no avail, and the airfield closed for good in 1968. The site is now totally built over with a combination of housing and the Pyson's Road Industrial Estate. The latter does at least make a nod to the past with roads named Hornet, Anson, Blenheim and Lysander Close.

Main features in 1934:
Landing ground: grass, maximum run 2,700ft E-W. *Hangars:* two. *Accommodation:* Aero Clubhouse.

The Avro 504s used by the School of Technical Training (Men) were likely to have been less immaculate than this example. (via DWL collection)

READING (Coley), Berkshire

51°26/00°58W 121ft amsl; SU711718. Quarter of a mile S of Reading town centre

The realisation in 1915 that the war was not going to be 'over by Christmas' caused the War Office to seek an expansion of the RFC. The first necessity was to increase the number of instructors, and in December 1915 the School of Instruction was established at University College, Reading. The School evolved into an initial training course for prospective pilots and observers, and on 27 October 1916 was re-titled No 1 School of Military Aeronautics. The original HQ was established in Yeomanry House on Castle Hill, but the main classrooms were in Wantage Hall (SU727724), with the students being billeted throughout the town.

A four-week course was the norm by 1917, covering artillery spotting, wireless, photography and machine-gun training. Old aeroplane fuselages were placed under the trees along Upper Redlands Road for practical instruction (if only they were still there!). That odd sight was exceeded by the experience of wingless machines being taxied on the Elmhurst Road playing fields. Also set up in Reading was the School of Technical Training (Men), for whom advanced instruction was provided at a small aerodrome near the River Kennet.

Created in low-lying land by joining up two fields, types reported in use included Avro 504s, Farman Longhorns and Shorthorns. The fields also served as an LG for visitors until September 1917, when the SoTT (Men) transferred to Halton. After the Armistice, the land was soon released and is now largely built over with housing and an industrial estate.

Main features in 1918:
Runways: grass. *Hangars:* none. *Accommodation:* none.

RUSTINGTON, West Sussex

50°48N/00°30W 22ft amsl; TQ058020. 2 miles E of Littlehampton off A259

Sited between Rustington and East Preston villages, Rustington was opened in 1917 as an LG for Gosport machines involved in gunnery practice, but in 1918 it was surveyed with a view to its redevelopment as a Training Depot Station for the US Air Service. The roughly rectangular site of 159 acres (64.4 hectares) was planned to have six large HP sheds capable of housing the 0/400, plus a pair of erection and repair sheds in addition to the standard RFC accommodation site.

One HP shed was almost complete when the Armistice stopped all further work. The buildings and site were cleared by the early 1920s and now the whole area is covered by houses and is known as West Preston.

Main features in 1918:
Runways: grass. *Hangars:* one HP shed. *Accommodation:* under construction.

SELSEY, West Sussex

50°45N/00°46W 20ft asl; SZ865957. 2 miles N of Selsey Bill beside B2145

The flat farmland land between the B2145 and the minor road to Church Norton, originally used as a private landing field in the 1930s, was surveyed as a potential ALG in early 1942. Overriding the objections from the Ministry of Agriculture to the loss of prime farmland, the site was requisitioned in July. The subsequent detailed survey proposed a pair of landing strips in the form of a cross, the NE/SW runway achieved 4,200ft (1,280m) and the SE/NW strip had a maximum of 3,900ft (1,189m). Although some farm buildings were scheduled for demolition, cottages near Coles Farm and Norton Priory were earmarked for accommodation.

Construction, which began early in 1943, was limited to the removal of trees and hedges and laying Sommerfeld tracking to create the two runways. All was ready when the Spitfire VBs of No 65 Squadron arrived from Fairlop on 31 May, followed on 2 June by the mighty Typhoons of 245 Squadron, also from Fairlop. Both Squadrons formed No 121 Airfield of the embryo Tactical Air Force and were at Selsey to gain experience of operations from virtually unprepared strips. Most personnel pitched their tents in the grounds of Norton Priory, which became the HQ for the Airfield. The Spitfires proceeded with their bomber escort duties while No 245 Squadron continued to work up on its relatively new mounts. Having proved the viability of the ALG, on 1 July both Squadrons departed, No 65 to Kingsnorth and No 245 to Lydd. Although the deployment had been a success, some necessary improvements had been identified before further use in the planned invasion of Europe.

Over the autumn and winter of 1943 four Extra Over Blister hangars were erected together with PSP temporary hardstandings, but no other permanent buildings. The improved airfield opened on 1 April 1944 and from 8 April the three Squadrons that were to make up No 135 Airfield began to arrive. The first was 485 (RNZAF) Squadron, followed by No 222 (Natal) and 349 (Belgian) Squadrons, all equipped with the Spitfire IX. All three Squadrons went into action immediately on armed recce sorties and bomber escort duties over France. Renamed 135 Wing on 15 May, on D-Day the Squadrons were patrolling over the beachhead from first light without sight of the Luftwaffe. It was No 349, on its third sortie, that intercepted a formation of Ju 88s and Ju 188s near Caen, claiming two destroyed and a further three damaged. The whole Wing was on patrol over the beaches on 8 June when it met a large mixed Fw 190 and Bf 109 fighter-bomber formation. The brunt of the combat fell to Nos 222 and 485 Squadrons, which jointly claimed seven destroyed.

On 10 June a section of No 349 Squadron landed at B2 (Bazenville) to refuel and rearm, the first unit to land in France. The New Zealanders followed just three days later when they began to operate from B-3 (Ste Croix-sur-Mer) during the day, permitting longer combat patrols over the battlefield. From 19 June No 135 Wing began to carry bombs in the fighter-bomber role until the end of the month, when No 145 (French) Wing replaced it at Selsey, also with the excellent all-round Spitfire IX. The three Squadrons, Nos 329, 340 and 341, were led by Wg Cdr Crawford-Compton and continued the armed recce patrols over the battlefield. They also undertook escort sorties for 'heavies' tasked with daylight attacks on the V-1 *Noball* sites. It was during one of these escort duties on 9 July that the Wing muscled into a fight between a group of P-47s and Bf 109s with somewhat mixed results. The Wing Leader and 340 Squadron's Commandant, J. A. M. Fournier, both bagged a 109, but Captain Boudier of No 341 was less fortunate. He attacked a 109 but a P-47, which was also after the German fighter, mistook the Spitfire for a Messerschmitt and promptly shot it down! The unfortunate Frenchman was captured, ending his war as a POW.

The Wing was briefly joined at Selsey during mid-July by No 74 Squadron, but by 6 August No 135 Wing had returned, displacing No 145 Wing, which moved to the relative luxury of Tangmere's pre-war accommodation. The Wing, in which No 33 Squadron had replaced 485 Squadron, was not to stay long, for on 19 August No 33 drew the short straw and left for the B10 strip while the other two Squadrons were attracted to the creature comforts of nearby Tangmere.

The brief but hectic life of Selsey as an ALG was in essence over, its job done as the battle moved further into France. Although officially retained until just after the war ended, its operational career was effectively finished when, in March 1945, local farmers were permitted to use the field for grazing cattle and sheep. The steel tracking was lifted, the road to Church Norton reopened and the Blister hangars removed. Soon there was little or no evidence of the important role played by this quiet corner of Sussex. Fortunately local people did not forget.

Today a marker stands beside the footpath that curves over the open fields of the former airfield from the Church Norton road (SZ866954). Erected by West Sussex County Council as part of the Selsey Heritage Trail, the plaque records:

'RAF SELSEY
1943-1945
From these fields Spitfires & Typhoons provided cover for the Allied Invasion Forces on D-Day 1944.
English, Belgian, French & New Zealand Squadrons were based here.'

Main features:
Runways: 045° 4,200ft, 135° 3,750ft, steel matting (Sommerfeld track). *Hangars:* four EO Blister. *Hardstandings:* temporary, Sommerfeld track. *Accommodation:* tented camp and requisitioned local housing.

The Selsey Heritage Trail marker records the role played by RAF Selsey in 1943-45. (DWL collection)

SHEERNESS, Kent

51°26N/00°45E 7ft asl; TQ913742/932748

On 10 January 1912 Lieutenant Charles Samson RN made history when he took off from a platform mounted on the forward gun turret of HMS *Africa* moored in the Thames Estuary off Sheerness. This flight by a Short S.38 pusher biplane was the first by an aircraft from a ship. In May the S.38 was back at Sheerness abroad HMS *Hibernia*, to which the platform had been fitted in preparation for the Naval Review at Weymouth, where Samson made the first take-off from a ship under way.

The Short S.38 being taken out from Sheerness to HMS Africa for Lt Samson's historic flight in January 1912. (JMB/GSL collection)

Flying ignored Sheerness until 1917 when two independent aviation sites were established. The first (TQ913742), a mile south of the dockyard, was a Naval Kite Balloon training school with an RFC ELG a mile to the east (TQ932748).

Located just inland of the railway line, No 1 Balloon Training Base (SE Area) was a 75-acre (30.4-hectare) site equipped with five canvas balloon sheds. The personnel establishment was 306, of whom 132 were trainees receiving advanced instruction prior to going to sea. Its sister establishment, the 50-acre (20.3-hectare) RFC ELG for Home Defence, was to the east of Marine Town and intended for emergency use by pilots in trouble due to weather or technical problems. With a maximum run of just 1,200 feet (366 metres), the site was very prone to flooding. It was used by detachments of No 37 Squadron operating from Rochford, Stow Maries and Goldhanger, and in 1918 by aircraft co-operating with the Artillery Co-operation Camp at Sheerness.

Both units closed down shortly after the Armistice and are now built over. An industrial estate covers the Balloon Base and a school and housing the RFC Landing Ground.

Main features of Naval Base in 1918:

Landing ground: grass, 75 acres. *Hangars:* five balloon sheds. *Accommodation:* not known.

SHEFFIELD FARM, Berkshire – see THEALE

SHELLBEACH, Kent – see LEYSDOWN

SHOREHAM, West Sussex

50°50N/00°17W 4ft asl; TQ203055. 1 mile NW of Shoreham-by-Sea alongside A27(T)

SHOREHAM, 1935

Shoreham was officially opened as the municipal airport for Brighton, Worthing and Hove in June 1936, but the Art Deco terminal and hangars had been in use from 1935. The two hangars were steel with asbestos cladding, both being 106ft (32.3m) wide by 100ft (30.5m) deep. The all-grass flying surface had a maximum dimension of 2,400ft (732m) in the N-S direction and an average of 2,250ft (686m) in the other orientations. The hangars were destroyed in May 1941 but the delightful terminal building continues in use to this day.

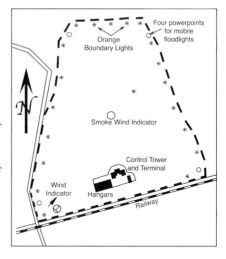

Shoreham is a delight to visit. Nestling beneath the soon-to-be South Downs National Park with the stunning architecture of Lancing College on the skyline, boasting a superb Grade II* listed 1930s Art-Deco-style terminal building, the oldest licensed airfield in the UK has a history dating back to the pioneer days of British aviation prior to the First World War.

In 1910 a former pupil of Lancing College, Harold Piffard, erected a shed in the south-east corner of a rather swampy area drained by many ditches, which was bounded by a high bank in the east with the River Adur beyond and the main railway line to the south. The land was leased from a local farmer by a local solicitor, George Wingfield, who set up a company called Aviators Finance Co Ltd in association with Piffard, whose shed contained his second aeroplane named 'Humming Bird'. The first hop was made in May 1910, and over the summer a number of flights were achieved but always in a straight line as turns inevitably ended in a crash. Finally, in October 1910 came the final crash from which the machine could not be resurrected. However, 'Piff', as he was known, had designed and built the first aeroplane to fly at Shoreham. The rudder, engine and propeller of 'Humming Bird' are preserved in London's Science Museum.

On 7 March 1911 Oscar Morison flew from Brighton to land at Shoreham in his Blériot, which he stored in Piffard's shed as Wingfield started to improve the aerodrome by filling in some of the ditches to give a maximum landing run of some 2,000 feet (610 metres). The choice of Shoreham as a turning point in the Brooklands to Brighton air race on 6 May 1911 put the new aerodrome on the map. The newly titled Brighton & Shoreham Aerodrome was officially opened on 20 June 1911, and among the dignitaries were the mayors of Brighton, Hove and Worthing. A line of six aeroplane sheds were placed alongside the railway embankment, supplementing Piffard's hangar.

The world's first air cargo flight was made from Shoreham on 4 July 1911 when Horatio Barber carried a load of Osram lamps to Hove aboard his Valkyrie biplane, landing safely at the Marine Park in Wish Road. As Shoreham grew in importance, it was chosen as a landing point in both the Circuit of Europe and Circuit of Britain Air Races. The Chanter Flying School was established late in 1911, joined in October 1912 by the Avro Flying School, which moved from Brooklands. In May 1913 the Avro 503 floatplane was first flown from the River Adur, as later was an Avro 504 with floats.

More sheds were erected, increasing the number to ten as the original Piffard building was converted into a restaurant. A number of very unorthodox designs appeared during 1913, the first being the Radley-England Waterplane. Designed by Gordon England, the pioneer glider soaring pilot, this extraordinary contraption was powered by three Gnome rotary engines mounted in tandem, driving a propeller nearly 10 feet (3 metres) in diameter. The twin floats each had seats for three with the pilot operating from the front of the right-hand float. Amazingly it did fly from the Adur until a float was damaged, causing it to sink. England then got involved with the amazing Lee-

Harold Piffard's fourth aeroplane being assembled outside his hangar at Shoreham in 1911. (JMB/GSL collection)

Richards Annular Wing Monoplane, which also flew – just – towards the end of November. A biplane version, very much non-flying, of this machine was built in 1965 for the movie *Those Magnificent Men in Their Flying Machines*.

    The Sussex County Aero Club was founded during 1913 by the Pashley Brothers, and in March 1914 they set up the Pashley Flying School, confirming a commitment to Shoreham that, for Cecil, was to last a lifetime. Around July 1914 a Flight of BE.2s from No 6 Squadron landed from Farnborough as an omen of things to come. However, the outbreak of war in August brought little change to Shoreham as the Pashleys continued training until December, when they closed their School, the RFC formally taking over on 15 January 1915.

Shoreham's Pashley brothers (Cecil is on the left) with their Farman-type aeroplane in 1913/14. (JMB/GSL collection)

No 3 Reserve Aeroplane Squadron took up residence on 21 January 1915 with the usual ad hoc collection of aeroplanes, Maurice Farman Longhorns and Shorthorns, FE.2Ds and Avro 504s. The formation of No 14 Squadron on 3 February was expedited using personnel from No 3 RAS, which did little to maintain the flow of trained pilots. During 1916 eight more aeroplane sheds were erected to the west of the existing line. The inappropriate Reserve title was dropped on 31 May 1917 when it became No 3 Training Squadron. The six-week course at that time included a minimum of 3 hours dual and 3 hours solo flying – no wonder the life of a pilot on the Western Front was so short!

Finally in July 1918 the long-time resident No 3 TS disbanded, being incorporated into No 21 TDS at Driffield. Its replacement was the South Eastern Area Flying Instructors School, created with nineteen Avro 504Ks and two each of every fighter then in service to provide a fourteen-day course. In October 1918 No 94 Squadron completed its work-up and departed to France with its SE.5As. A month later the end of hostilities meant a rapid run-down and the start of demobilisation, the first being No 82 Squadron in February 1919 followed shortly after by the closure of the Flying Instructors School.

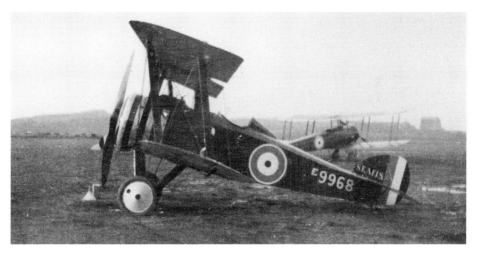

A two-seat Camel, E9908, operated by SEAFIS in 1918, with Lancing College on the skyline. (JMB/GSL collection)

Shoreham became home in April to No 1 Wing, Canadian Air Force, which consisted of No 1 Squadron with SE.5As and No 2 with DH.9A bombers. During the time the Canadians were there, a number of captured German aircraft arrived for storage and the lure of flying them was too much for the rather bored pilots. Sadly, on 22 May Major Carter, the CO of No 2 Squadron, was killed aerobatting a Fokker D.VII when the top wing detached. A subdued Shoreham returned to normal flying. Financial constraints led to a decision to disband the Wing on 28 January 1920 and ship its aircraft to Canada, including many of the captured machines. By December 1921 Shoreham had been cleared of all military structures and aircraft and closed, reverting to grazing land.

In 1925 F. G. Miles sought out Cecil Pashley (his brother had been killed in the war) to form the Gnat Aero Company to carry out pleasure flying with an Avro 504K from New Salts Farm to the south of the railway line (TQ204045). The aerodrome was called Easter's Field. Pashley also taught Miles to fly, his first solo being on 19 May 1926. However, during June a move was made to a slightly larger field over the railway line on the western edge of the modern Shoreham as the company was renamed Southern Aircraft Ltd, with a subsidiary, Southern Aero Club, providing training and the pleasure flights.

The partnership continued to flourish and expand as F. G. Miles, in a shrewd investment, persuaded his father to invest in the land to the east of their aerodrome, which included part of the old aerodrome. An ambitious Flying Meeting was held at Shoreham on 19 May 1928, which included the demolition of an Arabian fort in grand style. During the year Siskins from nearby Tangmere were frequent visitors during cross-country flights. Around this time Sir Alan Cobham was trying to persuade local authorities to establish municipal airports, and the Mayor of Worthing proposed that a joint Brighton, Worthing and Hove airport committee commission a report from Sir Alan. His recommendation was that the original site was the most suitable, but expanded to include land up to the Worthing to Brighton road.

The land was bought for £10,000, netting Miles a tidy profit, and a further £31,000 was allocated for a terminal building and hangars. Work began in November 1934 and Olley Air Service Ltd was appointed as controlling authority on behalf of the Corporations of Brighton, Hove and Worthing. Two hangars were provided, of steel with asbestos cladding, both being 106ft (32.3m) wide by 100ft (30.5m) deep. The all-grass flying surface had a maximum dimension of 2,400ft (732m) in the N-S direction and an average of 2,250ft (686m) in the other orientations. However, the 3rd Edition of the Air Ministry's *Air Pilot* publication insisted that 'in conditions of no wind, aircraft must land and take off in the direction of NE-SW'. That high bank to the River Adur could never be forgotten, nor the railway embankment to the south.

The aerodrome remained in use while the building work continued, with Railway Air Services including the aerodrome in its timetable from May 1935. The new terminal and hangars were completed ahead of schedule on 1 September 1935. The official opening was delayed until 13 June 1936 to give time to organise an international rally and RAF participation in the form of the Gloster Gauntlets of No 19 Squadron from Duxford. A year later, the Martin School of Air Navigation at Shoreham received a contract from the RAF to train volunteer reserve pilots as part of the expansion of the service. Designated No 16 E&RFTS, its fleet initially consisted of Air Ministry-supplied Tiger Moths, which were later joined by a number of Hinds, Harts and also Battles. Two Bellman hangars were erected to the east of the terminal to house the E&RFTS fleet, but on 1 September 1939, in common with the other E&RFTS units, No 16 was shut down as EFTS units were enlarged.

With the closure of all flying training, Shoreham became an international airport as places nearer to London like Croydon were considered too hazardous. For a time, neutral airlines like KLM and Sabena used the airport with DC-2s, DC-3s, Lockheed 10s and 14s, Fokker FX.IIs and even an FW 200 Condor of the Danish Airline DDL. The previously gleaming white terminal was daubed with green camouflage paint and, as the neutral airlines were painted in high-visibility neutral orange, they were covered in camouflage netting when on the ground. The brief period of international airport fame ended with the German blitzkrieg through the Low Countries into France in May 1940, and Shoreham was requisitioned as an advanced fighter airfield in No 11 Group.

The terminal and hangars photographed in May 1987. (DWL collection)

The first military occupants were Lysanders of No 225 Squadron on anti-invasion coastal patrols, but on 18 August the Fighter Interception Unit arrived from bombed-out Tangmere with just one surviving aircraft, its new AI-equipped Beaufighter; a second arrived shortly afterwards, which made the first night sortie from Shoreham on 4/5 September, but its early AI equipment failed. The Luftwaffe finally realised that Shoreham was a military aerodrome on 8 October when three Bf 109s bombed and strafed the field causing some damage. Additional night defence arrived on 14 October when No 422 Flight was formed with Hurricanes, although their primary role was to evaluate the effectiveness of using single-seat night-fighters. As military accommodation was nonexistent, the Sussex Par hotel became the Officers' Mess, the Sergeants' Mess and quarters were in the Ricardo Engineering Works, and airmen were billeted in the town. No 422 left in early December, followed in late January by the FIU, which moved to Ford.

Enlargement of the aerodrome began in early 1941, to incorporate the area to the west over the New Salts Road that had been the 1926-35 aerodrome; ditches were buried in conduits to give a maximum landing run of 3,600 feet (1,097 metres). Sadly the work attracted the attention of the Luftwaffe with a series of attacks; the first, on 13 March by seven Bf 109s, caused slight damage, and on 26 March a solitary bomber cratered the grass, but it was on the night of 8/9 May that serious damage was done to Shoreham. Although the hangars either side of it were destroyed, miraculously the terminal building was untouched.

To replace the hangars, four Over Blisters were dispersed around the aerodrome, one of which was placed beneath the burned-out skeleton of one of the original hangars. Two Lysanders arrived in May 1941 to provide an ASR Flight, the aircraft being equipped with a dinghy on each bomb rack and smoke floats under the fuselage. More Lysanders arrived for No 1488 Flight (Target Towing), which was formed on 1 December 1941 to provide air gunnery refresher training for No 11 Group squadrons. No 277 Squadron came into being at Stapleford Tawney on 22 December, incorporating the ASR detachment at Shoreham as 'D' Flight, which then had three Lysanders and two Walruses on strength.

9 February 1942 saw the departure of No 1488 Flight to Southend, and in May Defiants arrived for No 277's 'D' Flight to supplement its existing types. Hurricanes visited briefly during June in connection with the abortive Operation 'Rutter', but returned on 14 August with Nos 3 and 245 Squadrons in preparation for Operation 'Jubilee', the combined op against Dieppe. There was an early start on 19 August, and in the pre-dawn half-light on an unlit and unfamiliar aerodrome two aircraft collided on the ground and had to abort. A rendezvous with No 43 Squadron from Tangmere was successful and all three squadrons attacked gun positions around the landing sites.

The flak defences were very strong and No 3 lost Sergeant Banks, but No 245 Squadron fared much worse, losing three of its number; its CO, Sqn Ldr H. Mould, just managed to get his severely damaged aircraft back to Shoreham ,but another pilot could only make Friston. No 254 was left with a solitary serviceable Hurricane IIc after the first sortie. Hurriedly refuelled and rearmed, at 07.50 No 3 linked up with No 43 again for a second strike, this time escorted by Spitfires of Nos 310 and 312 Squadrons. Valiant efforts by No 245's groundcrew got seven aircraft ready for the second attack at 12.55. All returned safely, but with more flak damage, leaving just three serviceable. The excitement over, the Hurricanes departed to Hunsdon and Middle Wallop as Shoreham returned to its ASR work.

The work of the ASR crews was as hazardous as any other RAF duty. On 12 October 1942 a Walrus landed in a minefield just 4 miles off the French coast to rescue a 616 Squadron pilot. Under constant shelling from shore batteries in addition to the mines, the pilot, Sgt Fletcher, and his gunner, Sgt Healey, got well-deserved DFMs for the successful rescue. The following year, on 14 April, a Walrus was set on by no fewer than fifteen Bf 109s. The very one-sided combat resulted in the amphibian crash-landing into the sea, but the crew managed to take to their dinghy to be picked up by a fellow 277 Squadron Walrus.

Also in April 1943 No 7 AA Practice Camp was formed to train RAF Regiment gunners, and their target-towing Lysanders formed as No 1631 Flight on 1 August. More RAF Regiment gunners arrived on 18 October when No 18 Armament Practice Camp was formed. It moved to Eastchurch at the end of 1943 when the AA Flight merged with No 1622 Flight based at Gosport to form No 667 Squadron, but remained at Shoreham as 'C' Flight, by then operating Defiant target tugs.

Shoreham had always been prone to flooding, and to ease that and to cater for the increased propensity for damaged Allied bombers to land at the first UK aerodrome they saw, in February 1944 the Pioneer Corps laid a 3,600-foot (1,097-metre) metal track runway on the 03/21 grass strip. Between 11 February and 12 March seven B-17s and two B-24s arrived at Shoreham, causing much damage to the aerodrome surface despite the new runway.

After Shoreham had been transferred to Tangmere's control, Sea Otters began to replace the Walruses. On 7 March Sqn Ldr Brown landed in the Somme estuary to rescue four American airmen right under the noses of the Germans, but, being overloaded, was unable to take off; nothing daunted, he taxied the 76 miles (122km) home. The HQ party of No 277 Squadron moved in from Gravesend in April 1944 and on 26 April No 345 (Free French) Squadron came to undertake an air firing course before starting operations with its Spitfire VBs on 2 May.

The busiest period in Shoreham's history followed in the build-up to Operation 'Overlord'. A number of VIP visits also preceded the day, which included the AOC 11 Group and General P. J. Koenig, Commander of all Free French forces. On 6 June No 345 Squadron flew four missions over the beaches and late in the day escorted tug/glider combinations to their LZ positions behind the German lines. The French pilots were continually operating over their homeland and weather problems on 26 July necessitated a diversion to B2 (Bazenville) for an emotional landing on French soil. They returned to Shoreham the following day, but moved to Deanland on 16 August as the activity level eased.

No 277 Squadron was also now flying early Spitfire Mk Vs on ASR duties and incredibly managed to shoot down a V-1 on 4 July, followed by two more the following day. Since the missile was faster than the Mk V in level flight, this was an amazing achievement. The transfer of No 277 HQ to Hawkinge on 5 October reduced Shoreham to C&M status. Although there was some military activity linked to Tangmere and later Nether Wallop, it was the transfer to the Ministry of Civil Aviation on 12 March 1946 that heralded the resurrection of Shoreham.

Although the South Coast FC was re-established when the airfield reopened on 29 June 1946, there was little other activity until the Brookside Flying Group was established in 1948 by L. J. 'Benjy' Benjamin with a solitary Miles Magister. The number of resident light aircraft gradually increased as Shoreham moved into the next decade, but there was no sign of any commercial activity until the Ministry agreed to hand control back to the Joint Airport Committee; the Committee leased Shoreham to F. G. Miles Ltd, which commenced aircraft design and construction. The first product was the M77 Sparrowjet, which flew for the first time on 14 December 1953. For a time East Anglian Flying Services used Shoreham for services to France and the Channel Islands, but these ceased after October 1962. The Miles Student made its first flight from Shoreham on 15 May 1957, but no orders were forthcoming and F. G. Miles Ltd became part of Beagle Aircraft in October 1960.

The new company built a factory and set up production of its new B.206 light executive twin. A prototype B.218 was also built and flown from Shoreham, but never went into production. Twenty of a military version of the 206 were sold to the RAF as the Basset, but were withdrawn from service after only nine years. In 1968 Beagle was in effect nationalised and produced the B.121 Pup, which flew on 8 April 1967. An order for a military version, to be called the Bulldog, was not enough to save Beagle, which went into liquidation on 20 February 1970. The valiant effort to re-establish Britain's pre-war dominance of the light aircraft market had failed.

A Shoreham legend also ended on 10 December 1969 when Cecil Pashley died. Over his lifetime – he was seventy-seven – he had logged more than 20,000 flying hours and almost certainly taught more people to fly than any other instructor. In his honour the road leading into the airport is now Cecil Pashley Way. Another legend was appointed Airport Manager when Shoreham again became the Brighton, Hove & Worthing Municipal Airport on 15 May 1971, when 'Ben' Gunn, the former Chief Test Pilot of Boulton Paul, and Beagle's Marketing manager, took the reins.

Another attempt to establish a scheduled service from Shoreham began in 1972 when John Fisher Airlines (JFA) operated Twin Pioneers to the Channel Islands, later changing to Islanders and Trislanders, but the venture failed after selling out to Jersey Ferry Airlines. After decades of waterlogging, particularly on the northern side, and many years of local opposition, approval for a hard runway was granted in 1981, which came into use the following year. Despite this major improvement, another short-lived scheduled service was Jersey European Airways, which flew Twin Otters from 1980 to 1984, followed by Brymon Airways, which used a DHC Dash 7s in 1991 but failed to make a profit. The most recent commercial service, operated for some three years by Skysouth to Normandy with a Navaho Chieftain, ceased operations in February 2009.

Airshows have been a feature of Shoreham almost from its beginning, and in 2009 the local RAF Association marked the twentieth anniversary of its first display. Over those years, well in excess of £1 million had been raised for the RAF Benevolent Fund. Sadly, the 2007 show was marred by the fatal crash of a Hurricane, and a memorial plaque to the pilot, Brian Brown, was unveiled at the 2008 event.

With the terminal building as a backdrop, a stunning memorial to all British, Commonwealth and Allied service personnel was unveiled in 1997. The main feature is a propeller from a Martin Marauder, which came down in the English Channel in June 1944. Among the many businesses that operate from Shoreham is the Transair Pilot Shop, but it stands out as the only one with an ex-RAF Tornado as a Gate Guardian. An increasingly rare survivor of wartime training architecture is the anti-aircraft dome trainer, and Shoreham boasts one in excellent condition, albeit on the north side of the airport but close to the last of the wartime Blister hangars.

The anti-aircraft gunnery dome trainer, modified Blister hangar and wartime building in 1987. (DWL collection)

The Shoreham terminal provides the backdrop for the Marauder propeller memorial in 2004. (DWL collection)

Shoreham is a delightfully relaxed airport to visit, in marked contrast to its larger brethren in the South East. Its excellent visitor centre is run by the Shoreham Airport Historical Association, and is the best place to learn more about this amazing hub of aviation history, which celebrates its centenary in 2010, an ideal year to visit Shoreham.

Main features:
Runways: NW-SE 3,600ft, NE-SW 3,450ft, grass. *Hangars:* four Over Blisters. *Hardstandings:* two twin- and four single-engined type. *Accommodation:* RAF: 0 Officers, 84 SNCOs, 530 ORs.

Polegate airship SSZ.30 at a mooring-out station, believed to be Slindon. (JMB/GSL collection)

SLINDON, West Sussex

50°53N/00°38W 301ft asl; SU952104. 6.5 miles NE of Chichester

When Germany renewed its indiscriminate submarine offensive in 1918, the British counter was to create more anti-submarine patrols by non-rigid airships. An additional mooring-out station for Polegate, Slindon came into use on 28 April 1918 and was located in a sheltered valley between the Folly and Eartham Wood through which runs the old Roman road of Stane Street.

Two SSZ blimps were usually stationed at Slindon, which was considered one of the best mooring-out stations. Together with the sister station of Upton, near Poole Harbour, Slindon held the patrolling record for such stations. With Polegate, the three stations flew day and night patrols totalling more than 1,000 hours in May 1918 alone, and played a major part in restricting the U-boats' activities. With no further role after the Armistice, Slindon was abandoned and no evidence survives of its vital Great War role.

Main features in 1918:
Runways: none. *Hangars:* none. Airship mooring facilities.

SOBERTON, Hampshire

50°55N/01°07W 247ft asl; SU620155. Three-quarters of a mile SE of Soberton village off minor road

In 1940 a number of locations were selected as scatter fields on which to disperse and safeguard aircraft in the event of the expected heavy air raids on permanent aerodromes. On a plateau close to Soberton, an LG of some 150 acres (61 hectares) was established for use by Gosport, but no records survive of any aerial activity, although it was still listed as an ELG in 1944.

Post-war the site was used for a time in the 1950s by AST at Hamble, but was replaced by Somerton on the Isle of Wight. The land is now farmed with substantial hedges giving no clues of its brief aeronautical use.

Main features:
Runways: grass, 150 acres. *Hangars:* none. *Accommodation:* none.

SOMERTON, Isle of Wight

50°44N/01°18W 195ft asl; SZ488944. 1 mile S of Cowes on A3020

Perhaps a few of the 400 employees of the BAE Systems Insyte (Integrated System Technologies) factory on Newport Road, Cowes, Isle of Wight, realise that their works have been manufacturing advanced technology equipment since 1916. Today it is the Samson multi-function radar system, designed to give new Royal Navy Type 45 'Daring' Class destroyers a world-beating air defence capability, but in 1916 it was Short-designed biplanes.

Renowned for its boat-building and naval aviation skills, J. Samuel White & Co Ltd was invited to tender for twenty Short Land Tractor bombers in early 1916, but the company had no suitable aerodrome from which to test such machines. To remedy this defect, some 60 acres (24.3 hectares) of farmland were bought from Somerton Farm between Cowes and Northwood. As ditches were being culverted and hedges removed, the company developed and offered an improved landplane version of the Type 840 seaplane.

After the new aerodrome had been inspected in late March 1916 a contract was placed and flight trials started almost immediately. Almost opposite the aerodrome on a 20-acre (8.1-hectare) site, a new factory was built to manufacture the new landplane and the licence-built version of the Short 184. The latter seaplanes were trundled down a track across the field on trolleys to the River Medina, from where they were towed to East Cowes for flight-testing.

Although Samuel White built and flew an amazing quadruplane scout at Somerton, no orders were forthcoming and production was concentrated on the Avro 504. The aerodrome also became an Air Park for all Isle of Wight landplane production. In 1918 the Gosport-based School of Coastal Artillery began to use Somerton as a day LG before moving into Wight aerodrome, as it was then called, with twelve BE.2Cs and 118 personnel in September 1918. It is unlikely that much happened at Somerton after the Armistice and the School closed in August 1919.

The sole Wight quadruplane fighter N546 at Somerton in early 1917. (JMB/GSL collection)

The unlicensed aerodrome was used by Captain F. W. Merriam AFC as a gliding school, which closed in 1923, and for his Aviation Bureau, which started in 1926. His Avro 504K was used for joy-riding during Whitsun 1928. The Saunders A10 fighter and licence-built Bluebird IV were test-flown from Somerton from early 1929. Two years later, in February 1931, Spartan Aircraft Ltd acquired the factory to produce the Arrow, Three-seater and Cruiser, and formed an operating company, Spartan Air Services, to demonstrate the Cruiser on routes between Heston and Cowes. In 1936 Spartan Airways was taken over by British Airways.

The aerodrome continued with Saunders-Roe as a communications field when all other IoW aerodromes closed at the outbreak of war. It was considered for redevelopment as an ALG, but because the two landing strips were barely 3,000 feet (914 metres) in length, it was eventually rejected, remaining in use for visitors to Saunders-Roe throughout the war.

Somerton Airways was formed in 1946 to operate the aerodrome and provide ad hoc charters. Morgan Aviation took over the operation in September 1947 and increased the grass runway to 3,600 feet (1,097 metres). For nearly two years, as a BEA associate operator, the company operated services to Portsmouth and Southampton, but ceased trading in early 1951 and the airfield closed. AST at Hamble bought the lease with the intention of using the field for practice forced-landings and as a relief airfield. A cutback in flying training made the site redundant and it was sold to Plessey, which expanded the factory site. British Aerospace acquired Siemens Plessey in April 1998 and, through a number of name changes, the factory is now BAE Systems Insyte.

Main features:
Runways: grass landing and take-off area, maximum 3,000ft run. *Hangars:* aeroplane factory. *Accommodation:* not known.

SOUTHAMPTON, Hampshire – see EASTLEIGH

SOUTHBOURNE, West Sussex

50°51N/00°55W 32ft asl; SU763065. 3 miles W of Chichester off a minor road

When the United States declared war on Germany in 1917, the generally immature state of its aircraft industry led to the recognition that its aero squadrons in Europe would be largely flying battle-proven British and French designs. Thus Southbourne was conceived as a large Training Depot Station to meet the need to prepare US personnel for service in France. Sited on land between Southbourne, Westbourne to the north-west and the River Ems, the new station covered some 247 acres, greater than most TDSs, as it was planned to house the Handley Page 0/400 heavy bomber. By August 1918 the flying field with its essential services was virtually ready and construction of the technical site adjacent to Southbourne was under way. Together with the standard three double GS sheds and the single-bay Aeroplane Repair Shed of a TDS, the aerodrome was also to have a large Handley Page shed, able to house up to twelve 0/400s with their wings folded. The rest of the buildings of a TDS, including the MT bay and workshops, were arranged behind the hangars.

Completion was scheduled for 1 November 1918, including a planned large domestic site to the west at Lumley Farm, but with construction still far from complete at the Armistice, Southbourne was never occupied. The partially complete buildings were auctioned off during 1919 and the land returned to cultivation. By the 21st century the Bourne Community College, with a new leisure centre, occupies part of the former technical site. Looking out over the old airfield, hedges and fences break up the otherwise apparently still open fields. However, the incessant roar of traffic is a reminder that the landing ground, which never saw an aeroplane, is now bisected by the new A27 trunk road.

Main features in 1918:
Landing ground: grass. *Hangars and Accommodation:* incomplete standard RFC TDS aerodrome.

ST MARGARET'S, Kent – see DOVER (St Margaret's)

STAPLEHURST, Kent

51°09'N/00°35'E 64ft asl; TQ808432. 8 miles SSE of Maidstone off A229

Like most of the future Kent ALGs, Staplehurst was initially surveyed in the spring of 1942. The detailed survey being completed by September, a go-ahead was given on 19 January 1943. The work, which started almost immediately, necessitated the demolition of one cottage and the felling of a few trees, but was very straightforward, being completed by early spring 1943. The primary strip was aligned 10/28 with the secondary runway almost at right angles.

The grazing cattle were evicted by the arrival on 6 August 1943 of a sixty-vehicle convoy carrying No 126 Airfield of No 83 Group, which had taken more than 3 hours to travel from Redhill. The Spitfire VBs of Nos 401, 411 and 412 (RCAF) Squadrons flew in the following day and were dispersed around the field. As usual most of the personnel were under canvas, but some accommodation had been requisitioned at Chickenden Farm, Spills Hill Farm and other cottages.

Ramrod operations started immediately although the first, on 8 August, was aborted through bad weather. A month later all outside contact was cut as Staplehurst prepared for Operation 'Starkey'. A heavy mist on 9 August delayed the start, but a patrol over the French coast around 09.00 saw no action. On the second mission the Canadians tangled, inconclusively, with a number of Fw 190s. The third trip, escorting Bostons to Courtrai, was also abortive. The results were disappointing, but the day had proved the Airfield's capability to operate under field conditions.

After a quiet period an escape exercise on 10 October proved a little more exciting than usual. The pilots were dropped off at various locations in south-east Kent with a brief to get back using their initiative. Fg Off J. T. Murchison and PO R. M. Davenport decided to get back as fast as possible by 'acquiring' a pair of Spitfires from No 129 Airfield at Ashford. Security at Ashford must have been lax as Fg Off D. P. Kelly also helped himself to a Tiger Moth from the same aerodrome. The Army was embarrassed as well when two more pilots liberated a bus from a camp near Headcorn. After a successful exercise, the Airfield returned to winter quarters at Biggin Hill on 13 October 1943.

A winter of improvements saw the creation of seventy hardstandings and a complete taxiway, all constructed from Sommerfeld tracking in preparation for the arrival of the 363rd FG on 14 April 1944. The three Squadrons, the 380th, 381st and 382nd of the IXth Air Force, operated the new P-51B Mustang and had the luxury of a Butler combat hangar to supplement the four original Blister hangars. The initial missions from Staplehurst went badly: on 22 April four Mustangs failed to return, another four on 29 April, and it wasn't until 28 May that the Group was able to claim sixteen victories including five on the ground for the loss of just two Mustangs, one of which had collided with a Thunderbolt.

On D-Day the Group escorted troop carrier and glider formations into Normandy before strafing enemy positions. In the two weeks following, the 363rd achieved nineteen confirmed victories but lost a similar number of Mustangs, mainly to flak. Overall it claimed forty-one enemy aircraft while flying from Staplehurst, but lost forty-three of its own. On 28 June 1944 a somewhat

Pilots from the 382nd FS, 363rd FG, gather around 'Big Mac Junior', the P-51B assigned to John R. Brown, post D-Day.
(Kent Messenger via A. Moor)

larger visitor arrived in the shape of a B-24 from the 489th BG, which arrived with battle damage. Two days later the Group was notified of a move to the continent, to A-15 at Maupertus, the transfer starting on 1 July and completed on 5 July.

The site was derequisitioned in October with most of the tracking lifted for reuse on the continent and the hangars removed before the end of the year. Clearance was complete by early 1945 and the land was handed back to its owners. Much of the area is still open and, with a little imagination, a visitor could still see Mustangs scattered around the aerodrome. However, there is no physical evidence of the hectic months of 1944.

Main features:
Runways: 100° 4,200ft, 010° 3,300ft, steel matting (Sommerfeld track). *Hangars:* none.
Hardstandings: seventy temporary, Sommerfeld track. *Accommodation:* tented camp.

SWINGATE DOWN (Dover), Kent – see DOVER (St Margaret's)

SWINGFIELD, Kent

51°09N/01°12E 459ft asl; TR240449. 6 miles N of Folkestone on minor road

The land on which the ALG called Swingfield was built had two earlier, but little-recorded, aeronautical experiences. The first was in 1916 when some 50 acres (20.25 hectares) of farmland between St Johns Farm and Park Wood were used as an ELG by No 50 Squadron to the end of hostilities. Officially a Second Class LG with a maximum landing run of 1,500 feet (457 metres), it quickly reverted to farmland in 1919, but was requisitioned again in 1940 for use by Swordfish patrolling the Dunkirk beaches, pretending to be Gladiators!

The best recorded period began with a survey in 1942. More land to the east and north-east of the original site was identified as required for the ALG, the plans for which were accepted in December 1942. Some grading and felling of a number of trees commenced soon after, and on 10 May 1943 No 16 Airfield Construction Group arrived to lay the two Sommerfeld track steel mesh runways and erect a pair of Blister hangars. Their work was tested on 16 June when a Spitfire flew in and, having pronounced it satisfactory, the aerodrome was released for grazing by cattle and sheep.

No 50 (Home Defence) Squadron flew rocket rail-equipped BE.2Es and used Swingfield as an ELG. (JMB/GSL collection)

During the autumn the construction team returned to lengthen the runways to bring Swingfield up to the latest ALG standard. Two more Blisters were added as well as a complete taxiway plus eventually fifty hardstandings. As with the other ALGs, Swingfield was intended for use leading up to and during the D-Day period, but it was kept in reserve and not used until August 1944.

With Manston overflowing with anti-*Diver* squadrons, some of the other residents were dispersed and the eleven Albacores of No 119 Squadron arrived on 9 August 1944, joined later by the Swordfishes of No 819 Squadron, both units transferring to No 157 (GR) Wing, based at Hawkinge. Anti-shipping patrols commenced immediately, and to facilitate night operations a makeshift flare path consisting of a single line of electric lights was laid out. The Wing's prey at night were the German E-boats, and attacks were made off Calais and Gravelines that resulted in at least one E-boat being set on fire.

An attempt by the Germans to evacuate Boulogne on 1 September was thwarted by No 157 Wing, although one Albacore was shot down. The following day the CO of 119 Squadron was lost on a similar operation. With operations in the Channel slackening, both units were transferred to Bircham Newton on 2 October, leaving Swingfield to return to its standby role. It was not required again and was finally derequisitioned on 28 April 1945 after the runways and hangars had been removed. The open nature of the site hints of its wartime use but no physical evidence of a little-used ALG can now be detected.

Main features:
Runways: N-S 4,200ft, NE-SW 4,800ft, steel matting (Sommerfeld track). *Hangars:* four Blister. *Hardstandings:* fifty hardcore and gravel. *Accommodation:* tented camp.

TANGMERE, West Sussex

50°50N/00°42W 50ft asl; SU910060. 3 miles E of Chichester, south of A278(T)

In May 1951 Geoffrey Dorman, an eminent aviation journalist, published a history of aviation titled *Fifty Years Fly Past*. In Chapter 15, headed 'First at Tangmere', he tells of how, on 19 November 1916, his forced-landing in sea-fog on George Bayley's Church Farm led to the creation of this famous aerodrome. Stationed at Gosport with No 28 Squadron for advanced training on the FE.2B pusher biplane, Dorman had been tasked to fly to Shoreham and back to complete the 25 hours necessary for the award of his wings. On his return to Gosport the following morning he reported that his emergency field would make a good landing ground.

On 25 September 1917 the required 200 acres (81 hectares) were requisitioned under the Defence of the Realm Act, and work to clear the site started almost immediately. The entry of the USA into the conflict caused a change of plan for Tangmere, the aerodrome being allocated in February 1918 to the United States Army Air Service as a Handley Page TDS. The necessary changes to the accommodation delayed the hand-over until September 1918; meanwhile, the camp was used by No 92 Squadron RFC for training on its SE.5As from March 1918 in preparation for its posting to France in July.

The seven GS sheds (Belfast Truss hangars), arranged in the standard three pairs, and a single ARS, plus the 330ft (100m) HP shed and extensive hutted accommodation were now ready, but the delay in delivery of the HP 0/400s prevented the start of training before the Armistice. Although USAAS personnel moved in from Ford on 17 November with BE.2Es, Farman F40s and DH.4s, their stay was brief and they soon returned to the USA.

In mid-December 1918 No 40 Training Squadron arrived from Croydon and immediately reformed as No 61 TDS with Avro 504Ks and F2Bs; the unit was redesignated 61 Training Squadron on 20 June 1918. The aerodrome also accepted squadrons returning from France, mostly without aircraft, starting with No 41 in early February. Most units disbanded at Tangmere during the year, and those still active by December 1919 moved on to Croydon; Tangmere closed in early 1920.

A potential purchase of the site by W. O. Bentley as a factory for his famous cars came to nothing, and in June 1925 Tangmere reopened as the Coastal Area Storage Unit with Fleet Air Arm aircraft occupying much of the extensive hangarage. A Station HQ was formed on 23 November 1926, and in early December No 43 Squadron, already nicknamed the 'Fighting Cocks', brought its Gamecock fighters from Henlow, being joined on 1 February 1927 by the reconstituted and Siskin IIIA-equipped No 1 Squadron. No 43 also received the Siskin in June 1928. Tangmere now became a premier fighter station, with Nos 1 and 43 Squadrons regularly beating other squadrons during exercises and at gunnery practice camps. All this was achieved despite, or because of, a summer flying programme from 07.00 to 13.00 leaving the rest of the day for leisure pursuits. This arrangement was unique to Tangmere, which was consequently a much sought-after posting.

The CASU disbanded on 1 August 1928 with its personnel transferring to Gosport. The RAF now embarked on an extensive domestic construction programme; the new permanent buildings included barrack blocks, messes for Officers, NCOs and airmen, SHQ, NAAFI, Guardroom and married quarters. Completed on time in 1930, the station now boasted a camp the equal of any, with a rectangular grass aerodrome having a maximum landing run of some 3,600 feet (1,097 metres) on an NE/SW alignment.

The rivalry between the two resident squadrons received a boost in May 1931 when the 'Fighting Cocks' was the first RAF squadron to receive the archetypal 1930s silver biplane fighter, the superlative Hawker Fury. The aerobatic display by three Furies was the highlight of that year's Hendon RAF Display. No 1 had to wait until February 1932 before the first of its Furies began to replace its ageing Siskins. The only other Fury unit was No 25 at Hawkinge, and the three deadly rivals vied to provide the best performance at the annual Hendon Display; the peak of perfection was perhaps the 1937 No 1 Squadron aerobatic team, which flew four Furies with unbelievable precision in a tight box formation. The idyll of peacetime Tangmere began to change in 1937 as the RAF reacted to the growing threat from Germany.

No 1 Squadron lost a Flight on 22 February when it was re-formed as No 72 Squadron with Gladiators; No 87 re-formed with Furies in March, then No 233 formed on 18 May as a GR Anson squadron in No 16 Group. None were to stay long. The two fighter units left in early June, No 72 to Church Fenton and No 87 to Debden; they were immediately replaced by No 217, another Anson squadron from Boscombe Down. No 233 left for Thornaby on 9 July, with No 217 moving to Bicester in mid-August. During this flurry of activity, the station had been experiencing yet more construction work. New workshops, MT and more accommodation were followed, in 1938, by an eastwards extension to give a maximum of 4,500 feet (1,327 metres) of landing ground, skirted by an all-weather perimeter track.

The Munich Crisis of September 1938 put Tangmere on a war footing. The beautiful silver Furies reappeared in dark green and brown camouflage, as did the airfield buildings; air raid trenches were dug throughout the camp and a flight of Hawker Demons arrived to provide night defence. Despite the easing of tension brought by the 'peace in our time' speech from Prime Minister Neville Chamberlain, the RAF continued to rearm as quickly as possible. At Tangmere it was now No 1 Squadron's turn to get new equipment first, when its Hurricanes began to arrive during October 1938, those for No 43 following in November. The winter months were spent working up on the new eight-gun monoplanes.

With tension growing, No 1 was appointed part of the Advanced Air Striking Force destined for France at the outbreak of war. Since Tangmere was its war station, No 605 (County of Warwick), Auxiliary Air Force, arrived on 27 August with ten Gladiators and six Hurricanes with which it was re-equipping. No 43 erected barbed-wire defences around its dispersed aircraft on the eastern side of the aerodrome and moved into tents to be at instant readiness as war was declared. On 9 September No 1 duly left for France, but tragedy struck 605 ten days later when it lost two pilots as their Gladiators collided near Tangmere. In mid-October No 92 re-formed at Tangmere with Blenheim I(F) fighters. After almost thirteen years at Tangmere, 43 Squadron transferred to No 13 Group at RAF Acklington in mid-November, being replaced by the Hurricanes of No 501 Squadron. Blenheim I(F)s of No 601, the so called 'Millionaires Squadron', arrived from Biggin Hill at the end of December as No 92 moved to Croydon.

With everything in place, Tangmere settled into the quiet period known as the 'Phoney War'. On 11 February 1940 No 605 Squadron was posted to Leuchars and a month later No 601 began to exchange its Blenheims for the single-seat Hurricane. The winter of 1939/40 saw weeks of frost and snow, then the thaw brought flooding to many aerodromes. Tangmere escaped flooding, unlike Shoreham, which had to transfer all its scheduled Channel Island services to Tangmere during February and March.

In mid-April Tangmere saw the formation of a most significant unit. Under the command of Wg Cdr G. P. Chamberlain, the Fighter Interception Unit with six Blenheim IV(F) fighters was charged with the 'further development of the Straight AI pulse method' of intercepting enemy aircraft at night. History was finally made on the night of 22/23 July when, for the first time, an enemy bomber (Dornier 17Z) was intercepted through the use of airborne radar and shot down by Flt Lt Ashfield and his two AI operators, Pilot Officer Morris and Flt Sgt Leyland.

The 'Phoney War' ended abruptly on 10 May as Germany attacked the Low Countries. On that day No 501 left for Bethienville and 145 Squadron arrived from Croydon. No 601's 'A' Flight reinforced No 3 Squadron at Merville from mid-May, both auxiliary squadrons in the thick of the action over Dunkirk. On 1 June No 43 Squadron returned to Tangmere and was immediately sent to patrol over the Dunkirk beaches. In a successful action, the Squadron claimed seven Bf 109s and two Bf 110s for the loss of two Hurricanes and one pilot. Tangmere had unusual visitors during this time: six Cherbourg-based Vought V-156Fs of the Aeronavale, which mounted an attack on the Germans at Furness before returning to base. Six days after its success over Dunkirk, No 43 suffered such losses that it became temporarily non-operational. No 1 Squadron returned on 23 June and all the squadrons used the welcome relative lull in activity to train their replacement pilots.

Nos 145 and 601 Squadrons were scrambled in the evening of 11 July 1940 to intercept a raid on Portsmouth by He 111s of KG55. Two Heinkels were shot down just off Selsey Beach and another force-landed on its return to base. The honours were even as three Hurricanes were hit, No 145 Squadron's Leader, J. Peel, being rescued by Selsey lifeboat as his aircraft sank, and the second 145 Squadron Hurricane making it back to Tangmere. No 601 Squadron's Sergeant A. Wooley bailed out of his blazing machine to survive with burns. No 43 Squadron lost PO R. de Mancha on 21 July when he collided with a Bf 109 during combat, the Messerschmitt pilot also being killed. Westhampnett became Tangmere's satellite station during May and was formally opened on 31 July when No 145 officially took up residence.

The intensity of the Luftwaffe attacks increased, with Thursday 8 August being especially hard for No 43 Squadron. In combat with Bf 109s over the Isle of Wight, it lost two Hurricanes and their pilots, another four being damaged with two pilots wounded. The following day No 266, with Spitfires, arrived from Wittering, but lost two aircraft and one pilot on 12 August when it was transferred to Eastchurch. The previous day No 601 had tangled with the Luftwaffe over Portland, but returned with four Hurricanes and their pilots missing. In this action the Luftwaffe also lost three Ju 88s of StabII/KG55 and five Bf 110s to defending RAF fighters.

Daily attacks on the South Coast and its airfields were now taking place. Tangmere's turn came on 16 August 1940, when the third raid of the day, consisting of more than 100 aircraft, was recorded over the Isle of Wight at 1300 hours. Although both Nos 43 and 601 Squadrons intercepted the formation, a force of Ju 87s from StG2 managed to evade the defenders and hit Tangmere in a classic 'Stuka' attack. Two hangars were totally destroyed and the remaining three seriously damaged. The station workshops, sick quarters, fire hydrant pump house and Officers' Mess were in ruins, and its power, Tannoy and water services were all put out of action. An air raid shelter received a direct hit; ten servicemen and three civilians were dead and another twenty wounded. Two Spitfires, seven Hurricanes and a Magister were destroyed or damaged, and the FIU lost all six of its Blenheims. Fortunately the RAF's first radar-equipped Beaufighter, which had arrived four days previously, was undamaged. .

In the air No 43 had two aircraft written off and two damaged, with no loss of pilots. 601 Squadron only lost one Hurricane, which force-landed in flames while the attack was in progress. The groundcrew rescued the pilot, PO W. Fiske, who sadly died of shock and his injuries in hospital the next day. 'Billy' Fiske was the first American volunteer to lose his life during the Battle of Britain. The attackers paid dearly: No 43 shot down seven Stukas and damaged three more, and two of the escorting Bf 109s of II/JG2 fell to the guns of 601 Squadron.

Lessons were learned. The Sector Operations room moved to St James School in Chichester, and the Officers' Mess took over Shopwyke House near Goodwood. Blast pens were provided for the more widely dispersed aircraft, and the FIU's solitary Beaufighter immediately moved to Shoreham. On 19 August No 601 exchanged with No 17 Squadron from Debden; six days later the new Squadron lost two Hurricanes and Squadron Leader C. Williams in combat off Portland with Bf 109s and Bf 110s. On 2 September 1940 No 601 Squadron returned after its 'rest', but at 0930 hours on 6 September, in combat with Bf 109s, four Hurricanes were shot down and two pilots killed, one of whom was Flt Lt W. H. Rhodes-Moorhouse. The next day the shocked Squadron was withdrawn to Exeter, exchanging with No 213. On that day Tangmere's other long-time resident squadron, No 43, lost three more Hurricanes and two pilots including Squadron Leader Caesar Hull. It was transferred north to Usworth on 8 September, swapping places with No 607 Squadron, which had arrived on 1 September.

A Luftwaffe target photograph of RAF Tangmere taken on 6 August 1940, ten days before the devastating attack. (Luftwaffe via P. H. T. Green collection)

The new arrivals had a gentle introduction to combat in the south until 9 September, when, at 1730 hours, they intercepted a formation of Do 17s escorted by Bf 109s over Mayfield, south of Tunbridge Wells. The untried Squadron lost six Hurricanes, with three pilots killed and two more wounded. Tangmere's casualties continued, albeit at a lower level, for the rest of September, but the Luftwaffe's target had shifted to London, particularly at night. To meet this new potential threat to Tangmere, a dummy flare path (Q-site) was laid out at Colworth to supplement the earlier decoy airfield at Gumber. During August and September the Squadrons of the Tangmere Sector claimed 275 enemy aircraft destroyed, 116 probables and 146 damaged. The station had fully justified its motto 'Attack to defend'.

On 5 October 1940 No 607 had one Hurricane shot down and another three made force-landings; thankfully all the pilots survived. Two days later a collision during an afternoon patrol cost two aircraft and one pilot. On 9 October No 145 returned from Dyce and the next day 607 Squadron left for the relative peace of Turnhouse. The longer nights had brought occasional visits by mysterious black-painted Lysanders, flown in by No 419 (Special Duties) Flight from Stradishall; questions about their role were firmly discouraged. The first of their 'special duties' from Tangmere took place over the night of 19/20 October 1940, their task and destination unknown.

At the end of November it was the turn of No 213 to move north, to Leconfield, and its successor was No 65 Squadron from Turnhouse with the Spitfire Mk 1. To strengthen the night-time protection of Portsmouth, it was joined on 10 December by the radar-equipped Beaufighters of 219 Squadron from Redhill, where it had been part of London's night defence. To No 219 Squadron's acute embarrassment, it was a 65 Squadron Spitfire, flown by Flight Lieutenant Smart, that on 10 January 1941 achieved Tangmere's first night combat victory over Portsmouth. Appropriately, it was the CO, Squadron Leader J. H. Little, who broke Tangmere's Beaufighter duck on 17 February, bringing down a Do 17. Nearly a month later, on the night of 13 March, the Squadron had a most successful night: four bombers were destroyed and another damaged for no losses. However, that night's target had been the airfield, where a barrack block was demolished; most of the occupants reached the shelters and there was only one casualty. In the raids of the night before, Tangmere had been hit more severely; the east wing of the Sergeants' Mess was destroyed, two barrack blocks were damaged and a third, housing the men of the MT section, was demolished, with five killed and fourteen wounded.

Tangmere personnel, including 'Cocky' Dundas (centre), inspect bomb damage in March 1941. (J. E. Johnson via P. H. T. Green collection)

No 145 Squadron finally gave up its trusty Hurricanes in early February 1941 for the Spitfire II and, together with No 65, went onto the offensive over the Channel and northern France. However, 65 was posted to Kirton-in-Lindsey at the end of February, changing places with 616 Squadron, also with Spitfires, although No 616 operated out of Westhampnett from early May and 145 Squadron moved to nearby Merston. On 18 March Wg Cdr Douglas Bader arrived as Wing Leader of the Tangmere Fighter Wing consisting of Nos 145, 610 and 616 Squadrons, although for most of the time the Squadrons operated from Tangmere's satellite landing grounds.

With the improving spring weather, Fighter Command's series of offensive operations received standard code names. A *Rodeo* was a pure fighter operation, while a *Circus* was a fighter sweep escorting a small formation of bombers, both aimed at bringing Luftwaffe fighters into combat. However, a *Ramrod*, although again fighters escorting a force of bombers, had a primary aim of destroying ground targets. A *Roadstead* was a low-level attack on shipping, coastal defences or ports. A *Rhubarb* was a low-level strike operation, whereas a *Ranger* was a freelance sweep by a fighter wing operating independently.

In early July 1941 No 1 Squadron returned to Tangmere with cannon-armed Hurricanes to operate alongside Turbinlite-equipped Havocs of No 1455 Flight, which was formed on 7 July. The Havocs carried AI radar and a powerful searchlight in the nose to illuminate the target bomber for the accompanying fighters. The Flight was renumbered 534 Squadron in September 1942, before finally disbanding at Tangmere on 25 January 1943 when the Turbinlite project was finally abandoned. No 1 continued in its night 'intruder' role; carrying two long-range tanks, the aircrafts' endurance over the continent exceeded 4 hours. The most successful pilot was Pilot Officer Karel 'Kut' Kuttelwascher, a Czech, who in just five weeks from 1 April destroyed eight enemy bombers including three in one night.

The occasional visits by black Lysanders, which had begun in October 1940, became more frequent from March 1941 as No 491 Flight became No 1491 Flight; on 25 August it was redesignated 138 Squadron. In the greatest secrecy and under cover of darkness, the Lysander pilots were carrying agents of the Special Operations Executive to and from tiny grass fields in enemy-occupied France. The still picturesque 'Tangmere Cottage', just outside the camp's main gate, provided a secluded hideaway for the agents or 'Joes' waiting for their flights.

For the first time Tangmere acquired 'hard' runway surfaces during 1941/42. The airfield was enlarged to the west and south-east to provide two asphalt strips, the longest being 5,850 feet (1,783 metres), which were linked by extended taxiways. The contractor, Wimpey, also provided sixteen Blister hangars scattered around the airfield to replace the GS sheds lost to the attentions of the Luftwaffe. A new two-storey Flying Control Tower was also completed; the ground floor housed the Duty Pilot, Duty Crew and night-flying equipment, and the first floor had the control room, radio room and crew rest areas.

Two old rivals and companions-in-arms were together again at Tangmere for three weeks in mid-1942. No 43 arrived from Acklington in mid-June to learn the problems of working with the Turbinlite Havocs, before No 1 moved to Acklington on 8 July to re-equip with the Hawker Typhoon. The transfer of No 501 from Ibsley on 3 July, followed by the other two Ibsley Squadrons, Nos 66 and 118, on 16 August, together with No 41 Squadron from Llanbedr, set the rumours flying. A visit by Air Chief Marshal Sir Sholto Douglas, C-in-C Fighter Command, confirmed that a major combined services operation against Dieppe, code-named 'Jubilee', was being planned for mid-August 1942.

Before dawn on 19 August No 43 Squadron's Hurricanes linked up with those of Nos 3 and 245 from Shoreham. Led by No 43's CO, Squadron Leader D. Le Roy du Vivier, the formation attacked gun emplacements west of Dieppe harbour. Despite flying low to avoid radar, the Hurricanes met alert defences, which had been forewarned by smoke-laying Bostons; two aircraft were lost and five more damaged. The Spitfires of No 41 Squadron provided top cover for the Canadians of No 412, who met with six Fw 190s over the assault fleet without loss on either side. By 07.50 No 43 Squadron was again airborne, searching, without success, for reported E-boats. Later, Spitfires of Nos 41, 42 and 501 Squadrons escorted 'Hurribombers' of No 175 (Warmwell) and No 87 (Charmy Down) to attack more gun positions.

Only when the decision was made to withdraw from Dieppe did No 66 get into the fight, escorting Nos 3 and 43 Squadrons on their third operation over the harbour. Shortly after 1500 hours, Nos 41, 118 and 501 Squadrons and the 309th FS from Westhampnett met with the Luftwaffe in a confused and costly battle, destroying two Do 217s but losing two Spitfires, including that of 41's CO, Sqn Ldr G. Hyde. Operation 'Jubilee' was singularly unsuccessful, but Tangmere had made a proud contribution of more than 400 sorties despite the losses and damage. The aerodrome then became host to a succession of Spitfire squadrons committed to *Rhubarbs* and *Ramrods*.

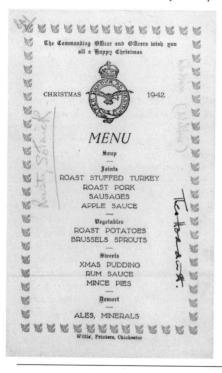

On 25 September 1942 No 823 Squadron arrived with Albacores, and was attached to 16 Group, Coastal Command, for Channel anti-shipping operations. Apart from eleven weeks at Manston from January 1943, the Squadron remained at Tangmere until 1 June 1943. It was joined, on 29 October, by No 486 (RNZAF) Squadron. Its Typhoons, faster at low level than other Fighter Command aircraft, were intended to counter the Luftwaffe's tip-and-run fighter-bomber attacks on South Coast towns; but with minimal radar warning of these low-level intruders, the defenders reverted to standing patrols. December was a particularly successful month, with No 486 claiming four Bf 109s, two Do 217s and a single Fw 190.

Tangmere's 1942 Christmas Menu signed by Operations Room WAAFs. (via S. Kellerman)

As this threat diminished No 486 went onto the offensive, initially escorting fighter-bomber *Ramrods* and *Roadsteads*, but also carrying a 250lb (114kg) bomb under each wing. Its role changed to fighter escort by early 1944 as the bombers of No 2 Group and the USAAF attacked the 'ski' launch sites for the V-1 missiles being constructed in France. Tangmere welcomed the Windmill Theatre Company on 28 February 1943 who gave two performances in the station theatre, formerly the Handley Page hangar, which had been remodelled by the Luftwaffe on 16 August 1940. At the end of March 1943 No 197 arrived from Drem, being joined on 4 August by 183 Squadron from Harrowbeer. During this time the Operations Room moved from the now cramped accommodation at St James School to the imposing Concert Hall of Bishop Otter College. Nos 41 and 91 Squadrons transferred from Westhampnett to the parent station in the first week of October 1943. Their Spitfire XIIs undertook *Rodeo* fighter sweeps, but it was not until 20 October that the Luftwaffe took the bait; the Wing was attacked from out of the sun by some twenty-five to thirty Fw 190s and Bf 109s, but the outcome was a resounding success for the RAF, with no losses but nine 'kills' claimed.

Gloster-built Typhoon 1B EK176 operated by No 1 Squadron in July 1943. (via DWL collection)

Being close to the coast, Tangmere was frequently a haven for damaged Allied bombers, most of which landed safely. That was not the case on 19 November 1943 when a Flight Engineer flying a Halifax in place of the mortally wounded pilot totally misjudged his approach. The aircraft crashed into one the few remaining hangars with the loss of all of its crew and six Typhoons of 197 and 486 Squadrons.

The creation of the 2nd Tactical Air Force on 1 June 1943 had a significant impact on Tangmere. Its task was to provide the air support for all military operations over the continent. In preparation for the Second Front, Tangmere, like all South Coast airfields, saw a bewildering succession of squadrons come and go – thirty-four units from January to August 1944. This was to ensure that squadrons could move anywhere at 3 hours' notice while maintaining 100% operational capability. The small boys watching at the boundary fence would see a squadron arrive, set up its tents and operate for a short period, before packing up as its replacements arrived. Bishop Otter College in Chichester, where Tangmere's Operations Room was sited, saw a vast increase in personnel as it became 2TAF's new signals organisation capable of handling all fifty-eight squadrons flying from eighteen airfields and ALGs between Friston and Lee-on-Solent.

In mid-April 1944 the six Canadian Spitfire Mk IX squadrons that made up 126 and 127 Airfield (redesignated Wing from 12 May 1944) arrived at Thorney. Nos 401, 411 and 412 Squadrons of 126 Airfield arrived from Biggin Hill via Fairwood Common and 127 Airfield's Nos 403, 416 and 421 Squadrons came directly from Kenley. In the build-up to D-Day their principal duty was the dive-bombing of *Noball* sites, but they also attacked communications and airfields. From before dawn on 6 June itself the Squadrons provided a continuous umbrella over the beaches, but saw little of the enemy. D-Day+1 was much more eventful for 126 Wing, which claimed eight out of twelve Ju 88s that were attacking the beachhead. During the afternoon the Wing shot down four Fw 190 fighter-bombers, one falling to the guns of the Wing Leader, Wg Cdr G. C. Keefer DFC and bar.

Tangmere's units began to operate from forward airstrips in France from mid-June, and were replaced on 22 June by No 132 Wing (Nos 66, 331 and 332 Squadrons) from Bognor and 134 (Czech) Wing (Nos 310, 312 and 313 Squadrons) from Appledram; these units too moved into Europe within a few weeks.

Tangmere had often been honoured by distinguished visitors. The Duke of Kent had been a frequent visitor before his death in 1942, and the Duchess of Gloucester had reviewed the WAAFs. Shortly before D-Day Air Chief Marshal Leigh Mallory as Air Commander of the Allied Expeditionary Air Force had entertained the Supreme Commander, General Eisenhower, and all the senior Air Commanders, including his deputy Air Chief Marshal Tedder, in Tangmere's Officers' Mess. However, this was eclipsed on 14 July when Their Majesties the King and Queen Elizabeth inspected some of Tangmere's sections and held an investiture.

No 132 Wing departed to Funtington in August, and the Spitfires of No 145 Wing (Nos 74, 329 and 341 Squadrons) arrived from Selsey. The Wing specialised in VIP escort duties, which included protecting the Dakota carrying Prime Minister Winston Churchill and a B-26 Marauder that held General Dwight Eisenhower. On 14 August No 341 Squadron arrived, and all four squadrons left five days later for airstrip B-8 (Sommervieu). Nos 222, 349 and 485 Squadrons of 135 Wing transferred from Selsey, and almost immediately joined the exodus to France. Tangmere's Station Diary recorded:

'At last No 135 Wing have gone to France. This, the last Wing of 84 Group, is the last that will come through the sausage machine as far as Tangmere is concerned. Since D-Day squadrons flying from Tangmere have destroyed 432 enemy aeroplanes.'

As the war moved further into the continent, Tangmere's main customers were American transports bringing back wounded for treatment in local hospitals. The Central Fighter Establishment began transferring to Tangmere from Wittering from September, completing the move in mid-January 1945; it was then joined by the Naval Air Fighting Development Unit (No 787 Squadron). No 787 took over the Westhampnett satellite on 12 July to make room for the Night Fighter Development Wing, which transferred from Ford on 15 July. When the Central Fighter Establishment, which included the Enemy Aircraft Flight, departed to West Raynham on 1 October 1945, it left behind a number of former Axis machines including a Ju 88 and a Fiat G-55.

A total of 811 enemy aircraft were destroyed by Tangmere's squadrons, a further 242 were 'probables' and no fewer than 432 were damaged. Tangmere's immediate peacetime role was to welcome many repatriated prisoners of war who were processed as speedily and sympathetically as possible. However, much of the camp was virtually derelict, and the damaged roof of the last of the pre-war Belfast hangars had collapsed during a storm on 17 November 1944. A refurbishment programme was implemented with three T2 hangars, built on the foundations of the bombed-out hangars, replacing the now scruffy Blisters. A further T2 was erected on the northern boundary for use as a maintenance hangar. The first post-war Squadron to return was No 85, which flew its Mosquitoes in from Castle Camps on 9 October 1945, and at the end of April 1946 No 1 returned to its old pre-war haunt with the Spitfire F.21, which it exchanged for Meteor F.3s from October 1946.

The Meteor and Tangmere hit the worldwide headlines during the summer of 1946 following the re-formation, on 14 June, of the High Speed Flight. Originally formed in 1926 to compete for the Schneider Trophy, the new Flight was tasked to raise the Absolute Air Speed Record using specially prepared Meteor F.4s. Under the command of Wg Cdr E. M. Donaldson, his other pilots were Sqn Ldrs W. A. Waterton and N. F. Duke. The two modified aircraft, named Star Meteors, arrived in August, and on 7 September 1946 Donaldson set a new record of 616mph (991kmph) over a 3km course between Rustington and Littlehampton.

A new Tangmere Day Fighter Wing was created on 1 October when No 222 brought its Meteor F.3s from Weston Zoyland to join No 1 Squadron, and No 266 arrived from Wattisham on 16 April. In August 1947 Tangmere's proud fighter heritage going back to 1915 took a knock when No 1 Squadron exchanged its Meteors for Harvards and Oxfords as it became 11 Group's instrument flying training unit! Common sense finally prevailed on 1 June 1948 when No 1 returned to front-line status with new Meteor F.4s.

No 1 received its first USAF Exchange Officer in October when Major Robin Olds arrived as a Flight Commander. A Second World War ace, Olds was destined to distinguish himself in both the Korean and Vietnam wars. He also made his mark with No 1, achieving the highest scores during the armament practice camp at Acklington in January 1949. When the CO was posted, Major Olds became the first officer from a foreign Air Force to command an RAF squadron in peacetime. Under his leadership the Squadron was the top scoring fighter unit during Exercise *Foil* in June 1949, claiming sixty aircraft destroyed and thirty-nine damaged, confirmed by gun-camera film.

Someone at the Air Ministry had a sense of tradition, for 266 Squadron was renumbered No 43 on 11 February 1949 and the old pre-war friendly rivalry was rekindled. It was during this nostalgic period that Geoffrey Dorman presented the FE.2B propeller, which had been damaged in his 1916 forced landing, for display in the Officers' Mess. Sadly, the new partnership was to last for only nineteen months as No 43 was posted to Leuchars on 9 November 1950, being replaced by 29 Squadron with Mosquito NF.36s. When No 29 got its long-nose, radar-equipped Meteor NF.11s in August 1951, it became the first RAF jet night-fighter unit. Tangmere was an all-Meteor station again.

The sun shone on 24 April 1953 when No 1 Squadron became the first RAF squadron to receive its Standard. The presentation was made by Air Vice-Marshal Sir Charles Longcroft who, nearly forty years earlier, had re-formed No 1 as an aeroplane unit at Farnborough. Three days later the Squadron moved to Biggin Hill, returning during July. During its absence a large concrete hardstanding was laid in front of the hangars, and Operational Readiness Platforms (ORPs) appeared at each end of the main runway.

A stunning all-red Hunter appeared at Tangmere in August 1953 when Hawker's Chief Test Pilot Neville Duke flew the modified prototype Mk 3 in for an attempt on the world speed record, then held by the USA. As the reserve pilot on the 1946 High Speed Flight, it must have been a satisfying moment for Duke when, on 7 September, he flew the Hunter to a new Absolute Speed Record of 727.63mph (1,171kmph) over the same 3km course.

Hunters finally came to Tangmere on a permanent basis in June 1955 when No 1 Squadron re-equipped with F.5s. No 34 Squadron, which came to Tangmere in August 1954, received its Hunter F5s from October 1955. Both Squadrons were sent to Cyprus from August to December 1956 to operate in a defensive role during the disastrous Suez campaign.

After more than six years at Tangmere, 29 Squadron moved to Acklington on 14 January 1957, to be replaced nine months later by No 25 Squadron with its mix of Meteor NF.12s and NF.14s, but now the fighter role of Tangmere was drawing to a close. The airfield was in the wrong place, as the need was for bases in the east to defend the V-Bomber bases and Britain's nuclear deterrent. All three Squadrons were disbanded, starting with No 34 on 10 January, No 1 on 23 June and No 25 on 1 July. The formal departure of Fighter Command on 23 June was marked by a massed flypast of Hunter and Meteor squadrons in the presence of the Air Officer Commanding.

No 90 (Signals) Group, renamed Signals Command in November 1958, became the new 'owner' of the historic station. No 2 Ground Servicing Squadron and a Ground Radio Calibration Flight moved in, followed on 25 August by two squadrons. The Varsities of 115 Squadron checked navigation and approach aids throughout the UK and abroad, and the Canberras of 245 undertook daily calibration of early warning radars. The station received the Freedom of the City of Chichester on 5 May 1960 with a scroll and a silver and enamel image of the City Arms presented to the Officers' Mess. The following year 'B' Flight of No 22 Squadron began to use the station for its yellow air-sea-rescue Whirlwind helicopters.

This period was enlivened by the spectacular arrival on 11 April 1962 of an 81st Tactical Fighter Wing Voodoo, which deposited its undercarriage all over the airfield. On 30 October the fire crew had more excitement when, after an engine fire, a Hawker P.1127 made an emergency wheels-up landing on the hallowed turf of Tangmere. Also that year the runway was used by Donald Campbell for early trials of his Bluebird jet-engined car, which later raised the Land Speed Record to 403mph (649kmph). On 19 April 1963 No 245 Squadron was renumbered 98 and moved, together with 115 Squadron, to Watton on 1 October as the station came under the auspices of No 38 Group, Transport Command. The change of role brought no new flying units and when, in May 1964, the Whirlwinds of 22 Squadron moved to Thorney Island, leaving the airfield to No 623 (Volunteer) Gliding School, the writing was on the wall! Transport Command became Air Support Command on 1 August 1967 and Hercules aircraft of No 242 OCU, Thorney Island, began to use Tangmere for practice parachute supply drops.

On 4 April 1968 four Hunters of No 1 Squadron flew in from West Raynham to perform the last fighter sortie from the station. Among the pilots was Flt Lt Alan Pollock, who broke away from the formation to fly under the top span of Tower Bridge. His protest achieved the publicity he wanted but abruptly curtailed his RAF career.

Tangmere was formally closed on 16 October 1970. The scroll was returned to the Mayor of Chichester for safe-keeping, but has since returned to Tangmere for display in the Tangmere Military Aviation Museum. The married quarters remained in use by Thorney Island, and while the station was officially under Care and Maintenance, the Gliding School continued to operate until disbanded in December 1974. In early 1979 the Royal Engineers used the Officers' Mess for anti-terrorist training, which involved explosives and demolition of internal walls. Later that year the site finally came up for auction through the Property Services Agency and was quickly sold off.

After disposal, the perimeter track was used for many years by the Sussex Police Driving School for training traffic officers in both cars and motorcycles. The embryo Tangmere Museum acquired part of the site in 1980, and after much hard work the museum opened in June 1982 to tell the story of the Battle of Britain and the history of a famous RAF station.

The three main T2 hangars were refurbished for use as grain stores and remain in good condition. However, plans for a Business Park and a new road called Chichester Drive saw the demolition of many buildings during the mid-1980s. Fortunately in 1985, with the help of Andy Saunders and the Tangmere Museum, the BBC produced a 30-minute programme on Tangmere titled *Requiem for an Airfield*. At the time of filming the Guardroom, Officers' Mess and many other buildings were still extant although much vandalised. The programme was broadcast on 16 June 1986 on BBC2 and included interviews with many significant Tangmere personnel.

During a visit I made in early May 1987 the surviving RAF buildings then included the control tower, fire station, the remains of the First World War Handley Page assembly shed (latterly the station theatre), the NAAFI and at least one barrack block. Into the 21st century one of the few surviving original station buildings is the now very derelict control tower. Andy Saunders records in his *RAF Tangmere Revisited* that the owners, the Church Commissioners, offered it to him for a nominal £1 in the early 1980s. Why didn't he take it? A new industrial park can be found to the north-east of the old tower and the north-south runway houses acres of glasshouses producing peppers for Tangmere Airfield Nurseries Ltd! Further east, the 1950s concrete blast walls remain along the boundary. A wartime building is used as the warden's office of the East Hampnett Caravan Park.

The control tower in May 1987. (DWL collection)

Main features:
Runways: 255° 6,000ft x 150ft, 170° 4,800ft x 150ft, concrete. *Hangars:* one T2, two Bessonneau, ten Over Blisters, six Extra Over Blisters. *Hardstandings:* fourteen single-engined type. *Accommodation:* RAF: 255 Officers, 238 SNCOs, 3,170 ORs; WAAF: 17 Officers, 16 SNCOs, 732 ORs.

Places of interest nearby:
The Tangmere Military Aviation Museum (SU906060) has gone from strength to strength and has three main exhibition areas. The Tangmere Hall tells the story of the station from 1917 to 1970, while the Battle of Britain Hall and the new Merston Hall house a unique part of Tangmere's history. On loan from the RAF Museum are two record-breakers, the Meteor F3 from the 1946 High Speed Flight and Neville Duke's Hunter Mk 3 of 1953. On 7 September 2003, the 50th anniversary of

The view from the control tower with the western taxiway and replacement T2 hangars. (DWL collection)

this historic flight, a two-seat Hunter painted in a celebration red colour scheme, flew over the museum as part of a commemorative function. With many other historic aircraft, the Tangmere Aviation Museum is a must-see collection.

A memorial stone, unveiled by Group Captain Douglas Bader on 18 December 1976, is still on the village green adjacent to the appropriately named Bader Arms, where other relics of the wartime period are displayed. In the graveyard of the village church, the neat rows of gravestones commemorate the dead of both sides; leading RAF fighter pilots like Sqn Ldr Caesar Hull and Flt Lt William Rhodes-Moorhouse lie in peace alongside the lesser-known aircrew of their opponents, the Luftwaffe.

The Tangmere Airfield commemorative stone was unveiled by Grp Capt Douglas Bader in 1976. (DWL collection)

TELSCOMBE CLIFFS, East Sussex

50°57N/00°01W 93ft asl; TQ406017. 2.5 miles W of Newhaven off A259

Portsmouth was subjected to a Zeppelin attack for the first time on 25 September 1916. This audacious raid caused a rethink of the deployment of Home Defence squadrons much further west than before. The formation of No 78 Squadron at Newhaven on 1 November was a direct consequence and one of its detachments was sent to Telscombe Cliffs.

The LG was located on the chalk down cliffs between Rottingdean and Newhaven on grassland roughly 1,500 feet (457 metres) square. The six BE.2/BE.12 biplanes were accommodated in temporary Bessonneau hangars but the personnel lived in tents, or the more fortunate found billets in the nearby town. That winter was particularly bleak, with no natural shelter from the bitter winds, and it was all unnecessary as the Zeppelins never attempted another attack that far west.

No 78 moved to Suttons' Farm in September 1917, reducing Telscombe LG to an emergency use status until the increased U-boat activity in the English Channel brought the very unwarlike DH.6 trainers to Telscombe Cliffs. It was the success of the convoy system and long-range seaplane and airship patrols that forced the submariners inshore where British shipping losses mounted. The counter was to have standing patrols along the coastline, and every available aeroplane was employed including the slow low-powered DH.6 trainer on what were 'scarecrow' duties.

Airco DH.6s were flown on anti-submarine 'scarecrow' duties during 1917/18. |(H. J. Dyer via P. Swan)

No 514 (Special Duty) Flight was formed on 7 June 1918 within No 253 Squadron, but was transferred to No 242 when that Squadron was formed at Newhaven in August. The DH.6 was capable of operating as a light bomber when flown solo but not if an observer was carried. The unglamorous boring but vital duties continued to the war's end, with just the measurable reduction in shipping losses as recognition of their worth.

The Flight was disbanded in January 1919 followed on 15 May by No 242 Squadron. The LG returned to farmland and is now totally subsumed under the new town of Peacehaven.

Main features in 1918:
Landing ground: grass. *Hangars:* a number of Bessonneaus. *Accommodation:* not known.

THEALE (Sheffield Farm), Berkshire

51°25N/01°03W 150ft asl; SU650700. 4 miles W of Reading on minor road off A4

The grass fields that were to become Theale airfield were requisitioned in 1940 for use as a Relief Landing Ground for the aircraft of the Woodley-based No 8 EFTS under the name of Sheffield Farm. Although the re-sown grass surface was expected to be ready by November, the wet conditions that were to plague the airfield meant that it was not ready for use until the spring of 1941. By then the role had evolved from RLG to fully fledged training field. Also, the planned occupants had changed. A new EFTS was to be formed by Phillips & Powis Aircraft Ltd (renamed Miles Aircraft in October 1943), which also operated No 8 EFTS, both to be under the overall control of No 50 (Training) Group. The standard population of a C Class EFTS was sixty pupils with an Initial Establishment (IE) of twenty-four aircraft, in this case Tiger Moths together with an Immediate Reserve (IR) of a further twelve aircraft.

All this required much more than just a grass field. As so frequently happened in wartime, when the new training unit, numbered No 26 EFTS, officially came into existence on 14 August 1941, much of the necessary infrastructure was still awaited. The airfield was renamed Theale, but persistent flooding had delayed much of the building works. Two Blister hangars, together with some of the crew huts, stores and offices, were ready but the airmen's mess was still a building site. Not only that, there was no permanent water supply to the airfield. To provide accommodation for the students and lecture rooms, Sulhamstead House, about a mile from the airfield, was requisitioned, but also needed conversion work to make it suitable for its new role. With the airfield's northern boundary being the Kennet & Avon Canal, the wet conditions did not improve; in fact, flooding was a constant threat, especially in winter, when only regular pumping kept the flood waters at bay.

Despite these severe handicaps, the first course started flying on 21 August, only a week after the unit came into existence. The sixty pupils were normally divided into two Flights, each ab initio course of six weeks overlapping the following by three weeks. However, due to the lack of accommodation, 'B' Flight did not start flying until October 1941, using a dispersed site (believed to be its RLG at Waltham St Lawrence) with two Nissen huts as the rather basic accommodation!

Back at Theale, the equally primitive conditions were slowly improving, although the aircraft were being given priority. A technical area was created near the village of Sheffield Bottom around a T1 hangar with its span of 90 feet and 19-foot door clearance. The smaller hangars were all Blisters, two being the Over type with a span of 65 feet and a length of 45 feet. The remaining three double Blisters were the standard type. A Watch Office/Control Tower was also constructed. The primary equipment of the EFTS was of course the Tiger Moth, but the unit also had support/communications aircraft that included at least one Hawker Hind, as well as Puss and Hornet Moths, the latter types being impressed former civilian aircraft. There were no facilities for night-flying at Theale, the better-equipped White Waltham being used for this stage of the training curriculum.

Flying training can be a hazardous occupation, especially under wartime pressures. However, despite, or perhaps because of, the unsuitability of the airfield, No 26 EFTS suffered fewer accidents than many other flying schools. One of the worst occurred on 19 May 1942 when two aircraft collided on approach. Later, in 1944, Morris Motors-built Tiger Moth DE261 crashed into the Nissen hut sleeping quarters. The role of the unit evolved as the war progressed, taking on a grading duty in 1943 whereby each pupil received about twelve hours' dual instruction before being superseded by an assessment course for potential instructors.

Another unit was created at Theale in July 1944 when No 128 Gliding School came into existence. Using Slingsby Cadet gliders housed in one of the Blister hangars, the School trained local ATC cadets to fly. It was destined to outlive No 26 EFTS, as the latter was the first to disband on 9 July 1945, just two months after the end of the war in Europe and with the Pacific war still in progress. Powered flying had ceased on 30 June and a total of twenty-eight Tiger Moths awaited disposal instructions. Sulhamstead House had also been vacated, leaving Theale to the gliding school and the Care and Maintenance party. For a few months until December 1945 an Aircrew Demobilisation Unit used some of the accommodation. Finally, by 1948, with the gliders also gone, Theale fell silent.

For an airfield that suffered more than its share of wet conditions throughout its service life, it is almost inevitable that today virtually the whole site is under water. However, this is not the result of global warming but the efforts of gravel extraction companies, which moved in as soon as the airfield was derequisitioned. The only recognisable area is part of the former technical site, located in the south-west corner of the former airfield. Here the T1 hangar survives together with a couple of original buildings, all still in use by the gravel company. The aeronautical origins are also acknowledged by Hangar Road, which leads from Shefford Bottom to the Theale swing bridge over the canal. To the north, between the railway line and the A4, is a large modern industrial estate, the Arlington Business Park, with a shiny new 'Merlin House'. Until 2002 Arlington was the development arm of BAE Systems, so it is possible that 'Merlin House' also acknowledges Theale airfield, although no Rolls-Royce Merlin-powered machine was ever based there.

Main features:
Runways: N-S 2,520ft, NE-SW 2,520ft, E-W 2,400ft, NW-SE 2,700ft, grass.
Hangars: one T1, two Over Blisters, three standard double Blisters. *Hardstandings:* none. *Accommodation:* RAF: 23 Officers, 52 SNCOs, 134 ORs.

A T1 hangar and Hangar Road in 2003. (DWL collection)

Place of interest nearby:

On the high ground to the south of the airfield between Burghfield and Burghfield Common can be found an imposing house called 'Highwoods'. Although having no administrative responsibility for the airfield, the house and grounds were, from the outbreak of war to March 1946, the HQ of No 42 Group. Formed in January 1939 at No 81 Weyhill Road, Andover, as an Ammunition and Fuel Group, it became responsible for providing all the RAF's UK ammunition and high explosive. Without 'bombs and bullets' the RAF could not have done what it had to do! Visitors to the area can enjoy bed & breakfast at 'Highwoods', and although evidence of its wartime role is virtually non-existent it doesn't take too much imagination to conjure up the frenetic activity of the war years.

THORNEY ISLAND, Hampshire

50°49N/00°55W 0ft asl; SU762025. 2 miles S of Emsworth on minor road

The Thorney Island story actually starts many miles away, at Tangmere. On 25 September 1933 Sergeant William Molesworth Hodge, flying Hawker Fury K2073 of No 1 Squadron, was killed in an emergency landing near St Nicholas's Church, West Thorney. This sad accident, however, led directly to the creation of RAF Thorney Island, and the event was recorded by a plaque unveiled to the east of the Officers' Mess in May 1949:

'In September 1938 the pilot of a Fury aircraft of No 1 Fighter Squadron crashed on this spot. Representatives of the RAF who came to investigate the crash observed the unique suitability of the adjoining land as an airfield. Their recommendations subsequently resulted in the building of this aerodrome. He died not in battle yet not in vain.'

West Thorney, with its historic 12th-century Norman church, was, even in the early 20th century, one of the smallest and most remote Sussex parishes. The formal announcement of the repercussions of the Fury accident appeared in the *Portsmouth Evening News* during the summer of 1935, revealing that the Air Ministry planned to build a large five-squadron aerodrome on the island.

Contractors started preparing the 1,450-acre site for a typical Expansion Period aerodrome on the land to either side of the village approach road. During December 1935 steel girders for the six impressive 'C'-type aircraft sheds arrived by rail at Emsworth, completing their journey by road. Behind the hangars the typical pre-war mix of brick-built technical and domestic buildings began to appear and a Watch Office was provided between the hangars. Throughout 1936 and into 1937 construction continued, including numerous substantial three-storey barrack blocks, parade ground, Station Headquarters, NAAFI and married quarters. Across the airfield, West Thorney village was overwhelmed by extensive officers' housing, including the imposing three-storey Officers' Mess. The size of the station can be judged by the fact that it eventually had accommodation for 3,634 officers and airmen, together with 508 WAAF officers and airwomen.

Thorney Island opened – five months later than intended – as part of 16 Group, Coastal Command, on 3 February 1938. The first squadron aircraft arrived on 10 March when No 22 Squadron flew in from Donibristle, joined the following day by No 42. These two Squadrons, operating the ancient Vickers Vildebeest Mk III and IV, comprised the entire home-based maritime strike force. The Vildebeest Squadrons were joined on 4 April 1938 by the School of General Reconnaissance (SoGR) formed in 17 (Training) Group, Lee-on-Solent, to take over from the School of Air Navigation, Manston, the navigation and reconnaissance training of Coastal Command crews. Thorney Island received a Royal seal of approval when, on 9 May 1938, His Majesty King George VI toured the new station.

The Munich Crisis saw 42 Squadron detached to its war station of Thornaby while No 22's Vildebeests were armed with live torpedoes and scattered around the airfield in sandbagged dispersals. With the crisis over, Thorney began a role for which its location made it ideally suited: ferry flights to the Middle East. The first deliveries were made during October when fifteen Anson Mark Is left for No 4 FTS at Abu Sueir, Egypt, and Blenheim Mark 1s were delivered to 55 Squadron at Habbaniya in Iraq from March to May 1930.

Thorney Island was briefly controlled by 17 (Training) Group on the formation of the SoGR, reverting to No 16 (Reconnaissance) Group on 1 November 1938. Although the School remained as a lodger unit, the aerodrome was an operational Coastal Command station for the next eleven years. On 12 August No 42 Squadron moved to Norfolk to the newly rebuilt Bircham Newton, its replacement being No 48 Squadron, arriving on 25 August with its Anson Mk 1s. With the station at war on 3 September 1939, both Squadrons started anti-submarine patrols over the Channel, and on 9 September six Ansons were sent to search for the German liner *Westerland*. A second biplane unit appeared on 15 September, No 1 Coast Artillery Co-operation Unit (CACU) arriving from Gosport with its Swordfishes. In October a pair of Vildebeests carried out 22 Squadron's first attack on a U-boat; the puny 100lb (45kg) bombs failed to even dent the submarine's pressure hull, let alone sink the craft!

No 22 Squadron began to re-equip with the much-delayed and anxiously awaited Bristol Beaufort in November 1939. While the crews explored the complexity of their new mounts, regular Channel patrols were maintained by the Ansons of 48 Squadron assisted by the Swordfishes of No 1 CACU. Around this time the landing ground was extended to the south of the road to West Thorney; with the village now virtually surrounded, most residents were evacuated.

Nos 22 and 42 Squadrons exchanged places during April 1940, with 22 taking its Beauforts to North Coates, Lincolnshire, on the 8th and being replaced on 27 April by No 42 with its first Beauforts. During this 'Phoney War' period, and especially after the fall of Norway, North Coates was very much a front-line station and Thorney Island was a quieter location for a squadron to work up on new equipment. A similar rear echelon philosophy reflected the move of the SoGR with its Ansons to Guernsey on 22 April.

On 10 May 1940 Germany's blitzkrieg attack through the Low Countries changed everything. No 1 CACU returned to Detling, leaving Thorney Island for operational units; the first to arrive were five Wellingtons of No 3 General Reconnaissance Unit (GRU). Under the portly fuselage, tail and wing, the former bombers carried a ring 48 feet (14.6 metres) in diameter, code-named Directional Wireless Installation (DWI). It was in reality a magnetic degaussing coil, powered by a 500-amp petrol-electric generator installed in the fuselage, and designed to counter the threat from German magnetic sea mines. The unit disbanded at the end of July as ships became equipped with their own counter-measures.

Swordfishes returned on 30 May 1940 when No 818 Squadron, FAA, arrived after a four-day journey from Campbeltown via Sealand and Ford. While the Swordfishes covered the armada of little ships evacuating troops from Dunkirk, Ansons of 48 Squadron undertook hazardous anti-E-boat patrols over the same area. Mid-June saw the Navy Swordfishes depart and No 42's Beauforts flew north to Wick, while detachments of Blenheim fighters from Nos 235 and 236 Squadrons arrived to provide fighter cover over Channel convoys. On 3 July Blenheim IV bombers of 59 Squadron arrived, tasked with attacking the French ports where 'invasion' barges were accumulating. The Ansons of 48 Squadron were withdrawn to Hooton Park on the Wirral for patrols over the Irish Sea as the Battle of Britain developed, and the Luftwaffe began to show an interest in Thorney Island.

The first attack came on 13 August when a Ju 88 dropped four bombs on the station without causing significant damage. Three days later another solitary Ju 88 was more successful, destroying four aircraft in a hangar. These were isolated raids; the real test of Thorney Island's defences came on Sunday 18 August, the RAF's 'Hardest Day' of the Battle. At 13.59 the radar station at Poling detected four large formations approaching the Isle of Wight, one of which broke off and headed for Thorney. The attackers were twenty-eight Ju 87Bs of the 1st Gruppe of Dive Bomber Geschwader 77, the famed I.Stukagruppe77 (I./StG77) escorted by Bf 109Es of JG27. Just as the Stukas moved into their pre-attack line-astern formation, they were engaged by eighteen Hurricanes of 43 and 601 Squadrons from Tangmere. The attack was disrupted, with three Junkers shot down over the aerodrome, but two hangars were hit with three aircraft destroyed and one damaged. One of the fuel dumps was hit and it is likely that the Watch Office was also destroyed at this time. The only casualties were five civilian workers injured in a shelter. The departing raiders were engaged by 235 and 152 Squadrons and lost ten Stukas, including that of their commander, Hauptmann Herbert Meisel. Of twenty-eight dispatched, only thirteen returned unscathed. By comparison, RAF Thorney Island had got off lightly, although other formations had hit the Royal Navy hard at Ford and put Poling RDF station out of action. Although the other Stuka squadrons did not suffer as badly as I./StG77, losses were such that no further attempt was made to use the type en masse during the Battle – a significant victory indeed for the RAF.

Another raid by three Ju 88s on 23 August caused little damage, but the following day a Blenheim of 235 Squadron was mistaken for a Ju 88, and was shot down by Hurricanes of No 1 (RCAF) Squadron. Blenheims of 235 and 236 were joined, on 11 September, by Swordfishes of 812 Squadron FAA, disembarked from HMS *Glorious* for minelaying and anti-U-boat duties with Coastal Command, and these aircraft stayed until early January 1941. Long-nosed Blenheim IVs of 53 Squadron came to Thorney to join 59 Squadron in carrying out night-bombing raids on the invasion barges in French ports, which continued until February 1941. Both were then posted away, No 53 to Bircham Newton and No 59 to Manston, although 59 returned in mid-March to spent the rest of the year sending detachments to Detling and Bircham Newton.

Station defences were regularly tested by sporadic tip-and-run raids by single Luftwaffe bombers for the remainder of the winter. Although little damage was done, it could have been worse, for on 5 December a 1,100lb (500kg) bomb landed on the bomb dump, fortunately without exploding. Two hangars were also damaged by a Ju 88 in February, and in mid-June a pair of parachute mines damaged dispersed Beauforts. To reduce the risk of such attacks, a dummy aerodrome was set up at West Wittering, a village some 3 miles to the south-east. This K-site was initially equipped with realistic dummy Blenheims, but later became a KQ-site, with an electric flare path being installed to attract night raiders.

During 1940/41 Thorney Island was frequently used as the departure point for monthly Blenheim IV non-stop ferry flights to Malta. Squadrons of No 2 Group were successively detailed to send a Corporal Fitter and about half a dozen ground staff to Thorney to service and prepare the aircraft. One such corporal was Philip 'Tivy' Pleace of Wyton-based 15 Squadron, who recalled his deployment for the *Journal of the Blenheim Society*:

'Batches of six aircraft were sent at night; weather conditions had to be perfect, obviously wind direction and strength were important. Most nights the trips were cancelled – not surprisingly as the flight path was straight across occupied France. One night, after despatching six aircraft, we went to bed and the next morning went across to dispersal to await the next six to arrive and, after a while, a Blenheim IV came into the circuit and landed... Seeing that it was a new one, we frantically waved to receive it but the pilot switched off and was stood at the edge of the airfield. 'Stupid ****!' we said and I sent the tractor out to bring it in. There was not a drop of petrol in the tanks; the pilot had just made Thorney Island, finished his run and both engines stopped. Apparently they had drifted off course over the Alps. The observer had calculated that they could not make it to Malta and that they were a few inches short of the "Point of No Return".

Another day at the briefing the Wing Commander gave out to all pilots a map of Pantellaria, an Italian island in the Mediterranean, similar in size to Malta. On a previous operation, one of our Blenheims had made a perfect landing there by mistake ... donating a brand new Blenheim with IFF to the Italians.'

Meanwhile, the resident No 59 Squadron was joined successively by three RCAF squadrons. The first, No 404, formed on 15 March with Blenheim IVFs, left in June for Scotland. No 407 officially formed on 8 May, but received no personnel until 22 May, its first Blenheim IV arriving on 28 May. From June these were replaced by Beauforts and the Squadron moved to North Coates in July, still non-operational. The final unit, No 415 Squadron, formed on 20 August as a torpedo-bomber unit. Initially equipped with Beauforts and Blenheims, it lost its Beauforts in January 1942 to No 86 Squadron, and received Hampdens in exchange before moving to St Eval in April 1942. Like so many Coastal Command squadrons, it was destined to return to Thorney Island on many occasions in the future.

The Station's first resident Squadron, No 22, returned on 25 June 1941 to undertake torpedo strikes against Channel shipping. The Air Staff was moving towards bombing as the primary anti-shipping weapon and a succession of Blenheim and Hudson squadrons made Thorney Island their temporary home as a suitable target appeared. It was such a visit by No 59 Squadron that produced one of Thorney's most tragic wartime incidents. On 29 September 1941 a Hudson swung off the runway, its undercarriage collapsed and it caught fire. The crew escaped with minor injuries as fire-fighters arrived, unaware of the bomb load still aboard. Knowing the true situation, the Station Commander, Gp Capt H. S. Scroggs, and Sqn Ldr P. D. Dear, 59's 'B' Flight Commander, intervened just as the aircraft exploded. They were among the seven killed, with a further thirteen wounded.

No 217 Squadron exchanged places with No 22 during October 1941, and on 10 December 1941 No 280 Squadron was formed with Ansons to undertake air-sea rescue duties. The activities of both Squadrons were affected by airfield construction work, which began towards the end of 1941. On 12 February No 217 was involved in one of the least satisfactory Coastal Command operations of the war, an attack on the German pocket battleships *Scharnhorst* and *Gneisenau* in Brest harbour. In Thorney Island's contribution, four torpedo-equipped Beauforts were sent to rendezvous over Manston with their fighter escort, which, with a new position report, had proceeded to the new location. Two Beauforts landed to update themselves, while the other pair proceeded to the original position. A second wave of three Beauforts had the correct location and found the targets with their ASV radar. Eventually, in appalling weather, all seven Beauforts attacked despite ferocious defence from the ships' guns and fighter escort. Despite their bravery, none of their torpedoes found its target. The very frustrated crews of No 217 Squadron left for Skitten on 16 February 1942.

The construction work that had made 217 Squadron's life more difficult was the conversion of the station from two, virtually separate, grass landing grounds on either side of the West Thorney road to a reasonable facsimile of a standard three-runway Class A aerodrome. Using the rubble from bomb-damaged Portsmouth housing to provide hardcore, the three concrete runways, 150ft (45.7m) wide, were joined by a lengthy perimeter track 50ft (15.2m) wide with forty-two hardstandings of 120ft (24.6m) diameter. When the work finished in mid-year, Thorney Island had a longest runway of 5,100ft (1,554m) on a NE-SW (06/24) heading, plus two secondary runways, one of some 4,800ft (1,463m) with N-S alignment (01/19) and a third (12/30) of 4,053ft (1,235m). A new Watch Office was constructed in West Thorney to give a better overall view of the aerodrome, replacing that originally located on the west side of the airfield. The two bomb-damaged 'C'-type hangars were not rebuilt, but seventeen Extra Over Blister hangars were dispersed around the airfield.

Despite all this building work, the necessities of war meant that the station never completely closed. No 415 Squadron had continued working-up on Hampden torpedo-bombers until April 1942, when it left for St Eval. Before departing it was joined by a New Zealand Squadron, No 489, which had received Hampdens in March. Detachments were sent to St Eval in May/June, to Abbotsinch in June/July, and to Tain until 5 August 1943, when the rest of the Squadron moved to Skitten. A series of Hudson, Hampden and Blenheim squadrons transited through Thorney Island in the spring/summer of 1942. More unusual visitors were the Spitfires of 129 Squadron, which arrived at the end of July in preparation for Operation 'Jubilee', joined by 130 Squadron on 16 August, in preparation for their role in the ambitious combined forces raid on the heavily defended port of Dieppe.

At first light on the morning of 19 August, two 129 Squadron Spitfires attacked the Point d'Ailly lighthouse, which was the observation position for the Hess gun battery sited to the west of Dieppe. The first aircraft was shot down by flak but the second completed the mission and also attacked two

Fw 190s that had just shot down a Boston. This was followed by a full squadron attack on the Hess battery, covering a Commando mission to destroy its six 150mm guns. A brief dogfight resulted in a claim for a possible Fw 190. At 08.00 No 130 left to provide top cover for the ships and also tangled with defending Fw 190s. Wg Cdr M. V. Blake DSO DFC destroyed one but was then shot down himself, becoming a POW. Mid-morning saw No 129 escorting Hurricanes of 43 Squadron in an attack on the Bismarck battery to the east of Dieppe. They intercepted and destroyed a Do 217 attacking a flotilla of ships before being recalled due to deteriorating weather. Only four Spitfires found Thorney Island, another crashing into high ground north of Tangmere. Although 130 returned to Perranporth the following day, 129 stayed on until 24 September when No 131 Squadron took over.

No 59 Squadron arrived on 28 August 1942 to work up on its new Liberators; it became an informal OTU when No 86 converted from the Beaufort II to the Liberator Mark III during October 1942. After a prolonged gestation period, No 59 became operational in October; in December it received another new type, the Fortress IIA. In February 1943 it was sent to Chivenor, only to be back with Liberator Vs on 27 March. No 86 finally built up to its full strength of nine Liberators by 19 March 1943 when it left for Aldergrove.

While Coastal Command played 'musical chairs' with its four-engined reconnaissance bombers, it was left to the FAA to provide the vital Channel cover. Swordfishes of Nos 816 and 819 carried out essential anti-E-boat and shipping strikes for much of the autumn. They were replaced by No 415 (RCAF) Squadron with the Hampden I, which – incredibly – was to stay for just over a year, albeit while providing detachments to Bircham Newton, Predannack and Tain during that time. The unit's role evolved from shipping strikes to anti-E-boat patrols using its airborne radar. When No 59 returned in March to re-equip with the Liberator V, it was joined a month later by No 53, similarly equipped, which stayed on when 59 moved to Aldergrove in May. The Liberator's long range permitted lengthy *Musketry* sorties out into the Bay of Biscay; during one, on 8 July 1944, 53 Squadron's Liberator B flown by Flying Officer Handasyde was subjected to attacks by seven Ju 88s for nearly 40 minutes. Despite losing an engine, the aircraft made it back to Thorney, but with one gunner dead and another wounded.

This sort of action was very much the exception. For most Coastal Command aircrew, the protection of Britain's sea lanes was an unrewarding but nevertheless vital part of the war effort. As the U-boat campaign came very close to success, air power was an essential tool in combating this menace.

Prior to its move to Bircham Newton on 15 November 1943, No 415 (RCAF) Squadron replaced its Hampdens with the Wellington GR XIII, except for 'A' Flight, which received six Albacores from 841 Squadron FAA, both types having been intended to counter German E-boat operations in the Channel. The unit's replacement at Thorney was No 547, which converted to the Liberator before transfer to St Eval in January 1944. This last move left Thorney Island virtually empty, its only flying residents being a Warwick detachment from the ASR Training Unit at Thornaby.

In a complete change of role, Thorney's new residents were various Typhoon squadrons of the 2nd Tactical Air Force, grouped into 'Airfields'. This was a new tactical linking of squadrons that had come into being during 1943 in preparation for the Second Front. Fortunately for future historians, all received the more acceptable 'Wing' designation on 12 May 1944. The first Typhoon Squadron, No 193, arrived on 15 March 1944, followed by Nos 183, 609, 164 and 198, organised into the two resident 136 and 123 Airfields. By the end of April the movements had sufficiently settled for No 136 Airfield to link with No 146 from Needs Oar Point in an attack, led by Wing Commander D. E. Gillam, on a *Noball* site in France.

On 18 May, six days after they had become a Wing, Nos 164 and 183 Squadrons were led by Wing Commander J. M. Bruce DFC in a tactical reconnaissance over the Gisen-Pontoise area, encountering a pair of Bf 109s that were overwhelmed by superior numbers. A succession of tactical operations ensued, all in preparation for the forthcoming invasion. No 123 Wing successfully attacked a radar station on 24 May, but the strong defences accounted for two of 198 Squadron's Typhoons. A similar operation four days later saw the loss of 164 Squadron's popular CO, Sqn Ldr A. B. Russell DFC. The Wing took its revenge the next day when a pair of 'Tiffies' intercepted two Fw 190s, both being shot down by Fg Off A. R. Taylor using just eighty rounds from his four 20mm cannon. Radar sites were attacked all along the French coast, not only in the Normandy area, to keep the Germans unaware of the chosen landing region.

On D-Day both of Thorney Island's Wings successfully targeted German armour, but it was a hazardous task. No 183 Squadron, bounced by a squadron of Bf 109s, lost three of its number. The balance sheet was redressed by 164 Squadron, which during its three sorties on D-Day claimed two Fw 190s. A couple of days later it was 164's turn to be bounced by Messerschmitts, but now it was the attackers that lost one Bf 109 and two more damaged. On 10 June the Wing lost its OC, Wing Commander Bryan, to flak during an attack on troop columns.

As the Allied armies advanced, temporary airfields were created behind the front lines, freeing many UK Advanced Landing Grounds. No 164 Squadron moved to Funtington on 17 June, with 183 and 198 joining it the next day. No 609 also left Thorney on 18 June, but went straight to France to the B-2 (Bazenville) ALG. Its successors at Thorney Island brought yet another new type to the station in the shape of the Mosquito FB.VI of 2 Group's No 140 Wing (Nos 21, 464 and 487 Squadrons), operating mainly as night interdictors behind the battle area. As well as attacks on the railway network, they carried out a pinpoint daylight bombing raid on 14 July when the Wing, led by the renowned Gp Capt P. G. Wykeham-Barnes, attacked the Gestapo headquarters at Bonneuil Matours, echoing the famous Amiens raid. Nine tons of high explosive destroyed the six buildings occupied by the Gestapo, but the adjacent village was untouched.

No 2 Group was closely involved in Operation 'Market Garden' with its airborne assault on Arnhem and Nijmegen, especially the Mosquitoes of 138 and 140 Wings; however, adverse weather affected the success of their sorties.

The Wing's growing expertise in daylight precision bombing led to its selection for one of the war's classic operations. On 31 October Gp Capt Wykeham-Barnes led twenty-four Mosquitoes on one of 140's longest ever flights, a round trip of 1,235 miles (1,988km,) which took 5½ hours. Their target was another Gestapo Headquarters, housed in two buildings of Aarhus University in Jutland, Denmark. Escorted by eight Mustangs, the four boxes came in at rooftop level, catching the defences by surprise. Only one Mosquito was lost to flak, although two were damaged by bomb blast, including that flown by Sqn Ldr F. H. Denton, which brought back a large piece of masonry lodged in the fuselage. Finally, on 6 February 1945 No 140 Wing moved to the continent and joined No 138 Wing at B-87 (Rosieres-en-Santerre).

A month prior to its departure, the New Year saw Thorney Island filled with as wide an assortment of aircraft as at any time in its history. The newcomer from Angle on 1 January was the Coastal Command Development Unit, which changed its title to the Air-Sea Warfare Development Unit on arrival. Its equipment included the more obvious types such as the Catalina, Hudson, Liberator, Beaufighter and Fortress, but also oddities like the Typhoon, Albemarle, Ventura and a lone Lancaster. No 16 Group had kept a presence on Thorney Island during most of its occupation by 2TAF, usually FAA squadrons under Coastal Command direction. The first had been No 848 Squadron, which arrived on 3 June 1944 and whose Avengers were used for *Channel Stop* operations until they left at the end of August to prepare for embarkation on HMS *Formidable*. No 848's replacement on 7 August was No 157 (GR) Wing, consisting of 854 and 855 Squadrons, which arrived from Hawkinge for anti-submarine patrols, shipping escorts and night *Rovers*. During one of the latter operations on 14 August, an Avenger flown by Lieutenant Voak achieved the seemingly impossible by downing a V-1 missile with the aircraft's front gun. At the end of August No 854 was withdrawn prior to joining HMS *Indomitable*, although 855 stayed a week longer.

Thorney Island's next resident was No 83 Group Support Unit, which had been formed at Redhill in March 1944 to maintain an immediate reserve of pilots and aircraft for 83 Group. It moved in from Bognor on 25 September and stayed until early November, when the FAA returned with Swordfishes, then Barracudas, for anti-submarine patrols. No 278 (ASR) Squadron was posted in on 15 February, providing air-sea rescue using the Supermarine Walrus, with detachments at Hawkinge, Beccles and Exeter. In May the Sea Otter began to replace the Walrus, but both types remained operational until the unit disbanded on 14 October 1945.

The ending of the war in Europe had no immediate effect at Thorney Island. The peacetime plan for Coastal Command envisaged anti-submarine Wings and a single Strike Wing based at Thorney Island. In May 1946 No 248 with Mosquito VIs and 254 with the Beaufighter TF.X arrived to convert to the Brigand torpedo-fighter, although that type was not yet ready for service. The Squadrons, renumbered 36 (ex-248) and 42 (ex-254) on 1 October, were joined in November 1946 by No 1 Torpedo Training Unit; the two squadrons and No 1 TTU disbanded in October 1947 when the Strike Wing concept was abandoned.

On 15 December 1947 Thorney Island was transferred to 11 Group, Fighter Command, with the arrival of the Spitfire LF.XVIs of No 63 Squadron, the last front-line fighter unit to operate the

An oblique aerial view of Thorney Island in 1946/47 looking WNW and showing bomb damage to two 'C' hangars. (Thorney Station records via P. H. T. Green collection)

type. No 63 was joined in February 1948 by Meteor F3/4s of 56 Squadron from Duxford. No 63 finally began to exchange its Spitfires for Meteors in May, and when 222 Squadron arrived on 1 July an all-Meteor Wing was established. During the next two years the only physical change to the station was the provision of Operational Readiness Platforms (ORPs) at either end of the N-S runway. To the north this necessitated the re-routing of the taxiway, increasing the length of Thorney Island's longest runway to 6,000 feet (1,829 metres). However, the Fighter Command era was to be brief as the Meteor Wing moved to Waterbeach in early May 1950 as Thorney Island was to have yet another new 'owner'.

May 1950 saw very familiar types in the circuit as Ansons and Wellingtons landed at Thorney Island, but these were no longer operational aircraft. The station had been transferred to No 21 Group, Flying Training Command, and the resident unit was No 2 Air Navigation School. Its Anson T21 and Wellington T10 navigation trainers were well-worn but replacements were in the pipeline. In November 1951 the Valetta T3 arrived, followed by the Varsity in August 1952. Around this time the Married Officers' housing to the south of the road to the church in West Thorney was significantly increased. Although the Wellingtons departed, the Ansons soldiered on until April 1954 when the problematic Miles (Handley Page) Marathon T11 replaced them. Designed in 1944 as a twenty-two-seat civilian transport to meet a Brabazon Committee requirement, the aircraft, with a crew of three and room for two pupil navigators, was eventually foisted onto a reluctant RAF. After three years, No 2 ANS was none too disappointed to pass the Marathon survivors on to No 1 ANS, forming at Topcliffe.

A transfer to 25 Group in mid-February 1955 coincided with the return of a familiar role – ASR – but with very unfamiliar aircraft. The underpowered Sycamore helicopter was the initial temporary equipment of No 22 Squadron when it re-formed on 15 February; from June these were replaced with the marginally better piston-engined Whirlwind HAR 2. Once fully familiar with its mounts, 'B' Flight was detached to Martlesham Heath, while the HQ and 'A' Flight remained as Coastal Command lodgers on the airfield that for so many years had been their own. The HQ and 'A' Flight moved to St Mawgan on 4 June 1956, leaving a new 'D' Flight in residence.

In the late 1950s a flight of
No 2 ANS Varsities breaks to
land over another, coded D.
(R. Hadlow)

A No 2 ANS mixed formation of single-seat
Vampires and two-seat Vampire NF10s.
(R. Hadlow)

Meteor NF.14 WS788/D of No 2 ANS breaks
away from the camera aircraft. (R. Hadlow)

Crash rescue vehicles and the post-war control tower at Thorney Island in 1963. (T. Mayes)

After nearly twelve years in residence, No 2 ANS departed for Hullavington in mid-January 1962. Having been variously controlled by Coastal Command, the 2nd Tactical Air Force, Fighter Command and Training Command, it seemed inevitable that yet another new task would be found for this versatile station. The new 'owner' was Transport Command in the shape of 38 Group, whose 242 OCU moved in from Dishforth on 29 January 1962 bringing its Hastings and mighty Beverleys. The Island reverberated to the rumble of powerful Bristol radial engines, and from April 1963 a very different sound when the Argosy C1 with its whining Rolls-Royce Dart turbines joined the fleet. Around this time the wartime Watch Office in West Thorney, sited near the runway intersections, was replaced by a modern ATC tower built near the technical site on the opposite side of the main runway.

No 22 Squadron's 'B' Flight returned on 5 May 1964 with the vastly improved turbine-powered Whirlwind HAR 10, and remained a resident for the rest of the station's RAF use. The need for operational conversion training for the Hastings and the Beverley ceased in the mid-1960s; their replacement, the Lockheed Hercules, arrived in April 1967. The last Argosy conversion course was completed in December 1968 and for a time the whine of Allison turbines was the predominant sound over the Island.

However, the Rolls-Royce Dart staged a comeback as the Andover C1s of No 46 Squadron and the Andover Training Flight both arrived on 9 September 1970 from Abingdon. The independent existence of the ATF ended on 1 November when it was merged into 242 OCU. The defence cuts of 1975 brought the withdrawal of the Andover as a tactical transport; the three OCU aircraft left in April 1975, followed by the disbandment of 46 Squadron on 31 August. The continued retrenchment of the RAF's Transport units saw the OCU officially move to Lyneham on 31 October 1975, although it was November before the last Hercules departed. The Search & Rescue headquarters was transferred to Finningley in January 1976 as an SAR wing, together with No 202 Squadron. After thirty-eight years of continuous use, RAF Thorney Island closed on 31 March 1976.

For a time it looked as if the Navy would use Thorney Island in lieu of Lee-on-Solent, but that plan was still-born, as was another suggestion that the northern half of the airfield would be used for general aviation, replacing Portsmouth Airport. Some of the hangarage was rented by Britten-Norman (Bembridge) Ltd to store Islanders and Trislanders awaiting sale; up to twenty aircraft were held there in mid-1977. Three years later the Officers' Mess and other adjacent accommodation were refurbished for use by the Vietnamese 'boat people' refugees, who stayed until 1982 before being assimilated into the population.

Finally a decision was made on the future of the station. It was announced in August 1982 that Thorney Island would become a Royal Artillery barracks for 580 officers and men. The conversion work took more than two years before RAF Thorney Island became Baker Barracks, named after Field Marshal Sir Geoffrey Harding Baker, who is commemorated by a plaque inside the main gate adjacent to the Headquarters building.

Since 1989 the barracks has been home to the 47th Regiment Royal Artillery, known as 'The Hampshire and Sussex Gunners', who provide close air defence for the 3rd (UK) Armoured Division and 16 Air Assault Brigade. The Regiment was reorganised in 1993; three batteries were brought together as one Air Defence Regiment, with a Headquarters Battery that had been resident at Thorney Island from the beginning. A further battery from Colchester has been a recent addition, giving the Regiment five in total: 31/Headquarters Battery; 10 (Assaye) Battery; 43 (Lloyds Company) Battery; 25/170 (Imjim) Battery; and 21 (Gibraltar) Battery. In addition there is a Royal Electrical & Mechanical Engineers (REME) workshop.

Externally the adaptations to the former RAF buildings for their new roles appear minimal. Most obviously the four surviving 'C'-type hangars no longer have their main sliding doors, and each side elevation now has one or more large vehicle-sized doors, depending on its role. The most southerly hangar, known as the 'Navy Hangar' for unclear reasons, has a single large access in its southern elevation and is used primarily for storage. The remaining hangars are used by the individual batteries to house their vehicles and equipment; the central hangar, with its multiple side doors, is also the REME workshop. Towards the end of 2001, the MOD announced a number of tenders for building developments at the barracks. These included upgrading of the SNCOs' and Junior Ranks' living accommodation, enhanced gymnasium and medical/dental facilities, and more covered parking; this involved the construction of a new 'hangar' on the site of one destroyed sixty years before.

Throughout the technical and accommodation areas the most obvious evidence of the Army's presence are artillery 'gate guardians' and the red and blue signs on buildings like the NAAFI, indicating that 47 Regiment, Royal Artillery, is their occupant. Out on the airfield, the most obvious change is the lack of a control tower. None of Thorney Island's three Watch Offices/Control Towers have survived. Only a concrete base reveals the previous location of the post-war tower, which was apparently demolished at the end of 2001/early 2002. The group of emergency vehicle garages are now the 'Thorney Island Saddle Club', with an adjacent paddock for the horses. The runways generally are still in good condition, particularly the main runway (01/19), which is retained in a useable state in connection with the rapid reaction role of 21 (Gibraltar) Battery. In support of 16 Air Assault Brigade, the unit may be deployed by a range of aircraft including the Hercules, the Globemaster III and the Chinook. So aviation has not totally left Thorney Island.

Main features:
Runways: 015° 4,890ft x 150ft, 057° 5,100ft x 150ft, 120° 4,050ft x 150ft, concrete.
Hangars: six 'C'-type, sixteen Blister. *Hardstandings:* forty-two, 120ft diameter.
Accommodation: RAF: 330 Officers, 276 SNCOs, 3.030 ORs; WAAF: 19 Officers, 489 SNCOs and ORs.

Places of interest nearby:
In West Thorney can be found a delightful ancient church dedicated to the patron saint of sailors, St Nicholas. Described as one of the lovelier, lonelier, most remote, least seen and less known churches in Sussex, it alone is worth a visit to Thorney Island. It is now the Garrison Church of Baker Barracks, the first resident chaplain being appointed in 1992. As such it holds Royal Artillery Standards and a board recording the Army units to have served there. Aeronautically, the church has a wealth of artefacts commemorating its aviation links. An RAF ensign hangs above two boards recording the RAF and Fleet Air Arm units to have served at RAF Thorney Island. To the right, inset into an original doorway, is a beautifully simple memorial window engraved with the Station Crest including its motto 'Fly To Assist' and the dates 1938-1976. The unusual oak and slate pulpit was presented to the church in 1962 to commemorate the stay of No 2 Air Navigation School, whose badge is carved on one of the panels. In front of the altar rail are kneelers carrying the RAF eagle and squadron numbers. Other kneelers record the present Royal Artillery use of the church. The once disused Rectory was, in 1995, converted into a Church Centre for the use of Army and civilian personnel and their families living within the parish.

Within the graveyard, a recent stone commemorates Group Captain W. G. Devas CBE DFC AFC, 1912-2001, Officer Commanding RAF Thorney Island 1958-61. The northern extension to the churchyard is in the care of the Imperial War Graves Commission, with the majority of the neatly tended graves those of Allied airmen

The interior of St Nicholas's Church showing RAF Thorney Island history boards, standards and memorial window. (DWL collection)

from virtually every nation of the Commonwealth. There are also some twenty graves of Luftwaffe aircrew, the majority dating from 1940, who also gave their lives in the service of their cause. Within the cemetery a simple plain Portland Stone marker under the dates 1939-1945 records in both English and German the words: 'In memory of those who gave their lives for their country'.

Thorney Island/Baker Barracks is of course a secure military establishment and the access road is guarded. However, the 1974 edition of Ordnance Survey Sheet 197 indicates a public right of way coastal footpath circumnavigating the island, which passes the church in West Thorney – a wonderful way to spend a summer afternoon.

THROWLEY, Kent

51°14N/00°51E 275ft asl; TQ991535. 5 miles S of Faversham on minor road

Throwley was one of No 50 Squadron's 1916 Home Defence landing grounds. Formed at Dover in May 1916, No 50 operated a mix of BE.2 and BE.12 biplanes on anti-Zeppelin patrols. As most of its work was at night, it needed a number of basic emergency LGs that included Harrietsham, Detling, Throwley and Bekesbourne. Throwley was approximately triangular in outline and covered 87 acres (35.24 hectares) between Bell's Forstal on its eastern side and Dodds Willows wood.

Improvements were put in hand in early summer 1917 as No 112 Squadron was created from 'B' Flight of 50 Squadron, equipped with the Sopwith Pup. Three Bessonneau hangars were erected on the edge of Dodds Willows to house the aeroplanes. A wooden hangar was also assembled for No 6 Motor Transport Squadron. Most of the airmen were under canvas adjacent to Bell's Forstal farmhouse, which became the Officers' Mess. Unusually a bore hole was sunk and a water tower erected to overcome a significant lack of water on the site.

No 112, led by Major Gerald Allen, had no success in its day and night patrols for the remainder of 1917 as the Pup was becoming obsolescent. It was joined by No 188 (Training) Squadron, which was formed at Throwley on 20 December 1917 with Avro 504Ks to train pilots in night-flying skills. When No 143 Squadron was formed on 1 February 1918 accommodation for all purposes was in very short supply. As more wooden huts were assembled in cleared areas of Dodds Willows, 143 was moved on to Detling in mid-February.

Major C. J. Q. Brand DSO MC DFC arrived to take command of 112 Squadron as it was converting to the more effective Camel in March 1918. The construction programme went on apace until accommodation for 450 personnel was provided, together with a technical site consisting of workshops, three MT sheds and an additional wooden hangar to supplement the three Bessonneaus.

May brought a return to night bombing by the Gothas of the German strategic bombing unit, Kagohl 3. In favourable weather conditions a force of thirty-eight Gothas and three Giants launched an attack on London on 19 May. The defending response was very strong with a deafening gun barrage and some eighty-four fighters airborne, among which was Major Quintin Brand who intercepted a Gotha between Canterbury and Faversham, which he eventually shot down in flames at Harty Ferry on the Isle of Sheppey. Only thirteen raiders managed to reach London and six were shot down, shared equally between the guns and the fighters. It was the last major attack on Britain and No 112's only victory of the war.

Camels were issued to No 188 from July 1918 to provide advanced night-fighting training on the type, as 112 Squadron built up to a total of twenty-four Camels on strength by September. Under a reorganisation of the Home Defence, gun belts were established with the fighters tasked to patrol between them. No 112 was given Line H, a north-south patrol from Throwley to Judd's Hill near Faversham, then to Warden Point on the north shore of Sheppey.

'Twinkle' Camel D6405 served with No 112 (HD) Squadron and was photographed on 14 June 1918. (JMB/GSL collection)

Work had started on a large brick hangar (presumably a General Service shed), but with the coming of the Armistice it was never completed. Activity reduced significantly and No 188 disbanded on 1 March 1919. Its sister unit, No 112, survived until 13 June before being closed down. Although Throwley was transferred to the Ministry of Munitions in October 1919, the site was soon cleared and returned to agriculture.

During the critical summer of 1940 Cadman's Farm was designated a scatter ELG for Detling. The farm was on the southern boundary of Throwley, but despite the pasting that Detling received during the Battle of Britain there is no evidence that its aircraft scattered to Throwley. By the beginning of the 21st century a little evidence of Throwley survives. The original guardroom was rebuilt on the same site in the 1990s and some building bases and debris can be found in Dodds Willows wood. Bell's Forstal farmhouse, which became the Officers' Mess, is still a very fine building. The land between the farmhouse and the wood is still open farmland awaiting the arrival of a Sopwith Camel.

Main features in 1918:

Landing ground: grass. *Hangars:* three Bessonneau, one wooden type and one GS shed. *Accommodation:* wooden hutting.

TIPNOR, Hampshire

50°49N/01°06W, 6ft asl; SU638034. 2.5 miles N of Portsmouth city centre alongside M275

A 12-acre (4.9-hectare) promontory adjacent to Whale Island was an obvious location in 1917 for a Kite Balloon station providing spotting and observation duties for the ships of Portsmouth Command. A line of six balloon and two MT sheds was erected across the site together with the necessary hydrogen gas production plant and accommodation for the establishment of 182 personnel.

After 1 April 1918 the unit became No 15 Kite Balloon Base RAF, formally part of No 10 Group, Calshot, but operationally under Portsmouth control. It was returned to the Admiralty in August 1919 and became a firing range, a role it continues to perform.

Main features in 1918:

Runways: none. *Hangars:* six balloon sheds. *Accommodation:* assumed to be wooden hutting.

WALMER, Kent

51°11N/01°24E, 76ft asl; TR375493. 2 miles S of Deal off minor road

Just 57 acres (23.1 hectares) of the Hawkshill Down plateau between Kingsdown and Deal was requisitioned for a satellite LG for Dover in May 1917. The Walmer Defence Flight covering shipping anchored off Deal used a range of types including the BE.2C, Sopwith Pup and Bristol Scout. Accommodation for the aeroplanes was the ubiquitous Bessonneau portable sheds, which together with the personnel tents were lined up along the narrow strip of wood called the Firs on the western edge of the field. Officers were initially accommodated at Mayes Farm but later moved to Leelands on Grams Road.

Sopwith Pup N6442 'Julia' served with the Walmer Defence Flight in June 1917 and again in November 1917. (JMB/GSL collection)

The Walmer Defence Flight was also tasked with Home Defence, without success until 8 August 1917 when a Canadian pilot, Flt Lt H. S. Kerby, shot down a Gotha from the Kagohl 3 unit into the sea off Southend. The Germans returned a fortnight later and Kerby again claimed a victory, although this was not confirmed. However, the total losses on these two daylight raids were nine Gothas, which convinced the Germans to turn to night operations.

After heavy fighting around Arras, No 3 (Naval) Squadron transferred from France for a rest in November 1917, being joined in December by No 4 Squadron. In January 1918 the Walmer Defence Flight personnel joined with No 11 Squadron to be re-formed as No 6 (Naval) Squadron based at Dover. Walmer's R&R role continued as No 3 (Naval) returned to France, being succeeded by No 8 (Naval) on 3 March to re-equip with the powerful Bentley BR.1-powered Camels. By the end of March all the Naval squadrons had returned to the Western Front, leaving Walmer deserted.

The creation of the RAF brought a small Flight, later numbered 471 as part of No 233 Squadron, to Walmer with six Camels to provide escorts for DH.9s on reconnaissance and shipping patrols. This work continued after 11 November 1918, and in January 1919 a further Flight, No 491, also with DH.9s, moved in from Guston Road followed in March by the HQ of 233 Squadron, which absorbed the Flights. But the need for coastal patrols had gone and 233 Squadron was disbanded on 15 May 1919.

The aerodrome was abandoned but, thanks to the Countess Beauchamp, the sacrifice of its men was not to be forgotten. A memorial taking the form of a thatched well-head was dedicated on 8 August 1920. An attached plaque with the RNAS crest records the names of fifteen airmen who served at Walmer and later lost their lives in action. During the Second World War the site was used as an RAF MT base but, apart from propaganda balloons, no flying took place. After the war the memorial was relocated to a footpath crossing Hawkshill Down, and after refurbishment was rededicated on 7 July 1952. It continues in the care of the local RAF Association. Part of the site became a holiday camp for London children, but is now privately owned paddocks and stables. However, an old metal sign relating to the former camp adjacent to the memorial suggests that 'you are invited to use this memorial as a place of remembrance and quiet meditation'. Much of the former aerodrome is now public open space purchased by Walmer Parish Council from the Leith Estate in 1999 and is a designated Site of Nature Conservation Interest (SNCI).

Main features in 1918:
Landing ground: grass. *Hangars:* a number of Bessonneaus. *Accommodation:* requisitioned local housing and tented camp.

A bench adjacent to the well-head memorial gives an opportunity for a quiet reflective rest. (DWL collection)

WANBOROUGH, Wiltshire

51°32N/01°41W 627ft asl; SU220820. 5 miles SE of Swindon alongside Ermine Way

The greatly increased demand for trained pilots led Flying Training Command to create a number of additional RLGs. The land on the plateau to the north-east of King Edward's Place, alongside the Ermine Street Roman road, was selected in 1940 as Wanborough. Although earmarked for No 14 SFTS at Lyneham, the first users in early 1941 were Oxfords of No 3 SFTS at South Cerney, which acquired squatters' rights and the Lyneham unit never appeared!

In early March 1942 No 3 SFTS was reformed as No 3 (P)AFU at South Cerney, leaving Wanborough to No 3 EFTS based at Shellingford and the circuit was quickly buzzing with Tiger Moths until November 1942 when the landing ground was to be upgraded for permanent occupation. The work began with laying concrete bases for a number of Laing huts in the eastern corner adjacent to the parkland of King Edward's Place for use accommodation and Officers'/NCOs' Messes. Along southern and western boundaries four Blister hangars were erected connected by a vehicle access track.

The new occupants on 14 June 1943 were 'A' and 'B' Flights of the School of Flying Control with forty trainee controllers undergoing initial instruction prior to transfer to Watchfield to complete their training. Having settled in well by December, they were turfed out by No 3 Glider Training School, whose base of Stoke Orchard was totally flooded, the changeover officially taking place on 18 and 19 December.

The GTS had a total establishment of thirty Master II tugs plus fifteen spares, twenty-nine Hotspur gliders and fourteen reserves, and five Tiger Moths with a pair of spares. It must have been crowded although the former satellite of North Leach continued to be used whenever possible. The majority of the twenty-three staff pilots were billeted out, as Wanborough had accommodation for just eight officers and SNCOs. With 117 places there was plenty of room for the other ranks.

Although there were initially just seventeen pupils, numbers expanded rapidly and with increased pressure came accidents. The first on 28 December occurred when a Hotspur undershot, hitting a hedge with one fatality, and later a student crashed on his first solo. The site's elevated location overlooking the Vale of the White Horse with even higher ground to the south must have been a factor in these incidents. In May 1944 No 3 GTS returned to Stoke Orchard and the Flying Control School retrieved its RLG, transferring its Airfield Controllers course to Wanborough. During June and July 1944 American personnel were included in the courses, which continued to the war's end. The RLG closed down on 21 May 1946 and, apart from a riding school and stables that occupy the area adjacent to King Edward's Place, the remainder of the site has returned to farmland.

Main features:
Runways: NE-SW 2,250ft, N-S 2,700ft, E-W 2,700ft, grass. *Hangars:* four Extra Over Blisters. *Hardstandings:* none. *Accommodation:* RAF: 8 Officers/SNCOs, 117 ORs.

WELFORD, Berkshire

51°28N/00°24W 450ft asl; SU418745. 6 miles NW of Newbury off minor road

For most of the Cold War a researcher interested in current or even old military airfields was regarded with deep suspicion and the 1 inch Ordnance Survey maps of the period were deliberately unhelpful. Where today a depiction of the buildings and runways can be studied, then only a bare empty field was ever depicted. By the late 1980s the Landranger OS sheet 174 showed details of a highly secret airfield like Greenham Common, but on the plateau to the north of Welford village – nothing but contour lines!

The site was selected in October 1941 for future use by No 92 Group and was planned to have all the standard features of a Bomber Command OTU. However, by the time construction started in the spring of 1943 it was decided that the base would be allocated to the growing influx of the United States Army Air Force. By June the three runways were finished, the main one of 6,000ft (1,829m) aligned 15/33 and two secondary strips of 4,200ft (1,280m), together with forty-six loop and four 'frying-pan' hardstandings. When the first USAAF ground personnel arrived in July only one T2 and a few of the buildings on the technical site were complete. However, by 6 September 1943, as the VIIIth Air Support Command took charge of USAAF Station 474, construction was complete including dispersed accommodation for a total of 2,368 officers and men. In the centre of the technical site the historic 11th-century house called The Priory was retained to become the CO's accommodation.

The station, which the USAAF often called Welford Park, from the area and the railway station to the south, was earmarked for a Troop Carrier Group, but it took until 6 November before the first arrived. When it did, it was only the 34th and 43rd TCS of the 315th TCG, as the bulk of the Group was overseas. They were joined on 10 December by the 434th from Fulbeck, but that detachment only lasted a month before the unit returned to Fulbeck. The next arrival, between 23 and 31 January, was the 435th from Langar with its 4 TCS, the 75th, 76th, 77th and 78th. All this shuffling around was in order to give the TCGs experience of working with the 101st Airborne Division, encamped on various sites between Reading and Marlborough. The final piece of juggling was the departure of the 315th, which began to leave on 31 January for Spanhoe, the move being completed on 6 February when the Group HQ finally left. As soon as it had gone, units of the 438th TCG began to arrive directly from the States, although most of the squadrons and their aircraft went to Langar. By 16 March the components of the 438th had all been reunited at Greenham Common.

This left the 435th as Welford's sole resident unit, a situation that was continue for the next twelve momentous months. The station had been formally transferred to the IXth Air Force on 22 February and the way was clear for the intensive training with the 101st Airborne, which the Group's future commitments demanded. The first major test of its readiness took place on 23 March when a large demonstration of the airborne forces was laid on in the fields to the east of Welford for Winston Churchill, General Eisenhower and other VIPs. Later that month, in another significant exercise, ninety-seven CG-4A gliders were launched on a formation cross-country navigation assignment before returning to base. Near Welford the gliders were cast off, landing back at regular 10-second intervals. Night towing practices using both Hadrian and Horsa gliders confirmed that the Group was nearing a peak of efficiency as its real test grew closer.

In the early hours of D-Day, 6 June 1944, the 435th was in the first wave carrying the paratroopers of the 501st PIR to a DZ just south of Cherbourg, with the lead aircraft carrying General Maxwell Taylor and his staff. Flak hit ten C-47s, and three were lost, the rest returning with varying degrees of damage. Immediately on their return all the serviceable aircraft were refuelled and marshalled into position to pick up their gliders. In the afternoon a total of fifty C-47s towed thirty-eight Horsas and twelve Hadrians to the same area in a reinforcement mission. They were accompanied by a solitary C-47 with paratroopers who had not been able to jump earlier that morning. Again the Group lost three C-47s, which had to ditch due to flak damage. Another glider mission was flown on the morning of 7 June, and the excellence of the Group's work during this period was recognised in the award of the coveted Distinguished Unit Citation.

Resupply missions became the norm, initially by parachute, but as airstrips became available, the C-47s were able to land and return with wounded who were transferred to Newbury hospitals. During these operations time was also found during June to carry out a trial snatch recovery of CG-4A gliders from the battlefield. On 20 July half of the Group was detached to Tarquinna in Italy to participate in the invasion of southern France. While they were away, aircraft of the 90th TCS, 438th TCG, were detached from Greenham Common, returning on 23 August as the 435th taskforce came back to prepare for its next assignment, Operation 'Market Garden'.

Together with the rest of the TCGs in the area, the 435th launched its C-47s during the morning of 17 September on their way to Holland. The first serial of thirty-six aircraft left at 10.00 carrying troops of the 101st, the 'Screaming Eagles', to a DZ near Eindhoven just north of their objective, the bridge over the Wilhelmina Canal. A second serial of twenty-eight C-47s followed shortly after. The flak defences were strong, with twelve aircraft being hit in the first serial; fortunately ten were able to return. A further eight from the second serial were also damaged. The next day, two serials, each of thirty aircraft towing gliders, were dispatched with reinforcements. The LZ was identified accurately and, although seventeen C-47s were hit by flak, all returned safely. The story on 19 September was not so happy – three aircraft were lost, but there were instances of special heroism. A typical case was that of 1st Lieutenant Jesse Harrison who, despite his aircraft being on fire, flew on until he identified the LZ and released his glider. Only then did he and his co-pilot bail out of the blazing aircraft. Further resupply missions followed until the failure of the 'Garden' part of the operation to relieve Arnhem brought the missions to a close. The 435th returned to its supply and casevac operations until it moved to Bretigny (A-48) from 13 February 1945. As with the rest of the local IXth stations, Welford acted as a transit base until finally, in June 1945, it was returned to the RAF.

On 30 June Welford came under the control of RAF Transport Command with the formation of No 1336 (Transport Support) Conversion Unit with an establishment of thirty-four Dakotas, fifteen Horsas, fourteen Oxfords and a solitary Proctor. Tasked with training crews in glider towing, paratroop and supply dropping, the first course arrived on 26 August 1945, by which time the war against Japan, for which they were training, had finished. Their raison d'être having gone, the unit disbanded on 1 March 1946.

Reduced to C&M, the station was transferred to 90 (Signals) Group in October 1946, which virtually meant the end of flying. However, the connection with gliders was not totally lost, as glider manufacturer Elliotts of Newbury obtained approval to use Welford for the flight-testing of the company's new four-seat light aircraft, the Newbury Eon. Elliotts had built a third of the Horsas used by the Allied airborne forces and were then building wings for the local Chilton Aircraft-designed Olympia sailplane. The attractive low-wing monoplane made its maiden flight on 8 August 1947 and embarked on a successful flight-test programme. To promote both its products (they had acquired the production rights to the Chilton sailplane), Elliotts used the Eon to tow the Olympia to events throughout the country. Although the Olympia was a success, the sole Eon was destroyed in an unmanned take-off at Lympne in April 1950.

During 1947 Welford had become the HQ of the Southern Signals Area, renamed HQ Radio Navigation Aids Wing three years later. In December 1950 the now silent airfield was transferred to Maintenance Command, then to C&M when the HQ RNAW disbanded on 1 August 1952.

Welford's future remained in limbo for another three years until 1 September 1955, when it became a USAF 3rd Air Force logistics station. A suffocating blanket of security descended on the airfield, far exceeding anything it had known in wartime. The large numbers of revetments and bunkers that spread over the whole airfield revealed the reason for the high security. Welford had become a vast bomb store, serving all the USAF bases in Britain, and continues in that role to this day. The 7531st Ammunition Squadron was the first unit to operate from Welford, but was replaced in 1959 by the 3115th Ammunition Squadron. A succession of 'Ammo' units and/or name changes followed as the size and role of the 3rd Air Force responded to the changing Cold War situation.

Initially the ordnance was delivered by rail, but in 1967 the Beeching axe closed the branch line from Newbury with the result that all munitions had to be brought by road on the narrow country lanes. This unsatisfactory situation continued until the building of the M4 in 1977 permitted the construction of a dedicated exit road from the eastbound carriageway on the line on the old railway. The anonymously named 'Works Unit only' exit between the Hungerford and Newbury junctions enables munitions to be transported from the South Wales Docks direct to Welford. Again the OS map from 1989 gives no hint of this road, although the dismantled railway is shown.

In April 1995 the resident unit was redesignated the 424th Airbase Squadron, and from 1996 the station was jointly administered by the 424th ABS and RAF Brize Norton. On 1 April 1999 the base was taken over by the newly formed MOD Defence Munitions Agency, but by November 2002 Welford was back in American hands, being the full responsibility of the 424th ABS with its HQ at RAF Fairford.

Welford's squash court and, on the right, the dining room Nissen huts. (DWL collection)

The former gymnasium and chapel was under sentence of demolition in 2003. (DWL collection)

Welford remains a highly secure establishment and is virtually invisible from ground level, but the advent of Google Earth has revealed everything to anyone with internet access. The bomb shelters are built over most of the runways but many of the wartime hardstandings remain. From a close inspection, it would appear that the two wartime T2 hangars were still there in 2004, if the Google imagery date is accurate. The only part of the former RAF Welford that is visible to a casual visitor by road is the former married quarters. Their brown USAF road signs, including Glenn Miller Close, betray their fairly recent private status.

Although unannounced visitors will be given short shrift, the USAF does permit entry to Welford to a select group of dedicated civilians. The Ridgeway Military & Aviation Research Group is committed to preserving the military history of the area, especially RAF Welford. In a modern building adjacent to the former rifle range and the Sportsman's Club (which does superb beefburgers), the Ridgeway Group has an excellent museum. Entering, the privileged visitor (by pre-arrangement only) is confronted by the nose of a C-47 and a treasure trove of aviation history. Highlights include the massive wooden wing spar of a DH.10 Amiens, a working D4 Link Trainer and recovered wall artwork from Greenham Common, Mount Farm and Membury. The mezzanine floor houses a photographic exhibition and memorabilia from Welford's history, as well as a lecture area and a small memorial area fronted by the preserved chapel door – the building itself was demolished shortly after my visit.

In the early 1990s a Welford Fifty Committee was formed to create a suitable memorial to mark the 50th anniversary of RAF Welford. To the left of the original entrance road, known as Ammo Alley, a commemorative grove of American and British trees was planted in 1992. The memorial stone of local sarsen rock carried a plaque carrying RAF, IXth Air Force and USAFE badges. Subsequently plaques commemorating the 435th TCG, the Millennium and Welford's 60th anniversary were added. Other separate memorials are dedicated to all the airborne forces that flew from the Newbury area during 1944, and to the crew of a Lancaster from 101 Squadron that crashed at Welford on 31 March 1944. On 11 November each year a well-attended Remembrance

The interior of the Ridgeway Military & Aviation Research Group's museum. (DWL collection)

Day service is held. The Memorial Grove can be seen from the road just before reaching the present entrance on the left, albeit at a distance, so that the details are not visible. Welford keeps its secrets – even those of the sacrifices of those who flew from and served there over the past sixty years.

Main features:
Runways: 330° 6,000ft x 150ft, 020° 4,200ft x 150ft, 370° 4,200ft x 150ft, concrete with wood chippings. *Hangars:* two T2. *Hardstandings:* forty-six concrete loop type, four 'frying-pan'. *Accommodation:* USAAF: 470 Officers, 1,898 enlisted men.

WESTENHANGER, Kent

51°05N/01°02E 230ft asl; TR120370. 3 miles NW of Hythe off A20

The first aeronautical use of this site was in 1910, when the Folkestone Racecourse held a flying meeting at the end of September attended by a very large crowd and three aeroplanes. However, no further aeroplanes were seen until 1940-41 when dummy aircraft provided the dressing for a decoy aerodrome, probably for the nearby Lympne.

Flying machines in the form of Auster AOP IVs arrived in April 1944 with No 660 Squadron to practise tactical operations with local Army units. After a brief deployment to Weston Zoyland in May to practise crossing the Bristol Channel, 660 returned to await its move to France, which finally came on 12 July 1944. An ASR Walrus led twelve Austers in a line-astern formation, its navigating role completed on arrival in France and its rescue role not required. After a brief tidy-up, Westenhanger became Folkestone Racecourse once again.

Main features:
Runways: grass. *Hangars:* none. *Accommodation:* tented camp.

WESTGATE, Kent

51°23N/01°20E 8ft asl; TR328705. 1.5 miles W of Margate off A28

With a concentration of naval assets around the Thames Estuary, in early 1914 the Admiralty sought to strengthen the area's defences against submarine or aerial attack. To supplement the Grain air station, additional seaplane bases were chosen at Clacton and in St Mildred's Bay near Westgate-on-Sea. Westgate was opened on 2 August 1914 with Flight Commander J. T. Babington in command of a small group of officers and ratings. They sought accommodation in the town but found that they were in competition with the seasonal holiday trade; however, they found room in the St Mildred's Hotel for the pilots.

For some months no aeroplanes were permanently stationed at Westgate, various Short seaplane types being flown in as necessary to be hauled up and down the beach and onto the grass slopes, to the great interest of the holidaymakers. The transfer of the BEF to France left the Admiralty very short of aeroplanes and Westgate was put into a C&M status as work to construct slipways and an aeroplane shed went ahead. St Mildred's Hotel was requisitioned for accommodation, and by December 1914 a pair of seaplanes were permanently stationed at Westgate.

The need for a landplane base in the area led to the acquisition of land at Mutrix Farm on the clifftop to the east of the seaplane station (TR335705). During April 1915 'A' flight of No 2 Squadron RNAS arrived from Eastchurch with a combination of Avro 504s, Curtiss JN3s and BE.2Cs to occupy the usual range of wooden sheds and huts. Its purpose was to provide aerial defence against the Zeppelin. At this time the airships could easily out-climb their opponents, which caused the commander of LZ38 to nearly pay the price for overconfidence on the night of 17 May 1915. He was intercepted at just 2,000 feet (610 metres) over Ramsgate by Flight Sub-Lieutenant Mulock in an Avro 504B armed with incendiary bombs and grenades. To escape, the Zeppelin had to jettison its bombs to climb above the Avro. As it was the first time a Zeppelin had been intercepted, Mulock was asked to make a report to the Admiralty.

Single-seat BE.2C 8298 served at Westgate from 11 June 1916 on anti-Zeppelin duties. (JMB/GSL collection)

Westgate suffered its first fatality on the night of 9/10 August when Flight Sub-Lieutenant Lord crashed on landing after an unsuccessful attempt to intercept an airship. He was buried with full military honours in Margate cemetery. After two more sheds were erected, together with even more wooden huts, the Ocean Hotel was also requisitioned as numbers were increased substantially. The first combat success was on 20 March 1916 when Flight Commander R. J. Bone, detached from

Detling in his Nieuport, attacked and crippled one of five German seaplanes that had bombed Margate. The limitations of Westgate aerodrome were brought to a head with an accident in March 1917, which led to the move to Manston. The latter airfield was already being used as an ELG, and Westgate aerodrome was abandoned.

The seaplane base in St Mildred's Bay continued to expand, first with Sopwith Schneider seaplanes and later the Sopwith Baby. A pair of the latter took off during 23/24 May 1917 on a patrol, but one failed to return and a search was started by Flight Sub-Lieutenant Morris and Air Mechanic Wright. The missing Baby was later found and towed home, but the searching Short 827 suffered engine failure and had to force-land, overturned and sank, leaving the two crew clinging to some wreckage. After five days and nights surviving on a few malted milk tablets, they were found by a Curtiss H.12 flying boat to end their terrible ordeal.

When the seaplane base became RAF Westgate on 1 April 1918, the primary type on strength was the excellent Short 184. On its long-range patrols the increasing threat of interception by German aeroplanes lead to the provision of a Camel escort, which sometimes failed to protect its charges. Such an incident occurred on 18 July when a pair of Short 184s was being escorted by two Camels. Seven German seaplanes attacked from out of the sun, forcing one Short down onto the sea. One attacker landed alongside to continue the fight, which resulted in the destruction of the RAF machine. The Camels returned to Manston after flying alongside the other Short 184, which appeared to be undamaged, but it never reached Westgate and its loss was never explained.

No 219 Squadron was formed at Westgate in August from the two Flights at Westgate and Manston; Westgate's Sopwith Babies and Short 184s had become No 406 (Seaplane) Flight and Manston's Camels No 470 (Fighter) Flight in May. The seaplanes were joined in November 1918 by the Fairey IIIB of No 442 Flight, but operations slowed dramatically after the Armistice. No 219 Squadron and No 442 Flight were both disbanded on 7 February 1920 when RAF Westgate was formally closed.

After an inventory had been taken, the station's buildings, machinery, plant and furniture were all auctioned on 15 December 1920 and removed. One hangar was dismantled and transferred to Manston, where it survived into the 21st century. The land on which the aerodrome stood was initially returned to farming, but in the 1920s was totally built over and houses now stand where Avros and Nieuports once flew. The seaplane base was similarly dismantled although the wide slipway was still extant during a visit in September 1987. St Mildred's Hotel was looking rather neglected, and was replaced around 2000 by an apartment block called Marine Height Flats; the wide slipway had gone when a visit was made in September 2004. However, the role of Westgate in the Great War is commemorated by a plaque titled 'Wings over Westgate', which sets out the history of the site.

The first in what became a famous line of Fairey seaplanes, the N9 Fairey III, at Westgate with St Mildred's Hotel in the background. (JMB/GSL collection)

Dismantling a hangar at Westgate aerodrome for re-erection at Manston. (GSL collection)

A view of Westgate in September 1987, with both slipways and St Mildred's Hotel visible.
(DWL collection)

Main features of seaplane base in 1918:
Take-off and alighting area: St Mildred's Bay. *Hangars:* one Admiralty seaplane
shed. *Facilities:* slipway and hardstanding. *Accommodation:* local accommodation.

WESTHAMPNETT, West Sussex

51°51N/00°45W 95ft asl; SU875075. 1.5 miles NE of Chichester on minor road off A285

The 100,000-plus visitors who annually flock to the Goodwood Revival meeting, which began in 1998 to mark the sixtieth anniversary of the opening of the Goodwood motor racing circuit, would not believe that it really all began on 7 December 1938 when the Air Ministry approved the acquisition of land on the Duke of Richmond's Goodwood estate as an ELG for nearby Tangmere. Initially Westhampnett, as the aerodrome was called, was retained as open meadow land for emergency use, but after the fall of France it was upgraded to full satellite status, reopening on 31 July 1940, when the Hurricanes of No 145 Squadron transferred from Tangmere.

What became known as the Battle of Britain had officially started a couple of weeks earlier, although the pilots of 145 Squadron had been in action since May. However, the next fortnight at Westhampnett was to be the most taxing they had experienced. It started badly on 1 August when Sub-Lt L. H. Kestin, seconded from the FAA, was killed by the rear gunner of a Henschel Hs 126 before it was sent into the Channel.

After a week of uneventful patrols, on 8 August No 145 Squadron was scrambled three times in a running battle over Convoy CW9, which had left the Medway ports the previous night. In desperate combat with almost overwhelming numbers of Ju 87 bombers and Bf 109 and Bf 110 fighters, the Squadron claimed seven Stukas and four Bf 109s destroyed and a further five Ju 87s and two Bf 110s damaged. The cost was very high, as the unit lost five Hurricanes whose pilots were lost in the English Channel. Among those tragic losses was Flying Officer Richard Kay-Shuttleworth, the second Lord Shuttleworth of Gawthorpe Hall, Lancashire.

Sqn Ldr J. R. A. Peel with his exhausted surviving pilots were loaded with congratulatory telegrams from the Secretary of State for Air downwards, and were visited by HRH the Duke of Gloucester and the AOC 11 Group, Keith Park, to personally thank them. Just three days later the Squadron was again in the thick of the battle when 100-plus 'hostiles' were approaching Portland Harbour and 145 with others intercepted them. In the mêlée that followed they claimed a Bf 109 and a Bf 110, but lost four Hurricanes; three pilots took to their parachutes but only two were picked up. The next day the battered Squadron again came off worst when sent to defend Portsmouth against a formation of Ju 88s from the 'Edelweiss' Geschwader, KG51, which were escorted by Bf 110s of ZGs 2 and 76 and Bf 109s from JG53, a total in excess of 150 aircraft. Against one Ju 88 destroyed, the Squadron lost three pilots with another badly damaged Hurricane just making it back to Westhampnett.

The handful of over-tired pilots were relieved on 14 August by the Spitfires of No 602 (City of Glasgow) Squadron from Drem, whence the remnants of No 145 retired to recoup and rebuild. The new Squadron arrived just as the Luftwaffe changed tactics. From attacks on convoys the new targets were Fighter Command's aerodromes. 16 August was to prove to be Tangmere's 'Black Friday' as the parent station's Hurricane squadrons sought to defend the aerodrome against a major attack by Ju 87s. The Spitfires of 602 Squadron took on the escorts and all returned safely, although two were badly damaged.

The Luftwaffe again attacked en masse on 16 August 1940 as it attempted to repeat its previous successes, dividing its formation to strike the airfields of Ford, Thorney Island and Gosport. The defending Squadrons were confused over the targets and all three were bombed and suffered varying degrees of damage and casualties. The attacking Ju 88s escaped without being intercepted but the Stukas were not so lucky. No 602 was among the three Squadrons that meted out severe punishment whereby eighteen Ju 87s were destroyed or had to be written off on their return. Westhampnett's share was four destroyed and four more damaged. Just one Spitfire was lost when it ditched, but the pilot was rescued. Four other fighters were damaged and two pilots wounded, but the Ju 87 never again appeared en masse over England.

The following weeks were not quite as frenetic, but the constant standbys and scrambles were wearing and casualties mounted, particularly on 7 September, the day when London became the target, when the Squadron lost two pilots. As the Luftwaffe began its night assault on the capital some night-flying training was undertaken, only to prove the unsuitability of the Spitfire with the loss of three aircraft. Standing patrols were started to counter the low-level fighter-bomber hit-and-run attacks on South Coast towns.

With the Battle over, No 602 was joined by 302 (Polish) Squadron from Northolt on 23 November, and in mid-December exchanged with No 610 (County of Chester) Squadron, retiring to Prestwick for some much-needed R&R.

Waterlogging of the aerodrome in heavy rain had been a problem since the beginning, and a start was made at the end of 1940 to ameliorate the situation. A continuous perimeter track was laid with hardstandings off it at regular intervals. At long last, as far as the groundcrews were concerned, Nissen huts replaced the bell tents, and eight Blister hangars were erected to provide some cover for maintenance and servicing. A small Watch Office built from corrugated iron was located in the north-eastern corner. Shopwyke Hall, a mile to the south-west, was requisitioned as the Officers' Mess.

Both 302 and 602 Squadrons were employed on escort duty for the No 2 Group *Circus* daylight raids over France and Belgium that commenced in January 1941, but gradually these evolved into pure fighter sweeps codenamed *Rodeos*. The Poles departed for Kenley in early April and a month later were replaced by No 616, which moved across from Tangmere. The Tangmere and Westhampnett Squadrons, together with No 145, which had moved back south to Merston, formed the famous Wing led by the legendary Wg Cdr Douglas Bader.

As the Wing re-equipped with the Spitfire V, *Rhubarbs* became the norm and it was on one of these that Bader was lost, historians disagree whether by collision with a 109, as Bader always maintained, or by being shot down – whichever, the result was the same. The Wing lost its leader and the Germans gained a very troublesome captive.

For the rest of 1941 squadrons were rotated regularly, including No 129, which replaced No 610, and No 65, which took over from No 616 and was then replaced by No 41, so that 1942 started with two Spitfire VB squadrons, but No 41 gave way to No 340 (Free French) Squadron in April. The cycle of operations continued until the end of July, when both No 129 and No 340 left for Thorney Island and Hornchurch respectively. In the last two weeks before No 129 left, olive drab uniforms joined the Squadron as six US Army Air Force pilots flew with them to gain experience prior to the arrival of the advanced party of the 31st FG on 30 July to create what became USAAF Station 352.

The uniforms had changed but the aircraft remained the same when the Spitfire VBs of the 309th FS flew in from Atcham on 1 August to fly with the Tangmere Wing in preparation for Operation 'Jubilee'. The CO of the 309th was Major Harrison 'Harry' Thyng, who had earlier

During July 1942, to gain experience, six USAAF pilots, including Captain H Thyng (No 5), later CO of 309th FS, flew with No 129 Squadron before Westhampnett became USAAF Station 352. (via DWL collection)

flown with No 129 Squadron and named his personal Spitfire 'Mary-James' in honour of his wife and young son. On 9 August he attacked and damaged a Ju 88 – the first fighter combat of many by the fighter pilots of the future Mighty Eighth.

The 309th was called to readiness at 03.47 on 19 August and, led by Thyng and in company with Nos 130 and 131 Squadrons from Tangmere, was over Dieppe by 08.50, where they were met by the Fw 190s of JG26. Lieutenant S. Junkin scored the first victory by an VIIIth Air Force pilot, but was immediately shot down himself, together with two more of his comrades. The 309th was off again just before midday in company with Nos 81 and 131 Squadrons escorting Bostons, but they lost another of their number. The final sortie was to cover the withdrawal of the ships, claiming one German bomber damaged. The long day had given the 309th much to chew over.

The second Squadron of the 31st FG, the 308th, arrived on 25 August as the 307th moved into Merston, so that for the first time the Group could operate as a complete unit. Transferred to the XIIth Air Force on 2 September, it continued to fly with the RAF until 9 October when, leaving its Spitfires behind, it left for North Africa and Operation 'Torch'.

No 616 transferred from Tangmere with its long-span Spitfire VI high-altitude variants at the end of October, linking up with No 131 Squadron for the regular *Ramrods* and *Rhubarbs*, although the Mark VI was not really suited to low-level operations. From January 1943 squadrons again rotated through as No 485 (New Zealand) and No 610 replaced Nos 616 and 131 before they were in their turn replaced by 167 and 501 Squadrons. At the end of June two Spitfire XII Squadrons, Nos 41 and 91, arrived to form a Wing concentrating on bomber escort duties.

In September 1943 No 91 became Fighter Command's top scoring Squadron before the Spitfires moved over to Tangmere, making way for a heavyweight machine. The Typhoons of Nos 174, 175 and 245 Squadrons made up No 121 Airfield and arrived during October to use Westhampnett as winter quarters. Operating as fighter-bombers against shipping and targets in France, the grass field soon became rutted as winter progressed. It is believed that additional dispersals and the T1 hangar in the north-east corner of the aerodrome were added at this time. The primary targets became the *Noball* V-1 launch sites, which were heavily defended, and losses each month averaged two or three per squadron during these operations.

In a typical low-level sweep on 8 January 1944 the 'Tiffies' ranged over much of France north of Paris. The leader, Wg Cdr R. T. P. Davidson DFC, dispatched a Luftwaffe transport, but Flt Sgt Waudby was last seen trailing white smoke – clear evidence of a coolant leak. During February and March the aircraft were modified to carry rockets as the tempo built up in the invasion preliminaries. A further reshuffle in April brought in No 144 Airfield as 121 Airfield moved to Holmsley South. The Canadians of Nos 441, 442 and 443 Squadrons flew Spitfire IXs, providing top cover to a bombing raid on Dieppe on 13 April, and the CO of 443, Sqn Ldr H. W. McLeod DSO DFC and bar, achieved the Squadron's first victory when he destroyed a Do 217 near Brussels on 19 April.

The next unit, No 129 Airfield, replaced the Canadians on 22 April 1944, but arrived with just one Squadron, No 184, which had trained in the specialised *cab-rank* operations under the direction of a forward air controller. The Airfield become No 129 Wing on 12 May, and at dawn on D-Day the Typhoons were into action attacking strong points and flak positions with rockets and guns, but lost three aircraft to the flak on D+1. On 17 June a move to Holmsley South preceded the transfer to France ten days later.

To defend Portsmouth and Southampton against V-1 attacks the Spitfire XIIs of No 41 Squadron and the Spitfire XIVs of No 610 Squadron passed through at the end of June before moving to Friston. A sequence of Spitfire units engaged on escort work passed through until the end of September, when Nos 118, 124 and 303 departed, leaving Westhampnett virtually deserted until the arrival of No 83 Group Support Unit from Thorney Island on 4 November. A succession of replacement aircraft and pilots passed through the aerodrome on their way to front-line squadrons. Not all made it safely, as a Spitfire skidded on the wet grass on 4 January 1945 and collided with two parked aircraft. A move to the more suitable Dunsfold was completed by 22 February but, according to the records of 11 Group, Westhampnett had been in C&M since 15 January.

A six-month hiatus ended in July 1945 when the aerodrome reopened to receive the Naval Air Fighting Development Squadron from the overcrowded Tangmere. Part of the Central Fighter Establishment, the NAFDU operated a fascinating collection of Naval machines flown by No 787 Squadron. When the CFE transferred to West Raynham in November, Westhampnett was again put into C&M, closing completely on 13 May 1946.

A completely new role for the aerodrome was envisaged by its new owner as the land reverted to the ninth Duke of Richmond and Gordon. As a pre-war racing driver known as Freddie March, he saw a potential racetrack in the almost 3 miles of the tarmac perimeter track. After the removal of the Blister hangars and other extraneous buildings, the Goodwood Motor Racing Circuit was opened by the Duke in September 1948, driving around the circuit in a Bristol 400, then the latest sports saloon. The renowned Reg Parnall won the first race, averaging 80.56mph. As speeds increased, the circuit became dangerous and, despite some safety improvements, Stirling Moss was severely injured in 1962. The cost of full safety measures was prohibitive and the circuit closed in 1965.

However, in 1958 flying had returned to Goodwood, as it was then known, when planning approval had been granted for the centre of the circuit to be used as an airfield with three grass landing strips. On the eastern side the operator, Goodwood Terrana Ltd, built a new hangar and flying clubhouse as the airfield increased in popularity. NDN Aircraft, formed by Desmond Norman, the co-founder of Britten Norman aircraft on the Isle of Wight, designed and built the NDN-1 Firecracker, which made its maiden flight from Goodwood on 26 May 1977. Sadly, the high-performance basic trainer did not attract any customers, although a turboprop version was built. The prototype G-NDNI and its three successors were all sold to the USA. Early work on the NDN Fieldmaster started at Goodwood before the company moved to Sandown on the Isle of Wight.

On 18 September 1998, fifty years exactly since the Goodwood circuit was opened, the Earl of March began the first Goodwood Revival Meeting by driving around the circuit in the very same Bristol 400 his grandfather had used in 1948. Spectators are encouraged to dress appropriately and the unique atmosphere is maintained by prohibiting any modern post-1966 vehicles on site during the event. Historic aircraft are also welcomed and Spitfires have flown again at Westhampnett during the Revival, although not yet a Typhoon – but we live in hope.

Sadly, on 8 April 2000 two-seat Spitfire Tr 9 G-TRIX crashed, killing both the pilot and the owner, who was under instruction. A new venture, the Ultimate High Academy, opened at Goodwood in June 2002, offering advanced flying training, including aerobatics and formation flying using Extra 300s, but transferred to Kemble during 2003. In 2004, during the Revival meeting, Lord March launched the Goodwood Aero Club, which he said 'is for anyone who just loves aviation and wants to share our passion for it.' With a programme of visits, talks and flights in historic aircraft, the membership had reached more than 450 by January 2005. The airfield continues to be a busy general aviation field, welcoming resident and visiting aeroplanes.

The 1941 control tower is a restaurant and bar adjacent to the circuit, and a memorial to the 31st Fighter Group is located adjacent to the external stairs. Other original wartime buildings such as the parachute packing shed survive in good condition. The T1 hangar is now off site and is used by Monro Horticulture Ltd. On 9 August 2001, at the airfield from which he made his last wartime flight, a statue of Douglas Bader, captured in characteristic pose looking skywards, was unveiled by his widow, Lady Bader. For the motor-sport fraternity a memorial garden and tablet commemorates the New Zealander Bruce McLaren, who was killed at Goodwood in June 1970, testing a sports car. He founded the McLaren F1 racing team in 1966. So, whatever your interests you are sure to find Westhampnett or Goodwood, whichever you prefer, well worth a visit.

The control tower is now a restaurant overlooking the circuit. (DWL collection)

The wartime parachute packing building is now the Circuit Shop. (DWL collection)

The statue of Douglas Bader was unveiled by his widow, Lady Bader, on 9 August 2001, exactly sixty years after he failed to return to Westhampnett. (DWL collection)

Main features:
Runways: WNW-ESE 3,300ft, NE-SW 3,000ft, NW-SE 4,200ft, grass. *Hangars:* one
T1, one Extra Over Blister, seven Over Blisters. *Hardstandings:* nineteen twin- and
thirty-two single-engined types. *Accommodation:* RAF: 91 Officers, 100 SNCOs,
1,171 ORs; WAAF: 0 Officers, 51 ORs.

Folkestone-built airship SSZ.4 moored-out at Wittersham in 1917/18. (JMB/GSL collection)

WITTERSHAM, Kent

51°01N/00°41E 106ft asl; TQ886281. 3 miles S of Tenterden off B2082

Established in 1918 as a mooring-out station for Capel airships, the site was frequently misspelled
as Withersham, West Mersham and West Hersham. As usual it was a heavily wooded area in a
slight valley, which made the site attractive to the Admiralty. A clearing was created in the
Sheepwash Plantation to house one SSZ airship, to enable patrols to be carried out if the parent
station was affected by sea fog or other climatic problems.

Wittersham closed shortly after the end of hostilities, and although there could be concrete
mooring blocks buried deep in the woods, no one has yet discovered them, nor found any other
physical evidence of the airship sub-station.

Main features:
Runways: none. *Hangars:* none; airship mooring facilities.

WOODCHURCH, Kent

51°05N/00°46E 160ft asl; TQ948362. 5.5 miles SW of Ashford off minor road

In recent years Woodchurch became synonymous with a superb event called 'Woodchurch Wings
'n' Things', which, with a garden party atmosphere, was held in the 'back garden' of Little
Engeham Farm, thanks to the generosity of Mr and Mrs Rob Davies. A charity event, it attracted a
unique collection of historic aircraft, vehicles and artefacts. If you never attended the show, you

missed something really special, for sadly, after eighteen years, ever-increasing bureaucracy, costs and health and safety limitations forced the cancellation of the planned 2007 show. Greatly missed!

Rob's 2,560-foot (780-metre) grass strip, although on virtually the same alignment as one of the original wartime runways, is about a quarter of a mile north of Woodchurch ALG, which was one of only two that were scheduled in 1942 for light bombers. Detailed plans placed the ALG immediately to the west of Hengherst village and north of the Shirkoak crossroads. The two runways were perpendicular to each other, the main N/S being 4,800ft (1,463m) with its shorter E/W strip cutting the Shirkoak to Engeham Farm road. The main accommodation site was placed in and around Hengherst House with room for some 400 personnel.

After approval of the plans, work started in December 1942 with a target completion date of 1 March 1943, but problems with the topography reduced the length of the E/W runway to 4,090ft (1,247m) of Sommerfeld tracking. Although a bomb dump was built nearby, the planned occupants had changed to fighters, which arrived on 28 July in the form of the Mustangs of Nos 231 and 400 (RCAF) Squadrons, No 128 Airfield. Low-level tactical recce sorties began in September, the first being over Dunkirk. Train-busting *Rhubarbs* soon became a speciality as the two Squadrons adjusted to the basic field conditions and assessed the suitability of the ALG.

No 39 (Recce) Wing HQ arrived on 11 August, also to sample rural living for a couple of months before returning to Redhill in mid-October, the two Squadrons joining them on 15 October to enjoy the winter comforts of a permanent aerodrome. No 5003 Airfield Construction Squadron moved in to repair and upgrade the facilities in the light of the summer's operations. The perimeter track was extended and additional aircraft hardstandings created, which eventually totalled seventy. A team of US Army engineers followed on to regrade the E/W runway and extend it to the east over the road from Hengherst and Woodchurch, which was only closed during operations. Five Blister hangars were erected to cater for the planned occupation by an American fighter group.

The Americans duly began to arrive in the first week of April 1944. The 373rd FG, IXth Air Force, with its 410th , 411th and 412th FS, arrived fresh from the USA as its P-47 Thunderbolts were delivered from depots, eventually totalling more than seventy by early May when the Group flew its first fighter sweep over Normandy . The usual mixture of escorts and fighter-bomber work followed while the pilots gained experience.

On D-Day the Group's task was top cover over the American beaches, then ground strafing of targets of opportunity including troops, tanks, and road and rail services. Unusually there was some

A 412th FS truck loaded with drop-tanks passes a P-47 V5-A of the same unit at Woodchurch in 1944. (Kent Messenger via A. Moor)

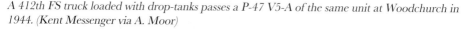

The CO of the 373rd FG briefs his pilots before their next mission. (Kent Messenger via A. Moor)

contact with enemy aircraft, and on June 7 six were credited as destroyed in a dogfight over Normandy. In total the Group destroyed thirty enemy aircraft while operating from Woodchurch, losing fifteen Thunderbolts. Transfer to France began in late July and most of the personnel and aircraft had left for Tour-en-Bessin (A-13) by the 31st.

Like all such ALGs Woodchurch had its share of disabled bombers. On 29 June a 458th BG Liberator landed without a nose wheel, writing off the aeroplane and bringing extra work for the runway repair team. In mid-July another B-24 landed safely.

As no further use was envisaged for Woodchurch, the American airfield crews began to lift the runway tracking immediately for reuse on the continent. They were followed in the autumn by an RAF Airfield Construction Squadron, which completed the dismantling of the ALG and the return of the site to agriculture. The only physical remnant of Woodchurch is the northern taxiway of the E/W runway, which is now used as the entrance drive to the Shirkoak Park estate.

Main features:
Runways: 010° 4,800ft, 110° 5,000ft, steel matting (pierced planking and Sommerfeld track). *Hangars:* none. *Hardstandings:* seventy temporary, Sommerfeld track. *Accommodation:* tented camp.

Places of interest nearby:
If a visitor wishes to learn more of the ALG and local history, the excellent Woodchurch Museum is the place to go. Housed in an 18th-century oak-framed barn not far from the village centre, its collection covers the history of the village from the Stone Age to the present day and has a detailed plan of the ALG, although the runway extension to the east by the American engineers is not depicted. Check the museum's website for opening times.

The layout of the ALG is illustrated in the Woodchurch Museum. (DWL collection)

WORTHY DOWN, Hampshire

51°06N/01°19W 345ft asl; SU470351. 3 miles N of Winchester on minor road parallel to A34(T)

Worthy Down has military connections going back much further than just the 20th century, for 'worthy' in the Roman era meant 'enclosure' and normally related to a plot of land given by the thankful Emperor to a legionnaire when he retired from active service. Even if that 'army' connection is ignored, the site's military history is now much more strongly biased towards the Army than the junior Royal Air Force. It was of course the Army that first brought aviation to Worthy Down.

The land on which the airfield was to be built had been a racecourse since the mid-1750s, but the last recorded use as such was in May 1896 and the site, including the wooden grandstand, was derelict when inspected by Lt Col J. A. Chamier RFC on 2 August 1917. He was looking for an alternative home for the Wireless & Observers School, which had been formed at Brooklands in March 1916 with Shorthorn, RE.7 and BE.2 aircraft. His favourable report noted that, although the field did slope from the grandstand towards the north-west, it was not enough to prejudice its use as a landing ground and the surrounding area was ideal for the inevitable forced landings. The associated undulation of the land, which was acceptable in 1917, was to cause more severe problems later. Forming the eastern boundary of the site was the then Didcot, Newbury & Southampton railway line. Although the nearest station was at Sutton Scotney, the proximity of the line was an important factor in the choice of the Worthy Down.

A roughly rectangular field of about 480 acres was requisitioned, giving a maximum landing run of some 4,800 feet (1,463 metres). It was decided to locate the technical area and hangarage at the bottom end of the site, with the railway as the eastern boundary. In October 1917 a platform and sidings were built on the aerodrome side of the railway, enabling both materials and workers to be brought to the site. In the twelve months from October 1917, around 6,000 wagons were unloaded at the sidings, and on 1 April 1918 Worthy Down station became a recognised public halt.

The planned hangarage consisted of two triple-bay GS sheds (Belfast hangars) and a single ARS. However, when the station was officially opened in early 1918 they were only some 50% usable, although the adjacent accommodation and administration facilities were virtually complete. In the interim the Wireless & Observers School had moved to nearby Hursley Park, being renamed the Artillery & Infantry Co-operation School on 7 November 1917, finally moving into Worthy Down at the end of May 1918. Nearly two months earlier, on 1 April 1918, Worthy Down changed to become part of the new Royal Air Force. However, the importance of the RAF's antecedents was recognised on 19 September 1918 when the School was redesignated the RAF & Army Co-operation School. Its task was to give advanced instruction in map-reading and artillery/infantry co-operation to pilots and observers. It was a busy station with up to 1,450 permanent personnel and 300 students, and an establishment of some eighty aircraft, mainly RE.8s but also FK.8s, F2Bs and 504Ks. A further name change to the School of Army Co-operation took place in December 1919.

The Armistice scuppered the plan to construct an aerodrome at nearby Flowerdown for No 1(T) Wireless School, so Worthy Down began to provide such flying facilities for the School. This was fortunate, as the Army Co-operation School was disbanded on 8 March 1920, being immediately reformed at Old Sarum. This left Worthy Down providing the flying wing of the renamed Electrical & Wireless School with 504Ks and Bristol F2B Fighters. This role continued until March 1927, although three years earlier things had begun to look up for Worthy Down.

After the virtual extinction of the RAF in the early 1920s, gradually money began to be released for modernisation and new equipment. For the first time the airfield was to have a front-line role as a heavy night-bomber station. On 1 April 1924 No 58 Squadron was re-formed with Vimys, initially on a single-flight basis, with the second being added from 1 January 1925. From December 1924 the promised new equipment began to supplement and eventually replaced the Vimys, as No 58 became the second squadron in the RAF to receive the Vickers Virginia. This magnificent biplane was to be one of the mainstays of the RAF's heavy night-bomber force during the inter-war period.

On 25 May, a new Squadron Commander was posted to No 58. The new boss, who was to play a significant role in the future of RAF Bomber Command, was of course Arthur Harris, then a Squadron Leader but later MRAF Sir Arthur 'Bomber' Harris. A Flight Commander of the Squadron was a young Flt Lt Bob Saundby, who was to become Harris's wartime deputy at Bomber Command. During Harris's service at Worthy Down, 10,000 gallons of aviation fuel apparently disappeared and the Air Ministry tried to make Harris pay for the loss. Not unreasonably he

Vickers Virginias of No 58 Squadron seen in the mid-1920s when Arthur Harris was the CO. (via N. Cullingford)

refused, and eventually it was found that the civilian works department had left a pipe open from an underground storage tank allowing the fuel to leak into the ditches below the Officers' Mess. Today a prosecution for environmental pollution would inevitably follow.

Shortly after the last of the E&WS aircraft had departed in March 1927, the second Virginia Squadron, No 7, arrived on 7 April from Bircham Newton. It had been the first squadron to receive the Virginia and its CO was also a name that was to resound through the history of the RAF. The then Wg Cdr C. F. A. 'Peter' Portal was of course to become MRAF Sir Charles Portal and, as Chief of Air Staff from October 1940 to January 1946, 'Bomber' Harris's boss.

With both Squadrons being part of the Wessex Bombing Area, with its Headquarters at Andover, the competition between them was very fierce, especially at the annual Armament Practice Camp. From 1927 until 1935 the holder of the Lawrence Minot Memorial Bombing Trophy was held by one or the other of the two Worthy Down Squadrons. Sadly accidents did occur. In 1931 a Virginia crashed into the Station Orderly Room, with just one of the four-man crew surviving. What should have been an accident took place when a Virginia was inadvertently flown by an 'erk' doing an engine ground run. Despite having never flown before, he managed to fly successfully around the circuit, landing safely to the relief of the substantial audience. On another occasion an 8lb smoke bomb was accidentally dropped onto the Winchester to Newbury road, fortunately without damage.

Much redevelopment occurred during the 1926 to 1930 period, including the substantial married quarters on the service road from the A34. On the main site, permanent barrack blocks, SHQ, Officers' Mess and Quartermaster's block were constructed. One of the last buildings to be completed during this period was a new chapel, which was dedicated by the Bishop of Winchester on 19 January 1930. On the airfield at least two attempts were made during the early 1930s to flatten and regrade the pronounced hump in the middle of the flying ground, together with improved drainage. Despite this the 1934 *Air Pilot* guide for Worthy Down recorded that the landing area could offer 1,200 yards (109 metres) in an E-W orientation, but exactly half that in the N-S direction, and cautioned that the north portion of the airfield sloped steeply and was very uneven.

In April 1935 No 7 Squadron began to re-equip with the Kestrel-engined Heyford, destined to be the RAF's last biplane heavy bomber. With its fuselage unusually attached to the upper of the biplane wings, the Heyford towered over the stately Virginias. During that summer Worthy Down played host to a number of Audax-equipped squadrons on Army Co-op exercises, but the growing threat from the continent was to bring changes to the two resident units. On 1 October two new Squadrons were created at Worthy Down as 'B' Flight of No 7 Squadron became No 102, and 'A' Flight of No 58 Squadron became No 215.

The contours and size of the airfield had always made Worthy Down a little tricky for the 1930s heavy bombers, and with the newer monoplane machines on the way the role of the station had to change. Nos 58 and 215 Squadrons took their Virginias to Upper Heyford on 14 January 1936. Nos 7 and 102 also left in early September with their Heyfords, this time further north to

Finningley. This was also part of the reorganisation of the RAF's bomber units following the formation on 14 July of Bomber Command. This had brought the Hinds of 49 Squadron to Worthy Down from Bircham Newton on 8 August 1936 and, just before Nos 7 and 102 departed, the Gordons of 35 and 207 Squadrons arrived in late August, fresh from their involvement in the Abyssinian crisis. The airfield was then transferred to No 2 Group.

The station opened to the public on 29 May 1937 for the Empire Air Day and nearly 2,000 visitors were attracted to see what the RAF could offer. Although still primarily a biplane air force, the new monoplanes were on their way. The first, in the shape of the Wellesley, arrived for No 35 Squadron in July, and by mid-September all twelve had arrived. No 207 Squadron also began to re-equip with the advanced machine, with all its complexities of retractable undercarriage, variable-pitch propeller and pneumatic brakes. In comparison with the compact biplanes, the wingspan of nearly 75 feet (22.9 metres) also seemed rather daunting. With its Barnes Wallis-designed geodetic construction, the airframe was very strong, unlike the undercarriage, which tended to collapse at the slightest provocation.

The rapid expansion of the RAF resulted in yet another change of role for Worthy Down, which was now earmarked for Coastal Command. Thus No 49 Squadron left with its Hinds for Scampton on 14 March, with the two Wellesley Squadrons following to Cottesmore on 20 April 1938. The station was formally transferred to No 17 (T) Group at Lee-on-Solent on 15 April. Although Ansons of Nos 206, 220 and 233 Squadrons exercised with HMS *Centurion* from Worthy Down during August, a further change of plan meant that the airfield itself would become a 'ship'. Thus, as a shore-based FAA establishment, the first Naval residents were Nimrods and Ospreys of 800 Squadron, which arrived on 7 July. A detachment was sent to join HMS *Courageous* during the Munich Crisis, while the main body of the Squadron began to re-equip with a mix of Skuas and Gladiators during October 1938. On 21 November No 803 Squadron was re-formed at Worthy Down from No 800's 'B' Flight, and by early January it had an establishment of nine Skuas. In early January 800 Squadron left with its Skuas for a ten-week cruise aboard HMS *Ark Royal*, returning for a few weeks in April and May before returning to its ship on 24 May.

Worthy Down officially became HMS *Kestrel* on 24 May, and on the same day No 1 Air Gunners School was created with the formation of its constituent Nos 755 and 757 Squadrons. Both were Telegraphist Air Gunners (TAG) training squadrons, equipped with Ospreys and Sharks. The planned third Squadron, No 756, did not appear until 1941, and 757 went into abeyance on 15 August 1939, also until 1941. Following the outbreak of hostilities, No 815 Squadron was formed at HMS *Kestrel* from the survivors of Nos 811 and 822 Squadrons, who had been aboard HMS *Courageous* when she was sunk on 17 September 1939. Equipped with the Swordfish, the unit carried out torpedo training but disbanded in early November, becoming No 774 Armament Training Squadron. Tasked with training Observers and TAGs, the aircraft establishment included three Skuas, three Rocs, four Shark target-tugs and four Swordfishes. On 15 December No 763 Squadron was formed as TSR Pool No 1 to train Swordfish crews required for HMS *Ark Royal* and HMS *Hermes* and as replacements for elsewhere. The unit was sent to Jersey Airport on 11 March 1940, but in the face of the German continental blitzkrieg was back at Lee-on-Solent by the end of May. No 755 also had a brief sojourn on Jersey, but was back at Worthy Down by 31 May.

Worthy Down's varied career took another turn on 1 February when it saw the formation of a new fighter Squadron, No 806. With its eight Skuas and four Rocs, the Squadron moved to Scotland at the end of March, but was back at Worthy Down on 26 May, where it supplied a detachment to Detling to provide cover for the Dunkirk evacuation. Before embarking aboard HMS *Illustrious* on 11 June, the Squadron had exchanged its Rocs for the first Fulmars to enter FAA service, working up on its new fighters at Eastleigh. The start-up fighter role of HMS *Kestrel* continued on 1 July with the formation of No 808 as a Fleet Fighter Squadron with twelve Fulmars. It must have been a shock for a new unit to find itself suddenly in the front line when, on Thursday 15 August, the airfield was attacked by Ju 88s. The raiders were part of a large formation from LG1 escorted by Bf 110s of ZG2. Intercepted in succession by the Hurricanes of 43 Squadron, then those of No 601 and finally No 609 Squadron with Spitfires, the Luftwaffe formation suffered heavy losses. At least five Ju 88s and one Bf 110 were brought down for the loss two 601 Squadron Hurricanes, plus a pair of 43 Squadron's aircraft damaged; only one RAF pilot was injured. Thanks to the RAF, the station got off lightly with one hangar roof being damaged, but there were no casualties. The humorous sequel to this attack was the broadcast by 'Lord Haw-Haw', who claimed that HMS *Kestrel* had been bombed and sunk!

After its fright, No 808 moved north on 5 September, making room for yet another new Squadron, No 807, which came into being on 15 September, again with Fulmars. Although intended for HMS *Victorious*, delays led to the Squadron embarking aboard HMS *Pegasus* in early December for fighter catapult operations. Supermarine's Southampton factories had been subjected to a devastating raid on 26 September, bringing the critical Spitfire production to a halt. The tentative plans for the dispersal of Spitfire production and flight-testing were put in hand immediately. A pair of Bellman hangars was hurriedly erected at Worthy Down and in December 1940 Jeffrey Quill's Spitfire Development Unit moved in from Eastleigh.

During 1941 a large dispersed storage facility was constructed to the west of the airfield in Worthy Groves between the A34 and the B3420, an old Roman road. There were forty-eight Dutch Barns (a sole example of the type still exists on the former airfield near South Wonston), two Bessonneau and a single Naval-type Fromson storage Blister hangar. Much of the hangarage was camouflaged in woodland. A single taxiway from the airfield crossed the A34 with the help of railway-type level crossing gates!

To help protect this increasingly valuable site, a decoy site was built at Micheldever to attract enemy bombers, and some especially strong ground defences were erected. A ring of some thirty-one pillboxes was built, many of which still exist. Most of the fixed defences were of the Royal Engineer Type 22 octagonal pillbox, either concrete or brick-built and crewed by one NCO and five men, with at least one LMG. Actually on the airfield there were at least two Pickett-Hamilton retractable forts. One, sited near the married quarters, has been sealed, but a second, on the top of the airfield, is believed to be still extant.

Throughout all the excitement of 1940 No 1 Air Gunner's School with its solitary No 755 Squadron continued to train its TAGs. On 6 March the School was expanded to its originally planned size with the formation of 756 and 757 Squadrons; 756 was equipped with Proctors to provide the advanced half of the TAG course, including cross-country flights using radio beacons. Its sister Squadron initially flew a few Ospreys, but these were withdrawn in May in favour of the Skua to provide the initial part of the air gunnery course. The trainee TAGs were often known as 'Goons' and lived in lines of wooden huts in the valley to the south of the Officers' Mess (this area is still sometimes referred to as Goon Valley). Two of the numerous trainees to pass through HMS *Kestrel* during this period later went on the stage and became better known as Sir Ralph Richardson and Sir Laurence Olivier. The latter subsequently recalled that he eventually made quite a good pilot 'after a ghastly first day of taxiing one Shark into another'.

The much-increased activity did lead to some problems, particularly in the co-ordination between the Spitfire test flying and the flying training. One accident in particular could have had serious consequences. Jeffrey Quill was testing a Spitfire when, cresting the infamous hump in the middle of the field, he was confronted by one of No 756's Proctors. A collision was inevitable, resulting in the Proctor being destroyed and the Spitfire badly damaged. Despite these problems, the first Griffon-powered Spitfire was tested at Worthy Down during November 1941. Much of the development of the Seafire took place on the airfield, continuing through into 1943.

The elderly Sharks of 755 Squadron began to be supplemented by Lysanders, although the last of them was not withdrawn until October 1943. Nearly a year earlier, on 1 December 1942, the three Squadrons of No 1 AGS were merged together into the single 755 Squadron. As the Sharks were finally beached, they were replaced by Tiger Moths and the much-reviled Curtiss Seamew. Finally, on 31 October 1944 No 755 Squadron was disbanded, all future TAG training being undertaken in Canada.

Trials of the Spitfire XIV had begun in November 1943 but the much-improved facilities at High Post led to all Spitfire development being transferred from Worthy Down in March 1944. HMS *Kestrel* became the home for a number of unusual units. No 739 (Blind Approach Development) Unit with Oxfords moved in from Hinstock, joined in February 1944 by the Whitleys of 734 Squadron. The latter had been converted by SS Cars (later Jaguar) to be flying classrooms with fuel-flow meters and other instrumentation to train pilots in Merlin engine handling techniques. Its customers were TBR crews converting from the likes of the gentle Swordfish to the much more powerful Merlin-engined Barracuda. Towards the end of August an ATA Ferry pilot, Peter George from No 6 Ferry Pool at Ratcliffe, made two visits to Worthy Down. On 24 August he delivered a Defiant from Desford, collecting an Avenger, which he took up to Sherburn-in-Elmet. Almost a week later he brought a different Avenger from Ratcliffe; it is unclear which of Worthy Down's resident units were the intended recipients. A pair of unusual visitors dropped in during a spell of bad

Two Liberators of the 832nd BS, 486th BG, from Sudbury have been diverted in with full bomb loads after their mission was aborted. (W. H. C. Blake via N. Cullingford)

Lt Cdr Blake, on the left, was Commander Flying at Worthy Down in 1944. His companion is Lt Clegg RNVR. (W. H. C. Blake via N. Cullingford)

weather, probably the largest aircraft ever to use the airfield. Two Liberators, which had full bomb loads on board, had to be offloaded before they could take off again! As the station gradually ran down, its last permanent flying unit, No 739 Squadron, left for Donibristle in October 1944.

Southampton University Air Squadron operated two Tiger Moth aircraft until late 1946 when it moved to Eastleigh; for a time the airfield was also used to store redundant aircraft awaiting disposal. For a short period the RN Regulating School (equivalent to Military Police) and the Rehabilitation & Vocational Training School were both based at HMS *Kestrel*, but with the inevitable post-war economies *Kestrel* was 'paid off' in November 1947.

In June 1952 the Naval Air Electrical School moved to Worthy Down from Warrington, the station being reopened as HMS *Ariel II*, with extra huts built to house the School. Worthy Down's flying swansong occurred in late 1959 when it played host to Whirlwind helicopters of No 848 Squadron working up to join the first Commando carrier, HMS *Bulwark*. The NAES role lasted until 1 November 1960 when the School moved to Lee-on-Solent, which meant that once again Worthy Down was surplus to Naval requirements.

After more than forty-two years, Worthy Down's original service returned to take over responsibility for the camp. The British Army, specifically the Royal Army Pay Corps, decided to make Worthy Down its new HQ and the centre for the new Electronic Accounting Development Unit. The old hangars were dismantled and other buildings replaced in a substantial rebuilding programme. The camp was officially opened on 20 June 1961 by the Rt Hon John Profumo OBE MP, the then Secretary of State for War.

On 6 April 1992 the Adjutant General's Corps was formed at Worthy Down, bringing together a number of other individual units, including of course the RAPC. The other four main constituents of the AGC are the Royal Military Police; the Royal Army Education Corps; the Army Legal Corps; and the Women's Royal Army Corps. Worthy Down still has a major training role, which has been a significant feature throughout the history of the station/camp. For the future, a rationalisation of the services provided at Worthy Down and similar establishments of the Navy and Air Force looks likely. The personnel at this historic site are confident that their exceptional efficiency will mean that Worthy Down will be chosen as the location for any future combined facility.

An oblique aerial view looking north, with the Adjutant General's Corps site in the foreground, what was the airfield beyond, and the married quarters on the left.
(Adjutant General's Corps via DWL collection)

A visitor to Worthy Down who turns off the minor road, the old A34, passes the large married quarters site on the left with a modern St Andrew's Church before reaching the security gate. Those with a reason to proceed further drive along the curving route of the original station road, pass the 1926 Officers' Mess on the right, to the modern administrative block of the Worthy Down Support Unit, flanked by the 1961 official opening commemorative stone. The site now consists of mainly modern buildings including Gould House, the Regimental HQ of the AGC, on the ground floor of which is a predominately photographic history of the Corps' constituent units; the history of the Pay Corps, for example, dates back to 1649. However, among the modern buildings are a few pre-war and wartime structures, including four imposing 1930s barrack blocks; the south elevation of one carries a depiction of the Corps cap badge and motto, 'Fide et Fiducia'. Other memorials can be found around the camp. On the roadside in front of the Officers' Mess is a memorial rose garden. which, a tablet records, was moved from the Women's Royal Army Corps Centre, Guildford, and dedicated on 4 June 1992 in the presence of Her Majesty the Queen, Colonel in Chief of the Adjutant General's Corps. Adjacent to the grass amphitheatre that replaces the former parade square, in front of the barrack blocks, is a general tribute to Worthy Down's history. On a substantial boulder, a granite tablet explains:

> 'This stone records Worthy Down's continuous military use from 1917 as an aerodrome and barracks and is dedicated to the servicemen and women of the Royal Flying Corps, the Royal Air Force, the Royal Navy, the Royal Army Pay Corps, and since 6 april 1992, the Adjutant General's Corps'

Worthy Down's memorial, with a barrack block beyond. (DWL collection)

Of the large storage area across the old A34 to the west, no structures have survived, although fragments of brick and concrete litter the area, which, being divided into two distinct levels, confirms the previous military use. On the old airfield itself, little has changed. From the road, the open landscape slopes away just as it has for centuries, but is of course now farmed. Of the numerous 'Dutch Barn' storage sheds that survived in the 1980s, just one now remains together with the base of another. The old perimeter track still encircles the field and leads to a solitary roofless brick building, which with its blast walls may have been a decontamination block. Just as the road, which is the southern boundary of South Wonston, degenerates into a bridleway, an old road with remnants of a gate leads from the airfield to a row of wooden huts. Although apparently pre-war barrack huts, I was assured that they were built in the 1930s as stables, the role that they perform to this day – an appropriate point at which to close the history of an historic military station built on an old racecourse!

Main features:
Runways: N-S 2,310ft, E-W 4,200ft, grass. *Hangars:* two triple GS sheds, two Bellman, two Bessonneau, one Fromson. *Hardstandings:* unknown. *Accommodation:* RN: 148 Officers, 1,740 Chiefs/POs/Ratings; WRNS: 4 Officers, 352 Chiefs/POs/Ratings.

WROUGHTON, Wiltshire

51°30N/01°48W 600ft asl; SU140788. 4 miles S of Swindon off A361

Sadly, the name Wroughton does not generate the same excitement and mental image as Duxford, Hendon or Cosford. In the 1970s, when the National Museums were building up their aeronautical collections and opening Hendon and Duxford, the Science Museum, the original technology museum, was, through its renowned Curator of Aeronautics, the late John Bagley, assembling a unique collection of primarily civil aircraft. Whereas the other museums sought to open to the public as soon as possible, public access to Wroughton was always strictly limited for policy and financial reasons. In the 'credit crunch' era of 2009, it was not even possible to find from the Science Museum website if any open days were planned. and email enquires went unanswered. Wroughton continues the very private controlled existence that it has had from the beginning.

Conceived as a combined Maintenance Unit and Electrical & Wireless School, work to drain and level the site on the northern edge of the escarpment overlooking Swindon began in 1938. The main technical area was located in the south-east corner with a single 'C' and a pair of 'D'-type hangars. Another pair of 'C' hangars was placed on the eastern boundary and two 'Ds' on the northern edge. The remaining seven 'L' hangars and twenty-seven Robins were dispersed around the remainder of the site.

By the time RAF Wroughton opened on 1 April 1940 the plans for an E&WS had been dropped, so it was No 15 MU of No 41 Group, Maintenance Command, that took up occupation. In common with so many new airfields, Wroughton was far from finished and when three new Lysanders arrived on 3 April there was only one hangar useable and just a temporary landing field in the east.

As building work progressed aeroplanes continued to fly in. Blenheims were the first to be processed, arriving in early May and being delivered to No 107 Squadron on 19 May. Hurricanes were the next arrivals, for storage, but three were set up as a Battle Flight, armed and flown by the unit's pilots as self-defence. The first air raid warning was on 25 June, but an attack on 13 August caused a little damage to a pair of Blenheims. Six days later four bombs were dropped near a still unfinished 'D' hangar without causing any significant damage. A pair of Hurricanes took off but failed to locate the raider.

Throughout the Battle of Britain Wroughton prepared and dispatched an average of sixty aeroplanes each month for Fighter Command; this tempo was maintained into the New Year. With aeroplane totals well in excess of available hangarage, outlying dispersal fields at Barbury Castle, Burderop Park, Uffcott and Upper Salthorp Farm were brought into use. The furthest was more than 2 miles from the aerodrome, and aeroplanes had to be towed to and from them over local roads and temporary tracks. Among the unusual types handled at Wroughton were the Curtiss Mohawk and Helldiver.

Waterlogging of the landing field had been a problem throughout the winter, and provision of hard runways became a priority after the arrival on 14 June 1941 of No 76 MU from Cosford, which packed aeroplanes for overseas shipment. It took over the pair of northern 'D' hangars on No 2 Site adjacent to Clouts Wood. The types handled included the Master, Albacore, Defiant, Fulmar, Gladiator, Oxford, Roc, Sea Hurricane, Spitfire, Swordfish and Walrus. Despite the stated priority, building of the permanent runways was much delayed, and when work did start it caused major disruption. Finally, on 13 March 1944 the unusual three-runway layout with a common intersection in the centre was brought into use.

Before No 76 MU took over the two 'L' hangars on No 3 Site in the north-west corner during August 1944, numbers of aircraft on site, including external storage at the dispersed locations, peaked in May at 573. Packing of aircraft, mainly for the FAA, employed some 220 RAF and 600 civilian personnel, but numbers were drastically cut after the surrender of Japan in August 1945. Although work at No 76 MU was much reduced, No 15 MU was busy, albeit scrapping rather than storing aircraft.

The post-war review confirmed the retention of No 76 MU, but a change of policy that even single-engined fighters were to be ferried to their overseas destinations caused its closure at the end of September 1946. No 15 MU was still accepting new aircraft, including Meteors and later Canberras, as the scrapping work tailed off. The latter type became the predominate task, but in August 1954 the first Whirlwind helicopters arrived, a foretaste of the future.

Vampires were employed as a Station Flight as Maintenance Command's Communications Squadron moved in from Andover in 1956. An unusual collection of aircraft also arrived during that year for storage pending the creation of the RAF Museum. The Nash Collection had been donated by the Royal Aeronautical Society and some of its aeroplanes, including the Camel, Shorthorn and Fokker Triplane, were refurbished at Wroughton.

A No 41 Group Test Pilots' pool was created at Wroughton in April 1958 with Meteor T7s, but moved to Lyneham after two years when the Station Flight was closed. The build-up of helicopter work meant that by 1968 Whirlwind, Sioux and Wessex aircraft formed the bulk of modification and updating tasks, although work on the Canberra continued until March 1972 when the last aircraft was processed, bringing to an end a nineteen-year commitment.

As a result of a Parliamentary report, the Admiralty was given responsibility for all helicopter maintenance and modification, so Wroughton became a Royal Navy Air Yard on 5 April 1972, the MU being simultaneously disbanded. A batch of twenty Scouts for the British Army was followed by Gazelles for the same customer, and the Sioux they replaced arrived for storage prior to sale. Further rationalisation proposed the closure of the Air Yard and the concentration of helicopter work at Fleetlands by April 1979. As this change was being implemented, it was realised that Fleetlands did not have the resources and Wroughton was partially reprieved for a while.

With the RNAY concentrated within the eastern site, this left the bulk of the site unused. The new occupant of six hangars on Nos 3 and 4 sites and the remainder of the airfield was the London Science Museum, which had been looking for an airfield to house its larger items and its expanded aeronautical collection. The first aircraft to arrive on 25 October 1978 was a DC-3, originally delivered to United Airlines in 1936 and, by 1978, the third oldest DC-3 in existence. A Comet 4B followed, and over the following years a superlative collection was amassed, including many unique in Britain such as a Boeing 247, a Constellation and a Lockheed 10 Electra. Just two of the hangars were used for the aircraft collection; the others housed vehicles including fire engines, cars, buses, trucks and a unique agricultural collection.

The world's first hovercraft, the SR-N1, made a historic crossing of the English Channel on 25 July 1959, fifty years after Louis Blériot. (DWL collection)

Although starting an airfield-based collection later than other national museums, Wroughton opened its doors to the public for the first time on Sunday 21 September 1980 and the future looked bright. Although never open on a daily basis, over the following years a series of open days and public events were held under, from 1989, the enthusiastic guidance of the Wroughton Site Manager, Ross Sharp. At the time we shared a common career path, he at Wroughton, me at Duxford, and we became good friends. A meeting of the British Aircraft (later Aviation) Preservation Council was held and from 1991 the annual PFA rally moved to Wroughton for three years.

For the August Bank Holiday in 1992, the Great Warbirds Air Display moved from West Malling. That year was the last season for the Vulcan as an historic RAF display aircraft; GWAD was its penultimate public outing and the display was awesome. As much as I welcomed the return of the flight of the Vulcan in 2008, its displays are inevitably much more restrained than before. Other events included the Great Vintage Flying Weekend; the fifth such feast of historic light aviation was held at Wroughton in 2001.

Although the RNAY had converted its hangars into sealed humidity-controlled buildings for long-term deep storage of helicopters, the need for such was much reduced and closure rumours began to circulate again in 1996. A sale was agreed, but it fell through and in an August 1998 an internal report recommended that the Science Museum acquire the RNAY, which then consisted of nearly 140,000 square feet (approximately 1,300 square metres) in the 'C' and two 'D' hangars as well as offices and other accommodation. During 1999 the RNAY site came under Science Museum control.

An environmental management consultant's report in October 2001 highlighted deterioration of the runway surfaces, which led to a decision in November that no further flying or vehicular events could be held at Wroughton. Instead of finding funds to resurface the runways, a grandiose scheme called Creative Planet was proposed. This envisaged taking up all the runways and taxiways and utilising the whole 562 acres (228 hectares) to demonstrate sustainable development! The blurb said that Wroughton's 'rather barren landscape' would be transformed 'almost beyond recognition'. Wroughton was to be the National Centre for Sustainable Development for industry, agriculture, housing and transport, with forests, fields, farms and villages all showing the sustainable way forward. Just how the aeronautical and other collections fitted into this somewhat nebulous concept is unclear, and perhaps fortunately it failed to get any financial support.

Yet another development plan surfaced in 2007 as part of a bid for £50 million from Big Lottery funding for 'Inspired', the £64 million interactive project aimed to transform Wroughton from a storage site with virtually no public access to a fully functioning museum in its own right. Public votes in a nationally televised programme decided how the money would be spent, and sadly they were not 'inspired' to support Wroughton's plans. In many ways that decision sums up the Wroughton story. Storage, however vitally important, is always a supporting role and it looks as if a store is what Wroughton is destined to remain.

The unusual control tower, with two of the 'C'-type hangars beyond. (DWL collection)

Wroughton's Guardroom. (DWL collection)

Overlooking Swindon and the Vale of the White Horse is a disused ROC underground post.
(DWL collection)

Main features:
Runways: 220° 4,890ft x 150ft, 180° 4,128ft x 150ft, 270° 4,000ft x 150ft, concrete.
Hangars: two 'B'-type B, three 'C'-type, four 'D'-type, twenty-seven Robins.
Hardstandings: sixty-six hardcore and asphalt. *Accommodation:* RAF: 44 Officers,
49 SNCOs, 112 ORs; WAAF: 1 Officer, 1 SNCO, 15 ORs.

WYE, Kent

51°11N/00°55E 133ft asl; TR044478. 4 miles NNE of Ashford on A28

Potential airmen posted to picturesque Wye for pilot training must have enjoyed the scenery when the pressures of wartime training permitted such luxury. The aerodrome was located on 86 acres (35 hectares) of low-lying meadow between the Canterbury to Ashford road and the railway line. The River Great Stour and its tributaries meandered nearby but the close proximity of the wooded North Downs posed an ever-present high-ground threat, especially in adverse weather.

The aerodrome opened in May 1916, and on 1 June No 20 Reserve Squadron, No 6 Wing RFC, moved in from Dover with a mix of Avro 504s, RE.8s and BE.2Cs. Accommodation was very basic: the aircraft had the standard Bessonneau hangars and staff and pupils were also under canvas. Another Reserve Squadron, No 51, arrived in January as the drive to produce pilots for service on the Western Front intensified, and on 1 May 1917 a third Squadron, No 66 RS, was formed from the two resident units. Built for a single squadron, Wye was now very overcrowded. Accidents were inevitable and after one such on 15 March 1917, Lieutenant O. C. Bryson rescued his pupil, 2nd Lt Hillebrandt, from the burning aircraft; sadly the injured man died of his burns but the then Captain Bryson was later awarded a well-deserved Albert Medal.

No 6 Wing set in motion a hurried reallocation of its resources as No 51 RS moved to Waddington in mid-May, followed on 20 May by No 66 transferring to Yatesbury. At the end of May all Reserve Squadrons were renamed Training Squadrons, and on 1 June No 20 TS moved to Wyton as there were plans for major expansion at Wye.

The aerodrome had been selected to house an Anglo-American training squadron; three large metal-clad aeroplane sheds, a transport shed and workshops were erected during the summer beside Maiden Wood, and a hutted accommodation camp was built in the south-east corner. Pending the arrival of the Americans, No 86 Squadron came from Dover with Pups and Camels to operate as an advanced training unit for three months from mid-September. The intended occupant, No 42 TS, arrived from Hounslow on 16 December 1917 and continued training British pilots. The first Americans came to Wye for training during the summer of 1918 and were soon making full use of the fleet of twelve Avro 504Js, a similar number of Camels and a Bristol M.1C, which apparently was intended solely the instructor's use.

A line-up of Avro 504Js of No 42 TS at Wye in 1918. (JMB/GSL collection)

Following the Armistice, the Americans were on their way home within a couple of weeks although training continued at a much slower tempo, before the TS was disbanded on 1 February 1919. Later that month the personnel of No 3 Squadron used the accommodation for a few months before moving to Dover. Wye was declared surplus and formally disposed of in October 1919. The land quickly returned to agriculture, although the land is still called Aerodrome Field. The only acknowledgment to Wye aerodrome can be found in the gravestones of at least fourteen men, eight of whom are buried in Wye churchyard, who died flying from this virtually forgotten field.

Main features in 1918:
Landing ground: grass. *Hangars:* Bessonneau and metal-clad aeroplane sheds. *Accommodation:* hutted camp.

YAPTON, West Sussex – see FORD

Index

RAF Wings

Royal Canadian Air Force (CAF)

Royal Flying Corps (RFC)

Flights/Squadrons

The Action Stations Revisited Series

Volume 1 Eastern England
9780859791459

Volume 2 Central England and the London Area
9780947554941

Volume 3 South East England
9780859791106

Volume 4 South West England
9780859791212

Volume 5 Wales and the Midlands
9780859791113

Volume 6 Northern England and Yorkshire
9780859791120

Volume 7 North East England, Scotland and
Northern Ireland
9780859791441

Published by Crécy Publishing Ltd
1a Ringway Trading Estate
Shadowmoss Rd
Manchester M22 5LH
www.crecy.co.uk